Korean Business and Management : the Reality and the Vision

Korean Business and Management:
the Reality and the Vision

Edited by Zusun Rhee, Eunmi Chang

HOLLYM
Elizabeth, NJ·Seoul

**Korean Business and Management:
the Reality and the Vision**

Copyright © 2002
by Zusun Rhee, Eunmi Chang, et al.,

All rights reserved.
No part of this book may be reproduced in any form
without the written permission of the author and the publisher.

First published in 2002
by Hollym International Corp.
18 Donald Place, Elizabeth, New Jersey 07208, USA
Phone (908)353-1655 Fax (908)353-0255
http://www.hollym.com

Published simultaneously in Korea
by Hollym Corporation; Publishers
13-13 Gwancheol-dong, Jongno-gu, Seoul 110-111, Korea
Phone (02)735-7551-4 Fax (02)730-5149, 8192
http://www.hollym.co.kr

ISBN: 1-56591-167-9 (hardcover)
Library of Congress Catalog Card Number: 2001098525

Printed in Korea

Preface

Whenever we confront an economic development that exceeds the general rate, we praise it as a miracle; when the economy stagnates, we then conclude the miracle was merely a bubble. It seems to be a common fallacy to declaim exclusively on the outputs or results of the economic development of a society while ignoring objective in-depth analyses on the characteristics and processes. Analyzing the business and management of a society is a formidable task, not only because such a critique should cover the dynamic reality of the society but also because it should be persuasive from academic and practical perspectives at the same time. Perhaps this explains why such attempts have been rare.

At the launch of the new century, scholars from a host of disciplines convened at Michigan State University, East Lansing, to comprehensively diagnose the reality of Korean management and to search for a visionary direction. The conference, entitled "Transforming Korean Business and Management Culture", was held on September 19 and 20, 2000, with participants from diverse areas worldwide. The following articles comprise a collection of the material presented at the conference, even though some have been in editing the current book.

In addition to the various disciplinary backgrounds and research perspectives of the authors, audiences will be able to enjoy a great amount of diversity in the way that each issue is delivered — some are macro while others are micro in their research perspectives; some are more academic while others are practical; some are largely explanatory while others are strictly backed up by statistical analyses. In spite of all the different approaches, each paper is manifestly the fruit of experienced insights and the painstaking examination of each author in each field. The opinions stated in the articles are strictly those of the authors.

Korea is one of the many partners to the United States and its people. In that sense, we wish to express our appreciation to the School of Labor and Industrial Relations, College of Social Science, Institute for Public Policy and Social Research, Center for

International Business and Education Research, Eli Broad College of Business, and International Studies and Programs at Michigan State University for their contributions to the conference on Korean business and management. The conference could not have been held so successfully without the invaluable collaboration of the Korea Economic Research Institute, the Korea Labor Institute, the Korea Development Institute, and the International School of Public Policy and Management, KDI. Finally, we are grateful to Mr. Ham Kiman, the president of the Hollym Corporation; Publishers for bringing together the conference papers into a published book.

KOREAN BUSINESS AND MANAGEMENT : THE REALITY AND THE VISION

TABLE OF CONTENTS

PART 1 | **Introduction__11**

13 | Roles of the Government and Private Corporations for a Viable Business and Management Culture
by Sung Hee Jwa

23 | Korean Financial Crisis in Global Political-Economic System
by Gill-Chin Lim

PART 2 | **Government Policy & Business Systems__49**

51 | Were Regulations on Economic Concentration in the Korean Fair Trade Act Effective?
by Zusun Rhee

79 | After the Economic Crisis: An Analysis of the Effects of Corporate Restructuring
by Hasung Jang

133 | Corporate Governance System in Korea: What Questions Should We Ask for Future Recommendations?
by Y. Peter Chung

151 | Do Agency Problems Explain the Post Asian Financial Crisis Performance of Korean Companies?
by Byung-Mo Kim and Inmoo Lee

171 | *Chaebol* Structure, Diversification and Performance
by Inhak Hwang

PART 3 — Management Philosophy & Strategic Choices __205

207 — The Impact of Confucianism on East Asian Business Enterprises
by Tai K. Oh and Eonsoo Kim

227 — Asian Management Styles? The Evidence from Korea
by Dennis P. Patterson

249 — Determinants of Competitive Advantage in the Network Organization Form: A Pilot Study
by Eonsoo Kim, Irene M. Duhaime, John C. Mc Intosh, and Sun-ah Yang

275 — An Empirical Study on the Change of Organizational Culture and Performance in Korean Firms
by Young-Joe Kim

PART 4 — Industrial Relations & Human Resource Management __307

309 — The Korean Industrial Relations System: from Post-Independence to Post-IMF
by Richard N. Block, Jeonghyun Lee, and Eunjong Shin

345 — Rapid Changes in Earning Inequality in Korea after the Financial Crisis
by Sung-Joon Park

367 — HRM in Korea: Transformation and New Patterns
by Woo-Sung Park and Gyu-Chang Yu

393 — Changes in Gender Differences in the Employment Structure
by Hae Un Rii

INTRODUCTION

1. **Roles of the Government and Private Corporations for a Viable Business and Management Culture**
   by Sung Hee Jwa

2. **Korean Financial Crisis in Global Political - Economic System**
   by Gill-Chin Lim

Roles of the Government and Private Corporations for a Viable Business and Management Culture

Sung Hee Jwa[1]

I. Introduction

Good afternoon. It is my pleasure to stand before such distinguished scholars and participants in what I believe to be a very important conference. I wish to talk about the role of the government and private corporations and their responsibilities in shaping business culture, as well as today's economy. This issue, perhaps, is not terribly important among U.S. policy makers and is usually taken for granted. However, in Korea, it is fast becoming an important and highly controversial topic that has drawn the attention of the public and academic scholars.

II. Philosophical background

To put into proper perspective, the nature of the roles of the government and private corporations, it is important that we have a good grasp of the philosophical thinking underlining the nature of Korea's economic

---

[1] President, Korea Economic Research Institute, Seoul, Korea.

management culture, which has been based on the philosophy of Confucianism. Confucianism stresses the fulfillment of human morality through learning and training. Moreover, it emphasizes that an elite group of "morally superior" men should lead the "morally inferior" general public by using principles and rules that they themselves have chosen. As such, we observe that Confucianism has often served as the philosophical basis for our paternal governments.

There exists, however, another equally important school of thought, which has been widely unrecognized in the process of industrialization: Taoism. In essence, Taoism, true to its liberal nature, is skeptical about confining people within specific moral values and an artificial order. To that effect, even defining the Tao and naming things is regarded as self-defeating. Taoism does not espouse any artificial social order but instead emphasizes spontaneity and "being natural without coercion." There is an interesting quote that I wish to share with you (by the Taoist master Lao Tsu):

> "The one who tries to possess the economy in a forced way will lose it. The economy is a mysterious thing that can not be controlled in an artificial way. The one acting contrary to being natural will fail and the one trying to hold with force will lose ···"(Lao Tsu, *Scriptures on Morality*)

In applying Confucianism and Taoism to the economic context, we find that Confucianism will emphasize government-led economic management while Taoism, akin to the Hayekian Philosophy of political economy, will stress the importance of a natural and spontaneous market order. I do not deny that government-led economic management based on Confucianism may have contributed to the rapid growth of East Asian economies, but my point is that it has resulted in more regulations and restrictions on economic activity than in Western countries. Moreover, the emphasis on an elite group as a leading social force has led to non-transparent business as well as national governance structures that have relied on a group of elite's, or the president or chairman's discretionary decisions rather than the rule of law.

I propose that we look at the role of the government and private corporations from the perspectives of Taoism and of Friedrich von Hayek. Put in another way, we must recognize that there exists a natural market order in the economy that arises endogenously and spontaneously, independent of any outside intervention. In this context, competition in the market place is the natural process of discovering an optimal outcome, and in fact, one cannot discover or dictate the optimal economic structure in advance of market competition.

As is well known, the Korean government often directly intervened in the decision-making process of the private sector thereby creating undesirable distortions in the economy's incentive structure. So, how should the role of government be defined so as to generate a viable business culture? Well, broadly speaking, the government should establish a regime of fair competition in the economic and social system so that the discovery function of the market order may become effective. Specifically, the role of the government should be limited to defining the external economic and social environments, and should be confined to preserving the spontaneity and endogeneity of the market order. What is important here is the distinction between exogenous and endogenous economic variables. The government should create an economic environment conducive to active competition in the market by providing proper economic institutions, that is to say, the rules of the game, which to the firm, constitute the exogenous variables, while allowing endogenous management decisions to be independently decided upon by private corporations.

III. Assessment of past economic policy

As way of evaluation, we find first that past policy measures often replaced market mechanisms thereby creating harmful distortions in the economic incentive structure. As a result, management and corporate decision-makers had not been presented with an environment that provided sufficient motivation to economize and innovate, but instead became increasingly dependent on the government for guidance.

Second, under the system of *"gwanchi-geumyung"* or "government-controlled finance," the financial sector was often used as a tool to support the government's industrial policies. Subsequently, the development of financial institutions became retarded, and gradually their function to discriminate between viable and non-viable firms became eroded.

Third, efficient economic policy-making usually requires informational superiority on the part of policy makers. This, however, was usually difficult to guarantee, and this is even more true in the increasingly globalized economy, and yet economic policymakers, accustomed to the mind-set conditioned by Confucianism, believe that it is in our interest to manage every detail of the economy. As a result, private corporations lost their sense of independence, often seeking for government favors, and this led to widespread "moral hazard" behavior not only in the private sector but also in government itself, which in turn provided an ideal setting for the 1997 crisis.

IV. *Chaebol* policy and economic management

Let me illustrate the consequences of the past government-led economic management system, whereby the government decided on determining and influencing the endogenous variables, by taking the example of the *Chaebol* policy. I have always emphasized that the *Chaebol* have evolved into powerful economic organizations under the umbrella of government protection and favor and are, in fact, the product of Korea's specific economic and institutional environment.

Despite this, the government's interventionist mode of thinking has led to policies relying upon the direct regulation of the *Chaebol*'s managerial behavior. And rather inappropriately, this has been done without a proper understanding of the issue of the institutional environment, which is a critical factor influencing business and management behavior of the *Chaebol*, and hence has led to sub-optimal behavior and widespread criticisms of the *"gwanchi-gyeongje"* or "government-controlled economy."

While the *Chaebol* have served as a vehicle to propel rapid economic growth, they have also been subject to huge public criticism. Amongst other things, the *Chaebol* have been criticized for concentrating their economic power, for their over-diversification activities, for failing to separate ownership from management and for the way that managerial power has been passed down to family members. As I have just mentioned, however, it is important to bear in mind that these factors are endogenous managerial activities or the outcomes of managerial decisions, which have evolved under the given economic as well as institutional environment. Therefore, one should not expect that such a direct regulation policy to be effective, because the underlying causes of the *Chaebol* behavior were not appropriately addressed.

V. Post-crisis government-led restructuring and evaluation

The economic crisis exposed the deep rifts between the post-war generation development strategy and the new paradigm to be adopted in the future. Despite some progress in corporate governance structures, essential parts of the post-crisis restructuring process, however, remain under strong governmental guidance and, like those of the 1970s and 80s, overlook some important considerations. Let's take for example, the government-guided swaps of large businesses in major industries, the reduction of the debt/equity ratios to 200% on all *Chaebols* disregard of their inherent differences, and the prohibition of cross-debt. We find that these measures all involve direct intervention on endogenous management variables. As such, a most noticeable characteristic of these post-crisis reforms is in their way of make-up, which tends to overlook or ignore the more important underlying causes of economic behavior. However, government-led restructuring without the necessary institutional reforms simply will not have any lasting effect as is amply evident by the pre-crisis *Chaebol* reform efforts. Rather than this forced restructuring, a more systematic approach should be adopted, with rules and institutions designed to increase market pressure and induce firms to restructure voluntarily.

VI. Corporate governance restructuring and business responsibility

As is evident from some of the presentations in this conference, there is much discussion recently about corporate governance structures. Applying our previous arguments on the role of the government to corporate governance should provide a concrete illustration of the analytical potential of the new paradigm.

To a business firm, the external market environment is an exogenous variable while internal control systems are strategic variables disposable to the management, and is therefore endogenously determined. As is well known among economists, we must bear in mind that the optimality of endogenous behavior is conditional on the effectiveness of exogenous market pressure.

Broadly speaking, there are two ways to monitor and discipline corporations: through external market mechanisms and through internal control systems. The external market mechanisms are the exogenous factors affecting business decisions, and usually emphasize the establishment of economic institutions to enhance the corporate monitoring role of the various markets for products, capital, debt, managers and so on. Internal control systems, on the other hand, constitute endogenous variables, and include mechanisms such as the holding company system or a planning and coordination office operating as a kind of holding company, as well as the board of directors.

Current debate about corporate governance tends to put more weight on internal control systems as can be seen in the OECD guidelines, which emphasize the proper role of the board of directors in corporate governance. This, however, is largely based on the experiences of advanced economies in which the external market for corporate control in the product, capital, debt, and CEO markets are well established and all operate competitively. The situation in Korea is somewhat different owing to the past interventionist development strategies that have hampered the development of various market institutions. On top of that, the OECD position seems to miss the point because they fail to recognize that the system of the board of directors is, in fact, part of the internal management system, which should be allowed to be strategically utilized to meet the objectives of the corporation, and hence the details of the internal management system should be left so as to be endogenously determined. Therefore, in the Korean context, it may be argued that the improvement of the role of the external disciplinary system becomes even more urgent and crucial in inducing corporate behavior towards enhancing the efficiency of internal governance systems, including the board of director system. I am not saying that the continued development of internal control systems is not important. On the contrary, internal control mechanisms must be continuously strengthened, but I am warning against the possibility of imposing excessive restrictions on management decision variables, which is likely to occur if we are not careful.

It follows, again, that the role of the government and public policy is to promote the effective functioning of external market mechanisms through institutional reforms, which will help discipline corporations while leaving internal control systems to be decided upon by the corporations in the pursuit to maximize their survival probabilities.

VII. The role of the private corporations in transforming business and management culture

What about the roles and responsibilities of the private corporations, particularly in creating a viable business and management culture that will prove to be competitive in the era of increased global competition? First of all, it goes without saying that market discipline rather than government intervention will effectively determine the success or failure of a firm in this new paradigm of economic management. Three important implications to the management of private corporations come to mind. First of all, Korean firms will have to engage in a fierce competition with world-class competitors and hence, inefficient firms will have to exit the market, no longer being able to rely on government protection, as has been the case in the past. A second point is that transparency will be a key determinant of business competitiveness, as potential investors and lenders are bound to turn their backs on firms that do not have a transparent internal corporate governance structure. Third, since the constant cycle of technological innovation is becoming increasingly shorter, firms failing to innovate on a regular basis will eventually fall behind in the competition.

Ensuring the autonomy and accountability of private corporations requires not only a paradigm shift in economic management, but also a constant effort to nurture market mechanisms. It is about time that the Korean government changed its half-century-long habit of economic intervention, and allowed the market to do its job. Of great importance is that firms will have the added responsibility of keeping track of and adapting to the changing economic environment.

Let me conclude by saying that the issue on the roles of the government and private corporations in economic management is a long-standing and as yet unresolved subject in the economics profession. The debate is as heated and controversial as ever, and I invite all of you here to think deeply about this most important matter.

Thank you for your kind attention.

Korean Financial Crisis in Global Political-Economic System

Gill-Chin Lim[1]

I. Introduction

An American writer Steven Schlossstein wrote in 1989 on Korea and Brazil in his book *The End of the American Century*.

> "In twenty-five years between 1962 and 1987, Korea's GNP increased more than ten times, from $12 billion to nearly $120 billion, and the countrys hard working population of 40 million people had accomplished more in a shorter period of time than Brazil with its 130 million or Mexico with 75 million. The two Latin American economies had also enjoyed better access to the paternalistic American market. ···And neither had experienced the devastating effects of civil war, which further delayed Korea's start."

Ten years after such an observation, the both nations were struggling to come out of severe economic crises. Both of their reform efforts rely heavily

---

[1] Distinguished Institute Professor, KDI School of International Policy and Management, Seoul, Korea. MSU Endowed Professor of Asian Studies in a Global Context, Michigan State University, USA

on a large sum of loans and policy prescriptions from the International Monetary Fund (IMF).

Korea achieved remarkable economic growth since the early 1960s with a series of five-year economic development plans. A nation with a relatively small population—about 46 million in 1999-quickly became one of the 11 largest economies in the world and earned an honorable title 'Asian Tiger' along with Hong Kong, Singapore and Taiwan. It also showed an overall improvement in education, health and housing during the rapid pace of industrialization. But, in 1997, it encountered a financial crisis symptomatically surfaced as an acute shortage of foreign reserve, which forced it to seek a rescue from IMF.

Since the financial crisis broke out in Asia and Latin America, scholars and policy analysts have investigated their causes and impacts. They also examined the policy prescription and evaluated its effects. However, existing studies and commentaries are fragmented and mostly concerned with economic aspects of financial crises and reform efforts. There have been few studies looking at the financial and economic crises from political and economic viewpoint of policy making in a more general framework.

In this remark, I evaluate the economic policy reform efforts of Korea led by the IMF guidelines with a methodological framework of Global Political-Economic System. I look at the Korean reform policies with a set of evaluation criteria and a normative theory of public decision-making process in a global context. Based on this evaluation, I propose that the international agencies, government and private agents restructure their policy-making framework with an expanded concept of sustainability. I also suggest that a global restructuring be considered by major actors in the global political-economic system to minimize the possibility of recurring crisis.

II. Theoretical Model: Global Political-Economic System

1. Shortcomings of Existing Theories

Financial and economic crises erupted in recent decades are the result of complex forces in both global and domestic scenes. Unlike in the years when countries conducted their social and economic affairs without substantial global interdependency, contemporary crises are an outcome of interactions among many actors in a complex global political and economic system. The existing theories on the causes of financial and economic crises are constructed around a small number of actors to blame or focus on macro economic variables, which are mere symptoms rather than root causes.

An earlier economic analysis looking at "fundamentals" and key economic variables conceals the real source of the trouble. Crisis is caused by weak economic fundamentals—excessive expansionary fiscal and monetary policies lead to a persistent loss of foreign reserves and ultimately abandonment of the parity (Krugman 1979, Flood and Garber 1983). The second-generation economic models and other variations do not establish a clear relationship between fundamentals and crisis, but use a similar set of variables. The government objective is to derive benefits from fixed exchange rate. The government abandons parity when the cost exceeds the benefit (Obstfeld 1994).

The existing explanations usually focus on the current affairs lacking perspectives on historical evolution of institutions, which govern economic system. The condition leading to a severe shortage of foreign reserves or current account deficit is a result of longstanding practice with an institutional inertia existing in the history of policy making. But most policy prescriptions are made with little reference to historical origin of the current events.

These theories also lack a proper understanding of political and cultural backgrounds. The Korean culture of favoritism based on kinship, schools and regional loyalty contributed to crony capitalism and a rampant abuse of power and corruption.

To understand the true causes of crises and prescribe effective cure, we need to develop a framework, which takes into account the complex interactions among various actors in the global and domestic scenes. Understanding global trends is prerequisite to identifying key actors and building a comprehensive framework.

2. Global Political-Economic System: A Model

I propose a methodological framework of Global Political-Economic System. There are a number of actors in this system.

- International organizations
    - International Monetary Fund
    - International Bank for Reconstruction and Development
    - OECD
    - United Nations
- Foreign governments
    - Creditor countries
    - Debtor countries
- Foreign financial agents
    - Financial institutions
    - Private investors
- Political actors
    - Parliament
    - Political parties
- Central decision makers
    - President and the Cabinet
    - Central Bank
    - Financial supervisory institutions
- Financial institutions and actors

Banks
  Other financial institutions
  Private investors
- Businesses
  Business conglomerates
  Small and medium size businesses
  Multinational businesses
- Labor
  Organized labor
  Unorganized labor
- Judiciary and law enforcement offices
  The judiciary
  Law enforcement offices
  Government auditing office
- Others
  The general public
  Civilian organizations
  Press
  Research institutes

Each of these actors has a set of nominal organizational objectives. In conducting their business to achieve their objectives, their professional competence can be evaluated in three categories: *technical competence, inter-subjective competence* and *ethical competence*. The relationships among the actors can be legitimate or illegitimate, efficient or inefficient, and truthful or deceptive.

An actor, that is technically, inter-subjectively and ethically competent, is in a state of stability being able to achieve its objectives. To have a well functioning, stable global system, all actors should be stable having technical, inter-subjective and ethical competence, and the relationships among all actors should be legitimate, efficient and truthful. When the majority of individual systems are unstable, a global political-economic system becomes unstable.

An actor at its younger age may be stable but later become unstable and go out of business. At the initial stage of development, an entire political-economic system may have stability, but changes in individual actors may create forces which destabilize the entire system. Whether an individual actor or a country in a global system at a given point of time can overcome a crisis depends on their ability to restructure their roles, functions and enhance their level of competence.

III. Crisis and Response

1. From Chung-Hee Park to Dae-Jung Kim

When Chung Hee Park took power by military coup in 1961, people were skeptical about the Korea's capability to develop its economy. Under his authoritarian regime, he carried out a series of five-year economic development plans. He was a dictatorial, undemocratic ruler, but there is little dispute that his regime achieved a remarkable economic progress to be called a miracle. He reigned over the nation until he was assassinated by his own CIA (Central Intelligence Agency) director in 1979. He was succeeded by two generals, Doo-Whan Chun and Tae-Woo Roh, during whose presidency Korea continued on the path to rapid growth.

In 1992, the first civilian politician Young Sam Kim was elected by popular vote and assumed the presidency until the 1997 financial disaster. During his presidency, Chun and Roh were convicted of treason and corruption.

Dae-Jung Kim of National Congress for New Politics (NCNP), 73 year old politician who faced death several times since Park, including a death sentence under Chun, won the Presidential election against Hoi-chang Lee of the governing Grand National Party (GNP) and In-je Rhee in December 1997. The victory with narrow margin—40.3 percent out of 80.6 percent of the 33 million eligible voters was won by a coalition with United Liberal Democrats (ULD), the leader of which is Jong Pil Kim, the former CIA Director under Park. Nonetheless, it was significant in that the transition of power was made from an incumbent to opposition party for the first time in Korean presidential election history.

From Chung Hee Park to Young Sam Kim, Korea grew continuously. Table 1 shows key indicators of growth, development and transformation of Korea

2. Korea's Political-Economic System before the 1997 Crisis: Identifying the Cause of Crisis

IMF and Other International Actors

In this section I examine the three competencies of the actors in the *Global Political-Economic System*. I begin with the IMF. How competent was IMF? In November 1996, the 24 member IMF Executive Board offered the following discussions on Korea.

> "Directors welcomed Korea's continued impressive macroeconomic performance: growth had decelerated from the unsustainably rapid pace of the previous two years, inflation had remained subdued notwithstanding some modest pickup in the months prior to the consultation and the widening of the current account deficit largely resulted from a temporary weakening of the terms of trade."

The above comments make us question the IMF's technical competency to judge macro economic performance of Korea.

The IMF also conducted a highly sophisticated research on early warning system to predict currency crisis (Kaminsky, Lizondo and Reinhart 1997). Published in July 1997, it proposes to look at the economic variables such as international reserves, the real exchange rate, domestic credit, credit to the public sector, domestic inflation, export, money growth, real GDP growth, and the fiscal deficit as useful indicators for detecting a possible crisis within the following 24 months. There is no clue that this early warning system was ever used to prevent the Korean crisis that broke out one and a half year after its publication. If this model had been used to a certain nation which faced a currency crisis, then we need to question the technical quality of this model. Otherwise, we need to dispute the inter-subjective competence of IMF—whether the technical materials they produce are conveyed to member nations decision-makers competently.

An evaluation of ethical competence involves an examination of the ability of the IMF's key decision makers to recognize critically their problems and restructure their decision making process. They must examine critically the legitimacy of their organizational structure and decision-making process. Their actions should be accountable and transparent. From the viewpoint of a governance system of modern organizations, the composition of the IMF Executive Board is abnormal. Twenty-four members out of 184 member nations cannot represent the true interest of small and economically weak nations. There is no input from outside the IMF. Some of the most critical decisions affecting human race are made without reasonable representative mechanisms. The 30-year embargo rule on program documents no doubt hampers transparency.

The objectives of foreign governments are to maximize the benefit of their own. For that reason rich nations lend money and poor nations borrow. The level of competence differs among nations. In general, it is believed that the advanced industrial countries have superior technical competence demonstrated by their ability to compete in the international market. The Global Competitiveness study conducted by IMD International (1998) demonstrates that advanced countries have stronger competitive edge over developing nations. In 1997, US was number one, Singapore 2, Japan 9, UK 11, Germany 14, Korea 30 and Russia 46 out of 46 countries. The advanced nations have better knowledge to handle international financial matters and can gain from international transactions-daily deals as well as long lasting treaties and conventions such as GATT, WTO, etc.

The advanced countries are supposedly more transparent, less corrupt than others. The indicators of transparency and corruption provided by Transparency International (1997) corroborate this point. Korea's Corruption Perception Index (CPI) ranked 34 among 52 surveyed. Denmark was one, Finland 2, UK 14, US 16, Russia 49 and Nigeria 52. Before the major financial crises in Korea, Latin America and other Asian countries, no advanced nations blew whistles. In terms of ethical competence, it is true that the governments of advanced nations are less corrupt, but they tended to acquiesce the corruption of other countries for political reasons.

Through various foreign financial agents, Korea borrowed heavily from other nations-totaling $10.1 billion from France, $10.8 billion from Germany, $2.8 billion from the Netherlands, $6.0 billion from the United Kingdom, $23.7 billion from Japan and $10.0 billion from the Unites States in 1997 (Delhaise 1998). Foreign financial intermediaries are in general more competent in using the world market to gain more profit and to minimize risks. The banks in the United States and Europe are more transparent. While the IMF, as an international organization to serve common goods, is obliged to have a concern over the ethical dimensions in their decision making process, the foreign governments and financial agents have little reason to consider ethical issues in international market. Anything can happen. For example, profit oriented investors set up companies in Cayman Island, tax haven, through which Malaysian and Indonesian Banks borrowed money.

In this context, the conspiracy theory emerged. Malaysian Prime Minister Mahathir Mohamad publicly expressed that Western speculators conspired the Asian financial melt down, and he imposed currency controls and prohibited foreign shareholders to take their money from Malaysia for one year from September 1, 1998. Whether it is a conspiracy or not, it is important to examine the effect of capital flight by foreign investors. Existing evidence suggests that capital flight by foreign investors is a small portion of the total outflow. Out of $6 billion that Mexico lost in

December 1994 in foreign exchange reserve, only $360 million was taken out by foreign investors. Kwang Jun (1993) shows that the turnover rate is higher among domestic investors in Korean stock market. The IMF report tells that there was unrecorded capital flight of $20 billion from Korea, Indonesia, Malaysia, Thailand and the Philippines in 1997. Among these nations, Korea had the largest amount—$8.7 billion. The trading data analyzed by Choi, Kho and Stulz (1997) showed positive feedback trading and hedging among foreign investors but no evidence that foreign investors exercised destabilizing effect on the Korean stock market (Kim 1998).

Key Domestic Actors
At the center of an inquiry into the Korean crisis are four groups of actors: political actors; central decision-makers; financial institutions and actors; and businesses. Comprehending the relationships among them is essential to understand the cause of the crisis.

The year 1997, when the financial crisis hit Korea, was a turbulent year. Early in January, Hanbo Steel went bankrupt leaving $6 billion debt. Other large conglomerates—Kia, Sammi and Jinro-followed the scenario of massive financial crunch. Some are of the opinion that the bankruptcy of these large business conglomerates in a chain reaction created a nation-wide disaster. But, evidences clearly show that Korean corporations and banks were technically incompetent for a long time well before the Hanbo scandal broke out.

The Korean corporate governance structure was known for its technical and ethical incompetencies long before the crisis. The presence of a small number of large business conglomerates—*Chaebol*s is thought to be one of the biggest problems in Korean society. The owner controls a group of a flagship company and subsidiaries. The board of directors has little voice of their own in making decision in the board. They lack a sense of ownership and creativity. This governance system was a fertile ground for inefficiency and corruption. A study shows that only 27 percent of the 570 non-financial firms created shareholder values during the five years before the

Korean crisis. Seventy three percent of the companies did not generate earnings to cover the capital costs (Kim 1998).

Top 30 *Chaebols* account for about 14 percent of GDP. Since *Chaebols* own a large share of equity, corporate bond and bank loans, they have a tight relationship with the financial sector. The performance of banks is directly related to the performance of businesses. Delhaise (1998) demonstrated that the efficiency rate of Korean banks was the lowest in Asia, and their gross profit margin (GPM) was absolutely poor. They were not able to yield decent returns for shareholders and to generate provisions for non-performing assets. The near bankruptcy of Korean banks was not revealed because of the untruthful financial statements and the loose supervision by the regulatory authorities. Delhaise said that the Korean banks were deep in trouble well ahead of the Asian crisis. It is more appropriate to say that the incompetence of the Korean banks was one of the root causes of the Korean crisis.

The lack of ethical competence of the Korean government, the financial sector and businesses are easily illustrated. *Chaebols* bribed Presidents Doo Whan Chun and Tae Woo Roh. The top aids of both Young Sam Kim and Dae Jung Kim were convicted of bribery in 1997. The former chairmen of the Bank Supervisory Commission and the Insurance Supervisory Commission were indicted for accepting bribes from the chairman of the Shin-Dong-Ah *Chaebol* group. Hanbo represented a case depicting the chain of Korean corruption among businesses, the financial sector, politicians and the government.

While the national crisis was approaching without much notice by the general public, the most intense campaign for presidential election in Korean political history was going on. It was the year the democratic capability of the nation was being tested. Railroading a labor bill by GNP took place in the National Assembly in 1996 and political confrontation repeated. The legislatures behavior before the crisis simply validates the old tradition of spiraling conflicts and position bargaining.

The three powerhouse decision makers in the economic decision making under President Young Sam Kim were the Deputy Prime Minister (also Minister of Finance and Economy), the Senior Secretary to the President on Economic Affairs, and the Governor of the Bank of Korea (BOK). The BOK Governor claimed that he submitted warning signals several times but they never reached the President. All of them denied any negligence on their part. But the fact that the Korean government made an official request for an emergency loan to the IMF only on November 21 clearly proves the incompetence of the central decision-makers. The date of the call to the IMF was just eleven days after the sharp reduction in foreign reserve-from $22.3 billion in October down to $7.3 billion in November-and a depreciation in exchange rate from 844.2 won to a dollar in 1996 to 1000. It seems apparent also that the communication among the key decision-makers surrounding the Blue House was pitifully inefficient and dysfunctional. This is partially due to the stringent leadership style of Young Sam Kim. The inconsistencies in the claims by the key decision-makers indicate illegitimate communication practice and deceptive reporting by the technocrats deeply imbedded in the Korean bureaucracy. The Office of Auditing has an accumulation of distortions in government agencies. Perhaps the single firmest evidence about the illegitimate relationship is the scandal involving collection of campaign fund for the governing party through the Office of Taxation.

Overall, the collusion among the government, politicians, business and the financial sectors weakened the economic efficiency, fostered corruption, avoided reform and justified the *status quo*.

Other Actors
As noted earlier, the Korean labor grew big and potentially powerful during the rapid expansion of the economy. However, political oppression under Park and Chun nurtured strong anti-government sentiments. Presidential candidate Roh promised the freedom to organize and to bargain collectively in his Declaration of Democracy in June 1987. After 1988 when labor unions could bargain collectively, labor union activism drove up wages and added to labor market rigidity. Labor became gradually

more confrontational and engaged in illegal strikes.

The Korean press, quite polemic with the government, was busy in sensational reporting of the Presidential campaign with intermittent stories about the investigation about the President's son. There was little evidence for competence of the press to give any alarms for the approaching crisis. It should be also noted that none of the government funded research institutes produced any official research giving a lucid warning. None of the civilian organizations such as Citizens Coalition for Economic Justice, which claims to be a watchdog for government incompetence, hinted anything.

The judiciary and the law enforcement entities in Korea were often questioned about their ability to make independent and prudential judgement and investigation. The lack of ethical competence of the judiciary and the law enforcement agencies was a reason why the candidate Dae-Jung Kim promised an establishment of independence counsel system during the campaign.

In Sum

The political-economic system of Korea in the years before the 1997 crisis was ripe for a collapse. Individual components in the system were mostly incompetent and the relationship among key decision-makers in the web was tainted with illegitimate, inefficient and deceptive practices. It had the conditions to be unstable, bound to have a crisis. The above analysis unveils that real cause of the Korean financial crisis was incompetence of individual actors at the micro level.

3. IMF's Prescription

Shortly after the sharp decrease in foreign reserve and depreciation in exchange rate, the Korean government sought IMF's help. On December 3, 1997, the Korean government represented by Vice Prime Minister Chang-Yuel Lim and the IMF led by Managing Director Michel Camdessus signed a Stand-by Arrangement. A wide range of reform measures are described in the Stand-by Arrangement titled "Summary of the Economic Program" (December 3, 1997) and it was reviewed nine times as of February 1999. The three groups of policies are (i) Macroeconomic Policies, (ii) Financial Sector Restructuring and (iii) Other Structural Measures.

Moody's downgraded Korea's credit rating to a junk bond status on December 10. Before the presidential election, the IMF obtained consent from all three candidates to abide by the arrangement. On December 16, the Korean government raised the maximum interest rate to 40 percent. A few days after the December 17 Presidential election, Korea got $4 billion emergency financial support from the Asia Development Bank (ADB). On December 21, Moodys rating was non-investment grading. On December 24, The World Bank (IBRD) offered $3 billion in financial assistance. Total borrowing of $57 billion consists of $21 billion from the IMF, $10 billion from the World Bank, $4 billion from the Asia Development Bank and $22 billion from industrial nations.

4. Korean Government's Policies

In response to the policy measures outlined in the Stand-by Arrangement, the Korean government under the new President Dae-Jung Kim put forward the following "four banners" (Ministry of Finance and Economy 1999a, 1999b, Financial Supervisory Services 1999).

- Swift and prudent reforms
- Coordinated, multi-faceted approach
- Prevention of moral hazard
- Maintenance of social stability

Under these directions, the Korean government implemented reforms in five areas: market liberalization, financial sector, corporate sector, labor sector and public sector. The results of government efforts can be summarized as follows (Ministry of Finance and Economy 1999a, 1999b).

Market Liberalization
Korea acted upon lifting barriers in capital market, foreign direct investment and foreign exchange transactions quite swiftly. For example, foreign equity ownership ceiling — an item in the Stand-by Arrangement — was completely eliminated in May 1998. The New Foreign Investment Promotion Act (FIPA), effective as of November 17, 1998, streamlined and consolidated all previous foreign direct investment laws. The new Foreign Exchange Transaction Act replaced the old Foreign Exchange Management Act.

Financial Sector
The government closed or suspended financial institutions lacking competitiveness. These are 16 merchant banks, 5 commercial banks, 6 securities companies, and 4 insurance companies--totaling 86 financial institutions. Banks went through restructuring to have a sound bank status with BIS ratio of 10 — 13 percent. The government provided fiscal support for restructuring to normalize financial flows and dispose of NPLs (Non-performing loans) and to recapitalize banks. Unsound loans in June 1998 were estimated 136 trillion won and precautionary loans amounted 72.5 trillion won. Government-guaranteed public bonds were issued and Korea Asset Management Corporation (KAMCO) was mobilized to purchase NPL. Korea Deposit Insurance Corporation (KDIC) was engaged in recapitalization of banks.

Corporate Sector
The Five Principles of Corporate Restructuring agreed upon between the government and the business leaders in early 1998 — enhancement of corporate governance, prohibition of cross-guarantees between business affiliated, improvement of corporate financial structure, concentration on core competence, and reinforcing responsibility of governing shareholders and management — are the guidelines for corporate sector reform. Businesses

are to put an end to financial cross-debt guarantees among subsidiaries by March 2000. They are to improve capital structure debt-equity ratio. To enhance transparency, they will use combined financial statement beginning FY 1999 and appoint outside directors. To promote the rights of the shareholders, they take measures to remove corruption and collusive relationship between government and big businesses. The big deals are going on between business conglomerates. Most recently President Kim clearly expressed his strong will to carry out necessary corporate restructuring.

Public Sector
To meet the goal of building a small and efficient government, the Korean government planned to reduce the size of the central government officials by 11 percent by 2000 (18,000 out of 162,000). In 1998, 9,084 were laid off. 35,070 local jobs, 12 percent of the total, were eliminated by September 1998. It also pursued privatization of state owned enterprises. Out of 109 State Owned Enterprises (SOEs), 20 public institutions including two public corporations were privatized. The Regulation Reform Committee abolished 4,465 of the previous 11,125 regulations.

Labor Market
To improve labor market flexibility, the Labor Standard Act (LSA) was revised in Feb 1998. There has been Tripartite Commission (government, business and labor) agreement about layoffs, rights for labor activities, political participation, back-pay and health care provisions.

5. Evaluation of the Policy Reform Effort

To assess the performance of the government's reform effort, I first review the changes in key indicators since the crisis (Ministry of Finance and Economy 1999a, 1999b).

Usable foreign reserve has increased from $8.9 billion in December 1997 to $79.7 billion in February 2000. Current account deficit of $8.7 billion in

December 1997 changed to a surplus of $25 billion in 1999. Exchange rate, which was nearly 2,000 won per dollar in 1997, stabilized to 1,147 won in September, 2000. Interest rate changed from 30 percent to 6--8 percent. Inflation was 0.8 percent in 1999. GDP growth rate was minus 6.7 percent during 1998 and 10.7 percent in 1999. The KOSPI (Korea Stock Price Index) is about 660 in September 2000. The effectiveness of IMF-led reform in Korea can be evaluated at three levels: Macroeconomic level; Microeconomic level for corporate sector; and Individual level.

Macroeconomic Level

A checking of the Korean government reform effort against the IMF guidelines reveals that the Korean government quite aggressively implemented reforms at the macro level. Macroeconomic reform has made substantial progresses at least in terms of quantitative measures. However, policy makers must recognize that the macro indicators hide some important aspects of the economy and society. For instance, foreign reserve is not an indicator of financial solvency but that of liquidity at best.

There are several areas of concern at the macro level reform. First of all, the total amount of external debt has not been reduced significantly. What has happened is a simple conversion of short-term debts to long-term debts, which Korea must pay back in the future. There is no guarantee that Korea will have enough cash when the long-term debts mature. Circumstances may arise under which the long-term debt burden can trigger a crisis. This is possible if the forces in the global political-economic system, which are beyond the control of Korean economic policy makers, strike Korea. Unexpected shocks originating from Chinese, Japanese or American economy could make Korean situation quite volatile. Korea may have to continuously seek new debts to pay old debts. The long-term costs of financing these debts—costs of managing debt postponement—from the national point of view must be estimated.

There is also a concern about government debt. Including debt guarantees, it could rise from $41.7 billion (50 trillion won) to $165 billion (200 trillion won) in 1999. The total government debt could escalate as high as 45 percent of GDP.

The high exchange rate gave a favorable condition for expansion of export after the financial crisis, but a lower exchange rate will alter the favorable import-export situation.

Korea was able to keep inflation low during the last couple of decades. Since the stringent monetary and fiscal policies and restructuring of business firms, there has been a sharp increase in unemployment. At the end of 1998, eight percent or 1.8 million were unemployed. There were 1.04 million unemployed (4.8 %) in December 1999. The income gap between the rich and poor has widened according to the Office of the Statistics report in March 1999. The size of the middle class has substantially dwindled. Unfortunately, all these lead to a divided society which runs counter to the IMF objective specified in the second item of Article I — maintenance of high level of employment and real income.

Due to the higher level of unemployment after the crisis, there was an ongoing dispute in the Tripartite Commission and a threat by labor to exit the Commission and go on a strike. Federation of Korea Labor Unions exited from Tripartite Commission in early 2000 and the Seoul Metropolitan Subway workers went on strike in May 2000. In the education sector, the Ministry of Education embarked on early retirement system. Unhappy teachers organized by the Korea Teacher Union demanded resignation of the Minister of Education.

The most noticeable action taken by the National Assembly after the crisis was the congressional hearing on 1997 financial crisis, questioning three central decision-makers under Young Sam Kim. The National Assembly members from NCNP-ULD coalition also wanted to call in the former President and his son who refused to appear in the hearing. The hearing was politically motivated by the ruling coalition of NCNP and ULD to discredit the Young Sam Kim's party and the government. NCNP-ULD tried to prove that the Young Sam Kim's bureaucrats were incompetent, unethical and lacked effective communication.

The tradition of confrontation and railroading— this time for NCCP-ULD's push for the government— restructuring bill-in the National Assembly continued in 1999. The public hearing debacle and the illegitimate, disorderly conducts at the legislature illustrate the Korean polity's immaturity: Korea is still far from having competent, democratic and legitimate governance in the political and executive arenas.

Microeconomic Level for Corporate Sector
The inability of having political consensus in Korean politics seriously limits the possibility to carry out reforms at the micro level for the corporate, financial, and labor sectors. Despite the Five Principles of Corporate Restructuring agreed upon between the government and the business leaders in early 1998, the responsiveness of the private sector has not been satisfactory. The Korea Stock Exchange released data showing that chairpersons of the ten largest *Chaebols* increased the ownership of the stock of their subsidiaries by 57.4 percent in volume (57.8 in amount) since 1999 (*Chosun Daily* March 6, 1999). Micro level reforms within *Chaebols* have been slow. They continue to be technically incompetent: the Korea Stock Exchange's recent analysis using consolidated financial statement disclosed that the 30 largest business groups were found to have a 20 percent increase in corporate loss.

In the financial sector, the Financial Supervisory Services (FSS) issued a warning to 10 banks for their negligence in complying with corporate financial restructuring agreement. An April report by FSS unveiled that non-performing loans by 22 banks have increased by 4.3 percent in 1998.

A rather dramatic event took place as an aftermath of the Korean Air's crash in China. Upon demand by President Kim, the Chairman of the Han Jin group — the business conglomerate for the Korean Air— resigned. The case was a warning against incompetent corporate owner-managers. In the meantime, the government announced that *Chaebols*, which do not expedite group level restructuring could be "worked out."

Individual Level

Perhaps the most difficult reform is the reform of individuals. Although a large number of public officials and private sector employees have been laid off, we cannot simply assume that those who stay on the job work efficiently and cleanly. Evidences for corruption in both public and private sectors are abundant. It has been observed that bureaucrats and business employees do not have proper professional knowledge to run efficient organizations. The intent of the public sector reform is to change the "large and inefficient" Korean government to a "small and efficient" one. However, without ongoing educational programs to enhance competence of bureaucrats, the government could become "small and inefficient" rather than "small and efficient."

An unwanted impact of the cuts in budgets and employment in the private sector has been the flight of the country's top-level scientists and engineers to other nations. According to a survey of 70 *Chaebol*-affiliated firms by the Korea Industrial Technology Association (KITA), domestic manufacturing firms cut their R&D investment by 9.9 percent from 1997 to 1998 forcing about 5,000 researchers to leave Korea since the IMF crisis. Another trend endangering sound long run economic recovery is substantial reduction in R&D spending. Between 1994 and 1997, Korea's annual increase in R&D spending was 15.5 percent. In 1998 it was minus 12.8 percent (*Chosun Daily* May 12, 1996).

In Sum

Korea has the appearance of successful reform in macro economy, as the basic macro economic indicators demonstrate. However, the reforms at the micro levels have not been effective.

The IMF prepared a preliminary assessment of IMF-supported programs in Indonesia, Korea and Thailand in January 1999. It reports that the program did not restore confidence and attract capital flows in the market rapidly enough in Korea (Lane et. al. 1999). The bulk of the report is an attempt to justify the IMF-prescribed monetary and fiscal policies and structural reforms. It also purports that stabilization effort without structural reforms would have been costly to treat the symptoms without dealing with the causes of the disease. Focusing on economic issues, it has a thin treatment of program impacts and policy process. The last paragraph of the report mentions the political context of policy implementation. It feels encouraged about Korea and Thailand, which had been successful in implementation of policies. But given the ongoing political turmoil observed in Korea, their assessment might be overly optimistic. Their competence in political analysis is questioned. The World Bank office in Korea was closed in August, 2000, implying that Korea had recovered from the crisis.

IV. Summary and Conclusion

Globalization hurts societies not able to compete with the big forces originating in the global scene. Societies, which lack political cohesion, social justice, knowledge and ethical norms, can easily fall prey to global forces. Some countries in Asia and Latin America have proved this thesis. Societies, which possess these positive qualities, are able to respond to global challenges and capture new opportunities for further social progress. Proponents of globalization are knowledge professionals, large businesses and advanced nations. Opposition often comes from those individuals, businesses and organizations under protective policies.

The web of the global political and economic system is complex enough not to render any meaningful prediction for an individual actor's fate. The increasing levels of the complexity in the system have not been accompanied by sufficient discoveries of knowledge about the system. Decision-makers at the national government and international organizations are like doctors without the knowledge of human anatomy. They tended to treat symptoms rather than true causes. The patient is physically and mentally ill, but the doctors address bodily injuries only.

In this remark, I inquired the causes of financial crisis in a broad framework. Technical, inter-subjective and ethical competencies of public and private, foreign and domestic actors were examined for Korea. In case of Korea, evidences clearly revealed that incompetence of the corporate sector, the financial sector, politicians and the government decision-makers led to the crisis. The Korean system before the crisis was unstable, lacking satisfactory degrees of legitimate, efficient and truthful relationships among them. Corruption and collusion among the four key actors were at the center of the financial and economic disaster.

The IMF, with its superior technical resources, was not able to help prevent the Korean financial crisis. The decision making process was hasty and did not have satisfactory representation of relevant parties. Reform measures in Korea at the macro level have been effective in terms of overall quantitative indicators, but they have not been successful at the micro and individual levels. Dubious behavior among corporate and financial sectors is still observed.

The policy making and implementation process involving financial crisis and reform paid little attention to the impacts of policies. They ignored to take necessary precautionary measures. Policies to reduce or ameliorate unwanted impacts were not included as explicit policy objectives. This is disappointing because, at various levels of governmental hierarchy, it is now a common practice to assess impacts of major public and private programs and projects. The exclusion of impact assessment in the IMF-led programs seriously damages its legitimacy as public institution.

The official document signed by the IMF and Korea has no discussion of the program's impact on unemployment and income distribution. Countermeasures on unemployment sponsored by the Ministries of Labor, Education, etc. came after the facts. The discernable social division created by the IMF's austere monetary and fiscal policies, unfortunately, will stay for a long time. Such a division adds to political costs, reduces social cohesion and decreases productivity. In light of the second item of the Article I, the IMF's negligence over social policies in the Korean-IMF case should not be repeated in other occasions.

Would Korea have embarked on reform programs without feeling the danger of national bankruptcy? Would Korea have adopted the austere monetary and fiscal policies and structural reforms without IMF directives given as conditions for loan? The immature democracy which depicts Korean political environment and incompetent and illegitimate practices of Korean economic actors and policy makers would not have made it possible to undertake reforms well before acute symptoms were detected. In spite of the problems the IMF programs brought about, much of what the Korean government achieved during the years after crisis could not have happened but for the IMF prescription.

Yet the IMF may well accept the criticisms about its governance that it is not operating legitimately with satisfactory levels of transparency, participation and inter-subjective competence. It should look at a possibility to amend its rules, decision-making procedures and organizational structure if not a thorough restructuring — for example, a merger with other organizations or abolishment. The IMF needs to learn more about making decisions more transparently and implement policies more effectively. It needs to develop a better way of working with other international organizations, notably the World Bank, the Inter-American Development Bank, the Asia Development Bank and the indigenous NGOs and research institutes in member nations.

Normatively speaking, the ultimate objective of public policy in a democratic society is to maximize the overall public well being by employing policy alternatives chosen in an open process. The role of public and international organizations can be debated (Bennett 1995). Nevertheless, at least nominally the Korean government, the IMF and the World Bank are to ensure sustained quality of life for all members of the society. The narrow objective of sustained growth is hurting some segments of people, natural environment and social cohesion. Requisite is a broadened concept of sustainability. (Lim and Lee, 1999) *I propose that public policy making encompass not only economic sustainability but also political, ecological, technological and cultural sustainability. By taking an approach to have a balance among* competing goals, policy makers can depreciate social conflicts and minimize the long-run social costs of policy implementation. In this regard, reforms are needed for all actors in the contemporary global political-economic system. They need to gain global competence — an ability to respond to the global problems and opportunities with technical, inter-subjective and ethical competence.

Major international organizations and countries concerned should seriously think about practical action for global restructuring. Until the global political-economic system is governed by a workable monitoring or coordinating mechanism, crises are likely to repeat without warning and economically fragile nations are unlikely to overcome them easily.

Table 1. Key Indicators: Korea

Indicator	Value	
Population (mil.)	38.1 (1980)	46.7 (1997)
Life Expectancy (years)	67 (1980)	72 (1997)
GDP (bil. of US $)	62.8 (1980)	442.5 (1997)
Real GDP/capita (US $)	1,648 (1980)	9,620 (1997)
Real annual GDP growth rate (%)	9.4 (1980-1990)	7.2 (1990-1997)
Import/export (bil. of $)	25.1/29.8 (1980)	171.3/164.9 (1997)
Inflation (%)	19.8 (1970-1980)	5.3 (1990-1997)
Unemployment (%)	5.2 (1980)	2.0 (1997)
Agriculture (% of GDP)	15 (1980)	6 (1997)
Industry (% of GDP)	40 (1980)	43 (1997)
Service (% of GDP)	45 (1980)	51 (1997)
Government deficit (% of GNP)	2.9 (1980)	4.9 (1994)
Balance of payment current account deficit (%)	-2.2 (1980)	-1.8 (1997)
International reserve (bil. of $)	2.9 (1980)	20.4 (1997)
Human Development Index Rank	32 (1992)	30 (1995)
Human Development Index Value	0.859 (1992)	0.894 (1995)

*Source: World Development Report 1998/1999, World Development Indicators 1999, Human Development Report 1994, Human Development Report 1998.

References

Bennett, A. LeRoy. (1995) *International Organizations: Principles and Issues*. 6th ed. New Jersey: Prentice Hall Inc.

Choe, Hyuk, Bong-Chan Kho, and Rene Stulz. (1998) Do Foreign Investors Destabilize Stock Markets? The Korean Experience in 1997. Ohio State University Working Paper. Ohio State University, June.

Delhaise, Philippe F. (1998) *Asia in Crisis: The Implosion of the Banking and Finance System*. Singapore: John Wiley & Sons (Asia) Pte Ltd.

Financial Supervisory Services. (1999) *Introducing a New Paradigm to Korea's Financial and Corporate Sectors*. Seoul: Financial Supervisory Commission, Jan.

Flood, R., and P. Garber. (1983) A Model of Stochastic Process Switching. *Econometica 51*. pp. 537-551.

IMD International. (1998). *The World Competitiveness Yearbook 1998*. New York: IMD International.

James, Harold. (1996). *International Monetary Cooperation since Bretton Woods*. Washington, D.C.: International Monetary Fund.

Jun, Kwang. (1993). Effects of Capital Market Liberalization in Korea: Empirical Evidence and Policy Implications. Edited by Stijn Claessens and Sudarshan Gooptu. *Portfolio Investment in Developing Countries*. Washington, D.C.: The World Bank. pp. 404-425.

Kaminsky, Graciela, Saul Lizondo, and Carmen M. Reinhart. (1997). Leading Indicators of Currency Crises. IMF Working Paper. International Monetary Fund, July.

Kim, E. Han. (1998). Globalization of Capital Markets and the Asian Financial Crisis. *Journal of Applied Corporate Finance*. Vol. 11. No. 3. pp. 30-39.

Korean Ministry of Finance and Economy. (1999a). *Reinventing the Korean Economy: A Year of Reform*. Seoul: Ministry of Finance and Economy.

_____. (1999b). *The Road to Recovery in 1999: Korea's Ongoing Economic Reform*. Seoul: Ministry of Finance and Economy, Feb.

Krugman, Paul. (1979). A Model of Balance of Payments Crises. *Journal of Money, Credit, and Banking*. 11, August. pp. 311-325.

Lane, Timothy, Atish R. Ghosh, Javier Hamann, Steven Phillips, Marianne Schulze Ghattas, and Tsidi Tsikata. (1999). *IMF-Supported Programs in Indonesia, Korea and Thailand: A Preliminary Assessment.* Jan.

Lim, Gill-Chin, and Man-Hyung Lee. Ed. (1999). *Global Transformation Toward a Sustainable Civil Society.* Seoul: Hanul Academy Publishing Co.

Obstfeld, Maurice. (1994). The Logic of Currency Crises. NBER Working Paper No. 4640. Cambridge, Massachusetts: National Bureau of Economic Research.

Schlossstein, S. (1989). *The End of the American Century.* New York: Congdon & Week, Inc.

Transparency International. (1997). *TI Press Release (July 31, 1997).* Berlin: Transparency International.

United Nations Development Programme. (1998) *Human Development Report 1998.* Oxford: Oxford University Press.

World Bank. East Asia Pacific Region. (1999). *The Republic of Korea and the World Bank: Partners in Economic Recovery.*

_____. (1999). *World Development Report 1998/1999.* Oxford: Oxford University Press,

_____. (1999). *World Development Indicators 1999.* Oxford: Oxford University Press,

GOVERNMENT POLICY & BUSINESS SYSTEMS

1. Were Regulations on Economic Concentration in the Korean Fair Trade Act Effective?
   by Zusun Rhee

2. After the Economic Crisis: An Analysis of the Effects of Corporate Restructuring
   by Hasung Jang

3. Corporate Governance System in Korea: What Questions Should We Ask for Future Recommendations?
   by Y. Peter Chung

4. Do Agency Problems Explain the Post Asian Financial Crisis Performance of Korean Companies?
   by Byung-Mo Kim and Inmoo Lee

5. *Chaebol* Structure, Diversification and Performance
   by Inhak Hwang

Were Regulations on Economic Concentration in the Korean Fair Trade Act Effective?

Zusun Rhee[1]

I. Introduction

Korea's antitrust policy came into effect in 1980. This policy was enacted under the Monopoly Regulation and Fair Trade Act (FTA). The Korean Fair Trade Commission (KFTC) was established as the institution responsible for enforcement of the act in the same year, although it was not granted status as an independent decision-making body. Since then, the FTA and KFTC have been looked upon as the guardian of fair and free market competition and have faced no serious criticism. Many economic experts, as well as the general public, tend to think that reinforcement of the FTA and KFTC is a good policy. This national sentiment has encouraged the continuous reinforcement of the FTA and KFTC over the past twenty years. At present, the FTA has become a core economic law and the KFTC has become an independent body within the administration, and one of the most powerful government authorities

The main objective of the FTA is to regulate economic concentration. At the outset, Korea's antitrust policy of restricting economic concentra-

---

[1] Research Fellow, Korea Economic Research Institute, Seoul, Korea.

tion was only a declaration without any practical enforcement mechanisms; these enforcement mechanisms were introduced a full six years after the enactment of the FTA. Five main regulations on economic concentration and two ancillary regulations have been consecutively introduced since 1986. The reinforcement of the FTA targeted the removal or significant mitigation of economic concentration in large business groups (LBGs) called the "*Chaebols*". The KFTC has published its *Fair Trade White Book,* every year, suggesting that the enforcement of regulations on economic concentration has been successful in achieving its intermediate targets. Many foreign and domestic economic experts suggest that the *Chaebol* structure was the main cause of the economic crisis of 1997. As such, the general public and the KFTC strongly feel that economic concentration of the *Chaebol*s should be removed or significantly mitigated. Paradoxically, this kind of argument may mean that the current regulations on economic concentration are not effective enough to prevent or to restrict the economic concentration of the *Chaebol*s. Although these regulations have been continuously strengthened during the last fourteen years and the KFTC has urged successful enforcement of these regulations, there still remains a serious degree of economic concentration of *Chaebol*s, and the *Chaebol* structure is regarded as the principal cause for the recent economic crisis. Despite this paradoxical situation, the KFTC and many economic experts still propagate the view that a need exists to strengthen the behavioral regulations on the economic concentration of the *Chaebol*s. This argument, however, is extremely dangerous and may not lead to a desirable resolution of the *Chaebol* problem in Korea because it imposes serious costs on the national economy without having many practical benefits.

This paper attempts to explain whether the regulatory measures on economic concentration in the FTA were effective or not, and will describe the various kinds of policy and regulatory alternatives that are feasible, given that past regulations have not proven effective.

First of all, we will examine explicitly the definition of *Chaebol*s', identifying key factors of economic concentration. Two different arguments about key factors and their corresponding policy alternatives will be presented in the next section. In this section we will also explain various economic measures of economic concentration such as aggregate concentration, industrial/market concentration, ownership concentration and conglomerate concentration. In addition, we will review the KFTC's interpretation of the *Chaebol* structure, which constitutes the background of the regulations on economic concentration to *Chaebols*.

The third section will provide historical review of changes in the regulations on economic concentration in the FTA. We will identify the motives and objectives of each regulation on economic concentration and the trend of reinforcement of these regulations within the last 20 years. We will judge whether a regulatory measure was effective or not based on the number of years that it has been in effect.

The fourth section will examine the data that is related to each economic measure explained above. According to the KFTC's recognition of economic concentration, we will focus on aggregate concentration, diversification and ownership concentration. Industrial/market concentration will not be addressed in this paper because it is not directly related to FTA regulations on economic concentration. Similarly, we will exclude a discussion on concentration of management control because there have been no direct regulatory tools that have restricted it.

Finally, we will discuss policy and regulatory alternatives, which should bring a true resolution to the *Chaebol* problems. The abolishment of economic regulations (e.g. price, entry and quantity regulation, etc.), more rapid and complete opening of domestic markets to foreign competitors, the removal of exit barriers, the transparent enforcement of laws and the reinforcement of property rights protection are suggested as appropriate alternatives.

II. Economic Concentration and KFTC's Recognition about the *Chaebols*

The *Chaebol* is a group of firms substantially owned and controlled by a specific individual and his family, although his or their share in affiliated firms may be relatively small. In general, the *Chaebols* have diversified into various industries through cross share-holdings and cross debt guarantees among affiliated firms. The *Chaebols* have also been criticized for preempting profitable opportunities, thereby gaining an advantage in market competition through intra-group transaction.

1. Why Did Economic Concentration of the Chaebols Occur?

What factors then resulted in the economic concentration of the *Chaebols*? There exists two different answers to this question. One is based on the historical background of Korean economic development since the 1960s. Another is based on the theoretical concept of transaction costs.

The former argues that economic concentration of *Chaebols* occurred because of special benefits granted to specific firms or persons by the government's industrial policy. For example, the government actively supported firms or entrepreneurs selected to enter the chemical and heavy industries in the 1970s, backed by financial and institutional arrangements. This policy was called the chemical and heavy industry promotion policy. In addition, the government rescued firms from the danger of bankruptcy through additional financial assistance or merger and acquisition procedures. It is argued that this kind of special treatment to selected firms or entrepreneurs caused the formation of economic concentration we call *Chaebols*.[2] Thus, advocates of this argument by and large conclude that the wealth accumulated by the *Chaebols* is not a result of their own entrepreneurship or competitiveness but rather derived from special

---
[2] Lee, K(1999) pp.4 -5.

benefits provided by the government. Thus, their economic behavior should be regulated because they tend to be economically inefficient.

The latter argues that *Chaebol*s were formed and grew because the *Chaebol* structure minimized transaction costs. According to this argument, large business groups in Korea were formed to avoid the transaction costs inherent in the Korea-specific business environment due to a politico-economic collusive structure, wide spread corruption, obscure law enforcement, difficulties in making and enforcing contracts, narrow markets, and the distorted banking system. That is, the *Chaebol* structure was established as the result of the internalization of market transactions. This argument implies that the *Chaebol* is an economically efficient business structure and that regulations of their behavior would lessen their economic competitiveness rather than improve their economic efficiency.

2. KFTC's Recognition of the *Chaebols*

Aggregate concentration, industrial/market concentration, ownership concentration, and conglomerate concentration are all general measures of economic concentration.[3] Aggregate concentration means the degree of dominance of a certain number of LBGs or large individual firms in the broad economic domain, like entire industries or the manufacturing industry. This concentration is measured by the ratio of the largest 30 LBGs, or largest 100 firms in terms of economic aggregates such as total sales, total assets, employment or value added of a broadly defined economic domain. Industrial/market concentration means the degree of dominance of leading firms in the specific industry or market, like the automobile industry or the semiconductor industry. The CR4, the Herfindahl-Herschman Index, or the Entropy Index are all measures of

---

[3] Some economists discuss economic concentration using only aggregate concentration and industrial/market concentration (Clarke and Davies (1983)). However, some economists add ownership concentration and conglomerate concentration as analytical tools when discussing economic concentration (Khemani, Shapiro and Stanbury (1988)).

industrial/market concentration. Ownership concentration means the degree of concentration of equities or residual claims of a few individuals or their families. Largely, ownership concentration can be classified as the concentration of wealth and of controlling power. Conglomerate concentration refers to the degree of dominance of large-scale diversified firms or business groups operating in several industries and markets in a country's economy. Aggregate concentration is similar to conglomerate concentration, however, the latter is different from the former because it reflects power of diversification.

In Korea, aggregate and conglomerate concentration and the concentration of controlling power by LBGs are generally recognized as more important problems than industrial/market concentration or the simple concentration of wealth. This is shown in Figure 1, which represents the KFTC's interpretation of economic concentration.

The KFTC recognizes concentration of ownership and fleet-like business management as the main problems of economic concentration. Ownership concentration problems include the owner family's father-to-son wealth succession, the obscure wealth accumulation process and inequality of income distribution. These ownership concentration problems eventually result in social injustices. The problems with fleet-like business management usually include imprudent and unrelated diversification, intra-group transaction and cross share-holdings, worsening core business capabilities and the obstruction of balanced growth by small-and-medium-sized enterprises (SMSE). Economic inefficiency occurs because of these business management problems. Moreover, the above two problems, inevitably give rise to ownership control by a few family members or appointed personnel representing the owner, and family-oriented business management.

Therefore, the KFTC has urged an inducement of ownership deconcentration and independent professional business management through regulations and incentives related to LBGs' behavior. That is, the KFTC's policy objective is to separate ownership from management

Figure 1. Problem of Economic Concentration and Policy Objective [4]

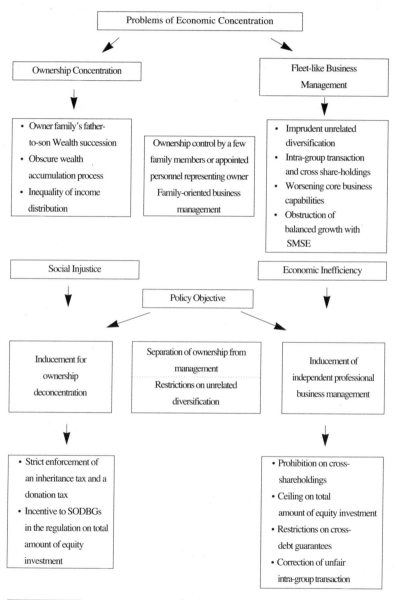

[4] Figure 1 is cited from the KFTC (1994).

through restrictions on unrelated diversification to non-core businesses. The KFTC listed strict enforcement of an inheritance tax and a donation tax, as well as an incentive for the sound ownership deconcentration business groups (SODBGs) through the regulation of the total allowed amount of equity investment, to be used as a tool of ownership deconcentration. It has also enumerated the prohibition of cross shareholdings, ceiling on total amount of equity investment, restrictions on cross debt guarantees and correction of unfair intra-group transactions, as the regulations to induce an independent professional business management. Thus, the KFTC's final objective of setting restrictions on economic concentration seems to guarantee social justice and to improve economic efficiency through the above regulatory measures. Was this objective indeed achieved by the KFTC's regulatory measures as listed above? First of all, we will historically review the regulatory measures in the next section to answer this question.

III. Historical Review of Regulations on Economic Concentration in FTA

The Korean government introduced the FTA in 1980 and established the KFTC to encourage fair and free competition, and to restrict the excessive concentration of economic power. Until now, this Act has been revised eight times. At the outset, the FTA had the article for the prohibition of business combinations for the purpose of restricting competition as the only tool suppressing excessive economic concentration. However, it was considered insufficient due to its exclusive focus on preventing the creation of new monopoly or oligopoly market structures. An ever-increasing number of critical opinions and concerns about the excessive economic concentration of LBGs, or so-called "*Chaebols*", have arisen since the late 1970s. These regulations on *Chaebols* have been steadily reinforced over the past 20 years. The major changes in the restrictions on excessive economic concentration occurred in the 1st, 3rd, 5th, 6th, 7th, and 8th amendments of the FTA. A summary of major regulatory changes during the last 20 years is shown in Table 1.

Table 1. Major Changes in Economic Concentration Regulations in FTA

Amendment	Article	Content
1st (1986.12.31)	7-2(8)	Prohibition of the establishment of holding companies
	7-4(9)	Prohibition of cross share-holdings
	7-3(10)	Ceiling on total amount of equity investment: 40% of the net assets of the LBG's affiliated corporations
	7-5(11)	Restrictions on the voting rights of finance or insurance companies
	8-2(13)	Report on status of share ownership
	8-3(14)	Designation of LBGs
3rd (1992. 12. 8)	10-2	Limitations on debt guarantees
	13	Inclusion of the report on status of debt guarantees
	14	Inclusion of the designation of LBGSLDGs and change of standard for the designation of LBGs and LBGSLDGs
4th (1994.12. 22)	10	Reinforcement of the ceiling on the total amount of equity investment from 40% to 25%
5th (1996. 12. 30)	10	Inclusion of the exemption of Article 10 to finance and insurance companies belonging to LBGs
	10-2	Reinforcement of the upper limit on debt guarantees from 200% to 100%
	23(7)	Prohibition of unreasonable supports
6th	10	Abolition of the ceiling on the total amount of equity investment.
	10-2	Prohibition of new debt guarantees
	10-3	Establishment of the deadline for complete removal of the existing debt guarantee
7th (1999. 2. 5)	8	Deregulation on the establishment of holding companies: from complete ban to report of establishment
	8-2	Restrictions on activities of holding companies
	8-3	Limitation on establishment of a holding company by LBGSLDGs
	50 (5)(6)(7)	Right to request financial transaction information to investigate unfair intra-group financial transactions
8th (1999. 12. 28)	10	Revival of the ceiling on the total amount of equity investment (25%)
	11-2	Decision of large-scale intra-group transactions by board of directors and notification thereof
	24-2	Imposition of a higher surcharge on the violation of prohibition on unfair intra-group financial transaction: 5% of the turnover

* LBGSLDG: Large Business Groups Subject to Limitations on Debt Guarantees

Direct behavioral regulations on excessive economic concentration were introduced in the first amendment of the FTA for the first time in 1986. The regulations in the first amendment prohibited the establishment of holding companies and cross share-holdings, put a ceiling on total capital investment, restricted voting rights of finance and insurance companies, designated large business groups, and requested reports on the status of share ownership. Let us take a closer look at the concrete contents of these regulations.

First, the establishment of a new holding company and the existing company's conversion to a holding company were completely prohibited. The exception to this rule is in the establishment of a holding company buttressed by the law and by the permission of KFTC for foreign investment projects pursuant to the Foreign Capital Inducement Act. This regulation was introduced to prohibit the LBG's control of many firms by small amounts of capital in the form of a holding company.

Second, the cross share-holdings among LBG's affiliated corporations were entirely prohibited. The only exceptions to this rule were cases of mergers, takeovers, the enforcement of security rights, and the receipt of accord and satisfaction. In addition, the owned or acquired cross held shares of LBG's affiliated firms were to be disposed within 6 months from the date of owning or acquisition, and a corporation that invested in SMSEs belonging to a LBG should not acquire or own other affiliated firms. This regulation was introduced to prohibit the fictitious increase in capital without the actual increase in production capability, and to eliminate the lending bias to LBGs according to the scale of equity capital.

Third, the ceiling on total capital investment to domestic companies was set at 40% of the net assets of the firm belonging to LBGs. This upper limit applied not only to the investment in affiliated firms but also to non-affiliated firms as well. There were, however, three exceptions to this regulation on share-owning or acquisition 1) according to firm rationalization by the law, 2) through the allocation of newly issued shares or stock dividends, 3) through the enforcement of security rights or the receipt of accord and satisfaction.⁵ This regulation was introduced to inhibit the excessive and imprudent extension or diversification of affiliated corporations.

Fourth, finance and insurance companies belonging to LBGs were entirely prohibited from exercising their voting rights with regard to their shares in domestic affiliated firms that they owned or had acquired. This regulation was introduced to prevent finance and insurance companies belonging to LBGs from becoming virtual holding companies that extended and controlled affiliated firms, not with equity capital, but with customers' deposits.

Fifth, the designation of LBGs was introduced to effectively enforce the regulations, including the above four. At the time of introduction, LBGs were designated according to the size of the total assets of a business group.⁶ According to the Presidential Decree of the FTA, the lower limit of the total assets was set at 400 billion Korean won. An exception to this standard is allowed only to a business group or a firm that engages in the finance and insurance businesses.

Sixth, the report on status of share ownership is another auxiliary regulation that is used to enforce the above four regulations, especially regarding the prohibition of cross share-holdings.

According to the third amendment in 1992, the Korean government initiated a limitation on debt guarantees for affiliated corporations of LBGs in Article 10-2 and added a reporting requirement on the status of the debt guarantees in Article 13. The limitation on debt guarantees for domestic affiliated corporations was established at a unilateral 200% of the

---

[5] This regulation is found also in the Japanese Antitrust Law. However, the Japanese regulation on the total capital investment is enforced not to LBGs but individual firms. Moreover, the ceiling is set to a larger amount between 100% of equity capital and 100% of net assets.

[6] A business group means a group of companies that is controlled by a person or a corporation, or a group of companies belonging to a person or a corporation. If a business group owns 30% or more of a company's shares, that company is an affiliated corporation of the business group.

shareholder's equity capital for each affiliated corporation belonging to a LBG. The government urged the implementation of this regulation for three reasons. First, the excessive cross debt guarantees between affiliate firms of LBGs tend to give rise to an unhealthy financial structure through excessive borrowing. Second, growing interdependency among firms with cross debt guarantees may reinforce economic concentration of LBGs and the contagion of insolvency may spread from one firm to another. Third, cross debt guarantees among affiliated firms of LBGs may cause lending bias to LBGs, and this bias results in the unfair competition between those firms belonging to LBGs and other non-affiliated independent firms.

In addition, a clause was added to the third amendment of Article 14 (Designation of LBGs) on the designation of large business groups subject to limitations on debt guarantees (LBGSLDGs) for enforcement of the regulation on debt guarantees. The conditions for the designation of LBGSLDGs are the same as those in defining LBGs according to the Presidential Decree of the FTA. The standard for the designation of LBGs also changed in this amendment from the size of total assets to the ranking of total assets. According to the Presidential Decree, any business group whose total assets rank within the top 30 should be designated as an LBG. The same standard was applied in designating LBGSLDGs.

With its inclusion of the FTA's fourth amendment in 1994, the Korean government reduced the upper limit of the total amount of equity investment from 40% to 25% of net assets. This amounted to a reinforcement of the regulation of the ceiling on total capital investment. However, there were two exceptions to this regulation. First, the ceiling was exempted within 20 years in case the social overhead capital investment pursuant to the Private Capital Inducement for Social Overhead Capital Act was activated by the approval of the KFTC. Second, the ceiling could be lifted if an affiliated corporation belonging to a LBG is be able to meet the requirements for ownership deconcentration and financial structure. That is, the ceiling could be lifted if an LBG were to be defined as an SODBG.[7]

In the fifth amendment of the FTA in 1996, the government added the clause that an application of the investment ceiling in Article 10 would not apply to the finance and insurance companies belonging to LBGs. This amendment also reduced the upper limit on debt guarantees from 200% to 100% of the shareholder's equity capital and relieved restrictions on voting rights of finance and insurance companies belonging to LBGs, in cases where the right was guaranteed by other related laws. Moreover, this amendment in Article 23 introduced the clause prohibiting unreasonable support to affiliated firms in order to sanction against unfair intra-group transactions, although this clause was not included in the chapter of restrictions on economic concentration.

With the sixth amendment in 1996, the government abolished the ceiling on the total amount of equity investment. This change occurred when LBGs and experts argued that this regulation discriminated between domestic and foreign firms in the domestic investment under a globalized competitive environment. The prohibition on new debt guarantees for affiliated corporations of LBGs was also introduced. Also, the removal of any existing debt guarantees by 2001 was called for, in the event a LBG was designated a LBGSLDG from 1998 to 2000.

In the seventh amendment in February 1999, the government deregulated the prohibition in the establishment and conversion of holding companies. However, this amendment stipulates very high standards for the establishment and conversion of holding companies. According to this amendment, the government restricted holding company's behavior to: 1) a holding company should not have liabilities in excess of net assets, 2) it should own more than 49% of the total shares of its subsidiaries,[8] 3) it

---

[7] The conditions for the SODBG can be found in Article 17(2) of the Presidential Decree of the FTA.

[8] In cases when the subsidiary is listed on the stock market, the lower limit of share holding for a holding company is 30%.

should not own shares of domestic firms other than subsidiaries, 4) a financial holding company should only own shares of companies engaging in financial or insurance business, 5) a general holding company should not own shares of domestic finance and insurance companies, 6) subsidiaries of a general holding company should not own shares of other domestic corporations. In addition to the above restrictions, the government imposed a limitation on the establishment of a holding company in LBGSLDGs. According to Article 8-3, debt guarantees 1) between a holding company and its subsidiary, 2) between a holding company and other domestic affiliates, 3) between subsidiaries, 4) between a subsidiary and other domestic affiliates should all be removed if a person desires to establish or convert to a holding company.

The seventh amendment also gave the KFTC the right to request financial transaction information in order to reinforce the investigative tools for unfair intra-group transactions. This, however, is only a two-year temporary right.

In the eighth amendment in December 1999, the government revived the ceiling on the total amount of equity investment arguing that its abolition would give rise to the rapid increase in circular investments among affiliated firms belonging to LBGs. They also argued that such opportunistic behavior results in the delay of structural reform of *Chaebols*. The ceiling was set at 25% of net assets.

This amendment also reinforced the monitoring and inspection mechanism in relation to unfair intra-group transactions. At first, the government imposed the duty of decision making concerning large-scale intra-group transactions to a board of directors and notification thereof on LBGs. In addition, it raised the surcharge on the prohibition violation of unfair intra-group financial transactions compared to that of other unfair business practices. For example, the upper limit of the surcharge against the former is 5% of the turnover, while that of the latter is 2%.

We can easily categorize any major regulatory tools that deal with restrictions on the excessive economic concentration in the FTA into five main regulations and two auxiliary regulations about LBGs in the above review. The five main regulations are as follows: 1) restrictions on the establishment of and the conversion into holding companies, 2) prohibition of cross share-holdings, 3) ceiling on total capital investment, 4) restrictions on voting rights of finance and insurance companies, and 5) limitations on the debt guarantees. The two subsidiary regulations are the designation of LBGs and LBGSLDGs, and their duty is to report on the status of share ownership and debt guarantees of affiliated corporations. In addition, another recently introduced and important regulation on excessive economic concentration is the reinforcement of the monitoring, inspection and punishment against unfair intra-group transaction. This is being used as a strong mechanism to promote the structural reform of LBGs by the Kim Dae Jung administration, but does not belong to the chapter of restriction on economic concentration in the FTA.

In conclusion, the above historical review shows that the regulations on excessive economic concentration have been consistently reinforced since the enactment of the FTA in 1980. This trend is summarized in Figure 2. However, many Korean people recognize that the excessive economic

Figure 2. Major Changes in Economic Concentration Regulation in FTA

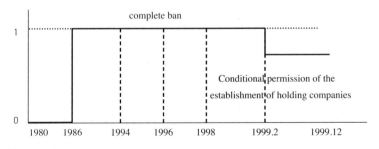

(2) Prohibition of Cross Share Holdings

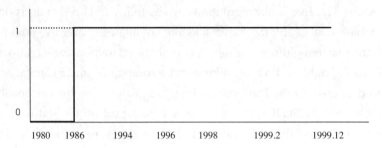

(3) Ceiling on Total Amount of Equality Capital

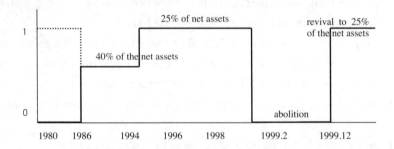

(4) Restrictions on the Voting Rights of Finance and Insurance Companies

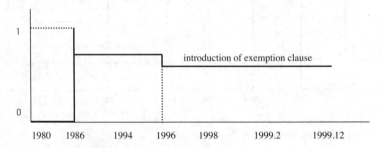

(5) Debt Guarantees

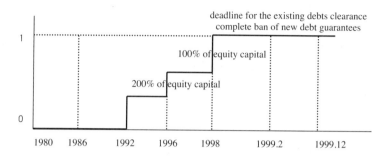

concentration of *Chaebol*s remains serious and thus should be corrected as soon as possible, notwithstanding the continuous reinforcement of the FTA as outlined above and other monetary regulations on LBGs.[9] Policymakers and bureaucrats also seem to have the same attitude towards the excessive economic concentration of *Chaebol*s.[10] Thus, it seems that this kind of national emotion resulted in the escalation of regulations on economic concentration over the past 20 years.[11]

---

[9] Monetary regulation on LBGs is referred to as a credit management system. The credit management system is composed of a ceiling on a credit line of affiliated corporations belonging to LBGs, regulation on the acquisition of real estate and the non-business purpose real estate, incentive for business specialization. For detailed contents, problems, and policy alternatives of these regulations, refer to Kwack, et al. (1995) pp. 265-307.

[10] "Almost all business groups have been acquiring the monopoly profits through debt financing at the sacrifice of laborer's, consumer's, and independent firm's interest. Besides this they have been investing the rents to high return nonproductive sectors and inducing government policy compatible with their private interest continuously." KFTC & KDI (1991) pp. 238-239.

[11] Lee, C. (1995) argued that regulations on LBGs' behavior was actually introduced according to political and social considerations rather than economic factors. According to his argument, the regulations were politically introduced in response to social complaints that the gap between the wealthy and the poor had been deepened by the excessive economic concentration of the Chaebols in the process of rapid economic growth.

IV. Effectiveness of Regulatory Measures on Economic Concentration

We have reviewed the regulatory measures on economic concentration in section III. If these measures had worked effectively, the economic concentration of LBGs should have been significantly mitigated or removed. Let us examine the data to see whether the KFTC's regulatory measures have been effective or not.

First, we examine the trend of aggregate concentration from 1985 to 1997.[12] The trend of aggregate concentration measured by major economic aggregates is almost steady without regard to the introduction and reinforcement of the regulation on economic concentration. The trends are summarized in Table 2 and Figure 3.

According to Table 2 and Figure 3, aggregate concentration with respect to total sales fluctuated 1) between about 27 to 32% of total sales in the top 5 LBGs, 2) between about 42 to 48% in the top 30 LBGs, and 3) between about 48 to 54% in the top 72 LBGs. This means that aggregate concentration in terms of total sales moved within a relatively narrow band

Figure3. Trend of Aggregate Concentration

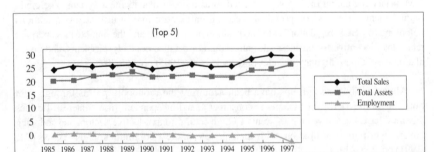

---

[12] Note the fact that in 1985 there were no actual regulations on economic concentration in the FTA. In the first amendment of the FTA in 1986, four major regulatory measures and two auxiliary regulations were introduced for the first time. For details of these regulations, refer to section III of this paper.

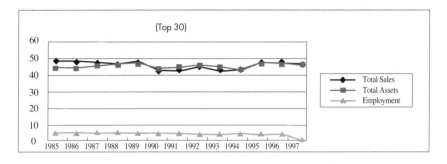

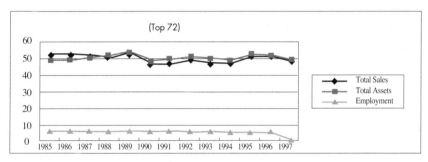

Table 2. Trends of Aggregate Concentration (1985-1997)

(Unit: %)

Year	Total Sales			Total Assets			Employment		
	Top 5	Top 30	Top 72	Top 5	Top 30	Top 72	Top 5	Top 30	Top 72
1985	26.77	48.11	53.84	22.49	43.99	50.76	2.71	4.60	5.61
1986	27.85	47.62	53.78	22.70	43.96	50.88	2.69	4.53	5.65
1987	28.25	46.88	53.12	24.33	45.24	52.44	2.70	4.56	5.66
1988	28.10	46.24	52.71	24.88	46.51	54.15	2.74	4.66	5.78
1989	28.64	47.51	54.25	26.09	48.30	56.32	2.69	4.64	5.72
1990	27.11	42.30	48.25	24.07	43.59	50.57	2.56	4.47	5.52
1991	27.50	42.80	48.83	24.55	45.00	52.25	2.59	4.51	5.50
1992	28.93	45.04	51.26	24.88	46.05	53.71	2.46	4.34	5.33
1993	27.99	43.11	48.73	24.39	44.91	52.46	2.47	4.35	5.31
1994	28.46	43.63	49.71	23.91	43.61	51.09	2.56	4.61	5.58
1995	31.27	47.75	53.59	26.86	47.25	55.18	2.73	4.68	5.62
1996	32.43	48.38	53.80	27.16	47.08	54.22	2.71	4.62	5.46
1997	32.38	46.62	50.51	28.88	46.64	51.38	-	-	-

* Top 5, Top 30, and Top 72 represent aggregate concentrations of the Top 5, Top 30 and Top 72 LBGs.
* Source: Hwang (1999), pp.116.

of 5 to 8% during that 12 year period. Aggregate concentration with respect to total assets fluctuated between about 22 to 29% in the top 5 LBGs, around 44 to 48% in the top 30, and between around 51 to 56% in the top 72. Thus, aggregate concentration in terms of total assets fluctuated within a 4 to 7% band. Aggregate concentration with respect to the employment level fluctuated between about 2.5 to 2.7% in the top 5, between about 4.3 to 4.7% in the top 30, between about 5.3 to 5.8% in the top 72. Thus, aggregate concentration in terms of the employment level fluctuated within a 0.2 to 0.5% range. These trends suggest that aggregate concentration remained at a certain level and was not related to the restrictions on economic concentration imposed by the FTA. Remarkably, in comparison to 1985, in which no actual regulations on economic concentration existed, statistics of other years show that no significant improvement of aggregate concentration occurred after introducing restrictions on economic concentrations. The trends of aggregate concentration, such as in the case of the top 5 LBGs, also show that aggregate concentration of these 5 LBGs has deepened during the same period. This may mean that aggregate concentration was in fact strengthened during this period.

Second, we will consider the degree of diversification from 1985 to 1997. The trends on the number of affiliated firms and types of industry are summarized in Table 3 and Figure 4. The average number of affiliated firms of the top 5 LBGs increased from 26 in 1985 to 44 in 1992 and only began to decrease substantially in 1996 and 1997. The average number of types of industry at which LBGs attended also had a similar trend during the same period, increasing from 14 to 18. From the top 30 LBG and top 72 LBG data, we again find the trend of continuous increase in the number of affiliated firms and types of industry. In the case of the top 30 LBGs, the average number of affiliated firms increased from 14 to 21 during this period the and average number of types of industry increased from 8 to 11. Although the government introduced and reinforced regulations on economic concentration and obstructed aggregate

Figure 4. Number of AF and TI

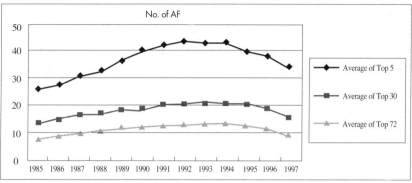

*AF : Affiliated Firms   *TI : Types of Industry

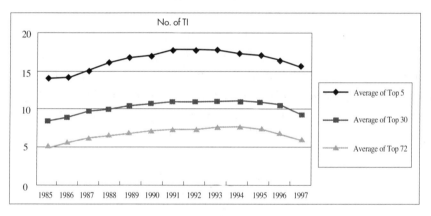

Table 3. Number of Affiliated Firms (AF) and of Types of Industry (TI) (1985 1997)

Year	Average of Top 5		Average of Top 30		Average of Top 72	
	No. of AF	No. of TI	No. of AF	No. of TI	No. of AF	No. of TI
1985	26.0	14.0	13.6	8.4	8.1	5.3
1986	27.8	14.2	14.8	8.9	9.0	5.7
1987	31.0	15.0	16.6	9.7	10.0	6.2
1988	33.2	16.2	17.3	10.0	10.9	6.7
1989	36.8	16.8	18.7	10.5	11.9	7.0
1990	40.8	17.0	19.0	10.6	12.3	7.2
1991	42.6	17.8	20.5	11.0	12.9	7.3
1992	44.0	17.8	21.1	11.0	13.3	7.4
1993	43.4	17.8	21.1	11.1	13.8	7.8
1994	43.8	17.4	21.2	11.0	13.9	7.8
1995	40.4	17.2	20.9	10.9	13.3	7.5
1996	38.8	16.4	19.6	10.6	12.1	7.0
1997	35.0	15.8	16.1	9.3	9.9	6.1

* Source: Hwang (1999) pp. 76.

concentration, this data shows that it could not prevent the extension of LBGs.

In addition, the Berry-Herfindahl Index (BHI) and Entropy Index (EI), which measure the degree of diversification and degree of unrelated diversification, show that the degree of diversification rose continuously in the same period, while the degree of unrelated diversification was somewhat reduced. These trends are summarized in Table 4, Figure 5, and Figure 6.

Figure 5 also shows that overall diversification was unobstructed despite the government's efforts to reinforce regulations on economic concentration. The BHI of each size of LBGs continuously rose before 1997. Although the regulations on economic concentration in the FTA peaked in 1997, overall diversification only began to fall slightly in the same year. These two facts constitute another important piece of evidence of the ineffectiveness of the regulations on economic concentration. Figure 6 shows that the related diversification ratio somewhat rose for all sizes of LBGs during this period, except in 1997. However, the top 5's related diversification ratio was always lower than those of the top 30s' except the top 5

Table 4. BHI and Relatedness Based on Group Size (1985-1997)

Year	1985	1988	1991	1994	1997
BHI					
Top 5 Average	0.7427	0.7660	0.8027	0.8102	0.7968
6th-30th Group Average	0.7240	0.7156	0.7407	0.7523	0.7363
31st-72nd Group Average	0.4012	0.4710	0.4879	0.5096	0.5090
Related Diversification Ratio (%)[13]					
Top 5 Average	16.7	17.7	18.8	20.5	19.4
6th-30th Group Average	21.7	22.2	24.8	25.7	24.8
31st-72nd Group Average	19.0	29.0	29.7	32.7	24.6

* Source: Hwang (1999) pp.184.

---

[13] Overall diversification index is the sum of related diversification index and unrelated diversification index. This relationship is described in detail in Palepu (1985). Therefore, the related diversification ratio is 1 less than the unrelated diversification ratio.

*Chaebol*s or top 72s' except top 30s'. Moreover, the related diversification ratio also fell in 1997. Therefore, it is difficult to say that the gradual decrease of the unrelated diversification ratio during this sample period is evidence of the effectiveness of the regulations on economic concentration.

Third, let us examine the trend of ownership structures in the *Chaebol*s

Figure5. Berry Herfindahl Index

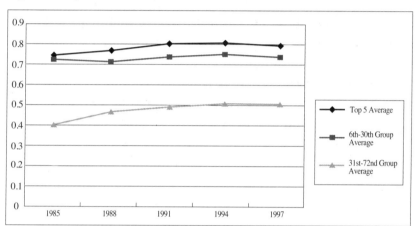

Figure 6. Related Diversification Ratio(%)

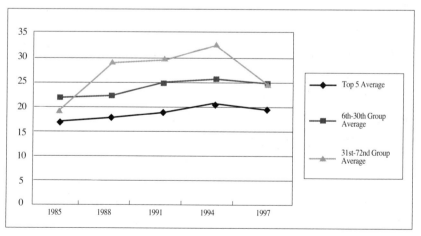

from 1987 to 1996. Table 5 and Figure 7 summarize this trend. The ownership structures show that owners' and their relatives' share of *Chaebols* fell from 15.8 to 10.3%, and affiliated firms' and self-owned shares also fell from 40.4 to 33.8%. Thus, insiders' shares also fell in the same period. In addition, the adjusted insider share ratio fell from 26.5 to 15.6%. However, these trends again cannot be regarded as evidence for the effectiveness of regulations on economic concentration.

In reference to ownership deconcentration, the government introduced an incentive to SODBGs in the regulation on the total equity investment with the fourth amendment of the FTA in 1994. Actually, this regulation is

Table 5. Trend of Ownership Structures in *Chaebols* (1987-1996)

(Unit: %)

Year	Owners & Relatives (A)	Affiliated Firms & Self-owned (B)	Insider's Shares (A+B)	Adjusted Shares of Owners A/(1-B)
1987	15.8	40.4	56.2	26.5
1989	14.9	31.3	46.2	21.4
1991	13.9	33.0	46.9	20.7
1993	10.2	33.2	43.4	15.3
1995	10.5	32.8	43.3	15.6
1996	10.3	33.8	44.1	15.6

· Source: Lee, K. (1999) pp. 6, Table 3.. The original source of this table is KFTC.

Figure 7. Trend of Ownership Structures in *Chaebols*

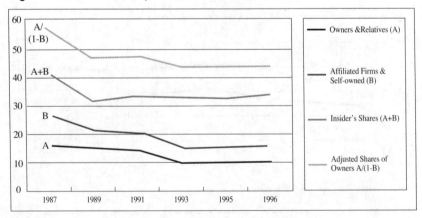

the only one to promote ownership deconcentration in the FTA. Hence, it should be carefully considered when checking the effectiveness of regulations on economic concentration in the FTA. When we examine Figure 7, we see that owners' and relatives' shares rapidly decreased between 1991 and 1993 and affiliated firms' and self-owned shares also sharply decreased between 1987 and 1989. Even adjusted shares of owners sharply decreased between 1987 and 1989 and between 1991 and 1993. Despite the introduction of this incentive, the ownership deconcentration did not advance further. The most important changes in ownership concentration occurred before 1994. This strongly suggests that the incentive to SODBGs was not effective on ownership deconcentration.

Thus far in this section we have examined the data, which reflects economic concentration of *Chaebol*s. This analysis reveals no significant effectiveness of the regulatory measures during the sample period. In spite of the KFTC's annual report about the successful enforcement of regulations on economic concentration,[14] our analysis shows that economic concentration has not been removed nor significantly mitigated.

V. Conclusion and Policy Implication

We have examined the effectiveness of regulatory measures on economic concentrations in the FTA through historical review of the regulations and data analysis according to the measurement tools for economic concentration. Our analysis provides the following conclusions:

First, regulations on economic concentration of *Chaebol*s have consecutively strengthened over the last twenty years. The actual introduction of the regulations occurred in 1986. The regulations essentially prohibited the establishment of holding companies and cross shareholdings, established a ceiling on the total amount of capital investment,

---

[14] KFTC (1998), pp.7-9.

restrictions on voting rights of finance and insurance companies, and so on. Another important regulation on economic concentration was introduced in the third amendment of the FTA in 1992, which was the limitation on debt guarantees. These five regulations were the basis for the restriction of economic concentration. Aside from these five, the prohibition of unreasonable support to affiliated corporations was added to Article 23. Although this is not limited to the LBGs, this regulation is frequently applied to the examination of LBGs' intra-group transaction. The regulations were intermittently introduced, as well as reinforced, during the past 20 years. In addition, in its annual *Fair Trade White Book* the KFTC has insisted that it has enforced the regulations effectively and has successfully achieved the intermediate target of restricting the economic concentration of *Chaebol*s. If that is the case, there should be no law enforcement problems within the KFTC. Thus, we can only consider the effectiveness of the regulations without considering the possibility of enforcement failure.

Second, the various economic measures of economic concentration did not support the effectiveness of regulations on economic concentration in all examined trends of data. The time series of aggregate concentration analysis shows that the trends of aggregate concentration only fluctuated within a certain band range without relation to the introduction or reinforcement of regulatory measures. The number of affiliated firms and types of industry also increased during the same sample period without any relation to the regulations on economic concentration. In addition, the BHI of top 5s', top 30s' except top 5s', top 72s' except top 30s' also rose gradually for the same sample period. Related diversification ratios also rose more or less in all sizes of LBGs during this period, except in 1997. However, the top 5s' related diversification ratio has always been lower than those of the top 30s' except top 5s' and top 72s' except top 30s'. Thus, these trends did not show the effectiveness of the regulations on economic concentrations.

Third, the trend of ownership structure in *Chaebol*s suggests that the insider's share fell rapidly between 1987 and 1989 and again between 1991 and 1993. However, the introduction of the incentive to SODBGs in the regulation on the total equity investment took place in 1994. Thus, there was no relation between rapid ownership deconcentration and the regulation on or incentive for economic deconcentration.

From our observation and analysis, we conclude that the regulations on economic concentration of *Chaebols* were not effective despite the claim of the KFTC who enforced them actively. That is, we suggest that the reinforcement of the existing regulations or active exercise of those regulations were, in fact, serious burdens to the national economy, and did not result in any practical benefits. Thus, the government should discard the existing ineffective regulations on economic concentration of *Chaebols* and pursue other effective policy tools for the resolution of the *Chaebol* problem.

Alternative policy tools should include market-oriented solutions rather than behavioral regulatory measures. More viable alternatives include the abolition of economic regulations, which pertain to price, entry and quantity regulation, etc., the more rapid and complete opening of domestic markets to foreign competitors, the removal of exit barriers, transparent law enforcement and reinforcement of property rights protection, and the establishment of independent and self-regulatory monetary institutions.

References

Chung, B. H. and Y. S. Yang. (1992). *Economic Analysis for Korean Chaebols*, Seoul: Korea Development Institute (KDI).

Clarke, R. and S.W. Davies. (1985). Internal organization, business groups, and corporate performances: An empirical test of the multidivisional hypothesis in Japan. *International Journal of Industrial Organization*, Vol. 3, pp. 401-420.

Hwang, I. (1999). *Chaebols' Diversification, Market Structure and Aggregate Concentration*. Seoul: Korea Economic Research Institute (KERI).

KFTC. (1998). *1998 Fair Trade White Book*. Seoul: KFTC.

KFTC. (1994). The realities of *Chaebol*s and the direction of revision for the fair trade act. Seoul: KFTC.

KFTC and KDI. (1991). *10 Years of Korean Fair Trade: Performance and Problems of Competition Policy*. Seoul: KFTC.

Khemani, R. S., D. M. Shapiro and W. T. Stanbury. (1988). *Mergers, Corporate Concentration and Power in Canada*. Seoul: The Institute for Research on Public Policy.

Kwack, M., S. Kim, J. Kim, J. Suh, H. Shin and I. W. Cheon. (1995). *Business Groups in Korea: Establishment of Top 30 LBGs and their Growth Factors*. Seoul: KERI.

Lee, C. (1995). *Jurisprudential Review of the Policy for the Obstruction of Economic Concentration*. Seoul: KERI.

Lee, J. (1997). *Is Fair Trade Policy Fair? : The Myths and Realities of Corporate Group Policy*. Seoul: KERI.

Lee, K. (1999). Corporate governance and growth in the Korean *Chaebol*s: A microeconomic foundation for the 1997 crisis. *Mimeo*. Seoul: Division of Economics, Seoul National University.

Palepu, K. (1985). Diversification strategy, profit performance and entropy measure. *Strategic Management Journal*, Vol. 6, pp. 239-255.

After the Economic Crisis: An Analysis of the Effects of Corporate Restructuring [1]

Hasung Jang [2]

I. Economic Crisis and Corporate Restructuring

1. Necessity of Corporate Restructuring

The economic crisis began in early 1997 when a number of *Chaebol*s became essentially bankrupt. The Korean government officially acknowledged the crisis in December 1997, when it negotiated a relief loan from the IMF and earnestly launched a series of corporate and financial sector reforms earnestly.

The purpose of restructuring was to recover from the growing economic crisis in the short term. In the long term, the restructuring campaign aimed at strengthening the competitiveness of the corporate and financial sectors, thus preventing the recurrence of an economic crisis

---

[1] The Korean version of this paper was presented at the Special Symposium of the Korea Finance Association in December 2000 and at the Symposium entitled "IMF Three Years: Accomplishment, Reflection and Future Directions" that was hosted by the Korea Development Institute in December 2000.

[2] Professor, Korea University, Seoul, Korea.

while transforming the country into an advanced market economy system. Three years have passed since Korea received its relief loan package from the IMF and undertook reform policies. It is now an appropriate time to evaluate government policies affecting corporate restructuring. This three-year evaluation will give us a yardstick to assess the possibility of crisis recurrence and to judge the direction and depth of future reform policies.

Analysis of the causes of economic crisis should precede an evaluation of the restructuring policy designed to relieve the crisis and to create an advanced economic structure. This paper focuses on the evaluation of policies because many scholars have already conducted in-depth discussions about the causes of the crisis. The widespread consensus is that all discussions about the causes of the crisis come down to two factors, one being external and the other internal. The following papers address the analysis and discussion of the causes of the economic crisis: Furman and Stiglitz (1998), H.W. Jang (1999), and Radelet and Sachs (1998). First, an explanation by the external factor suggests that the crisis started in Southeast Asian countries and spread to Korea. Second, the internal factor argument holds that the crisis was due to weaknesses inherent in domestic Korean corporations and financial institutions.

The foreign exchange crisis in Southeast Asian markets was triggered by the rapid withdrawal of foreign investment capital from these regions and the subsequently deteriorating value of currencies that such a withdrawal created. Given this external factor diagnosis, it is necessary to discover what caused the flight of foreign investment capital. A decline in investor confidence due to the insolvent operations of corporate and financial institutions was one of the fundamental causes. Countries such as Taiwan and Singapore that did not go through a foreign exchange crisis had competent domestic corporations and a financial industry that could absorb external shocks. In those two countries, external shocks did not lead to an extreme economic crisis. On the other hand, in the Korean case, it also makes sense to claim that there would not have been an extreme economic crisis without these external shocks, despite the inherently weak domestic corporations and financial institutions. That is why the internal factor and external factor arguments are not mutually exclusive, but instead mutually complementary in explaining the causes of the economic crisis.

In the case of Korea, investors rapidly lost their confidence in financial institutions after Hanbo Iron & Steel went bankrupt in January 1997, following the revelation of the insolvency of Korea First Bank. Since then, eight out of 30 *Chaebol* groups have gone bankrupt. Shortly before the government received the IMF relief loan package in December 1997, Jinro and Kia Motors went bankrupt and Halla was declared insolvent. These consecutive firm failures led to the insolvency of financial institutions and precipitated a plunge in market confidence. As more and more *Chaebol*s went bankrupt, those same *Chaebol*s disclosed more and more of the debt obligations that they had accumulated over the last 10 years. The disclosure of these ever-expanding debt obligations led to an additional fall in investor confidence.

In sum, insolvent obligations due to careless management of corporations and of financial institutions triggered a domestic economic crisis. Because financial mismanagement was a cause of the crisis, financial reform should be one of the most important elements in the economic reform. Yet the formulation of more fundamental economic reform policies requires analysis of why the financial institutions in Korea were giving out so many non-performing loans.

Loans were non-performing because financial institutions were giving their resources to already insolvent corporations. Weakness in the financial sector was not caused by excess operating expenses in financial institutions. Kookmin Bank, Housing and Commercial Bank, and Hana Bank, all of which focused on retail banking and small and medium enterprise banking, emerged as the best performing banks after the economic crisis. On the other hand, banks that mainly lent to *Chaebol*s, such as Korea First Bank, Seoul Bank, Hanvit Bank, Chohung Bank and Foreign Exchange Bank, proved to be insolvent. This record shows that non-performing loans stemmed largely from giving loans to insolvent *Chaebols*. Although crony capitalism and the backward management of financial institutions also played a major role in producing the non-performing loans, the core problem was the widespread mismanagement inside *Chaebols*.

For that reason, corporate restructuring—especially *Chaebol* reform—is the most indispensable piece of the reform agenda. It is natural that *Chaebol* reform should be accompanied both by settlement of non-performing loans and by financial reforms that upgrade credit analysis and risk management to the level of international best practices. Still, fundamental economic restructuring cannot be achieved without corporate restructuring because corporate mismanagement is most to blame for the non-performing loans. Without corporate restructuring, it is impossible to realize the short-term objective of overcoming the crisis, not to mention the long-term objective of transforming Korea into an advanced market economy.

2. Government Policy for Corporate Restructuring

The objective of corporate restructuring is to transform the internal structure of insolvent corporations, thus turning them into competitive firms. To accomplish this objective, in January 1998 the Kim Dae-Jung government and business leaders together established reform principles encompassing five main areas: enhancement of the financial structure, building competence core businesses, strengthening of cooperative ties with small and medium enterprises, strengthening the accountability of controlling shareholders and management, elimination of cross-debt payment guarantees, and the adoption of combined financial statements.

In September 1999, these leaders agreed to make progress in the above areas by the end of 1999. In addition, four additional reform priorities were announced: improvement of corporate governance structure, prevention of illicit inheritance and gifts, ban on unfair intra-group transactions, and improvement of the governance structure of the secondary financial market.

As part of the reform agenda, the elimination of cross-debt payment guarantees, the adoption of combined financial statements, and the prevention of illicit inheritances and gifts are to be enforced by law. The enhancement of the financial structure, building competence in core businesses, improvement of corporate governance structure, and ban on unfair intra-group transactions are to be voluntarily implemented by corporations.

3. Evaluation of Restructuring and Purpose of this Paper

Among the corporate reform policies, those that were written into law and enforced by prosecutors and regulators have been among the most successful. The elimination of cross-debt payment guarantees was enacted in April 1998, nevertheless, off sheet agreements among subsidiaries and indirect debt payment guarantees have not been eliminated. At least, the law eliminating cross-debt payment guarantees has helped in curbing the trend of intragroup bankruptcies. Combined financial statements, introduced in 2000, are also regarded as contributing to the improvement of accounting transparency. Yet there has been no legal amendment to prevent illicit inheritance and gifts. The National Tax Service and related government departments did not actively implement most reform policies.

There is no consensus about the success of the voluntary reforms pledged by corporations. The fact that there now exist public debates on the possibility of another economic crisis, despite the partial implementation of the reform agenda, suggests that corporate restructuring has not been successful in achieving positive results. Had corporate restructuring, especially *Chaebol* reforms, obtained expected performance, the recurrence of economic crisis would not be a significant threat unless there were external shocks. In this context, one can judge the quality and effectiveness of the reforms in an objective manner by estimating whether Korea is likely to encounter another round of economic crisis in the absence of external shocks.

The objective of this paper is to assess the accomplishments in the reform agenda pledged voluntarily by corporations. In doing so, this paper categorizes the change in the corporate management structure into seven areas — management structure, ownership structure, cost structure, financial structure, investment assets structure, corporate governance structure, and profitability — and analyzes each of them.

In this paper, management indices have been calculated to assess the change in the seven management areas, and statistical averages have been calculated from 1990 to 1999 for both *Chaebol*s and non-*Chaebol*s. At the same time, the management indices before and after the economic crisis of 1997 have been compared to find out whether there are any differences. Furthermore, this paper looks at any differences between *Chaebol*s and non-*Chaebol*s in terms of management performance to assess accomplishments in restructuring.

II. Data and Sample

Analyses in this paper is limited to non-financial listed companies, except in cases where analysis conducted by the Korea Fair Trade Commission and the Korea Stock Exchange are used as secondary data. Financial data for listed companies come from KIS2000, a database provided by Korea Information Service (KIS), and missing data from this source are supplemented with original data in the individual companies annual report and auditors report. The period of analysis is from 1990 to 1999, and data on the share ownership of listed companies since 1996 were obtained from the database of the Korea Stock Exchange.

The full sample of companies was divided into the top 30 *Chaebol*s and non-*Chaebol*s and then compared. The list of affiliates of the top 30 *Chaebol*s comes from the annual announcement by the Korea Fair Trade

Commission. For non-*Chaebols*, only companies with asset size over KRW 50 billion are included, in order to leave out firms that are so much smaller than *Chaebols* as to reduce comparability. The threshold of KRW 50 billion is logical considering that only two listed *Chaebol* affiliates have an asset size below KRW 50 billion.

In the case of non-*Chaebols*, the sample also changes annually because of newly listed companies and because of changes in firm asset size. Except for when the secondary data by the Korea Fair Trade Commission are used for assessing the change in management structure, otherwise the number of listed companies used for financial data analysis stands at 454, of which 111 companies belong to *Chaebols* and 343 belong to non-*Chaebols*. There may be a small difference in the number of companies used for calculating a particular management index because of partially missing data.

III. Change of Business Structure

1. Affiliates of Chaebols and Number of Business Categories

The *Chaebols* continuously increased their number of affiliates after 1990 and reached an average of 27.3 affiliates per *Chaebol* in 1997 when the economic crisis occurred.[3] The number of affiliates grew steadily after 1990 but increased most sharply in 1997. This trend is common both for the top 5 *Chaebols* as well as the top 6 to 30 *Chaebols*. After 1998, when restructuring began, the average number of affiliates decreased to 22.9 in 1999 but never again reached the pre-crisis period level. In 2000, the average number dropped remarkably to 18.1, as Daewoo Group went bankrupt and

---

[3] Table 1, Table 2 and Table 3 show the number of affiliates of the top 30 *Chaebols* as well as the change in the number of business segments during the 1990s. It is based on the announcement each April by the Korea Fair Trade Commission, which selects the top 30 *Chaebols* by asset size.

Hyundai Group spun off some affiliates. Another reason for the drop-off is that six out of the top 30 *Chaebols*, including Halla, Haitai, and Shinho, dropped out of the list in 1999 and were replaced by *Chaebols* with a comparatively small numbers of affiliates.[4]

The average number of business categories managed by the top 30 *Chaebols* was 19.1 in 1999, nearly the same as 19.5 in 1996. In 2000, existing *Chaebols* exited and new *Chaebols* entered the top 30 *Chaebol* list. This led to a significant reduction in the average number of business categories. For the top 5 *Chaebols*, the average number of business categories was 29.8 in 1999, a number unchanged from 1996. In 2000, the Daewoo bankruptcy and Hyundai's spin-off of affiliates resulted in a smaller reported number of average business categories.

As a result, restructuring has not achieved significant success in terms of reducing the number of affiliates and business categories, considering that Daewoo's bankruptcy and Hyundai's spin-off of affiliates are responsible for the change in the numbers. This indicates that reform policies designed to make *Chaebols* focus on core businesses have achieved little in reality. For the top 6 to 30 *Chaebols*, the reduction in the average number of business categories in 2000 was also a result of the exit of existing *Chaebols* and the entrance of other *Chaebols* in the top 30 list.

In conclusion, the decrease in the average number of subsidiaries and business categories only appears effective until it is realized that Daewoo, Halla, Haitai, and Shinho Group went bankrupt and dropped off the top 30 list. The voluntary corporate reforms do not appear to have brought about a significant improvement in business-line structure.

---

[4] Subsidiaries of Daewoo decreased from 34 in 1999 to 2 in 2000, and Hyundai Group also suffered a radical decrease from 62 to 35. The decrease in the number of Daewoo subsidiaries is due to bankruptcy. In the case of Hyundai, it mainly resulted from the split-up of subsidiaries. Also, *Chaebols* with many affiliates were left off the list of the top 30 *Chaebols* in 2000, including Halla (17), Haitai (15), Shinho (21), Daesang (14), and Kangwon Industry (13). *Chaebols* with a comparatively smaller number of affiliates, but with a large total asset size, entered the top 30 list, including Hyundai Oil (3), S-Oil (2), Daewoo Electronics (2), Hyundai Industrial Development (7), Shinsegae (10), and Yungpung (21). Numbers in parentheses indicate the number of affiliate companies.

Table 1. Average Number of Affiliates of the Top 30 Chaebols

	Top 5 Chaebols	Top 6-30 Chaebols	Total Top 30 Chaebols
1990	37.2	14.8	18.6
1991	41.4	14.5	19.0
1992	41.2	15.4	19.7
1993	41.6	15.8	20.1
1994	41.6	16.3	20.5
1995	41.4	16.6	20.8
1996	41.2	18.5	22.3
1997	52.4	22.3	27.3
1998	51.4	21.9	26.8
1999	46.8	18.1	22.9
2000	36.0 [1]	14.5	18.1 [1]

Source: Korea Fair Trade Commission, Annual data announced in each April.
Note: The radical reduction in 2000 is due to the bankruptcy of Daewoo; Hyundai's spin-off of affiliates; the exclusion of the many affiliates of the Halla, Haitai, and Shinho Chaebols that fell off the list; as well as the inclusion of the Hyundai Oil, S-Oil, and Hyundai Industrial Development Chaebols and their small number of affiliates into the top 30 list.

Table 2. Average Number of Business Types Managed by the Top 30 Chaebols

	Top 5 Chaebols	Top 6-30 Chaebols	Total Top 30 Chaebols
1990	18.0	10.8	12.0
1991	30.6	15.3	17.9
1992	31.2	15.7	18.3
1993	30.4	16.8	19.1
1994	29.6	16.3	18.5
1995	30.6	16.5	18.8
1996	29.8	17.5	19.5
1997	30.8	14.5	19.1
1998	31.0	13.9	17.3
1999	29.8	16.2	19.1
2000	25.4	13.3(15.7)	15.3(17.8)

Source: Korea Fair Trade Commission
Note: The number of business types is based on the two digits KSIC Industry categorization. The numbers in parentheses in the year 2000 represent the 23 Chaebols that were in the list of top 30 Chaebols in 1999 after excluding the 7 newly entered groups.

2. Asset Size of Chaebols

An examination of asset size reinforces the earlier analysis detailing the meager accomplishment of restructuring. As suggested in Table 3, as of April 2000, the asset size of the top 30 *Chaebols* has shot up compared with that of April 1996. In April 1999, that is, before Daewoo went into receivership, the assets of the top 30 *Chaebols* increased by 64.6 percent compared with April 1997, and this upward trend is most noticeable among the top 5 *Chaebols*. During the same period, the asset growth rate of the top 5 *Chaebols* posted at 92.2 percent while that of the top 6 to 30 *Chaebols* recorded 29.1 percent growth. As the Daewoo Group went insolvent in July 1999, assets of the top 30 *Chaebols* declined in 2000, but the level is still much higher than in the pre-crisis period.

It can also be observed that the asset size proportion of the top 5 among the top 30 *Chaebols* increased after the crisis. From 1990 to 1995, the percentage of asset size of the top 5 *Chaebols* out of the top 30 *Chaebols* had been stable at 54-55 percent. After the economic crisis, however, the percentage soared to 65.8 percent in 1999. Even after 2000, when Daewoo went bankrupt, the percentage rose to 62.6 percent. In conclusion, the scale of *Chaebols*' assets, if any, increased during the restructuring, and the assets of the top 5 groups especially increased, thus reinforced their market power.

Table 4 shows the fluctuation in asset size of the top 5 *Chaebols*. The asset size of all the top 5 groups rose after the crisis. In particular, Daewoo doubled its asset size from 1997 to 1999, as evidence of the fact that it pursued a very aggressive expansion policy during the crisis. Hyundai and SK had reached an asset size level in 2000 that was twice their respective asset sizes in 1996. The fact that restructuring not only failed to reduce the size of *Chaebols*, but instead served to increase their asset size, shows that the reforms designed specifically to prevent expansion of the top 5 *Chaebols* have been futile. It cannot be considered a coincidence that Daewoo went into receivership and that Hyundai encountered a serious managerial crisis because both companies pursued aggressive expansion policies in the midst of the crisis.

Table 3. Total Asset Size of the Top 30 Chaebols (Unit: KRW Billion)

	Top 5	Top 6-30	Total 30	Proportion of Top 5 in Top 30
1990	52,386	44,306	96,692	54.2%
1991	68,576	56,707	125,283	54.7%
1992	84,869	71,409	156,278	54.3%
1993	97,709	80,757	178,466	54.7%
1994	110,879	88,148	199,027	55.7%
1995	129,936	103,509	233,445	55.7%
1996(B)	161,713	125,373	287,086	56.3%
1997	202,006	146,358	348,364	58.0%
1998	273,090	162,228	435,318	62.7%
1999(A)	310,870	161,887	472,757	65.8%
2000	264,563	158,234	422,797	62.6%
A/B growth rates	92.2%	29.1%	64.6%	

Source: Korea Fair Trade Commission, Annual Announcement Data in April

Table 4. Total Asset Size of the Top 5 Chaebols (Unit: KRW Billion)

	Hyundai	Samsung	Daewoo (Hanjin)	LG	SK
1995	37,221	29,414	26,144	24,351	12,806
1996(B)	43,743	40,761	31,313	31,395	14,501
1997	53,597	51,651	35,455	38,376	22,927
1998	73,520	64,536	52,994	52,773	29,267
1999(A)	88,806	61,606	78,168	49,524	32,766
2000	88,649	67,384	(20,771)	47,612	40,147
A/B growth rates	102.7%	65.3%	120.5%[1]	51.6%	176.8%

Source: Korea Fair Trade Commission, Annual Announcement Data in April
Note: Daewoo Group, Growth rates up to 1999 based on 1996 data. Number in the parenthesis for 2000 is for Hanjin that became the 5th largest Chaebol in 2000 replacing Daewoo.

IV. Change in Ownership Structure

1. Ownership Structure of Chaebols

To examine the change in ownership structure, we will first look at the percentage of internally held shares, that is, shares under the influence of controlling shareholders. Internally held shares are calculated as the sum of shares owned by controlling shareholders and related parties of controlling shareholders, treasury stocks, and shares owned by *Chaebol* affiliates.

The percentage of internally held shares as announced by the Korea Fair Trade Commission in Table 5 is based on all listed and non-listed companies that belong to the top 30 *Chaebols*. The ratio of internally held shares increased to 50.5 percent in 1999 from 44.1 percent in 1996, and came back down to the pre-crisis level the of 43.4 percent in 2000. Still, the reduction in 2000 is due to the exclusion of the Daewoo Group.

As part of corporate restructuring, the percentage of internally held shares increased dramatically. For example, shares owned by individual

Table 5. The Ratio of Internally Held Shares of the Top 30 *Chaebols* (Including Both Their Listed and Non-listed Affiliates) (%)

	Individual Controlling Shareholder	Related party	Affiliates	Treasury Stock	Total internally held shares
1990	5.84	8.00	31.83		45.66
1991	5.78	8.15	33.18		47.11
1992	5.02	7.91	33.50		39.43
1993	4.14	6.18	33.05		43.37
1994	4.17	5.47	33.07		42.70
1995	4.95	5.61	32.38	0.41	43.35
1996	4.84	5.48	33.32	0.50	44.14
1997	3.70	4.80	33.74	0.76	43.00
1998	3.09	4.83	35.68	0.87	44.50
1999	2.00	3.36	44.06	1.08	50.50
2000	1.49	3.00	36.62	2.26	43.37

Source: Korea Fair Trade Commission, Annual Announcement Data in April

controlling shareholders and related parties decreased, and shares owned by affiliates increased. This led to a rise in the aggregate percentage of internally held shares. Shares of individual controlling shareholders decreased from 4.85 percent in 1996 to 2.00 percent in 1999. Shares of related parties also shrank from 5.48 percent to 3.36 percent. Yet subsidiaries increased their shares from 33.3 percent in 1996 to 44.06 percent in 1999.[5]

The increase in internally held shares and the overall structural change in ownership of the top 5 *Chaebols* can be seen in Table 6. For the top 5 *Chaebols*, personal shares of controlling shareholders decreased from 3.65 percent in 1996 to 0.99 percent in 2000. Shares of related parties also went down from 6.60 percent to 2.81 percent during the same period. Shares of affiliates, however, escalated from 36.9 percent in 1997 to 48.1 percent in 1999. This percentage fell to 38.5 percent in 2000 only after the Daewoo affiliates were excluded from the list.

In sum, at first examination, controlling shareholders seemed to lose

Table 6. The Ratio of Internally Held Shares of the Top 5 Chaebols (Including Both Their Listed and Non-listed Affiliates)(%)

	Individual Controlling Shareholder	Related party	Affiliates	Treasury Stock	Total internally held shares
1990	5.26	8.00	36.34		49.45
1991	5.10	8.09	38.42		51.61
1992	3.84	8.40	38.84		51.08
1993	3.96	6.84	37.91		48.70
1994	3.26	5.75	38.49		47.50
1995	3.06	5.50	38.77	0.30	47.64
1996	3.65	6.60	48.99	0.54	47.86
1997	2.51	5.07	36.90	0.76	45.24
1998	2.69	4.31	38.70	0.91	46.61
1999	1.68	2.90	48.10	0.84	53.51
2000	0.99	2.81	38.52	2.49	44.81

Source: Korea Fair Trade Commission, Annual Announcement Data in April

[5] The sum of the equity owned by affiliate companies and internally held shares decreased because the Daewoo Group was excluded.

their ownership stakes during the restructuring process, but in reality they managed to reinforce their management control by using a circular investment strategy to secure other group affiliates' shares at the expense of minority shareholders. An analysis of listed companies shows more clearly how controlling shareholders consolidated their management control using affiliates. Table 7 shows the percentage of internally held shares of listed affiliates that belong to the top 10 *Chaebols*. Shares owned by controlling shareholders and related parties totaled 6.56 percent in January 1998, but that percentage decreased to 3.52 percent in June 2000. Nevertheless, shares owned by subsidiaries surged from 17.34 percent to 24.48 percent in the same period. Other shares such as treasury stocks also increased from 1.29 percent to 4.53 percent. Hence, the ratio of internally held shares to total shares jumped from 25.18 percent up to 32.54 percent. In conclusion, an analysis of ownership structure shows evidence of deterioration due to the fact that majority shareholders fortified their management rights at the expense of minority shareholders.

In the process of restructuring, the percentage of internally held shares increased contrary to expectations, mostly due to the abolishment in early 1998 of the required ceiling on the total sum of equity investment into affiliated companies. After the ceiling was removed, an increase in affiliates' shares led to an increase in internally held shares. Even though cross shareholding among subsidiaries was officially banned, the abolishment of a ceiling precipitated an increase in shareholding through circular equity investment among affiliates. In particular, through the large paid-in capital

Table 7. The Ratio of Internally Held Shares of the Top 10 Chaebols' Listed Companies (%)

	98.1.1(A)	99.1.1(B)	2000.6.16(C)	C-A
Related party	6.56	6.02	3.53	-3.03
Affiliates	17.34	28.00	24.48	7.14
Etc	1.29	2.43	4.53	3.24
Total	25.18	36.45	32.54	

Source: Korea Stock Exchange Disclosure of Equity Ownership

increases in 1998 and 1999, subsidiaries bypassed the ban on cross shareholding via circular equity investment.

To ban "mutual equity investment" is to prevent the creation of "paper money" other than through the injection of external capital. Under the current policy banning mutual equity investments among subsidiaries, affiliates have still increased cross ownership through circular equity investments. Figure 1 illustrates the circular equity investment scheme among affiliates of the Hyundai group. Circular equity investment can amplify the risk of increase in paper money, for example, if company A invests $10 million in company B, and company B invests $5 million in company C, and company C invests $3 million in company A. The increase in equity capital amounts to $18 million, but no real capital was actually raised. In this manner, circular equity investment can potentially cause more serious governance problems than mutual equity investments caused previously.

Figure 1 Inter-company Shareholding in Hyundai Group

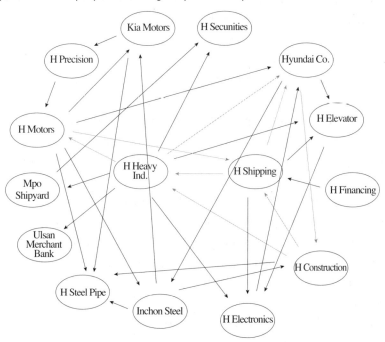

2. Ownership Structure of Chaebols and Non-Chaebols: Listed Companies

Table 8 compares the ownership structure of *Chaebols* and non-*Chaebols*. This analysis excludes listed financial companies. For non-*Chaebols*, only companies with assets over KRW 50 billion are included in the sample to avoid problems stemming from asset size difference. The Korea Fair Trade Commission bases the categorization of *Chaebols* and non-*Chaebols* on the annual announcement of the top 30 *Chaebol* groups. Data on equity ownership comes from the Korea Stock Exchange.

Chaebols and non-*Chaebols* rapidly increased their percentage of internally held shares after the economic crisis. As of the end of 1999, the average percentage of internally held shares among *Chaebols* amounted to 32.6 percent, and the average percentage among non-*Chaebols* amounted to 34.2 percent, showing little significant difference. The *Chaebols* increased their percentage of internally held shares by 12.6 percent from 20.2 percent at the end of 1996, and non-*Chaebols* increased their percentage by 7 percent from 27.8 percent at the end of 1996. Even compared to 1997, when IMF relief loans were provided, *Chaebols* and non-*Chaebols* increased their ratio to some extent, of internally held shares to total shares.

Hence, the percentage of internally held shares increased during the process of restructuring, and this increase was the largest among *Chaebols*. Most importantly, the *Chaebols* stepped up their acquisition of affiliates' shares as part of the restructuring process, and controlling shareholders consolidated their management control at the expense of minority shareholders.

Although there is no difference between *Chaebols* and non-*Chaebols* in terms of the percentage of internally held shares, the exact composition of those internally held shares is different. While the controlling shareholders in *Chaebols* maintain management rights by shares owned by subsidiaries, the controlling shareholders in non-*Chaebols* do so directly or through related parties. As of the end of 1999, the sum of shares owned by controlling shareholders and related parties in *Chaebols* equaled 9.02

percent and subsidiaries' ownership amounted to 18.93 percent. For non-*Chaebols*, the sum of shares owned by controlling shareholders and related parties added up to 21.96 percent but subsidiaries' ownership is a mere 8.83 percent.

It is clear that non-*Chaebols* have for several years had significantly higher ratios of individual equity ownership by controlling shareholders and of equity ownership by related parties. In terms of affiliate share ownership ratio, however, *Chaebols* have much higher values. *Chaebols* and non-*Chaebols*, nonetheless, do not show any significant difference in terms of the total percentage of internally held shares, except in 1996. In summary, the two groups do not show a difference in the ratio of internally held shares, although there is a statistically significant difference in terms of the precise composition of those internally held shares.

Table 8. Composition of Internally Held Shares in Listed Companies (Unit: Percent)

Year	Percentage of Shareholding by Individual Majority Shareholder			Percentage of Shareholding by Related Party			Sample Number	
	Chaebol	Non-*Chaebol*	t-value	*Chaebol*	Non-*Chaebol*	t-value	*Chaebol*	Non-*Chaebol*
1996	0.0425	0.1379	-10.59***	0.0332	0.0745	-5.40***	109	302
1997	0.0546	0.1436	-9.85***	0.0417	0.0952	-6.71***	119	333
1998	0.0533	0.1420	-9.62***	0.0357	0.0973	-7.86***	116	320
1999	0.0624	0.1308	-5.56***	0.0278	0.0888	-8.83***	111	340
Year	Equity Owned by Affiliates			Total Internally Held Shares			Sample Number	
	Chaebol	Non-*Chaebol*	t-value	*Chaebol*	Non-*Chaebol*	t-value	*Chaebol*	Non-*Chaebol*
1996	0.1131	0.0507	4.58***	0.2002	0.2718	-5.23**	109	302
1997	0.1936	0.0749	7.59***	0.3021	0.3211	-1.12	119	333
1998	0.2165	0.0795	7.38***	0.3396	0.3430	-0.19	116	320
1999	0.1893	0.0868	5.56***	0.3261	0.3417	-0.84	111	340

Source: Korea Stock Exchange Disclosure of Equity Ownership and Final Statement of Listed Companies
Note: t-values were tested to see whether Chaebols and non-Chaebols are significantly different. *** Means 1%, ** means 5% and * means 10% significance level. Sample size is identical in Table 12 and Table 13. Sample size varies by year because the list of the top 30 Chaebols announced by Korea Fair Trade Commission varies, and also because the number of non-Chaebols with an asset size over KRW 50 billion is limited.

V. Cost Structure

1. Change in Employment and Labor Expenses

Change in Employment

For listed companies among the top 30 *Chaebols*, the average number of workers per company began to decline in 1997 when the economic crisis set in. The number of workers fell drastically in 1998 and 1999. Non-*Chaebols*, however, increased their average number of workers in 1998 and 1999. This increase is evidence of the fact that unlike *Chaebols*, non-*Chaebols* that survived the crisis were more than able to maintain their previous employment levels.

At the end of 1999, *Chaebols* had an average of 3,652 workers per company, a figure 30.3 percent lower than the average of 5,245 workers in 1996, and 21.8 percent lower than the average in 1997. Non-*Chaebols*, on the other hand, had an average of 1,068.8 workers at the end of 1999, 5.6 percent lower than in 1996, but still 14.9 percent higher than in early 1997. In conclusion, the *Chaebols* went through an effective restructuring by reducing their work forces while non-*Chaebols*, on the other hand, increased their average number of employees.

Change in Labor Expenses

The Average annual labor expenses per worker grew continuously after 1990. Even after 1997, when the economic crisis broke out, the average annual labor expenses continued to grow.[6] Between 1996 and 1999, labor expenses increased by 20.3 percent for *Chaebols* and by 8.6 percent for non-*Chaebols*. The upward trend for labor expenses paid by *Chaebols* was slightly higher than the consumer price indices growth rate of 12.8 percent

---

[6] Labor expenses are calculated by adding up labor costs, welfare costs in the manufacturing costs, and labor expenses on the income statement. Average labor expenses are calculated by dividing labor expenses by the number of workers.

Table 9. Average Number of Workers per Company

	Chaebols	Non-Chaebols	Sample Number Chaebol	Non-Chaebol
1990	5,310.2	1,978.2	77	172
1991	5,331.3	1,744.6	84	198
1992	4,964.1	1,628.6	86	207
1993	4,913.2	1,477.1	89	221
1994	5,199.1	1,365.5	93	255
1995	5,299.7	1,253.3	102	274
1996 (B)	5,245.6	1,132.6	112	306
1997	4,672.9	929.8	119	336
1998	3,604.9	1,074.2	118	322
1999 (A)	3,652.5	1,068.8	111	341
A/B growth rates	-30.3%	-5.6%		

Note: The sample is only for non-financial listed companies. Data for listed companies comes from KIS2000, a database provided by Korea Information Service (KIS), and missing data from this source is supplemented with original data in the individual companies annual report and auditors report. The list of affiliates of the top 30 Chaebols comes from the annual announcement by the Korea Fair Trade Commission. For non-Chaebols, only companies with asset size over KRW 50 billion are included, in order to leave out firms that are so much smaller than Chaebols as to reduce comparability. The threshold of KRW 50 billion is logical considering that only two listed Chaebol affiliates have an asset size below KRW 50 billion.

in the same period. The growth rate in labor expenses of non-Chaebols was lower than the growth rate in the consumer price indices. Employees of non-Chaebols, therefore, saw a reduction in real labor income.

The average labor expenses of the top 30 Chaebols had been higher than that of non-Chaebols since 1990, and this difference is also statistically significant. After the occurrence of the economic crisis, the labor expense gap between the top 30 Chaebols and non-Chaebols has widened even more. Non-Chaebols continued to pay approximately 80 percent compared to what the Chaebols were paying in labor expenses per worker since 1990. That relative percentage decreased slightly from 84.6 percent in 1996 to 76.4 percent in 1999 because of restructuring.

Despite the increase in labor expenses per worker, the proportion of labor expense to the total expenses has decreased since the end of 1990 and,

Table 10. Average Annual Labor Expense per Worker

Year	Chaebol(C)	Non-Chaebol(D)	t-value	D/C Ratio	Consumer Price indices
1990	18,150.7	15,187.6	1.98**	83.7%	75.7
1991	21,613.0	18,659.6	1.56	86.3%	82.8
1992	25,880.6	20,547.5	2.23**	79.4%	86.8
1993	23,822.2	20,228.9	2.44**	84.9%	91.5
1994	27,020.7	22,079.8	3.85***	81.7%	96.8
1995	29,580.5	24,575.9	3.55***	83.1%	101.1
1996 (B)	32,671.9	27,646.3	3.29***	84.6%	106.2
1997	35,076.3	29,765.4	3.29***	84.8%	111.6
1998	37,532.9	28,618.0	4.49***	76.2%	118.3
1999 (A)	39,305.6	30,034.4	4.48***	76.4%	119.8
A/B growth rate	20.3%	8.6%			12.8%

Note: Sample is identical to Table 9. Note: t-value is to test whether Chaebols and non-Chaebols are significantly different. *** means 1%, ** means 5% and * means 10% significance level. A labor expense is the sum of labor costs and welfare costs in the manufacturing expense and labor costs on the income statement. Average labor expense per worker is the division of labor expenses by the number of workers.

Table 11. Proportion of Labor Expense in Total Expenses

Year	Chaebol	Non-Chaebol	t-value	Sample Number Chaebol	Non-Chaebol
1990	0.1400	0.1527	-0.97	77	172
1991	0.1414	0.1586	-1.39	84	198
1992	0.1383	0.1509	-1.03	86	207
1993	0.1301	0.1456	-1.31	89	221
1994	0.1298	0.1398	-0.89	93	255
1995	0.1239	0.1341	-0.97	102	274
1996	0.1220	0.1336	-1.21	112	306
1997	0.1067	0.1131	-0.73	119	336
1998	0.0898	0.0899	-0.02	118	322
1999	0.0844	0.0980	-1.77*	111	341

Note: Sample is identical to Table 9. Note: t-value is to test whether Chaebols and non-Chaebols are significantly different. *** means 1%, ** means 5% and * means 10% significance level. Total expense is the sum of cost of sales that is a part of manufacturing expenses, sales costs on the income statement, administrative expenses, non-operating expenses, and extraordinary loss. Labor expense is the sum of labor costs and welfare costs in the manufacturing expense and labor costs on the income statement.

in particularly rapid fashion, during the restructuring period.[7] The proportion of labor expenses in total expenses reached 12.2 percent in 1996, but declined to 8.4 percent at the end of 1999. This trend is also demonstrated in non-*Chaebols*, which have experienced a comparatively lower growth in nominal labor expenses. Since 1990, there has not been any significant difference between *Chaebols* and non-*Chaebols* in terms of the proportion of labor expense in total expenses. Non-*Chaebols* did, however, pay a significantly higher proportion of labor expense in total expenses in 1999, when restructuring was in progress.

2. Financial Costs

The proportion of interest expense in total cost has increased consistently since 1990, and has increased most dramatically in the years after the economic crisis. Even in 1999, the proportion of interest expense in total cost stood at a higher level than during the pre-crisis period.[8]

The same trend in interest expense is common for *Chaebols* and non-*Chaebols* alike. For *Chaebols*, the proportion of interest expense in total expenses reached 6.84 percent in 1996, the highest level since 1990. Since then, the proportion peaked at 9.05 percent during the restructuring process and fell to 7.36 percent in 1999, but still stood at a level higher than during the pre-restructuring period. For non-*Chaebols*, the proportion of interest expense plummeted in 1997 to its lowest level since 1992, but the proportion increased during the restructuring period.

To check whether the result was due to negative net asset value or to

---

[7] Total expense is the sum of cost of sales that is a part of manufacturing expenses, sales costs on the income statement, administrative expenses, non-operating expenses, and extraordinary loss.

[8] Total expense is the sum of sales expense that amounts to total manufacturing costs, sales expense on the income statement, administrative costs, non-operating expense and extraordinary loss. Interest expense is the sum of interest payments on debt and corporate bonds.

outliers with extraordinarily high debt to equity ratios, firms with debt to equity ratios over 1000 percent and negative net asset value were then excluded in the analysis. The result is shown in Table 13.[9]

For *Chaebols*, the trend in the proportion of interest expense in total expenses was the same even after excluding companies with negative net asset value and for firms with debt to equity ratios over 1000 percent. For non-*Chaebols*, the proportion of interest expense plummeted in 1999 to a point that was not only lower than the pre-crisis period but also the lowest since 1990. This shows that the reduction of the interest expense through decreased debt to equity ratio was more effective for non-*Chaebols*.

It is noteworthy that the proportion of interest expenses in total expenses did not decrease after restructuring, considering that the strengthening of the financial market conditions allowed for single digit interest rates and reductions in debt to equity ratios through share issuance.[10] The *Chaebols* sustained a higher proportion of interest expense in total expenses than non-*Chaebols* since 1990, but the difference was not significant. Still, the proportion of interest expense for *Chaebols* was significantly higher than for non-*Chaebols* both when the economic crisis broke out in 1998 and during the 1999 restructuring campaign.

---

[9] The difference between Table 18 and Table 19 is explained by the exclusion of companies with negative net asset value and debt to equity ratios over 1000%.

[10] Market rates for corporate bonds decreased from 12.57 percent in 1996 and 24.31 percent in 1997 to 8.30 percent in 1998 and 9.85 percent in 1999. Interest rate data comes from the Bank of Korea. A sharp contrast can be drawn between the dramatic fall in interest rates and the lack of any concomitant decrease in the proportion of interest expense in total expenses. It should be seen that debt to equity ratio reduction did not bring about a real reduction in financial costs despite decreased interest rates.) The question of why financial costs increased despite the reduction in interest rates and in the debt to equity ratios is discussed in the financial restructuring section of this paper.

Table 12. Proportion of Financial Costs in Total Expenses: Full Company Sample

	Financial Costs/total expenses			Sample Number	
Year	*Chaebol*	Non-*Chaebol*	t-value	*Chaebol*	Non-*Chaebol*
1990	0.0503	0.0550	-1.13	96	202
1991	0.0579	0.0608	-0.66	100	231
1992	0.0647	0.0681	-0.72	102	241
1993	0.0614	0.0656	-0.92	105	259
1994	0.0639	0.0659	-0.42	106	290
1995	0.0672	0.0674	-0.04	113	303
1996	0.0684	0.0667	0.37	117	322
1997	0.0651	0.0655	-0.09	120	346
1998	0.0905	0.0830	1.31	118	333
1999	0.0736	0.0709	0.43	111	343

Note: The sample was drawn from the same data set used in Table 9. The sample number is different from Table 9 since some companies did not report number of employee. t-value is to test whether *Chaebols* and non-*Chaebols* are significantly different. *** means 1%, ** means 5% and * means 10% significance level.

Table 13. The Proportion of Financial Costs in Total Expenses: All Companies Except Those with Negative Net Asset Value and Debt to Equity Ratios Over 1000%

	The proportion of financial costs in total expenses			Sample numbers	
	Chaebol	Non-*Chaebol*	t-value	*Chaebol*	Non-*Chaebol*
1990	0.0483	0.0534	-1.31	89	196
1991	0.0563	0.0597	-0.75	92	224
1992	0.0632	0.0669	-0.78	95	232
1993	0.0610	0.0631	-0.46	100	248
1994	0.0638	0.0612	0.61	103	271
1995	0.0643	0.0644	-0.02	104	286
1996	0.0623	0.0641	-0.42	107	299
1997	0.0611	0.0606	0.11	101	303
1998	0.0866	0.0732	2.53**	108	267
1999	0.0686	0.0517	3.07***	102	282

Note: The sample was drawn from the same data set used in Table 12. t-value is to test whether *Chaebols* and non-*Chaebols* are significantly different. *** means 1%, ** means 5% and * means 10% significance level.

VI. Financial Structure

1. Debt to Equity Ratio

The debt to equity ratio kept increasing after 1990 and peaked in 1997 when the economic crisis took place, before dropping in 1998 and 1999 when restructuring began. This trend has been common among *Chaebol*s and non-*Chaebol*s. It was the government's debt reduction policy that precipitated a drop in debt to equity ratio after the economic crisis. On the other hand, most of the improvement took place because many corporations with an exceptionally high debt to equity ratio went bankrupt in 1997.

Table 14 shows the average debt to equity ratio for the sample companies excluding those with negative net asset value. According to the official data, the average debt to equity ratio of *Chaebol*s was as high as 1,258 percent in 1997 when the economic crisis began. This high ratio, however, resulted from a small number of companies that had extremely high debt to equity ratios. For this reason, the ratio lacks statistical merit. For this reason, in this analysis, companies with negative net asset value or with debt to equity ratios over 1000 percent were then excluded. The result is shown in Table 15.

After excluding the companies with debt to equity ratios over 1000 percent, it is found that the average debt to equity ratio of *Chaebol*s in 1997 hit a record high of 396.4 percent, which was the highest since 1990. Yet the average debt to equity ratio dropped to 296.2 percent during the 1998 restructuring process and dropped further to 180.1 percent in 1999. The decline in debt to equity ratios was the result of the government's strong restructuring policy. For non-*Chaebol*s, the debt to equity ratio increased to 274.3 percent in 1997, the highest level since 1990, before dropping off to 191.7 percent in 1998 and to 143.4 percent in 1999.

Both before and after the economic crisis, *Chaebol*s have had higher debt to equity ratios than non-*Chaebol*s, and the difference in the ratio for the two

Table 14. Debt to Equity Ratios After Excluding Companies with Negative Net Asset Value

Year	Chaebol	Non-Chaebol	t-value	Sample Number	
				Chaebol	Non-Chaebol
1990	3.713	3.204	0.88	94	199
1991	4.711	3.082	2.51**	99	229
1992	14.620	3.034	1.13	101	238
1993	3.757	7.419	-0.86	103	256
1994	3.936	3.209	1.33	105	279
1995	4.143	4.861	-0.33	113	293
1996	6.149	3.191	2.32**	116	310
1997	12.587	5.103	1.01	113	323
1998	4.578	3.793	0.54	112	281
1999	9.385	3.947	0.76	106	297

Note: The sample was drawn from the same data set used in Table 9. t-value is to test whether Chaebols and non-Chaebols are significantly different. *** means 1%, ** means 5% and * means 10% significance level.

Table 15. Debt to Equity Ratios After Excluding Companies with Negative Net Asset Value and Debt to Equity Ratios over 1000 percent

Year	Chaebol	Non-Chaebol	t-value	Sample Number	
				Chaebol	Non-Chaebol
1990	2.9391	2.6755	1.24	89	196
1991	3.3197	2.8554	2.08**	92	224
1992	3.5657	2.8190	3.33***	95	232
1993	3.3739	2.5653	3.95***	100	248
1994	3.6235	2.4286	5.81***	*103	271
1995	3.3872	2.3884	5.40***	104	286
1996	3.4962	2.3703	5.84***	107	299
1997	3.9644	2.7434	5.22***	101	303
1998	2.9623	1.9175	5.31***	108	267
1999	1.8080	1.4344	2.53***	102	282

Note: The sample was drawn from the same data set used in Table 9. t-value is to test whether Chaebols and non-Chaebols are significantly different. *** means 1%, ** means 5% and * means 10% significance level.

groups has been statistically significant for the entire period. Yet the convergence in the debt to equity ratios between the two groups after the economic crisis indicates that the *Chaebols* have decreased their debt to equity ratio the most since the crisis. This is also evident in the distribution of debt to equity ratios shown in Table 16 and Table 17. When the economic

Table 16. Distribution of Debt to Equity Ratios among *Chaebols*

	<100%	<200%	<300%	<400%	<500%	<1000%>	1000%	negative net asset value
1990	5.21	30.2	19.79	12.50	17.71	7.29	5.21	2.08
1991	4.00	20.00	26.00	13.00	16.00	13.00	7.00	1.00
1992	0.98	14.71	29.41	18.63	12.75	16.67	5.88	0.98
1993	1.90	20.00	24.76	19.05	14.29	15.24	2.86	1.90
1994	2.83	12.26	28.30	22.6	48.49	22.64	1.89	0.94
1995	2.65	16.81	26.55	19.47	7.96	18.58	7.96	0.00
1996	2.56	17.09	23.93	18.80	11.11	17.95	7.69	0.85
1997	4.17	8.33	16.67	21.67	12.50	20.83	10.00	5.83
1998	5.08	30.51	18.64	18.64	6.78	11.86	3.39	5.08
1999	22.52	45.95	14.4	12.70	2.70	3.60	3.60	4.50

Note: The sample was drawn from the same data set used in Table 9. t-value is to test whether *Chaebols* and non-*Chaebols* are significantly different. *** means 1%, ** means 5% and * means 10% significance level.

Table 17. Distribution of Debt to Equity Ratios among Non-*Chaebols*

	<100%	<200%	<300%	<400%	<500%	<1000%>	1000%	negative net asset value
1990	7.43 3	3.17	27.23	12.38	8.91	7.92	1.49	1.49
1991	10.39	25.97	25.97	17.75	4.76	12.12	2.16	0.87
1992	11.20	26.56	22.41	19.50	5.39	11.20	2.49	1.24
1993	13.13	30.89	23.17	13.13	5.79	9.65	3.09	1.16
1994	12.41	31.38	25.52	11.03	6.55	6.55	2.76	3.79
1995	11.88	34.65	24.42	11.22	6.60	5.61	2.31	3.30
1996	16.15	32.92	21.12	10.56	3.73	8.39	3.42	3.73
1997	13.01	28.32	17.92	9.25	7.51	11.56	5.78	6.65
1998	26.13	30.63	8.71	7.51	2.70	4.50	4.20	15.62
1999	38.19	29.15	7.29	3.79	2.04	1.75	4.37	13.41

Note: The sample was drawn from the same data set used in Table 9. t-value is to test whether *Chaebols* and non-*Chaebols* are significantly different. *** means 1%, ** means 5% and * means 10% significance level.

crisis took place in 1997, only 12.5 percent of *Chaebols* maintained debt to equity ratios below 200 percent, whereas 41.33 percent of non-*Chaebols* had debt to equity ratios below 200 percent. While restructuring was taking place in 1999, however, 68.5 percent of *Chaebols* and 67.3 percent of non-*Chaebols* kept debt to equity ratios below 200%. In 1999, the debt to equity ratio gap between the two groups narrowed considerably. In terms of the proportion of companies with debt to equity ratio over 500 percent in 1997, the gap between the two groups still remained wide: 30.8 percent for *Chaebols* and 17.3 percent for non-*Chaebols*. Yet the gap was narrowed in 1999 as *Chaebols* scored 7.2 percent and non-*Chaebols* 6.12 percent.

2. Change in Debt and Equity Capital

In spite of the notable decline in debt to equity ratios, the proportion of financial costs did not decrease because the reduction in debt to equity ratios was not realized through debt reduction, but rather through a large increase in equity capital that could overshadow a real increase in debt. Changes in the amount of debt and equity capital during the restructuring period are summarized in Table 18 and Table 19. Even though debt to equity ratios dropped to half the level of 1996, the amount of real corporate debt actually increased. As shown in Table 18, *Chaebols* increased their average amount of debt per company by 12.3 percent in 1999, and the average amount of equity capital per company increased by 133.5 percent. For non-*Chaebols*, the average amount of debt increased by 27.2 percent, and the average amount of equity capital increased by 98.6 percent from 1996 to 1999.

Although there was a sharp decrease in debt to equity ratios, the proportion of financial costs in fixed expenses and in total expenses increased between 1998 and 1999. The proportion of financial costs reached a higher level than in 1996, during the pre-crisis period, in part because the real amount of corporate debt increased. Compared to when the economic crisis broke out in 1997, *Chaebols* decreased their average amount of debt by

20.3 percent in late 1999, and the average amount of equity capital increased by 104.7 percent. For non-*Chaebols*, in contrast, the average amount of debt and the average amount of equity capital increased at the same rate following the crisis. The amount of debt in *Chaebols* decreased, but the reduction in debt was smaller than the increase in equity capital. Hence, it appears that equity capital was not used to service debts.

Upon first examination, it is seen that the average amount of debt in *Chaebols* decreased in 1999, and that the average amount of debt was lower than during the 1997 pre-crisis period. The apparent reduction in the average amount of debt, however, is greatly exaggerated because the official data excludes companies that had gone bankrupt in 1997 and 1998 due to excessive debt.

Table 18. Average Amount of Debt and Equity Capital per Company After Excluding those with Negative Net Asset Value and Debt to Equity Ratios over 1000 percent (Unit: KRW Million)

	Chaebol		Non-Chaebol		Sample Number	
	Average Debt	Average Capital	Average Debt	Average Capital	Chaebol	Non-Chaebol
1990	537,333.5	173,125.1	212,772.1	128,537.4	89	196
1991	685,314.9	208,209.6	225,924.5	127,101.6	92	224
1992	774,525.6	228,294.8	253,726.6	136,283.3	95	232
1993	817,144.7	262,833.1	257,591.8	154,026.6	100	248
1994	988,550.2	314,177.4	270,473.9	160,141.2	103	271
1995	1,189,866.6	412,301.0	297,690.7	172,974.8	104	286
1996 (C)	1,410,807.0	442,388.4	323,344.4	188,565.8	107	299
1997 (B)	1,985,934.6	504,665.1	397,026.3	186,133.4	101	303
1998	1,913,638.8	650,685.9	421,930.4	256,148.4	108	267
1999 (A)	1,583,653.2	1,032,804.3	411,399.6	374,521.3	102	282
A-C	172,846.1	590,415.9	88,055.1	185,955.5		
A/C growth rates	12.3percent	133.5percent	27.2percent	98.6percent		
A-B	-402,281.4	528,139.1	14,373.2	188,387.9		
A/B growth rates	-20.3percent	104.7percent	3.6percent	101.2percent		

Note: The sample was drawn from the same data set used in Table 9.

When companies that were consecutively listed since 1990 (even if they were both listed and effectively bankrupt)are sampled, it is found that *Chaebol*s increased the average amount of debt per company by 1.7 percent from 1997 to 1999, as illustrated in Table 19, and that the average amount of equity capital increased by 53.6 percent. Thus, it is reaffirmed that the decrease in debt to equity ratios did not occur through a reduction in corporate debt. In the same period, non-*Chaebol*s decreased the average amount of debt by 1.3 percent and increased the average amount of equity capital by 68.7 percent.

In conclusion, the restructuring policy was not able to bring about an effective reduction in financial costs because the notable 50 percent reduction in the average debt to equity ratio was not achieved through a reduction in debt, but rather through an increase in equity capital.

Table 19. Average Debt and Average Equity Capital per Company for All Consecutively Listed Companies during 1990-1999

	Chaebol		Non-*Chaebol*		Sample Number	
	Average Debt	Average Capital	Average Debt	Average Capital	*Chaebol*	Non-*Chaebol*
1990	533,306.3	157,301.8	95,577.3	59,488.0	94.0	436.0
1991	675,996.0	194,011.1	114,950.7	65,619.9	94.0	441.0
1992	779,114.6	218,900.8	134,135.4	72,238.3	94.0	440.0
1993	832,125.5	264,061.2	149,181.8	87,594.2	94.0	441.0
1994	1,021,493.8	327,597.4	172,612.4	98,802.1	94.0	442.0
1995	1,274,657.1	427,834.1	199,601.8	112,121.3	94.0	444.0
1996 (C)	1,553,325.7	462,483.4	237,469.2	127,752.1	94.0	444.0
1997 (B)	2,188,004.5	502,298.2	306,377.3	128,596.2	94.0	444.0
1998	2,291,812.0	689,811.4	316,765.7	144,009.7	94.0	444.0
1999 (A)	2,225,009.4	771,552.3	302,372.1	216,936.2	94.0	444.0
A-C	671,683.6	309,068.9	64,902.9	89,184.1		
A/C growth rates	43.2percent	66.8percent	27.3percent	69.8percent		
A-B	37,004.8	269,254.1	-4,005.1	88,340.0		
A/B growth rates	1.7percent	53.6percent	-1.3percent	68.7percent		

Note: The sample was drawn from the same data set used in Table 9.

3. Debt Structure

Since the economic crisis, there has been a significant change in debt structure as part of restructuring. The most important change was that *Chaebols* began to increase their proportion of corporate bonds in long-term liabilities amid a swift fall in the proportion of debt owed to banks. For non-*Chaebols*, the proportion of corporate bonds in long term liabilities dropped sharply as the proportion of debts owed to banks soared, thus showing the opposite trend.

Chaebols continuously increased the proportion of corporate bonds in long-term liabilities after 1990, and the proportion of corporate bonds had grown larger than the proportion of bank loans since 1993. In particular after the outbreak of the economic crisis, there has been a significant financial change. The proportion of corporate bonds rose swiftly and that of bank loan plunged. The proportion of corporate bonds in fixed liabilities was only 32.2 percent in 1990, but then it increased to 40.4 percent in 1996 and escalated to 49.4 percent in 1998. In 1999, it was reduced but still stood at 45.0 percent. On the other hand, the proportion of bank loan in long-term liabilities was 38.5 percent in 1990 but dropped to 31.8 percent in 1996. It declined to as low as 26.3 percent in 1998 and to 26.5 percent in 1999. The change in debt structure was the same, even after excluding companies with negative net asset values and debt to equity ratios above 1000 percent.

Non-*Chaebols* went through a different change. The proportion of corporate bonds in fixed liabilities grew incrementally from 34.0 percent in 1990 to 38.7 percent in 1996. Soon after the economic crisis, however, the proportion of corporate bonds dropped suddenly from 28.4 percent in 1998 to 26.9 percent in 1999. The proportion of debt decreased gradually from 34.3 percent in 1990 to 27.5 percent in 1996. After the economic crisis, the proportion of debt bounced back to 36.3 percent in 1998 before falling again to 30.3 percent in 1999.

Table 20. Corporate Bonds/Long-Term Liabilities

Year	Total Samples			Excluding companies with negative net asset value and debt to equity ratios over 1000 percent		
	Chaebol	Non-Chaebol	t-value	Chaebol	Non-Chaebol	t-value
1990	0.3218	0.3404	-0.52	0.3450	0.3472	-0.06
1991	0.3605	0.3594	0.03	0.3897	0.3626	0.77
1992	0.3447	0.3605	-0.51	0.3660	0.3642	0.05
1993	0.3684	0.3708	-0.08	0.3828	0.3729	0.32
1994	0.3889	0.3939	-0.15	0.3967	0.3999	-0.09
1995	0.3892	0.3890	0.00	0.3917	0.3984	-0.22
1996	0.4037	0.3873	0.58	0.4000	0.3961	0.13
1997	0.4003	0.3639	1.19	0.4059	0.3646	1.38
1998	0.4936	0.2842	6.63***	0.4986	0.3080	5.55***
1999	0.4497	0.2686	5.40***	0.4769	0.3005	4.86***

Note: sample is identical to those in Table 18.

Table 21. Debts/Fixed Liabilities

Year	Total Samples			Excluding companies with negative net asset value and debt to equity ratios over 1000 percent		
	Chaebol	Non-Chaebol	t-value	Chaebol	Non-Chaebol	t-value
1990	0.3846	0.3427	-1.36	0.3657	0.3384	0.89
1991	0.3632	0.3256	-1.31	0.3474	0.3272	0.69
1992	0.3497	0.3174	-1.26	0.3275	0.3167	0.43
1993	0.3290	0.2944	-1.46	0.3232	0.2946	1.21
1994	0.3185	0.2606	-2.48***	0.3154	0.2587	2.44**
1995	0.3173	0.2724	-2.09**	0.3165	0.2721	2.02**
1996	0.3175	0.2751	-1.78*	0.3140	0.2717	1.74
1997	0.3426	0.3321	-0.44	0.3552	0.3312	0.95
1998	0.2629	0.3633	3.73***	0.2620	0.3435	-2.94***
1999	0.2651	0.3032	1.24	0.2512	0.2718	-0.70

Note: The sample is identical to those in Table 18.

VII. Investment Assets

Investment assets are defined as investment into securities and it was calculated as the sum of long-term deposit, investment in securities including equity and securities of affiliates, long-term loans, long-term notes and accounts receivable. For *Chaebol*s, the proportion of investment asset in total asset decreased steadily until 1996 and it decreased sharply in 1997 and rebounded to 20.6 percent in 1999. For non-*Chaebol*s, it has increased steadily since 1990. Investments in securities of affiliates soared during the restructuring process, with the trend being most conspicuous for *Chaebol*s.

The proportion of investment in affiliates' securities by *Chaebol*s was 19.9 percent of total investment assets in 1990 and reached 26.9 percent in 1996. It jumped even further to 32.4 percent in 1997 and went as high as 38.2 percent when restructuring was in progress in 1999. *Chaebol*s had a higher proportion of investment in securities of affiliates than did non-*Chaebol*s, and the difference between the two groups increased after the economic crisis. This was because *Chaebol*s increased their investments in affiliates securities through circular equity investment among affiliates.

Non-*Chaebol*s gradually increased the proportion of investment in affiliates securities from 20.2 percent in 1990 to 22.4 percent in 1996. In 1997, their investment in affiliates increased to 26.1 percent, and in 1998, to 28.3 percent. In 1999, in contrast, it decreased to 25.1 percent.

After the economic crisis, *Chaebol*s invested in securities of affiliates and concentrated on acquiring subsidiary stocks. This practice was made possible because subsidiaries actively participated in large-scale paid-in capital increases that occurred in 1998 and in 1999. Large equity capital increases enabled the *Chaebol*s to increase their ownership of affiliates securities dramatically during restructuring, as was illustrated in the earlier analysis of the change in ownership structure. Circular equity investment among affiliates was designed to secure management control for majority shareholders, and majority shareholders reinforced their management rights at the expense of minority shareholders.

Table 22. Investment Assets and Investment in Marketable Securities of Affiliates

Year	Investment Assets/Total Assets			Securities of Affiliates/Investment Assets		
	Chaebol	Non-Chaebol	t-value	Chaebol	Non-Chaebol	t-value
1990	0.1826	0.1363	2.90***	0.1989	0.2002	-0.04
1991	0.1776	0.1356	3.00***	0.2388	0.1925	1.64*
1992	0.1833	0.1392	3.39***	0.2319	0.1857	1.70*
1993	0.1752	0.1424	2.72***	0.2485	0.1988	1.83*
1994	0.1756	0.1406	3.40***	0.2497	0.2165	1.22
1995	0.1730	0.1456	2.89***	0.2584	0.2290	1.14
1996	0.1795	0.1605	2.05**	0.2688	0.2244	1.81*
1997	0.1559	0.1610	-0.57	0.3242	0.2605	2.55***
1998	0.1700	0.1562	1.33	0.3334	0.2833	1.78*
1999	0.2060	0.1687	2.56***	0.3815	0.2508	2.85***

Note: The sample number is identical to those used in Table 18

This circular equity investment came about because of the abolishment of a regulation in 1998 that previously imposed a ceiling on the amount of investment in affiliates. At that time, business leaders demanded that the government abolish the regulation in order to accelerate restructuring, and the government approved the request. The facts show that majority shareholders used the change in policy to secure additional management rights, rather than using the change to promote real restructuring.

VIII. Governance Structure

1. Dividends and Donations

It is shown here that, even after restructuring, the majority of *Chaebols* continue to spend more on donations than on dividends. In 1995, the total amount of donations by *Chaebols* was greater than that of dividends. The following year, donations decreased and dividends increased. In 1997, donations amounted to 58.7 percent of dividends. Yet the proportion of donations to dividends increased in 1998 and 1999, even though restructur-

Table 23. Total Value of Donations and Dividends (Unit: KRW Million)

	Chaebol			Non-Chaebol		
	Total Donation (A)	Total Dividend (B)	A/B	Total Donation (A)	Total Dividend (B)	A/B
1995	601,623.1	526,475.5	114.3	322,521.0	457,174.4	70.5
1996	436,011.9	783,881.2	55.6	334,244.0	560,262.8	59.7
1997	439,820.4	748,631.8	58.7	125,504.7	517,041.9	24.3
1998	257,868.9	425,741.4	60.6	318,052.3	537,841.9	59.1
1999	484,235.4	622,258.1	77.8	358,375.8	681,912.6	52.6

Note: The sample number is identical to those used in Table 18.

Table 24. Distribution of Companies with Comparative Size of Dividends and Donation Amount (Unit: percent)

	Dividend>Donation		Dividend<Donation		Donation=Dividend=0	
	Chaebols	Non-Chaebols	Chaebols	Non-Chaebols	Chaebols	Non-Chaebols
1995	61.8	71.5	38.2	27.4	0.0	1.1
1996	54.5	72.2	44.6	25.8	0.9	2.0
1997	57.1	69.6	40.3	27.4	2.5	3.0
1998	46.6	52.8	46.6	41.3	6.8	6.0
1999	42.3	46.3	53.1	47.5	4.5	6.2

Note: The sample number is identical to those used in Table 18.

ing was under way. Especially in 1999, dividends grew at a slower rate than before the crisis in 1996, while, in contrast, donations increased and reached up to 77.8 percent of dividends. Non-*Chaebols* had a lower proportion of donations to dividends than *Chaebols*, but even for non-*Chaebols*, donations in 1999 were larger than they were in 1996.

Corporations continued to spend more on donations than on dividends even during restructuring, as illustrated in Table 24. In 1996, 44.6 percent of the companies in the full sample that are affiliated to *Chaebols* paid out more in donations than in dividends. This ratio increased to 53.1 percent in 1999, when only 42.3 percent of the total sample paid out higher dividends than donations. Non-*Chaebols* have experienced the same trend.

Considering the preponderance of untransparent accounting practices, companies may have actually spent more on donations than was reported.

Table 25. Who Recommended Current Outside Directors

	1999		2000	
Controlling Shareholders	124	(41.8 percent)	71	(39.9 percent)
Management	138	(46.4 percent)	71	(39.9 percent)
Institutional Investors	1	(0.3 percent)	3	(1.7 percent)
Related Associations	18	(6.1 percent)	8	(4.5 percent)
Creditor Banks	15	(5.1 percent)	8	(4.5 percent)
Etc	1	(0.3 percent)	17	(9.6 percent)
Total	297	(100.0 percent)	178	(100.0 percent)

Source: Korean Association of Listed Companies. The survey was conducted in August of 1999 and 2000.

Table 26. Who Recommended Current Outside Director Elections

Recommendation by Principal Shareholder	Recommendation by Creditor	Recommendation by Employees	Etc
343 Companies	25 Companies	20 Companies	77 Companies
(73.8 percent)	(5.3 percent)	(4.3 percent)	(16.6 percent)

Source: Korea Stock Exchange. The survey was conducted in November 2000.

For dividends, the book value and the value that was really paid should be identical. Yet donations can be larger than the reported book value since payment through other accounts is also possible.

This phenomenon raises the question of whether donations in fact represent the "restoration of profits to society" by *Chaebols*, or alternatively, represent the neglect of shareholder-focused management. A large percentage of donations have been granted to *Chaebol*-affiliated cultural foundations or social groups.

2. Current Status of Outside Director System

Table 25 and Table 26 show the results of a survey of listed companies that was conducted by the Korean Association of Listed Companies and by the Korea Stock Exchange. The Korean Association of Listed Companies surveyed who recommended outside directors. The results show that controlling shareholders and managers recommended 80 percent of elected outside directors, and that a further 4.5 percent of elected outside directors was recommended by related associations or creditor banks. It is noteworthy that managers and controlling shareholders handpick the majority of outside directors. This trend is confirmed in another survey conducted by the Korea Stock Exchange in November 2000. The survey was conducted for 465 listed companies. According to the survey, majority shareholders recommended outside directors in 73.8 percent of companies, creditors recommended outside directors in 5.3 percent of companies, and labor unions recommended outside directors in 4.3 percent of companies. Clearly independent people are being excluded in the process of electing outside directors, and this exclusion keeps outside directors from independently monitoring the management.

Although the attendance rates of outside directors at board meetings is on the rise, only 53.5 percent of outside directors took part in meetings during the first half of 2000. Data announced by the Korea Stock Exchange in July and November of 2000 also indicates that attendance rates of outside directors at board meetings stood recently at approximately 60 percent, suggesting that outside directors do not play any active roles.

3. Cumulative Voting

Cumulative voting was adopted through a revision of the Commercial Code in 1998. As of October 2000, however, none of the 702 listed corporations has implemented the cumulative voting system, since 80 percent of the total listed companies have excluded from their articles of incorporation. In particular, 93 percent of the top 30 *Chaebol*s has excluded cumulative voting from their articles of incorporation.

Among the subsidiaries of the top 4 groups, only Dacom and Hyundai Pipe Co., Ltd., have yet to purposely exclude cumulative voting from their articles of corporations. Dacom accepted demands from minority shareholders. Hyundai Pipe Co., Ltd., is the only other company among the top 4 groups affiliates that has chosen voluntarily not to exclude a cumulative voting system. Hyundai Pipe Co., Ltd., however, did not need to exclude cumulative voting from its articles of incorporation because 46.9 percent of the company is owned by controlling shareholders and subsidiaries, and because 40.70 percent of the company is owned by Otemachi Ltd., a joint venture, thus raising the proportion of internally held shares to 87.6 percent. In conclusion, there isn't a company among the affiliates of the top 4 *Chaebols* that has chosen voluntarily to still allow for the possibility of a cumulative voting system.

There are nine companies among the affiliates of the top 5-30 *Chaebols* that do not exclude a cumulative voting system. Yet among those nine companies, only five remain after separating out insolvent firms such as The Korea Express Co., Dong Ah Construction, Kohap, and Jinro General Foods. Among these five companies, some could not exclude cumulative voting because of the existence of a second large shareholders influence, and thus there are few companies that have chosen voluntarily to not exclude a cumulative voting system. In terms of non-*Chaebols*, 23.6 percent of them do not exclude a cumulative voting system, but many of them are financial institutions or government-invested companies. In conclusion, a cumulative voting system that was designed by law to allow minority shareholders to elect independent outside directors is evaluated as being rarely implemented and thus ineffective.

Table 27. Current Status of Cumulative Voting Adoption by Listed Companies

	Number of listed companies	Number of companies that do not exclude from articles of incorporation	Number of companies that implemented cumulative voting
Affiliates of Top 4 Groups	47	2 (4.2 percent)	0
Affiliates of Top 5-30 Groups	79	9 (11.4 percent)	0
Non-Chaebols	576	136 (23.6 percent)	0
Total	702	147 (20.9 percent)	0

Source: People's Solidarity for Participatory Democracy

4. Evaluation of Corporations Governance Structure by Investors

A survey conducted by the People's Solidarity for Participatory Democracy in December 2000 provided investors' evaluation on the governance structure of listed companies in Korea.[11] In early December 2000, the People's Solidarity for Participatory Democracy carried out a survey of 87 domestic fund managers and 66 foreign fund managers on the governance structure of Korean firms. According to the survey, both domestic and foreign investors voiced their belief that Korean firms fall short of having a transparent and accountable governance structure.

A full 77.0 percent of domestic fund managers and 98.5 percent of foreign fund managers responded that Korean firms do not operate on a transparent basis. An 88.5 percent of domestic fund managers and 95.5 percent of foreign fund managers responded that Korean firms do not have management systems that demand accountability from management. Furthermore, 77.0 percent of domestic and 93.9 percent of foreign fund managers think that managers in Korean companies do not consider shareholders to be important. It is known that both domestic and foreign investors share very negative views toward Korean firms' governance structure.

In response to the question of whether they would increase their investments if corporate governance structure was enhanced, 100 percent of for-

---

[11] The original data was retrieved from the website of People's Solidarity for Participatory Democracy (www.peoplepower21.org). Foreign investors responding to the survey had the following distribution by national identity: the United States, 28.2 percent; Singapore, 22.7 percent; Hong Kong, 12.1 percent; the United Kingdom, 9.1 percent; the Netherlands, 4.5 percent; Australia, 3.0 percent; and other countries. 89.4 percent of respondents were investing in Korea, and the others had previously invested in Korean firms.

[12] For foreign fund managers, they were asked whether they would increase their investments or not. Domestic fund managers were asked whether stock investment in general would be increased or not. Since domestic fund managers operated with existing funds and since their potential injection of new capital was quite limited, domestic investors were asked about their reaction in the stock market. Foreign investors were asked whether they would increase their investment since they could draw new capital into Korea.

eign fund managers and 88.5 percent of domestic fund managers answered "yes".[12] More importantly, 78.8 percent of foreign fund managers expressed positive investment intentions, and 59.8 percent of domestic fund managers agreed about the possibility of a stock market boom. Considering that 72.4 percent of domestic fund managers and 71.2 percent of foreign fund managers consider that stocks of Korean firms are currently undervalued, it can be inferred that positive changes to the corporate governance system would play a major role in promoting the health of the stock market.

When asked about whether investors in Korea should be allowed to bring class action lawsuits, 94.3 percent of domestic fund managers and 98.5 percent of foreign fund managers agreed that Korea should amend its corporate governance structure to allow for such lawsuits. Among those managers, 77.0 percent of domestic fund managers and 97.0 percent of foreign fund managers said that class action lawsuits should be introduced at once. In regard to cumulative voting, 88.5 percent of domestic fund managers and 92.4 percent of foreign fund managers maintained that it should be implemented. Among those managers in favor of cumulative voting, 55.2 percent of domestic fund managers and 87.9 percent of foreign fund managers said that the adoption of cumulative voting is urgent.

Question 1. Are Korean Corporations Managed Based on Transparent Management Systems? (Unit: percent)

	① Absolutely Yes	② Somewhat Yes	③ Somewhat No	④ Absolutely No	⑤ No Reply/ Don't Know	Total
Domestic	2.3	20.7	44.8	32.2	0	100.0
Foreign	0	0	45.5	53.0	1.5	100.0

Question 2. Do You Think Korean Firms Have Management Systems that Demand Accountability from Management? (Unit: percent)

	① Absolutely Yes	② Somewhat Yes	③ Somewhat No	④ Absolutely No	⑤ No Reply/ Don't Know	Total
Domestic	0	11.5	55.2	33.3	0	100.0
Foreign	0	1.5	45.5	50.0	3.0	100.0

Question 3. Do You Think Korean Firms are Operated Based on Shareholder Value? (Unit: percent)

	① Absolutely Yes	② Somewhat Yes	③ Somewhat No	④ Absolutely No	⑤ No Reply/ Don't Know	Total
Domestic	0	23.0	52.9	24.1	0	100.0
Foreign	1.5	3.0	53.0	40.9	1.5	100.0

Question 4. How are Korean Firms' Shares Being Evaluated Relative to Their Profitability? (Unit: percent)

	① Very Overvalued	② Somewhat Overvalued	③ Adequately Evaluated	④ Undervalued	⑤ Very Undervalued	⑥ No Reply/ Don't Know	Total
Domestic	0	5.7	20.7	57.5	14.9	1.1	100.0
Foreign	1.5	6.1	16.7	54.5	16.7	4.5	100.0

Question 5-1. Do You Think Equity Investment will Increase if the Governance Structure of Korean Firms is Improved? (Unit: percent)

	① Absolutely Yes	② Somewhat Yes	③ Somewhat No	④ Absolutely No	⑤ No Reply/ Don't Know	Total
Domestic	59.8	28.7	9.2	1.1	1.1	100.0

Question 5-2. Would You Increase Your Investment in Korean Firms if Their Governance Structure Were Improved? (Unit: percent)

	① Absolutely Yes	② Somewhat Yes	③ Somewhat No	④ Absolutely No	⑤ No Reply/ Don't Know	Total
Foreign	78.8	21.2	0	0	0	100.0

Question 6. Even Though Cumulative Voting was Introduced, Few Corporations are Implementing the System Since it is not Required by Law. Do You Think Cumulative Voting Should be Mandatory? (Unit: percent)

	① Absolutely Yes	② Somewhat Yes	③ Should be mandatory but not yet	④ No Reply/ Don't Know	Total
Domestic	55.2	2.3	33.3	9.2	100.0
Foreign	87.9	3.0	4.5	4.5	100.0

Question 7. To Achieve Transparency in Management and Improvements Governance Structure, Think Class Action Lawsuits Should be Introduced to Cheek Illegal Behavior Majority Shareholders and Management? (Unit: percent)

	① Absolutely Yes	② Somewhat Yes	③ Need to be adopted but not yet	④ No Reply/ Don't Know	Total
Domestic	77.0	5.7	17.2	0	100.0
Foreign	97.0	0	1.5	1.5	100.0

IX. Profitability

1. Ratio of Profit to Sales

The *Chaebol*s have maintained a stable ratio of gross profit to sales since 1990, and they increased the ratio after the economic crisis. In contrast, non-*Chaebol*s suffered a drastic decline in the ratio of gross profit to sales after the crisis. The ratio of gross profit to sales had been higher in non-*Chaebol*s than in *Chaebol*s from 1990 to 1996, but after the crisis, *Chaebol*s began to have a significantly higher ratio. This means that the economic crisis had a more negative effect on the relative profitability of non-*Chaebol*s.

It is indeed evident from both the ratio of operating profits to sales and from the ratio of net profits to sales that the economic crisis had a more devastating effect on profitability among non-*Chaebol*s. The ratio of operating profits to sales and the ratio of net profits to sales had not been significantly different between *Chaebol*s and non-*Chaebol*s after 1990, but since 1997, *Chaebol*s have enjoyed significantly higher ratios than non-*Chaebol*s.

For *Chaebol*s, the ratio of operating profits to sales dropped by 4.5 percent in 1998, but then recovered to the 1996 level of 6.2 percent in 1999. Nonetheless, non-*Chaebol*s recorded a ratio of -7.3 percent in 1998, a net loss on the average operating profits, and greatly worsened profitability. In 1999, non-*Chaebol*s ended up with a ratio of 2.5 percent, half the level of

1996. This illustrates how the economic crisis wreaked greater havoc on the profitability of non-*Chaebols*, as measured by the ratio of net profits to sales.

Table 28. Gross Sales Profit Ratio

	Gross Sales Profit Ratio			Sample Number	
	Chaebol	Non-*Chaebol*	t-value	*Chaebol*	Non-*Chaebol*
1990	0.16294	0.19578	-2.33**	77	172
1991	0.16754	0.21074	-3.08***	84	198
1992	0.16276	0.21187	-3.51***	86	207
1993	0.16353	0.20449	-2.83***	89	221
1994	0.16950	0.20725	-2.67***	93	255
1995	0.16721	0.19884	-2.40**	102	274
1996	0.16389	0.19577	-2.51***	112	306
1997	0.17867	0.17844	0.02	119	336
1998	0.16875	0.14566	1.28	118	322
1999	0.17753	0.18686	-0.66	111	341

Note: The sample was drawn from the same data set used in Table 9. t-value is to test whether *Chaebols* and non-*Chaebols* are significantly different. *** means 1%, ** means 5% and * means 10% significance level.

Table 29. Ratio of Operating Profits to Sales & Net Profits Ratio

	Ratio of Operating Profits to Sales			Net Profit Ratio		
	Chaebol	Non-*Chaebol*	t-value	*Chaebol*	Non-*Chaebol*	t-value
1990	0.071187	0.076351	-0.70	0.01966	0.02646	-1.09
1991	0.074341	0.083381	-1.32	0.01696	0.02408	-0.99
1992	0.064443	0.078982	-1.89*	0.00382	0.02897	-1.68
1993	0.063089	0.068988	-0.64	0.00269	0.01116	-0.83
1994	0.068036	0.069648	-0.21	0.01235	0.00750	0.64
1995	0.064541	0.063670	0.12	0.00276	0.01201	-1.33
1996	0.060367	0.059106	0.17	-0.00868	0.00084	-1.15
1997	0.069874	0.039416	3.77***	-0.02357	-0.06589	1.92*
1998	0.045175	0.073440	2.50***	-0.07355	-0.39942	2.59***
1999	0.061665	0.024687	2.41**	0.01324	-0.04807	1.83*

Note: The sample is identical to those used in Table 28. t-value is to test whether *Chaebols* and non-*Chaebols* are significantly different. *** means 1%, ** means 5% and * means 10% significance level.

2. Net Profit to Equity Ratio

The net profit to equity ratio is estimated using, alternatively, equity capital in book value and equity capital in market value.[13] The average net profit to equity ratio using equity capital in book value suddenly began to decrease in 1996, before the economic crisis took place. In 1997 and 1998, Korean companies recorded a net loss. However, when restructuring was in progress in 1999, net profits returned. The average net profit to equity ratio using equity capital in market value continued to record a net loss after 1995, and the net loss persisted even during the process of restructuring in 1999. In this regard, it is estimated that restructuring did not help Korean firms to recover profitability.

For *Chaebols*, the average net profit to equity ratio using equity capital in market value was only 2 to 3 percent in the early 1990s, but that at least meant that *Chaebols* had generated net profits. Yet *Chaebols* began to record net losses from the pre-crisis period in 1995 and suffered a tremendous loss of as much as -127.6 percent in 1998 and of -65.0 percent in 1999. Despite this mild recovery, restructuring still does not seem to have restored profitability to Korean *Chaebols*. Even though net profits were recorded in terms of the average net profit to equity ratio to book value in 1999, a net loss occurred relative to market value. It is evident that there is a wide gap between market value and book value. At the same time, it reflects the fact that firms with a comparatively larger net loss or with smaller net profits have a narrower gap between market value and book value.

For non-*Chaebols*, the average net profit to equity ratio as measured using equity capital in market value continued to record a net loss after 1996. Profitability dropped to -608 percent in 1998, indicating that the profitability of non-*Chaebols* suffered the most after the crisis. Even though the net loss recovered slightly to -75.6 percent in 1999, the ratio of net profit to

---

[13] Equity capital in market value is calculated by multiplying the number of outstanding shares at the end of the year by the aggregate market price.

Table 30. Net Profits to Equity Ratio

	Net profit to equity ratio: market value			Net profit to equity ratio: book value		
	Chaebol	Non-Chaebol	t-value	Chaebol	Non-Chaebol	t-value
1990	0.05033	0.05754	-0.36	0.19532	0.29163	-1.96**
1991	0.03108	0.04105	-0.23	0.17127	0.23962	-1.06
1992	0.02470	0.00023	0.43	0.12688	0.26432	-1.88*
1993	0.02076	0.02593	-0.24	0.13367	0.27365	-1.91*
1994	0.03160	-0.03994	2.42**	0.21830	0.20421	0.21
1995	-0.01131	0.01387	-0.96	0.16146	0.20991	-0.59
1996	-0.05111	-0.05076	-0.01	0.00221	0.08321	-0.96
1997	-0.16302	-0.32374	1.50	-0.13309	-0.16421	0.30
1998	-1.27556	-6.08543	3.26***	-0.01971	-1.08427	3.83***
1999	-0.65016	-0.75586	0.19	0.13614	0.01637	0.35

Note: The sample is identical to those used in Table 28. t-value is to test whether Chaebols and non-Chaebols are significantly different. *** means 1%, ** means 5% and * means 10% significance level.

equity remained much lower than even before the crisis. This is evidence that restructuring did not help non-*Chaebol*s to regain profitability.

3. Interest Coverage Ratio

To find out whether operating profits are enough to pay back interest expenses, the interest coverage ratio is calculated by dividing operating profits by interest expenses. To prevent a handful of outliers from distorting the average, companies with a net loss in operating profits and companies with extreme interest coverage ratio above 100 are excluded from the sample in Table 31. The average interest coverage ratio that is calculated using the full sample is shown in Table 33.

For *Chaebol*s, the average interest coverage ratio recorded 1.81 in 1990 if companies with a net loss on operating profits or an interest coverage ratio above 100 are excluded. Since 1990, the ratio continued on a downward spiral and dropped to 1.02 in 1998, when operating profits were barely enough to pay back interest expenses after the economic crisis occurred. The ratio bounced back to 1.35 in 1999. Non-*Chaebol*s also experienced a deteriorating trend after hitting 1.87 in 1990. The ratio stood at 1.58 in 1998, the same as before the crisis. In 1999, the ratio had hit 1.84, its highest level since 1990. Yet after a close examination of the distribution of the interest coverage ratio in Table 32, it is revealed that restructuring did not improve firm profitability. For *Chaebols*, operating profits fell short of interest expenses, and 26.0 percent of total affiliates recorded an interest coverage ratio that is less than 1 in 1990. Yet after that it continued to increase up to 42.9 percent right before the economic crisis in 1996. In 1998, more than 59.3 percent recorded operating profits that are smaller than interest expenses, and 11.2 percent suffered a net operating loss. It means that, in 1998, 70.3 percent of sample companies could not cover their interest expenses with their operating profits. In the middle of restructuring in 1999, although the losses were more moderate, 44.1 percent had an interest coverage ratio that is less than 1 and 7.2 percent scored a net operating loss. More than 51.35 percent of the total corporations still could not cover interest expenses with their operating profits.

Table 31. Interest Coverage Ratio: Excluding Companies with Operating Loss and with Extreme Interest Coverage above 100

Year	Interest coverage ratio: excluding companies with operating loss and over 100			Sample number	
	Chaebol	Non-*Chaebol*	t value	*Chaebol*	Non-*Chaebol*
1990	1.8086	1.8699	-0.30	74	160
1991	1.4923	1.7013	-1.44	81	182
1992	1.2469	1.4811	-1.82*	82	189
1993	1.3307	1.6154	-2.22**	84	195
1994	1.3456	1.5557	-1.35	88	233
1995	1.2160	1.5223	-2.38**	96	246
1996	1.2426	1.4641	-1.77*	106	268
1997	1.5223	1.5800	-0.34	109	266
1998	1.0271	1.5863	-3.54***	104	230
1999	1.3565	1.8425	-2.89***	99	264

Note: The sample was drawn from the same data set used in Table 9. t-value is to test whether *Chaebols* and non-*Chaebols* are significantly different. *** means 1%, ** means 5% and * means 10% significance level.

Table 32. Distribution of Interest Coverage Ratio (Unit: percent)

	Interest coverage ratio > 1 interest coverage ratio		Interest coverage ratio < 1 (Operating Profits<interest expenses)		Operating Profit< 0	
	Chaebol	Non-Chaebol	Chaebol	Non-Chaebol	Chaebol	Non-Chaebol
1990	71.43	70.35	25.97	24.42	2.60	5.23
1991	69.05	72.22	28.57	21.72	2.38	6.06
1992	58.14	63.77	37.21	28.99	4.65	7.25
1993	61.80	61.54	32.58	28.51	5.62	9.95
1994	53.76	62.75	40.86	30.98	5.38	6.27
1995	47.06	54.74	48.04	35.77	4.90	9.49
1996	51.79	51.31	42.86	38.24	5.36	10.46
1997	57.98	44.94	35.29	35.42	6.72	19.64
1998	29.66	42.24	59.32	31.06	11.02	26.71
1999	48.65	54.25	44.14	29.91	7.21	15.84

Note: The sample is identical to those used in Table 31.

Table 33. Interest Coverage Ratio After Excluding Companies with an Operating Loss

Year	Chaebol	Non-Chaebol	t-value	Sample number	
				Chaebol	Non-Chaebol
1990	1.9360	36.1546	1.00	75	163
1991	1.5988	4.6148	1.11	82	186
1992	1.2468	57.3610	1.00	82	192
1993	1.3307	1.9292	2.86***	84	199
1994	1.3455	15.0682	1.08	88	239
1995	1.3212	1.6036	1.54	97	248
1996	1.2426	1.8266	2.80***	106	274
1997	2.9953	1.8158	-0.84	111	270
1998	3.9672	1.8449	-0.72	105	236
1999	6.8358	12.4198	0.73	103	287

Note: The sample is identical to those used in Table 31 except that those companies with interest coverage above 100 are included.

Non-*Chaebol*s had scored a higher interest coverage ratio than *Chaebol*s since 1990, but the economic crisis caused non-*Chaebol*s to even further more severe falls in profitability. The number of non-*Chaebol*s that scored a net loss on operating profits has increased most dramatically since the economic crisis, reaching up to 26.7 percent in 1998 and 15.8 percent in 1999. 54.2 percent of the total non-*Chaebol*s, however, did score higher operating profits than interest expenses in 1999, and that is a larger percentage than that of the *Chaebol*s.

An analysis of the interest coverage ratio makes it clear that the economic crisis resulted in a fall in corporate profitability. Even in 1999, when restructuring was in progress, profitability did not recover to pre-crisis levels despite a sharp reduction in debt to equity ratios and market interest rates.

X. Summary of Restructuring Results and Conclusion

To assess the effectiveness of corporate restructuring reforms during the three years following the economic crisis, this paper selected and analyzed management indices in the following six areas: business structure, ownership structure, cost structure, finance structure, investment asset structure, and governance structure. A summary of the results are as follows:

Business Structure
After the crisis, restructuring helped to decrease the average number of subsidiaries and business categories on a small scale. The progress shown in the official data, however, was mainly due to the exit of several insolvent *Chaebol*s from the top 30. Furthermore, the aggregate size of the top 30 *Chaebol*s soared relative to pre-crisis levels. Although Daewoo's bankruptcy and Hyundai's spin-off affiliates reduced the average number of affiliates, the top 5 *Chaebol*s rapidly built up their average asset size and growth rates in asset accumulation for the top 5 far surpassed growth rates for the top 6-30 *Chaebol*s. Thus, restructuring resulted in strengthening the

market power exercised by the top 5 *Chaebols*. It is assumed that corporate restructuring failed to reform the *Chaebols* portfolio of businesses towards a focus on core businesses.

Ownership Structure

During the restructuring process, the ratio of internally held shares rapidly increased. The quality of the ownership structure in *Chaebols* worsened due to circular equity investment among subsidiaries. Furthermore, despite the increase in the ratio of internally held shares, shares owned directly by major shareholders decreased. Major shareholders used circular equity investment to strengthen their management rights in subsidiaries at the expense of minority shareholders. Deregulation designed to accelerate the restructuring process actually served to worsen the governance structure inside most Korean firms. Even though mutual equity investment was banned in 1998, *Chaebols* were able to circumvent the government ban through an increase in circular equity investment.

Cost Structure

In the employment area, the restructuring plan was relatively successful. *Chaebols* laid off employees during the restructuring process, but in contrast, non-*Chaebols* increased employment. Average labor expense per capita increased during the process of restructuring. Growth rates of labor expense per capita in *Chaebols* slightly surpassed the growth rate in the consumer price indices. Growth rates for labor expense per capita in non-*Chaebols* lagged behind the growth rate in the consumer price indices. As a result, there was a decrease in real income. Despite the increase in labor expense per capita, the actual proportion of labor expense in total cost structure decreased during the restructuring process. The proportion of labor expense in manufacturing expenses, administrative expenses and sales expenses all decreased.

In spite of restructuring, the burden of interest expenses did not materially decrease. The proportion of interest expenses in total expense went down after restructuring. *Chaebol*s, however, did not reduce the proportion of interest expenses in fixed liabilities to the pre-crisis level. Considering the improved financial market conditions and the existence of single-digit interest rates, the absence of a decrease in interest expenses indicates the new equity capital was not used to bring down financial costs.

Financial Structure

Restructuring significantly reduced the average debt to equity ratio. Though the reduction was common in all types of firms, *Chaebol*s enjoyed a larger reduction in their average debt to equity ratio. Nonetheless, the overall debt level for *Chaebol*s has not decreased significantly because the reduction in debt to equity ratios was achieved through increases in equity capital. Restructuring, therefore, failed to achieve its original purpose of decreasing the debt burden faced by Korean firms. In the process of restructuring, there was a tremendous change in debt structure. *Chaebol*s increased their reliance on corporate bonds while decreasing their reliance on bank debt. For non-*Chaebol*s, the proportion of corporate bonds plummeted and the proportion of bank debt in long-term liabilities surged.

Investment Asset Structure

The proportion of investment assets of marketable securities and equity investments in total assets radically increased after the economic crisis. Investment in securities of affiliates rapidly increased, with this trend being most notable for *Chaebol*s. Through circular investment, controlling shareholders were able to strengthen their own management rights at the expense of minority shareholders. Following restructuring, there was a marked deterioration in the quality of ownership structure and governance structure.

Governance Structure

It is evident that there has not been an effective change in governance structure despite the introduction of laws designed to transform governance structure. During restructuring, *Chaebol*s increased internally held shares through circular equity investments among affiliates, thus intensifying the moral hazard of reinforcing their management right at the expense of minority shareholders. Even though the outside director system was introduced, majority shareholders and managers were able to handpick most outside directors. Though a cumulative voting system was also introduced, the system soon became ineffective as 80 percent of all corporations and 93 percent of the top 30 *Chaebol*s excluded it from their articles of incorporations. More than 50 percent of *Chaebol*s spent more on donations than dividends, showing that there has not been a real improvement in the corporate governance system that focuses on shareholder value.

Profitability

The economic crisis hurt profitability among all Korean firms, but especially among non-*Chaebol*. The average net profit to equity ratio based on book value recorded a net loss but had recovered to some extent in 1999. Yet the average net profit to equity market value ratio recorded a net loss even when restructuring was in progress, despite the reduction in the average debt to equity ratio and a rapid fall in the market interest rate. Consequently, profitability did not improve relative to the pre-crisis period. As of 1999, when restructuring was in progress, 51 percent of *Chaebol*s and 46 percent of non-*Chaebol*s could not afford to pay their interest expenses using operating profits.

According to the analysis of management indices through 1999, the performance of corporate restructuring is evaluated as poor. Significant accomplishments were realized through reductions in debt to equity ratio and reductions in the *Chaebol* labor force and the decreased proportion of labor cost in total costs. By most criteria, however, management performance was evaluated to be no better or even worse than before the crisis.

Significant accomplishments in indices such as the debt to equity ratio, did not translate into a real reduction in debts or financial costs. Business structure reform failed to realign business portfolios towards a focus on core businesses. Asset size radically increased, and the controlling market power of the top 5 *Chaebol*s was reinforced. Corporate governance structure did not improve greatly despite institutional changes, and ownership structure deteriorated during restructuring. Controlling shareholders created paper money through circular equity investments among subsidiaries and buttressed their management rights at the expense of minority shareholders. Compared to the pre-crisis period, profitability recovered only to a limited degree. About half of the total companies still cannot pay their interest expenses using operating profits.

In conclusion, the corporate restructuring policy that was aimed at restructuring *Chaebol*s was not successful based on an examination of management performance through the end of 1999. It is unlikely that the performance of corporate restructuring would pick up in the 2000 data since the implementation of the *Chaebol* reform program lost its momentum after 1999, and because restructuring slowed down as the financial markets became tighter and the business community braced for a renewed economic downturn.

The objective of corporate restructuring was to overcome an economic crisis in the short term. In the long term, it aimed at preventing a recurrence of the economic crisis and to transform the current market state into an advanced market economy system. The government policy that has been implemented since the economic crisis did not gain many real achievements, and the government policy failed to fulfill the original objective of corporate restructuring. Consequently, the fact that there is the possibility of another crisis, despite the fact that there has not been any external shock, reflects the fact that corporate restructuring has failed to achieve positive results.

Corporate restructuring is a national agenda that should be pursued consistently over a long period of time, and therefore it would be premature to label the reform policy as a complete failure based upon the outcome of the last three years. Future reform policy, nevertheless, will never be able to succeed if there is no reflection on why the past three years policies have had such a dismal outcome. During the past three years, Korea has experienced extreme hardships, such as a series of *Chaebols* going bankrupt, an increase in unemployment, and a severe economic contraction.

For reform policy to be successful, there are three elements that must be more effectively linked: the reform program, the main body of reform, and national consensus. Reform programs to decide what to reform, why to reform, and how to reform have been formulated after numerous discussions. Furthermore, there has been a national consensus about reform since right after the economic crisis. People actively participated in the National Movement to Collect Gold, and workers supported reform by restraining themselves from striking on a large scale even though they suffered severe layoffs. Thus, there cannot be any other reason but the main body of reform to rend the last three years of reform efforts unsuccessful. The primary cause of unsuccessful *Chaebol* reform is the lack of political leadership to muster a national consensus, to overcome the reaction of vested interests, and to use the government bodies' capabilities to implement the reform policy.

In summary, the future success of *Chaebol* reform hinges on political leadership and the will of government regulatory bodies to actively implement the reform policy. It is doubtful, however, to expect that economic departments in the government will play a new and active role that they could not assume even in the economic crisis. It is also doubtful to expect the current political leadership to form a national consensus, especially when the momentum for reform dissipated after the early part of the crisis. In the final analysis, a shift in the thinking of government policymakers and an injection of political leadership must take place before *Chaebol* reform and corporate restructuring will be successful.

References

Bae, Kee-Hong, Jun-Koo Kang and Jin-Mo Kim. (2000). Does group affiliation destroy shareholder wealth in emerging markets?: Evidence from mergers by Korean business group. Working Paper. Seoul: Korea University.

Furman, Jason and Joseph E. Stiglitz. (1998). Economic crises: Evidence and insights from east asia. Brookings Papers on Economic Activity, 2.

Jang, Hasung. (1999). Corporate governance and economic development: Korean experience. Working Paper. World Bank.

Jang, Ha Won. (1999). The undercurrent of the crisis in Korea. International Centre for the Study of East Asian Development, Kitakyushu.

Kim, E. Han. (1998). Globalization of capital markets and the Asian financial crisis. *Journal of Applied Corporate Finance*, Vol 11, No 3, Fall, pp.30-39.

Lee, Inmoo and Byungmo Kim. (2000). Do agency problems explain the post Asian financial crisis performance of Korean companies?: *Chaebol* vs. non-*Chaebol*s. Working Paper. Seoul: Korea University.

Lee, Keun, Keunkwan Ryu and Jung Mo Lee. (2000). Productive efficiency of *Chaebol*s and non-*Chaebol*s in Korea: Stochastic production frontier estimation using panel data. Discussion Paper, No. 36. Seoul: Institute of Economic Research, Seoul National University.

Radelet, S and J. Sachs. (1998). The east Asian financial crisis: diagnosis, remedies, prospects. Brookings Papers on Economic Activity.

Yoo, Jong-Il. (1999). Economic crisis, democracy and inequality: South Korean experience. Working Paper. Seoul: School of Public Policy and Global Management, Korea Development Institute.

Corporate Governance System in Korea: What Questions Should We Ask for Future Recommendations?[1]

Y. Peter Chung [2]

I. Introduction

Discussion on Korean *Chaebol*'s controversial governance emerged among media, regulators, and academics long before the IMF liquidity crisis began in November 1997. A typical Korean conglomerate (*Chaebol*), such as Hyundai or Samsung, is a network of several dozen affiliates interlocked through cross-funding. By holding large share portions in a few key companies, founding families influence the entire business group. In this regard, Korean *Chaebol*s are closer to Japan's keirestu than to the U.S. conglomerates like GM or GE. Most of discussion has been centered on *Chaebol*s' reckless borrowing and social anger at them.

The discussion and social anger accentuated when the sibling rivalry in Hyundai group, a major Korean *Chaebol* established in May 1947 by its

---

[1] I am grateful to Charles Hadlock, Tae-Hyun Ju, Jun-Koo Kang, and the participants at the 2000 Conference, Transforming Korean Management: Strategic Directions in the New Millennium, held at the Michigan State University for helpful discussions, comments, and other assistance.

[2] Associate Professor, University of California, Riverside, USA.

founder, Chung Joo Young, erupted in March 2000 when two sons claimed to be chosen as successor. Chung Mong Gu, the third son of the founder, was the chairman of Hyundai Motor Company and some other affiliated firms. He has been also the chairman of the entire group since 1998. Chung Mong Heon, the fifth son, was the chairman of Hyundai Electronics Inc. and has been the co-chairman of the group. As government regulators sought to break up Chung's empire, two ambitious sons squabble over their aging father's empire.[3] Until the 8.8 trillion Korean Won (KRW) mighty Hyundai was known to have a liquidity problem of mere 50 billion KRW in early spring 2000, however, the regulators did not have any effective tool. As Korean bond market is not deep enough and issuing additional equity would take time in then-depressed Korean stock market, if not impossible, borrowing more from its banks was the only viable option to Hyundai. The government and Hyundai's creditor banks subsequently demanded senior Chung to relinquish his control over the group in return for liquidity provision for the Hyundai's liquidity-squeezed firms. Hyundai had no other choice but promised to change its governance, and senior Chung announced that the two brothers and himself would resign from all board memberships for Hyundai affiliated firms. This episode is a significant event in the sense that other *Chaebol*s would eventually follow Hyundai's steps and change their governance structure.

Even during such a period of dramatic developments, a few important questions have not been raised. In this paper, I raise those research questions that need to be answered in the *Chaebol* debate. First, the paper raises the fundamental question: What has made *Chaebol*'s ownership structure survive for such a long period of time? Second but more importantly, is *Chaebol*'s ownership structure truly inconsistent with the goal of the modern firm, shareholder wealth maximization? In other words, do we have enough empirical evidence that can be used to argue

---

[3] Senior Chung died in March 2001.

against concentrated ownership structure for *Chaebol* firms? Researchers have hypothesized that corporate ownership structure has important influence on the firm value. Regulators as well as academics would find it interesting to examine if there is strong empirical evidence that is consistent with the hypothesis that the ownership structure of equity has an important influence on corporate value in Korea.

The paper is organized as follows. Section 2 reviews controversies around *Chaebol* corporate governance in Korea. Section III reviews the literature and applies concepts and hypotheses to *Chaebol* corporate governance. Section IV evaluates the major recommendations proposed by Korean media and government. Finally Section V summarizes the paper and encourages future research.

II. Controversies around *Chaebol* Corporate Governance

As Korean *Chaebol*s heavily rely on bank borrowing for their source of capital, one can naturally wonder why Korean government has not seriously influenced *Chaebol*s for the last four decades when it had power to do so through government-run or controlled banks. Is it because *Chaebol* governance has had its own merits? Also, it is said that *Chaebol* families own only an average 3% of their conglomerates but still run them like their own fiefdoms. Is it really possible to control the whole group with just 3% equity ownership? If yes, how can it be possible?

Cross-funding can reinforce the owner/manger's control and entrenchment like funding (or debt consignment) into unprofitable affiliated firms and therefore eventually weaken the financial health of the entire business group. It can create a moral hazard. Potential explanations for why the government has allowed such cross-funding for a long time are numerous, including friendly relationships between the political regimes and *Chaebol*s, entrepreneurial spirit admired, unique corporate culture favoring founders, efficiency achieved through cooperation and economies of scale, and diversification among affiliated firms. In sum, it was perhaps the best alternative for growth in the past when the modern capital market was not established and therefore internal cross-funding could supplement the incomplete external financing.

Government attitude toward *Chaebol*s, however, has dramatically changed as Korea went through its humiliating IMF liquidity crisis. First, several conglomerates, including one of the big four, Daewoo Group, have collapsed. As a result *Chaebol*s' reckless expansion has become the target of public anger related to the crisis. Second, the political regime has shifted from business-friendly regime to less friendly civilian-regime. Finally, the Korean equity market has become more efficient as ownership held by institutional investors and foreigners has grown and public's access to information has become easier, and therefore the government can no longer ignore the market's negative view of the *Chaebol*'s governance structure.

It is true that the controlling owners of *Chaebol* firms have only 3% (or less) equity of the affiliated firms. For example, Hyundai's Mr. Chung owns 0.9% of all affiliated firms, S.K's Mr. Choi owns 3.1%, Samsung's Mr. Lee owns 0.6%, and LG's Mr. Koo owns 0.4%.[4] But, their influence can go way beyond 3% because of cross-holding. Figure 1 illustrates examples of controlling stake by the two rival Chung brothers and makes us understand how family members can influence other affiliated firms of the group by holding large share portions in a few key companies. Table 1 shows the ownership concentration of Korean *Chaebol* firms in 1995. Again, even if the owner himself has less than 3% shareholdings on average, the holdings combined for the owner, family, and relatives are 10.6% on average. Furthermore, average holdings by affiliated firms are 32.8%. Thus, the controlling stake held by the founder is 43.3%, if not 50%. Mostly uninterested individuals and other friendly firms that might have business

---

[4] Source: Yonhap News, July 19, 2000.

Figure 1. Cross Holdings of Hyundai Affiliated Firms Controlled by the Two Rival Chung Brothers
(Source: 1999 Annual Reports and Various Newspapers)

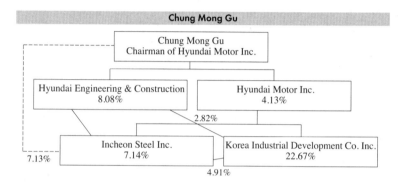

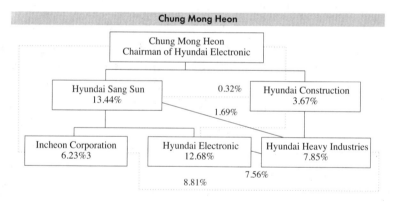

relationships hold the rest of ownership. In comparison, the average holding of a big U.S. firm in 1996 by institutional investors like pension funds is 45.6% (pension funds accounts for 22.4%) while foreign investors hold 6.1% and individual investors hold 47.7%. In the case of Japan, financial institutions hold 42.8%, other corporations hold 23.6%, individual investors hold 23.4%, and foreign investors 9.4% in 1995.[5] So, unlike in Japan and the U.S., lack of monitoring shareholders, such as blockholders,

---

[5] Source: Korean Economic Research Institute (1999).

Table 1. Percentage of Shares Controlled by Group Owner/Manager of Korean Chaebols (Source: Cho (1997))*

	Owner, family, and relatives	Affiliated firms	Total
Hyundai	15.7%	44.6%	60.4%
Samsung	2.8	46.5	49.3
Daewoo	6.7	34.7	41.4
LG	5.7	33.9	39.7
SK	17.4	33.8	51.2
Kia	17.4	4.4	21.9
All 30 *Chaebols*	10.6	32.8	43.3

* As of April 1, 1995.

financial institutions, and institutional investors, is the key characteristic of Korean *Chaebol*'s governance structure.

Corporate governance is an important issue, but the question whether *Chaebol*'s unique governance structure should be thrown away is subject to empirical evidence. Should the *Chaebol* firms be run by non-owner/managers? A good counter example is Kia Motor Group that collapsed in 1997, right before the IMF crisis began. Its former CEO and chairman of the board, Mr. S. Kim, was a non-owner/manager, and so Kia firms were not *Chaebol* firms. Mr. Kim, however, did cross-funding, excessive borrowing for expansion and other governance-related management actions similar to what *Chaebol* owner/managers had been doing. So, change in corporate governance to non-owner management may not be the answer unless there is effective monitoring system accompanies. As *Chaebols*' governance may have its own merits, we need more careful investigation into the issue whether the change in *Chaebol* governance is indeed consistent with shareholder wealth maximization. It appears that this issue has been generally neglected in the midst of debate about controversial governance of Korean *Chaebols*.

III. Theories and Empirical Evidence for the U.S. and Japan and their Implications for Corporate Governance of Korean *Chaebols*

Morck, Shleifer, and Vishny (1988) examine a 1980 cross section of 371 Fortune 500 firms to investigate the cross-sectional relationship between ownership and market value of the firm. They find evidence of a significant nonmonotonic relationship. The market value of the firm, proxied by Tobin's Q, first increases, then declines, and finally rises slightly as ownership by the board of directors rises.[6] Interestingly, however, for older firms, there is evidence that Tobin's Q is lower when the firm is run by a member of the founding family than when it is run by an officer unrelated to the founder.

Morck, Shleifer, and Vishny (1988) focus on two competing hypotheses. The first one is the convergence-of-interest hypothesis. If firms are run by managers who hold little equity in the firm and shareholders are too dispersed to enforce value maximization, corporate assets may be deployed to benefit managers rather than shareholders. Those managerial benefits include shirking and perquisite-taking, but also encompass pursuit of such non-value-maximizing objectives as sales growth and empire building. According to Jensen and Meckling (1976), as their stake becomes larger, these managers pay a larger share of such costs of deviation from value-maximization and therefore are less likely to squander corporate wealth. In contrast, the entrenchment hypothesis argues that a manager who controls a substantial fraction of the firm's equity may have enough voting power or influence more generally to guarantee his employment with the firm at an attractive salary and reputation. A related issue is the market for corporate control. Even in the U.S., it is very rare that firms

---

[6] Tobin's Q is generally defined as market value of the firm's assets divided by replacement value of the assets. A Tobin's Q ratio greater than 1 indicates the firm has done well with its investment decision.

whose insiders own more than 30% are acquired in a hostile takeover. In Korea, the government has banned the hostile takeover of most *Chaebol* firms in the name of economic stability. As a result, market discipline (the managerial labor market and the market for corporate control) may not force the owner/manager toward value maximization. With effective control but without external threat of takeover, the owner/manager may indulge his preference for non-value-maximizing behavior, although perhaps to a more limited extent than in the case where manager had effective control but no equity holding. Thus, the entrenchment hypothesis predicts that corporate assets can be less valuable when managed by an individual free from checks on his control.

The empirical endeavor in Morck, Shleifer, and Vishny (1988), though it is for the U.S. sample, leads us to several research questions for Korean *Chaebol*s. Whereas the convergence-of-interest hypothesis predicts that larger managerial stakes should be associated with higher market valuation of the firm, the predictions of the entrenchment hypothesis are much less obvious, particularly for Korean *Chaebol* firms. The reason is that some managers, by virtue of their tenure with the firm (for example, Kia's Mr. Kim) or status as a founder can be entrenched with relatively small stakes as we can see from Korean *Chaebol*s. Thus, theoretical arguments alone cannot unambiguously predict the relationship between ownership structure of *Chaebol* firms and market valuation of the their assets: Whether the owner/manager is good or bad for *Chaebol* firms is an empirical issue. Therefore one can study the relationship between owner/manager ownership and a proxy for market valuation of the *Chaebol* firm's assets, such as Tobin's Q.

There are several considerations in such attempts. First, one can look at the shareholdings of owner/manager and all owner/manager-controlled holdings. Other conditions necessary for entrenchment (for example, who elects the outside board members?) should be also incorporated. As for the performance of the owner/manager- managed firm, one can examine the firm's profitability instead of its Tobin's Q. Also, one can evaluate the impact on Tobin's Q of having a member of the founding family as one of the top officers because it would be interesting to see if a management team can become entrenched for reasons other than its control of voting rights. Results in Morck, Shleifer, and Vishny (1988) suggest that the presence of the founding family adversely affects Tobin's Q in older firms, where entrepreneurial talent of the founder might be less valuable. Whether the similar results are obtained from Korean *Chaebol* samples is an interesting question. Note that Korean *Chaebol*-affiliated firms are, in Korean standard, older firms. As results in Morck, Shleifer, and Vishny (1988) suggest, founders in younger firms might have an important leadership role to play. So, the age of the firms can be another control variables.

IV. Review of Some Recommended Measures

Much has been discussed among regulators, media, and academics on Korean *Chaebols*' governance, but little has changed. I would like to examine major recommendations that Korean government has suggested in light of previous theoretical and empirical research done for the U.S. and Japanese firms. By doing so, I can toss up the question whether those measures will effectively work. The ultimate question is, of course, "Do we need to force the owner/manager reduce his shareholdings? Do we need to curb down cross-funding? That is, do we need to dissolve the *Chaebol* conglomerates?"

1. Institutional Investors

The relation between corporate value and institutional ownership has been explored for the U.S. firms during the last ten years. Results in McConnell and Servaes (1990) are perhaps most typical for the U.S. firms: Corporate values are an increasing function of the institutional equity ownership.

Their results are therefore consistent with the hypothesis that corporate value is a function of the structure of equity ownership, but inconsistent with the classical view that the stockholders of an individual firm could be characterized as a widely dispersed and homogeneous group of relatively uninvolved absentee owners. Such relationship is yet relatively unexplored terrain for Korean firms, in particular for *Chaebol*-affiliated firms. One can advance three hypotheses. The efficient-monitoring hypothesis argues that institutional investors have greater expertise and therefore can monitor management at lower cost than can small atomistic shareholders. Thus, this hypothesis predicts a positive relation between institutional ownership and corporate value. According to the conflict-of-interest hypothesis, however, because of other profitable business relationships with the firm, institutional investors are coerced into voting their shares with management. The strategic-alignment hypothesis suggests that institutional investors and managers find it mutually advantageous to cooperate. This cooperation reduces the beneficial effects on firm value that could result from monitoring by institutional investors. Thus, the conflict-of-interest and the strategic-alignment hypotheses both predict a negative relation between institutional ownership and the value of the firm.

In the case of the U.S. firms, McConnell and Servaes (1990) find a strong positive relation between Tobin's Q and the fraction of shares held by institutional investors, a result which is consistent with the efficient-monitoring hypothesis. It might be interesting to see if we would find the similar results because such results would suggest that increasing institutional ownership for *Chaebol* firms is a good recommendation. Note that, as of April 1999, institutional equity ownership in Korea is 13.6%, compared to 47.7% (the biggest institution is pension funds) in the U.S. and 42.8% (mostly financial institutions) in Japan. [7]

---

[7] Source: Korea Stock Exchange.

2. Large Blockholders

Large blockholders can exert works as an effective device for monitoring owner/manager as well as the market for corporate control. Holderness and Sheehan (1985), for example, report positive excess returns around the announcement date when outsiders acquire large equity positions. Blockholders, however, can decrease the corporate value. Barclay, Holderness, and Pontiff (1993) find that the average discount for the U.S. close-end funds that have blockholders is 14.2% whereas the average discount for funds that do not have blockholders is only 4.1%. Relatives and close associates of blockholders are often employed by the firm. There can be other nonpecuniary benefits accrued to blockholders. For example, the firm may be associated with the blockholder's name, promoting its name and furthering its family pride and prestige. Thus, the evidence in Barclay, Holderness, and Pontiff (1993) imply that different blockholders have different effects on the value of the firms. Some blockholders accumulate their shares as a part of an attempt to monitor the firm. If they succeed, they can increase the firm value. Management-affiliated blockholders, in contrast, can consume private benefits and resist value maximization. These blockholders tend to decrease firm value. One of the recommendations proposed by Korean regulators is the increase in block ownership for *Chaebol*-affiliated firms. But, what really is needed may not be the outside blockholders who might be owner/manager-friendly, but truly outside, monitoring blockholders who might be interested in taking the firm to the 'market for corporate control.'

3. Financial Institutions

Prowse (1992) examines the corporate ownership structure for a sample of 734 Japanese firms in the mid 1980s and finds that ownership is highly concentrated in Japan, with financial institutions by far the most important large shareholders.

Interestingly enough, Prowse (1992) find that ownership concentration in independent Japanese firms is positively related to the returns from exerting greater control over management. This is, however, not the case in keiretsu firms.[8] Nonetheless Prowse's results suggest that the large shareholders, particularly financial institutions, of keiretsu firms do monitor and influence management using perhaps alternative channels.

4. Outside Board Members

It has been recommended that outside board membership for *Chaebol* firms should increase from the current 25% to 50% in 2001, which will be much higher than that (about 25%) in Japan. Inside board members can be puppets of the owner/manager. In some cases, the same thing can be true to outside board members. What really is needed is monitoring outside board members who are willing to take the firm to the corporate control market. Management-friendly outside board members can consume private benefits and therefore can be coerced into voting with owner/managers. For this reason, in conducting cross-sectional studies for *Chaebol* firms, one should control such variable as who elects outside board members.' Table 2 reports board composition for two Hyundai affiliated

Table 2. Board Composition of two Hyundai Affiliated Firms

	HD Heavy Industries	HD Sangsun
Founder and Family	1	
Officers		
W/ Shares	44	4
W/O Shares	36	
External Members		
W/Shares		
W/O Shares	5	3

[8] Keiretsu represents groups of enterprises composed of firms based in different industries, but bound by ties of fractional ownership, and reliant on a large commercial bank as the major lender. Note that large shareholders of keiretsu firms also typically have strong commercial and trading relationships with them.

firms, Hyundai Sangsun and Hyundai Heavy Industries. Insiders dominate the board of Hyundai Heavy Industries, accounting for 81 out of the total 86 seats. In the case of the younger Hyundai Sangsun, the board is more balanced with four insiders and three external members.

5. Market for Corporate Control

Stulz (1988) focuses on the importance of the takeover market for disciplining corporate managers. Korean government hasn't allowed for the 'market for corporate control,' protecting *Chaebol* firms from hostile takeover and therefor eliminating a presumably effective disciplinary tool for *Chaebol* owner/managers. As the government has been recently deregulating the corporate control market, one can implement some event studies for the change in *Chaebol* firm values around the change in the regulations.

In sum, there needs to be an investigation that the value of the firm is a function of the distribution of equity ownership among corporate insiders (i.e., owner/manager, family, officers and directors), individual shareholder, block shareholders, and institutional investors. The first attempt would be to regress Tobin's Q ratio against various measures of ownership (and other control variables) to gauge their impact on the value of the firm. Again, only accumulated empirical evidence can be used for an argument against concentrated ownership structure for *Chaebol* firms. Table 3 provides ownership of insiders, institutional investors, blockholders, and other types of shareholders for five major Hyundai firms, HD Motor, HD Construction, HD Heavy Industries, HD Electronics, and HD Sangsun. It indicates that the affiliated firms are the largest shareholders of major Hyundai firms. Unlike in Japan, government-run or influenced banks do not have much shareholdings and therefore do not own board membership.

Table 3. Distribution of Share Ownership for Five Major Hyundai Firms as of December 31, 1999 (Source: Annual reports and the Korea Stock Exchange)*

	HD Motor	HD Electronics	HD Construction	HD Heavy Industries	HD Sangsun
Founder and family	4.11%	1.70%	8.16%	19.62%	16.67%
Officers			0.12	0.03	
Affiliated Firms	16.86	32.17	3.49	8.34	15.80
Employees			3.48	5.99	
Government	0.14	0.14	0.51	0.10	0.83
Other Corporations	3.10	3.12	5.37	9.13	16.48
Financial Institutions	0.23	0.04	0.17	0.25	0.18
Institutional Investors	24.85	8.07	1.18	4.75	8.80
Individual Investors	35.30	44.26	64.64	49.74	35.35
Foreigners	15.40	10.31	12.81	2.05	5.85
Shareholders that own at least 5%	HD Jung Gong (7.33%) HDHeavy Ind(6.77%)	HD Sangsun (12.68%) HD Heavy Ind (7.56%) HD Elec. Ind (10.44%)		Chung Joo Yong (11.56%) Chung MongJoon (8.06%) Employees (5.99%) HD Construction (7.85%)	Chung Mong Heon (13.44%) HD Construction (12.60%)

* Employees mean employee stock ownership plans. Individual investors exclude those individual insiders (founder, family, and officers). Institutional investors include security firms, insurance companies, mutual funds, and other investment firms. Financial institutions include banks and other lending institutions.

V. Conclusion

It has been suggested that the *Chaebol* conglomerate system in Korea is outdated and needs to be structurally changed. Existing research on corporate governance of Korean *Chaebols* does not extend much beyond the aggregate statistics on the shareownership of their owner/managers and their affiliated firms published by Korean Stock Exchange and some research institutions. Such limitation should be obviously related to the lack of readily-obtainable ownership data because of massive cross-holding for *Chaebol* firms.

Following Jensen and Meckling (1976), interest in the relationship between corporate value and the ownership structure has continued to evolve on both the theoretical and the empirical front. Stulz (1988) develops a model in which the corporate value first increases, then decreases, as equity ownership is concentrated in the hands of insiders. Morck, Shleifer, and Vishny (1988) also advance an argument that suggests the nonlinear relation between corporate value and inside equity ownership. For cross-sections of U.S. firms, Demsetz and Lehn (1985), Morck, Shleifer, and Vishny (1988), Holderness and Sheehan (1988), and McConnell and Servaes (1990) present evidence on the relation between corporate performance and its ownership structure. Though the ownership data for Korean *Chaebol* firms might not be as easy to obtain as in the U.S., these theoretical and empirical researches for the U.S. firms have much implication for cross-sectional studies, times-series regressions, and even studies.

I argue that one should carefully investigate the relationship between the corporate value and the governance for *Chaebol* firms (and non-*Chaebol* firms) to see if its governance indeed needs to be dramatically changed. I also review some of the measures that have been recommended to improve corporate governance of *Chaebol*-affiliated firms in light of the existing theoretical and empirical research for the U.S. and the Japanese firms.

There are some other measures that I do not attempt to examine in this paper. Those include charging the controlling board members for more responsibility and guaranteeing small shareholders' rights. Whether these measures would work effectively is also subject to theoretical support and empirical evidence.

References

Barclay, M., C. Holderness, and J. Pontiff. (1993). Private benefits from block ownership and discounts on closed-end funds. *Journal of Financial Economics*, pp. 263-291.

Cho, D. (1997). *Korean Chaebol*. Seoul: Daily Economic Newspaper, Inc.

Demsetz, H. and K. Lehn. (1985). The structure of corporate ownership: Causes and consequences. *Journal of Political Economy*, 93, pp. 1155-1177.

Holderness, C. and D. Sheehan. (1985). Raiders or saviors? The evidence on six controversial investors, *Journal of Financial Economics*, 14, pp. 555-579.

Jensen, M. and W. Meckling. (1976). Theory of the firm: Managerial behavior, agency costs and ownership structure. *Journal of Financial Economics*, 3, pp. 305-360.

Korean Economic Research Institute. (1999). *In search of new paradigm for Korean corporate governance structure*. Policy report, 99-03.

McConnell, J. and H. Servaes. (1990). Additional evidence on equity ownership and corporate value. *Journal of Financial Economics*, 27, pp. 595-612.

Morck, R., A. Shleifer, and R. Vishny. (1988). Management ownership and market valuation: An empirical analysis. *Journal of Financial Economics*, 20, pp. 293-315.

Prowse, S. (1992). The structure of corporate ownership in Japan. *Journal of Finance*, 47, pp. 1121-1140.

Shleifer, A. and R. Vishny. (1998). *Grabbing hand; Government pathologies and their cures*. Cambridge, Massachusetts: Harvard University Press.

Stulz, M. (1988). Managerial control of voting rights, financing policies and the market for corporate control. *Journal of Financial Economics*, 20, pp. 25-54.

Weston, J. (1979). The tender takeover. *Mergers and Acquisitions*, pp. 74-82.

Do Agency Problems Explain the Post Asian Financial Crisis Performance of Korean Companies?[1]

Byung-Mo Kim[2] and Inmoo Lee[3]

I. Introduction

The lack of an effective corporate governance system in most Korean companies has been cited as one of the major problems that Korea should overcome for further economic development. Korean companies are likely to be more subject to various agency problems due to the inefficient corporate governance system. For example, Johnson, Boone, Breach and Friedman (2000) show that Korea has low scores in their measures of corporate governance among emerging market countries.

This paper examines whether agency problems explain the post-Asian financial crisis performance of Korean companies. Agency problems may become more important factors around a crisis since the crisis would cause more companies to fall into a situation of financial distress. The financial

---

[1] We would like to thank Charles Hadlock, Joonho Hwang, Tim Loughran, Jay Ritter, and Ben Sopranzetti for their useful comments.

[2] Korea Advanced Institute of Science and Technology

[3] Assistant professor, Korea University, Seoul, Korea.

crisis which Korea has recently experienced provides an interesting experimental setting to test the role of agency problems in explaining the cross-sectional differences in performance in an economy-wide financially distressed situation.

In a recent paper, Johnson, Boone, Breach and Friedman (2000) show that countries with weak corporate governance experienced a larger fall in asset prices during the Asian crisis. Moreover, Hahm and Mishkin (2000) present some evidence that the financial crisis in Korea can be partly explained by moral hazard and adverse selection problems caused by asymmetric information. At the individual company level, Mitton (2000) shows that companies with higher outside ownership concentration had significantly better stock price performance during the Asian financial crisis. Mitton uses a sample of 399 firms from Indonesia, Korea, Malaysia, the Philippines and Thailand. All firms in his sample are among the largest and most liquid firms in their respective markets, and are included in the International Finance Corporation (IFC) global index.

To further study the role of agency problems during the Korean financial crisis, this paper examines whether agency problems explain the stock price performance during the financial crisis period using a more comprehensive data set and various agency cost proxy variables.

We analyze the performance of 590 non-financial companies that were listed in the Korean Stock Exchange as of May 1, 1997. We use seven variables that would proxy for different degrees of potential agency problems: Three ownership structure variables (largest shareholder ownership, manager ownership, and blockholder ownership), one free cash flow measure (free cash flow over total assets), two leverage variables (short-term debt over total assets and long-term debt over total assets) and a variable showing the degree of diversification (number of business segments). All these proxy variables are measured based on the financial statement information at the 1996 fiscal year end. Stock returns are measured starting from May 1, 1997, shortly before the onset of the Asian financial crisis.

The results show that ownership structure does not significantly explain the post Asian financial crisis stock return performance of Korean companies. On the other hand, leverage, especially short-term debt, significantly explains the stock price performance. There is a significantly negative relation between the short-term debt ratio and the stock price performance. Moreover, the firms with more free cash flow show significantly better stock performance than the firms with less free cash flow. This indicates that the stock market has paid more attention to the positive role of free cash flow (i.e., providing the ability to overcome a short-term credit problem) than the negative role (i.e., potential agency problems between shareholders and managers). The high leverage ratios of most Korean companies and the relatively small amounts of free cash flow may explain why the stock market behaved in such a way.

For our sample firms, the average short-term debt over total assets is 42% and the average long-term debt over total assets is 25%. The average free cash flow over total assets is -0.4% (the median is -0.4% and the 70th percentile is 1.1%). This contrasts with the median free cash flow over total assets of around 5% for the industries in Lie (2000). The sample in Lie (2000) includes 8,194 announcements of special dividends, regular dividend increase, or self-tender offers by the U. S. firms.

The significant role of leverage in explaining the performance of Korean companies after the crisis might be consistent with the agency-based theory that a highly leveraged firm in financial distress makes inefficient investment decisions and this leads to a value decrease. An alternative explanation is that the Korean stock market pays a lot of attention to the firm's ability to repay loans, especially short-term loans, when most financial institutions are not willing to renew short-term credit due to their own liquidity problems during the economy-wide financial distress. This might lead to very poor performance of the firms with very high leverage, especially those with high short-term leverage.

Overall, it turns out that agency problems do not play such an important role in explaining the post-crisis stock price performance of Korean companies: at least up to the end of 1999.

The paper proceeds as follows: Section II reviews related studies, and Section III describes the data, provides some summary statistics, and defines variables used in the analysis. Section IV presents the empirical results. Section V discusses the results and its implications, and concludes.

II. Related Studies

Previous studies use various measures to proxy for the degree of agency problems. One of the most popular measures is the ownership structure. As pointed out by Jensen and Meckling (1976), agency costs can arise when the interests of a firm's managers are not aligned with those of the firm's shareholders. Many studies have shown that the ownership structure is closely related to the agency costs of a company (e.g., Morck, Shleifer and Vishny (1988)[4], Ang, Cole and Lin (2000), and Lins (2000)). Kim and Lee (2000) show that there is a curvilinear relation between the largest shareholder ownership and the corporate value using a sample of 168 Korean companies during the period from 1987 to 1996. Mitton (2000) shows that ownership concentration by managers is not significantly related to the performance of the firms in five East Asian countries while outside ownership concentration has significant explanatory power during the Asian financial crisis period. Regarding the role of outsiders, Weisbach (1988) and Brickley, Coles, and Terry (1994) present evidence that the presence of outsiders on the board reduces potential agency problems. Moreover, Shleifer and Vishny (1986) discuss the potential positive role of large block holders as an effective monitor, and Denis, Denis and Sarin

---

[4] They show that the positive effects of high ownership concentration (aligning the interests of managers with those of shareholders) initially dominate but the negative effects (management entrenchment) become more serious as the manager ownership increases too high.

(1997b) present supporting evidence.

Jensen (1986) shows that a company with a large amount of free cash flow can be subject to more agency problems. Lang, Stulz and Walking (1991) and Lie (2000) present empirical results that are consistent with the free cash flow theory in tender offers and self-tender offers, respectively. In addition, Maloney, McCormick and Mitchell (1993) show that tender offer firms with more debt perform better. This is consistent with the free cash flow scenario in that debt reduces agency problems between shareholders and managers, and leads to a better decision-making by the managers. On the other hand, leverage can also increase potential agency problems since companies in financial distress will be subject to more agency problems. Jensen and Meckling (1976) point out that financial distress can intensify the conflicts of interests between bondholders and shareholders.

Denis, Denis and Sarin (1997a) and Rajan, Servaes and Zingales (2000) show that corporate diversification reduces value, and that agency problems are the cause of value-reducing diversification. Yun and Kim (1999) show that corporate diversification in Korea reduces value, and that agency problems can explain this value decrease.

III. Data and Summary Statistics

1. Sample

Initially, we identify all firms listed on the Korean Stock Exchange (KSE) as of May 1, 1997. From this initial sample, we exclude the following firms: i) firms without stock price data on the 1999 Korea Securities Research Institute (KSRI)'s Stock Database; ii) firms without financial statement data on the Korea Listed Companies Association (KLCA)'s Listed Companies Database; and iii) firms in the financial industry. Our final sample includes 590 companies.

Table 1 shows the summary statistics. The average market capitalization was 170 billion Korean Won and the average total assets size was 633 billion Korean Won. Right before the crisis, Korean companies performed well on average. The average one-year return, ending April 30, 1997 was 20%. However, the equally-weighted average return over the period from May 1997 through April 1998 went down to -57%, while the average return of the Korea Composite Stock Price Index (KOSPI) was -40%. Since the KOSPI is a value-weighted index, the higher return of the KOSPI than the equally weighted average return of our sample firms indicates that larger firms performed better than smaller firms during this period. The average book-to-market equity ratio (B/M) was 0.98, indicating that on average the stock market was not very optimistic about the growth prospects of Korean companies even prior to the crisis.

Table 1. Summary Statistics

The sample is composed of all firms listed on the Korean Stock Exchange as of May 1, 1997, except for the following: i) firms without stock price data on the 1999 Korea Securities Research Institute (KSRI)'s Stock Database; ii) firms without financial statement data on the Korea Listed Companies Association (KLCA)'s Listed Companies Database; and iii) firms in the financial industry. The financial statement information is based on the 1996 fiscal year end data. The market capitalization is as of April 30, 1997. B/M represents the book-to-market equity ratio, based on the book value of equity (excluding preferred stock) at the 1996 fiscal year end and the market value of equity on April 30, 1997. Return on assets (ROA) is for the fiscal year ending in 1996. The return of the KOSPI index during the analogous period is reported in parenthesis. Post Return is the one-year holding period return starting from May 1, 1997. If a firm is delisted before the end of the one-year holding period, then the return is calculated only up to the date of de-listing, assuming zero returns afterwards.

	All
# of Firms	590
Market Capitalization	₩ 170 billion
Total Assets	₩ 633 billion
Sales	₩ 601 billion
B/M	0.98
ROA	0.84%
Prior Return	20.22%
	(-27.08%)
Post Return	-56.77%
	(-40.10%)

2. Proxy Variables for Potential Agency Problems

Based on the findings in previous studies, we use the following variables to proxy for the degree of potential agency problems: i) largest shareholder ownership; ii) manager ownership; iii) blockholder ownership; iv) free cash flow; v) leverage ratio; vi) number of business segments.

Each of the above mentioned proxy variables are measured in the following way using the financial statement information at the 1996 fiscal year end from the KLCA's Listed Company Database. The KLCA database also includes detailed information on the ownership structure of each company. The largest shareholder ownership includes the ownership of those who have a special relationship (e.g., family members) with the largest shareholder. Manager ownership is the total percentage ownership held by the managers of each company. Blockholder ownership is the total percentage ownership held by those individuals and corporations that own more than 5% of total shares outstanding. Blockholder ownership does not include the largest shareholder ownership. Free cash flow is defined similarly to Lehn and Poulsen's(1989). We define free cash flow as operating income before depreciation and amortization. We use two proxy variables for the leverage ratio, short-term debt over total assets and long-term debt over total assets. This is to check the role of heavy short-term debt burden, which has been cited as one of the major causes of the Korean financial crisis (Choi, Jen and Shin (2000)). To measure the degree of diversification, we use the number of business segments that are responsible for more than 10% of total sales. This is reported in the KLCA's Listed Company Database. However, KLCA reports only up to 5 business segments per firm, so this variable could be underestimated for some companies in our sample.

Table 2 shows the descriptive statistics of various agency problem proxy variables. The average largest shareholder ownership is 27% and the average manager ownership is 17%, which is bigger than the average blockholder ownership of 10%. The mean and median free cash over total assets are negative. Even the value at the 70th percentile is not that high: around 1%. This could be indicating that most Korean firms were in need of cash even right before the IMF crisis. This also indicates that free cash flow problems may not have been a major concern for most Korean companies around the crisis period. The average short-term debt over total assets is 42% and the average long-term debt over total assets is 25% for our sample firms. As previously mentioned, Choi, Jen and Sin (2000) argue that such a high short-term leverage is one of the major causes for the Korean financial crisis.

Considering the high short-term leverages of Korean companies (a median of 41% of total assets) and the small amounts of free cash flow (a median of -0.4% of total assets), most Korean companies were not subject to free cash flow problems around the crisis period.

Table 2. Descriptive Statistics for the Agency Costs Related Variables

The sample is composed of all firms listed on the Korean Stock Exchange as of May 1, 1997, except for the following: i) firms without stock price data on the 1999 Korea Securities Research Institute (KSRI)'s Stock Database; ii) firms without financial statement data on the Korea Listed Companies Association (KLCA)'s Listed Companies Database; and iii) firms in the financial industry. The financial statement information, including ownership information, is based on the 1996 fiscal year end data. The largest shareholder ownership includes the ownership of those who have a special relationship (e.g., family members) with the largest shareholder. Manager ownership represents the total percentage ownership held by managers of the company. Blockholder ownership represents the ownership held by those individuals and corporations that own more than 5% of total outstanding shares. Free CF represents free cash flow, and is defined similar, to Lehn and Poulsen's(1989) (i.e, operating income before depreciation, minus income taxes, minus interest expenses, minus preferred stock dividends, and minus common stock dividends). # of business segments represents the number of business segments that are responsible for more than 10% of the total sales. The average percentage is listed in the left with the 30th percentile, median, and the 70th percentile following in parenthesis.

	All (590)
Largest shareholder Ownership	26.72% (18.8, 25.6, 32.9)
Manager Ownership	16.57% (6.8, 15.0, 23.0)
Blockholder Ownership	9.79% (0.0, 5.8%, 11.7)
Free CF / Total Asset	-0.4% (-1.6, -0.4, 1.1)
Short-term Debt/Total Asset	41.9% (33.4, 41.2, 49.5)
Long-term Debt/Total Asset	24.8% (18.3, 24.0, 29.7)
# of Business Segments	2.09 (1, 2, 3)

3. Other Control Variables

Fama and French (1992) show that book-to-market equity ratio (B/M) and size are the two most important factors that explain the cross-sectional distribution of stock returns in the U. S. Kim and Kim (1998) also show that B/M and size have significant explanatory power in Korea. Therefore, we use market capitalization and B/M of each firm as control variables in our study. Market capitalization estimation is measured as of April 30, 1997. B/M is calculated based on the book value of equity (excluding preferred stocks) at the 1996 fiscal year end and on the market value of equity on April 30, 1997.

In addition to size and B/M, we also use beta from the Capital Asset Pricing Model to control risk, and prior one-year return to control the possible impact of prior stock returns on future stock returns (e.g., Jegadeesh and Titman (1993)). Beta is measured based on the market model by regressing individual company's daily returns on the KOSPI's daily returns over the one-year period ending on April 30, 1997.

4. Performance Measure

We measured the stock price performance of sample firms from May 1, 1997 through December 31, 1999. Even though we would like to measure the performance for a longer time period, we had to stop in December 1999 due to data availability. This period starts from right before the beginning of the Asian financial crisis and includes the recovery period.[5] Then on May 14, 1997, Thailand's currency was first hit by a massive attack by speculators. On November 17, 1997, the Korean government gave up defending its battered currency. Figure 1 shows the KOSPI levels

---

[5] In a related study, Mitton (2000) defines the Asian financial crisis period as the period from the end of June 1997 to August 1998. The beginning of this period corresponds with the devaluation of the Thai baht on July 2, 1997, and the ending point corresponds with the date on which the indices of five countries began a sustained upward trend.

Figure 1. Korea Composite Stock Price Index (KOSPI)

The following graph shows the KOSPI levels at the end of each month from January 1996 through December 1999.

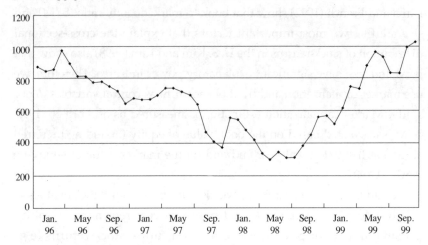

at the end of each month during the period from January 1996 through December 1999. The KOSPI was close to 1000 in April 1996, was around 700 in May 1997, and dropped below 400 by the end of 1997.

Buy-and-hold stock returns are measured over different periods starting from May 1, 1997, by compounding daily returns. If a company is delisted before the end of 1999, then the return calculation stops on the delisting date.

IV. Empirical Results

1. Comparison of Performance

We examine the differences in stock returns between the firms with different agency problem proxy variables. Table 3 reports the average returns for companies with various proxy variables in the top 30th percentile (high) and the average returns for the companies with proxy variables in the bottom 30th percentile (low). In addition, Table 3 reports the differences between high and low groups. The cutoff points used to classify the sample firms into high or low groups for each variable are reported in Table 2. The minimum difference in largest shareholder ownership between the high and the low group is around 14% and the minimum difference of manager ownership is around 16%. The 30th percentile of blockholder ownership is zero while the 70th percentile is 12 %. The difference in free cash flow over total assets between two groups is at least 2.7%. Regarding the leverage ratios, there are at least 10% in differences for both short-term and long-term debt ratios. The firms in the high diversification group have at least 3 business segments while the firms in the low diversification group have only one business segment.

On the left hand side, the average one-year returns before the crisis (from May 1996 to April 1997) and the average one-year returns during the crisis (from May 1997 to April 1998) are reported for the high and low groups.

For our sample firms, significant (at least at the 10% significance level) differences in one-year returns during the crisis between the high and low groups appear for all agency problem proxy variable groups except for the number of business segments variable groups. Consistent with Mitton (2000), blockholder ownership has significant explanatory power for the one-year stock return performance at the 1% significance level. The holding period is similar to the crisis period defined in Mitton (2000). The largest shareholder ownership and the manager ownership also have significantly explanatory power. Moreover, high free cash flow firms generated returns which were 17% higher than low free cash flow firms, and the difference between two groups is significant at the 1% significance level using the non-parametric two-sided Wilcoxon rank-sum test. Our sample firms with low short-term leverage generated returns that were 21% significantly (at the 1% significance level) higher than the returns for the sample firms with high short-term leverage.

On the right hand side in Table 3 we report the average return over a longer period, from May 1997 to December 1999. We also report the aver-

Table 3. Stock Returns Categorized by Agency Cost Variables

The sample is composed of all non-financial firms listed on the Korean Stock Exchange as of May 1, 1997. The financial statement information, including ownership information, is based on the 1996 fiscal year end data. The largest shareholder ownership (Large Sh) includes the ownership of those who have special relationship (e.g., family members) with the largest shareholder. Manager ownership (Manager) represents the total percentage ownership held by managers of the company. Blockholder represents the ownership held by those individuals and corporations that own more than 5% of total outstanding shares. FCF represents free cash flow, and is defined similar to Lehn and Poulsen (1989). ST Debt/TA represents short-term debt over total assets and LT Debt/TA represents long-term debt over total assets. # of business segments (# of Seg.) represents the number of business segments that are responsible for more than 10% of the total sales for each company. High includes the firms with each agency problem proxy variable in the top 30 percentiles and Low includes the firms with each agency problem proxy variable in the bottom 30 percentiles. Diff represents the return of High minus the return of Low. *** (** or *) represents the case where the differences are significant at the 1% (5% or 10%) significance level when the Wilcoxon rank-sum test is used. On the left hand side, the average post 1-year return starting from May 1997 is reported on top and the average prior 1-year return is reported in parenthesis. On the right hand side, the average return over the period from May 1997 through December 1999 is reported on top and the average return over the post Korean Financial Crisis period (from December 1997 to December 1999) is reported in parenthesis.

	Post (05/01/97-04/30/98) and Prior Return (05/01/96-04/30/97)			Post Return (05/01/97 12/31/99) and Post Korea Financial Crisis Return (12/01/97 12/31/99)		
	High	Low	Diff	High	Low	Diff
Large Sh	-55.96%	-61.74%	5.78%**	-36.51%	-29.64%	-6.87%**
	(28.89%)	(7.59%)	(21.30%)***	(16.63%)	(47.96%)	(-31.33%)
Manager	-55.03%	-57.47%	2.44%*	-36.53%	-20.19%	-16.34%*
	(37.59%)	(-6.51%)	(44.10%)***	(22.34%)	(54.70%)	(-32.36%)
Blockholder	-47.34%	-60.18%	12.84%***	-19.82%	-34.14%	14.32%***
	(11.79%)	(18.11%)	(-6.32%)	(49.93%)	(34.59%)	(15.34%)
FCF/TA	-43.98%	-60.93%	16.95%***	-2.32%	-49.40%	47.08%***
	(32.20%)	(15.17%)	(17.03%)***	(67.59%)	(2.82%)	(64.77%)***
ST Debt/TA	-67.93%	-47.26%	-20.67%***	-50.08%	-15.64%	-34.44%***
	(18.51%)	(20.50%)	(-1.99%)**	(20.01%)	(43.37%)	(-23.36%)***
LT Debt/TA	-61.74%	-48.71%	-13.03%***	-36.41%	-30.83%	-5.58%***
	(3.42%)	(35.45%)	(-32.03%)***	(23.38%)	(16.94%)	(6.44%)*
# of Seg.	-58.85%	-55.97%	-2.88%	-28.34%	-30.88%	2.54%
	(7.95%)	(37.18%)	(-29.23%)***	(32.84%)	(43.95%)	(-11.11%)

age return starting in December 1997, right after Korea gave up defending its currency.[6] For the post stock return during May 1997 through December 1999, all agency proxy variables, except for the diversification variable, have significant explanatory power (at least at the 10% significance level). However, for the post Korean financial crisis return over the period of December 1997 through December 1999, only the free cash flow and leverage variables are significant. Among the ownership variables, only the blockholder ownership has a significantly positive relation with the post return. The largest shareholder ownership and the manager ownership have a negative relation to the performance which contradicts our conjecture.

To summarize, the results in Table 3 show that free cash flow and leverage are the two most important variables to explain the cross-sectional variations in stock returns after the start of the Asian financial crisis. However, these results can be derived by differences in characteristics among the firms in different agency problem proxy variable groups. We later examine this issue.

In Table 4, we examine whether the results in Table 3 hold even after controlling for size. Table 4 reports the differences in average returns over the period from May 1997 through December 1999 between the high and low groups, holding size constant. We divide our sample firms into three size groups based on the market capitalization on April 30, 1997. Small firms are those in the bottom 30th percentile, medium firms are those in the next 40th percentile, and large firms are those in the top 30th percentile.

For the small firms, only the leverage variables are significant. For the medium sized firms, all agency problem proxy variables, except for the diversification variable, are significant. For the large firms, only the free

---

[6] On November 17, 1997, Korea abandoned its defense of the falling Korean won. On November 21, 1997, Korea announced that it would seek a rescue plan from the IMF and on December 1, 1997, Korea and the IMF resumed talks on the rescue plan after an initial deal failed. On December 4, 1997, the IMF announced a rescue package including a record amount of loan. Kho and Stulz (1999) include a more detailed description of these eventful days during the Asian financial crisis.

Table 4. Stock Returns for each Size and Agency Problem Proxy Variables Group

The sample is composed of all non-financial firms listed on the Korean Stock Exchange as of May 1, 1997. The financial statement information, including ownership information, is based on the 1996 fiscal year end data. The largest shareholder ownership (Large Sh) includes the ownership of those who have a special relationship (e.g., family members) with the largest shareholder. Manager ownership (Manager) represents the total percentage ownership held by managers of the company. Blockholder represents the ownership held by those individuals and corporations that own more than 5% of total outstanding shares. FCF represents free cash flow, and is defined similarly to Lehn and Poulsen's (1989). ST Debt/TA represents short-term debt over total assets and LT Debt/TA represents long-term debt over total assets. # of business segments (# of Seg.) represents the number of business segments that are responsible for more than 10% of the total sales for each company. The difference between the average return of High and the average of Low is on top. The average return of High is on the left-hand side and the average of Low is on the right-hand side in parenthesis. All returns are the returns over a holding period from May 1997 through December 1999. High includes the firms with each agency problem proxy variable in the top 30 percentiles and Low includes the firms with each agency problem proxy variable in the bottom 30 percentiles. *** (** or *) represents the case where the differences are significant at the 1% (5% or 10%) significance level when the Wilcoxon rank-sum test is used. Small (Medium or Large) represents the firms, the market capitalization of which is in the bottom 30 percentiles (the next 40 percentiles, or the top 30 percentiles).

	Small	Medium	Large
Large Sh	0.10%	14.24%***	-7.41%*
	(-47.7, -47.8)	(-43.8, -58.0)	(-2.9, 4.5)
Manager	5.78%	26.19%***	-41.17%
	(-46.0, -51.8)	(-37.9, -64.0)	(-15.4, 25.7)
Blockholder	15.14%	7.92%*	17.31%
	(-41,.0, -56.1)	(-38.3, -46.3)	(9.4, -8.0)
FCF/TA	5.61%	20.39%**	88.49%***
	(-41.3, -47.0)	(-35.6, -56.1)	(46.7, -41.8)
ST Debt/TA	-25.67%***	-26.85%***	-33.66%
	(-62.6, -37.0)	(-62.4, -35.5)	(-14.2, 19.5)
LT Debt/TA	-14.11%**	-35.14%***	19.34%
	(-53.1, -39.0)	(-68.8, -33.7)	(4.9, -14.5)
# of Seg.	12.84%	-1.70%	-43.15%
	(-42.8, -55.7)	(-43.0, -41.3)	(8.8, 51.9)

cash flow variable is significant. Even though it is hard to get to a strong conclusion based on the results in Table 4 due to the small sample size, the results suggest that the effects of agency problem proxy variables on performance are different for different size groups. For example, blockholder ownership, which is significant for the total sample, is not significant for large firms. Therefore, in the next section, we examine the explanatory powers after controlling for size and other factors.

2. Regression Analysis

We statistically test the significance of various agency problem proxy variables by using the regression analysis. We control for prior return, beta, size and B/M in each regression. The following is used in Table 5.

$$Return_i = a + \beta_1 PR1_i + \beta_2 Beta_i + \beta_3 LMKT_i + \beta_4 LBM_i + \beta_5 CH_i$$
$$\beta_6 LAR_i + \beta_7 MAN_i + \beta_8 OUT_i + \beta_9 FCF_i + \beta_{10} STD_i + \beta_{11} LTD_i + \beta_{12} DIV_i + \varepsilon_i$$

Return represents the stock return over the period of May 1997 through December 1999, and $PR1_i$ represents the return from May 1996 through April 1997. $Beta_i$ is the beta of the company i, $LMKT_i$ is the natural log market capitalization (= Ln (market capitalization in billion won)), LBM_i is the natural log book-to-market equity ratio, and CH_i is the dummy variable for a *Chaebol* company. LAR_i is the largest shareholder ownership, MAN_i is the manager's ownership, OUT_i is the blockholder ownership, FCF_i is the free cash flow over total assets, STD_i is the short-term debt over total assets, LTD_i is the long-term debt over total assets and DIV_i represents the # of business segments. A firm is classified as one of the *Chaebol* firms if it belongs to one of the top 30 *Chaebols* (as of April 1997). In April of each year, the Korea Fair Trade Commission (KFTC) ranks Korean conglomerates (*Chaebols*) based on their total assets, and identifies the 30 largest *Chaebols*.[7]

Among the control variables, prior returns, sizes, and B/M have significant explanatory power for stock returns. Among agency problem proxy variables, the coefficients of free cash flow and leverage are significant in the regression. Ownership structure variables do not have any significant explanatory power.

---

[7] Bae, Kang and Kim (2000) discuss the characteristics of the top 30 *Chaebol* firms based on the statistics at the end of 1997. They show that *Chaebol* firms are more diversified, represent 46% of the KSE's total market capitalization, and have higher leverage ratios (the average debt-to-equity ratio of 693%). In addition, the degree of cross-shareholding among member firms is significantly higher and an individual owner-manager (either a founder or his/her family) has almost complete control over all firms within the *Chaebol*.

Table 5. Regression Results

The following describe the regressions used in the subsequent table:

$$Return_i = a + \beta_1 PR1_i + \beta_2 Beta_i + \beta_3 LMKT_i + \beta_4 LBM_i + \beta_5 CH_i$$
$$\beta_6 LAR_i + \beta_7 MAN_i + \beta_8 OUT_i + \beta_9 FCF_i + \beta_{10} STD_i + \beta_{11} LTD_i + \beta_{12} DIV_i + \varepsilon_i$$

Return presents the stock return of the holding period from May 1997 through December 1999, and $PR1_i$ represents the return over May 1996 through April 1997. $Beta_i$ is the beta of the company i, $LMKT_i$ is the natural log market capitalization (= Ln (market capitalization in billion won)), LBM_i is the natural log book-to-market equity ratio, and CH_i is the dummy variable for a *Chaebol* company. LAR_i is the largest shareholder ownership, MAN_i is the manager's ownership, OUT_i is the blockholder ownership, FCF_i is the free cash flow over total assets, STD_i is the short-term debt over total assets, LTD_i is the long-term debt over total assets and DIV_i represents the # of business segments. Coefficients are reported on top and White's heteroskedasticity-consistent t-statistics are reported in parenthesis.

	Return
Constant	-5.312***
	(-3.35)
PR1	-0.159***
	(-2.70)
Beta	-0.204
	(-0.28)
LMKT	0.217***
	(3.26)
LBM	-0.124**
	(-2.03)
CH	0.136
	(1.36)
LAR	-0.181
	(-0.55)
MAN	0.148
	(0.64)
OUT	-0.110
	(-0.53)
FCF	2.126***
	(2.59)
STD	-0.803***
	(-3.80)
LTD	-0.092
	(-0.31)
DIV	-0.016
	(-0.51)
Adj-R2	12.54%

V. Summary and Conclusion

This paper examines whether agency problems explain the post Asian financial crisis performance of Korean companies. Agency problems might become more important around a crisis since the crisis would cause more companies to fall into a situation of financial distress. The financial crisis, which Korea has recently experienced, provides an interesting experimental setting to test the role of agency problems in explaining the cross-sectional differences in performance under an economy-wide financially distressed situation.

The performance of 590 non-financial companies that were listed in the Korean Stock Exchange as of May 1, 1997 is analyzed in the paper. We use seven variables that would proxy for different degrees of potential agency problems: i) three ownership structure variables (largest shareholder ownership, manager ownership and blockholder ownership); ii) one free cash flow variable (free cash flow over total assets); iii) two leverage variables (short-term debt over total assets and long-term debt over total assets); and iv) one variable to show the degree of diversification (number of business segments). Stock returns are used to measure the performance. Stock returns are calculated starting from May 1, 1997, right before the start of the Asian financial crisis.

The results show that ownership structure does not significantly explain the post- Asian financial crisis stock return performance of Korean companies. On the other hand, the leverage, especially short-term debt, significantly explains the performance. Moreover, the firms with more free cash flow show significantly better stock price performance. This indicates that the stock market has paid more attention to the positive role of free cash flows (i.e., providing the buffer to overcome a short-term credit problem) than the negative role (i.e., potential agency problems between shareholders and managers). The high leverage ratios of most Korean companies and the relatively small amount of free cash flows may explain why the stock market behaved that way.

The significant role of leverage in explaining the performance of Korean companies after the crisis may be consistent with the agency based theory that a highly leveraged firm in financial distress makes inefficient investment decisions and this leads to a value decrease. An alternative explanation is that the stock market pays a lot of attention to the firm's ability to repay loans, especially short-term loans, when most financial institutions are not willing to renew short-term credit due to their own liquidity problems under an economy-wide financial distress. This might lead to an extremely poor performance of the firms with very high leverage, especially with very high short-term leverage.

Overall, it turns out that agency problems did not play such an important role in explaining the post crisis stock price performance of Korean companies, at least up to the end of 1999. Agency problems could get more serious after a crisis. However, the poor explanatory power of agency problem proxy variables indicates that the stock market seems to pay more attention to the ability of a firm to go through a crisis by focusing on the amount of free cash flow and the short-term debt ratio. It would be interesting to examine whether agency problems play a more important role in explaining the cross-sectional differences in stock returns over a longer-term as more data become available.

References

Ang, James S., Rebel A. Cole and James Wuh Lin. (2000). Agency costs and ownership structure. *Journal of Finance*, 55, pp. 81-106.

Bae, Kee-Hong, Jun-Koo Kang and Jin-Mo Kim. (2000). Does group affiliation destroy shareholder wealth in emerging markets?: Evidence from mergers by Korean business groups. Working Paper. Seoul: Korea University.

Brickley, J. A., J. L. Coles, and R. L. Terry. (1994). Outside directors and the adoption of poison pills. *Journal of Financial Economics*, 35, pp. 371-390.

Choi, Dosoung, Frank C. Jen, and Han Shin. (2000). Causes and consequences of the Korean financial crisis. *Review of Pacific Basic Financial Markets and Policies*, 3, pp. 1-26.

Denis, David J., Diane K. Denis, and Atulya Sarin. (1997a). Agency problems, equity ownership, and corporate diversification. *Journal of Finance*, 52, pp. 135-160.

Denis, David J., Diane K. Denis, and Atulya Sarin. (1997b). Ownership structure and top executive turnover. *Journal of Financial Economics*, 45, pp. 193-221.

Fama, Eugene F., and Kenneth R. French. (1992). The cross-section of expected returns. *Journal of Finance*, 47, pp. 427-466.

Hahm, Joon-ho, and Frederic S. Mishkin. (2000). The Korean financial crisis: An asymmetric information perspective. *Emerging Markets Review*, 1, pp. 21-52.

Jegadeesh, Narasimhan, and Sheridan Titman. (1993). Returns to buying winners and selling losers: Implications for market efficiency. *Journal of Finance*, 48, pp. 65-91.

Jensen, Michael. (1986). Agency costs of free cash flow, corporate finance and takeovers. *American Economic Review*, 76, pp. 323-329.

Jensen, Michael C., and William H. Meckling. (1976). Theory of the firm: Managerial behavior, agency costs and ownership structure. *Journal of Financial Economics*, 3, pp. 305-360.

Johnson, Simon, Peter Boone, Alasdair Breach, and Eric Friedman. (2000). Corporate governance in the Asian financial crisis. *Journal of Financial Economics*, 58, pp. 141-186.

Kho, Bong-Chan, and Rene M. Stulz. (1999). Banks, the IMF, and the Asian crisis.

Working paper. Seoul: Seoul National University.

Kim, Kyu-Young, and Young-Bin Kim. (1998). What are the determinants of expected stock returns in the Korean stock market? Working Paper. Gwangju: Chosun University (in Korean).

Kim, Young Sook, and Jae Choon Lee. (2000). The relationship between corporate value and ownership structure. *The Journal of Korean Securities Association*, 26, pp. 173-197 (in Korean).

Lang, Larry, Rene Stulz and Ralph Walkling. (1991). A test of the free cash flow hypothesis. *Journal of Financial Economics*, 29, pp. 315-335.

Lehn, Kenneth and Annette Poulsen. (1989). Free cash flow and stockholder gains in going private transactions. *Journal of Finance*, 44, pp. 771-787.

Lie, Erik. (2000). Excess funds and agency problems: An empirical study of incremental cash disbursements. *Review of Financial Studies*, 13, pp. 219-248.

Lins, Kar V. (2000). Equity ownership and firm value in emerging markets. Working Paper. University of North Carolina.

Maloney, Michael T., Robert E. McCormick, and Mark L. Mitchell. (1993). Managerial decision making and capital structure. *Journal of Business*, 66, pp. 189-217.

Mitton, Todd. (2000). A cross-firm analysis of the impact of corporate governance on the east Asian financial crisis. Working paper. MIT.

Morck, Randall, Andrei Shleifer, and Robert W. Vishny. (1988). Management ownership and market valuation: An empirical analysis. *Journal of Financial Economics*, 20, pp. 293-315.

Rajan, Raghuram G., Henri Servaes, and Luigi Zingales. (2000). The cost of diversity: The diversification discount and inefficient investment. *Journal of Finance*, 55, pp. 35-80.

Shleifer, Andrei, and Robert Vishny. (1986). Large shareholders and corporate control. *Journal of Political Economy* 94, pp. 461-488.

Weisbach, M. S. (1988). Outside Directors and CEO Turnover. *Journal of Financial Economics* 20, pp. 431-460.

Yun, Young-Sup, and Sung-Pyo Kim. (1999). The value impacts of business diversification and agency problems. *The Korean Journal of Finance* 12, pp. 1-37. (in Korean)

Chaebol Structure, Diversification and Performance

Inhak Hwang

I. Introduction

For more than four decades, *Chaebols*, largely diversified business groups in Korea, have formed the major feature of Korean industrial organization.[1] A typical *Chaebol* consists of legally independent and financially partial-interlocked firms that act like a single entity under the effective control of a controlling shareholder and/ or his family. As of 1997, for example, the top 30 *Chaebols* consisted of about 27 affiliated firms on average and accounted for 46.6% of total corporate assets in the non-financial sector. There is no doubt that the *Chaebols* have contributed to the rapid growth of the Korean economy. But they started to face the difficulty from the mid-1990s, and the half of the top 30 *Chaebols* went into bankruptcy or debt restructuring program around the time of financial crisis in the late 1997. What went wrong with the *Chaebols*? Which of their structure and/ or strategies made them fragile at the shock of crisis? Among various features of *Chaebol* structure, this paper focuses on the business portfolio to examine how they affected the

---

[1] The *Chaebols* clearly belongs to the category of business groups, defined by Granovetter (1994) and Ghemawat and Khanna (1998).

management performance at the group level before the crisis.

Even before the crisis the *Chaebols* have always been under public attack primarily due to their predominant position in the national economy, as well as because of their diversification behavior and strong familial control. Especially, in Korea, the prohibition of excessive concentration of economic power is considered an important social value to be pursued and is well expressed in the Constitution (Article 119) and Fair Trade Act (Article 1). The business diversification of large *Chaebols* is also a focal point of social concern because it is widely believed to strengthen their economic concentration. Reflecting this social concern, the government has adopted various policy measures and regulations to restrain the diversification behavior of large *Chaebols*. And each year the Korea Fair Trade Commission (KFTC) designates the top 30 *Chaebols* in terms of asset size, placing them under special monitoring and restricting guidelines.

The hostile tradition of public policy toward diversification has been further reinforced by the economic crisis. Since the outbreak of the financial crisis in late 1997, many scholars have blamed the uncompetitive structure and reckless diversification strategy of the *Chaebols* as the main culprits of the economic turmoil. The new administration inaugurated right after the crisis initiated "the *Chaebol* reform policy" and treated the *Chaebols* and their organizational structure as "something to be discarded or dismantled." In this context, the government strongly demanded that the *Chaebols* restructure themselves in every activity including their organizational form, governance structure, business and debt structure.[2] As for the business structure, the government has urged *Chaebols* to de-diversify and rather concentrate on a few core business areas. While eager to achieve the goals of

---

[2] The 'Chaebol reform policy' is based on the following eight principles. The five principles announced on January 1998 include: ① improving management transparency ② eliminating debt-payment guarantees between affiliates (by March 2000) ③ improving capital structure and reducing the debt-equity ratio to 200 % ④ focusing on core businesses, and ⑤ enhancing the accountability of controlling shareholders and management; plus three further principles announced on August 1999, which include prohibiting ⑥ circular equity investment among affiliates ⑦ unfair trading among affiliates, and ⑧ unlawful bequests.

'*Chaebol* reform', it also has introduced much-controversial policies such as the "big deal" (business swap plan), which is currently being applied to eight industries.[3]

Now it should be clear that over the two past decades the government has always believed that *Chaebols*' diversification hurt their own performance as well as adversely affected allocative efficiency. But despite this consistent and unambiguous policy stance, we do not have any sufficient information concerning the extent of diversification of the *Chaebols* and how this has affected management performance and economic concentration. Recently some scholars, together with the regulatory bodies claimed that the excessive diversification of large *Chaebols* has been the primary cause for the fragile economy. However, little empirical evidence exists to either support or disclaim these arguments so far. Considering that there are plenty of arguments for and against diversification strategy, we urgently need empirical work to examine the linkage between diversification and performance, as well as the linkage between diversification and allocative efficiency.

This paper aims at addressing some of the above issues by examining the data of 72 *Chaebols* over the period of 1985-1997; which is about one decade before the infamous Asian economic crisis. Some understand the *Chaebols* to be a synonym of the top 30 business groups designated by the KFTC each year. However, in this paper, we use the term '*Chaebol*' to denote Korean conglomerates in general because there is no need to differentiate between *Chaebols* in the top 30 and others not in the top 30. The next section provides an overview of *Chaebol* structure including their ownership and governance, business portfolio and organizational structure. Section 3 addresses questions surrounding the *Chaebol*'s business structure and explains how their diversification strategy is related with other structural factors. Section 4 uses a panel data of 72 *Chaebols* covering the period of 1985-1997 to investigate some stylized facts about diversification.

---

[3] The eight industries are semiconductors, power generation equipment, petro-chemicals, aircraft manufacturing, railway vehicles, ship engines, oil refining, and automobiles.

Furthermore, we also conduct a regression analysis to test the excess diversification hypothesis that an extensive diversifying strategy has a negative impact on business performance using a sample of the *Chaebols* that showed signs of trouble around the time of the financial crisis. Section 5 provides a short summary and discusses the tasks for *Chaebol* restructuring ahead.

II. Features of *Chaebol* Structure

1. Largely Diversified Group

We have taken the example of the top 30 *Chaebols* to briefly outline some features of the *Chaebol* with special regard to their diversification behavior. Table 1 provides summary statistics about the top 30, as designated by the KFTC from 1987 to 1997. The top 30 *Chaebols* occupy a critical position in the allocation of economic resources. As of 1997, they consisted of about twenty-seven affiliated firms on average and accounted for 46.6% of total corporate assets in the non-financial sector.

We see from Table 1 that the *Chaebols* are largely diversified. For example, in 1997 each *Chaebol* operated in about 20 industries at the two-digit KSIC level, which comprised a total of 60 industries. Moreover, the top 5 are so highly diversified that they engage in about 30 industries. Of course, the *Chaebols* are not the only cases of engaging in multiple-line businesses and having a significant effect on economic activity. According to Montgomery (1994), the top 500 U.S. public companies engage in an average of about 11 industries, and of those, 40 companies engage in more than 30 industries (at the 4-digit level SIC Codes). It is thus true that diversification of a large corporation is also pronounced even in advanced countries. Despite this fact, however, we must admit that the level of diversification in the *Chaebols* is rather high compared to that in the U.S., after having taken into consideration the differences between the 2-digit and 4-digit level of industry classification.

2. Affiliates - Expanding Strategy

The second important feature of the *Chaebol*s is that they diversify through the creation of new firms and/ or the acquisition of existing firms. As a result, the number of affiliates belonging to each *Chaebol* tends to exceed the number of lines of businesses, as shown in Table 1. This way of expanding the business scope is distinguished from the way in which large corporations in some advanced countries diversify within a single

Table 1. Summary Statistics of Top 30 Chaebols: 1987-1997

year \ structure	1987	1993	1994	1995	1996	1997
Ownership Structure (%)						
Equity Investment Ratio	43.9	28.0	26.8	26.3	24.8	27.5
In-Group Shareholdings	56.2	43.4	42.7	43.3	44.1	43.0
Controlling family	15.8	10.3	9.7	10.5	10.3	8.5
Cross-shareholdings	40.4	33.1	33.1	32.8	33.8	34.5
Capital Structure (%)						
Equity-asset ratio		22.2	21.9	22.3	20.6	16.1
Debt-equity ratio		349.7	355.7	347.5	386.5	518.9
Cross-debt guarantee		469.8	258.1	161.9	107.3	92.2
Business Structure (numbers)						
Average number of Affiliates		16.4	20.1	20.5	20.8	22.3	27.2
Average number of industries engaged (KSIC 2-Digit)		18.3 (31.2)	19.1 (30.4)	18.5 (29.6)	18.8 (29.6)	19.8 (30.0)
Total number of Affiliates		509	604	616	623	669	819
Aggregate Concentration of Economic Power (%)						
Asset concentration		44.9	43.6	47.3	47.1	46.6	
Value-added concentration		13.6	14.2	16.2	14.7	13.0	

Note: 1) The statistics in the 1987 column are based on the 32 top *Chaebols*.
2) The figures in parenthesis denote the number of industries that the top five *Chaebols* engage in.
3) KSIC 2-digit comprises the 60 industries in total.

corporation through their divisional expansion. These different ways of diversification may have affected the organizational structure, namely one leading to business groups consisting of formally independent affiliates like *Chaebols* and the other leading to a multi-divisional form of large corporations. Nevertheless, the *Chaebols*, like other forms of business organizations, should be seen as a device via which diversified firms realize economic benefits from internalizing transactions.

One may ask why Korean corporations have diversified in this manner. That is, what factors make the entrepreneur to prefer diversification through the absorption of affiliates rather than through the divisional expansion? Among others, cross-equity investments and cross-debt guarantees between affiliates are the institutional factors behind 'the business group forming diversification strategy.' For example, cross-equity investments help the entrepreneurs to diversify through the affiliate expansion since this allows full control of all affiliates with only a relatively small amount of investment on the part of the entrepreneurs. Cross-debt guarantees also facilitate the affiliate-adding-diversification strategy since they increase the availability of external capital. In addition, the fact that *Chaebols* have pursued unrelated diversification might have another effect on the entrepreneur's choice of organizational structure.

3. CM-form Structure

Third, from the operational perspective of their organizational structure, the *Chaebols* can be classified as a CM-form (centralized multidivisional form). Even though a *Chaebol*'s affiliates are legally independent and financially partially-interlocked, they are under the authoritative and hierarchical control of the head office, which is often called the Secretarial Office or Planning and Coordination Office. Samsung may be considered the first group to form the current structure of business organization by establishing its head office in 1959, and other groups followed this example: LG in 1968, SK in 1974, Daewoo in 1976, and Hyundai in 1979

(Hwang and Seo, 2000).

The head office in a typical *Chaebol* assumes the role of centralizing the capital allocation decisions and also coordinates the business activities of each affiliate, treating the affiliate firms as divisions of a single corporation. Because of this stylized fact, Chang and Choi (1988) assume that the *Chaebols* have the organizational structure of an M-form type, and test the M-form hypothesis that, above a certain specified size, an M-form type corporation will outperform their traditional U-form counterparts, which retain an hierarchical, functionally-divided structure [Williamson (1975)]. But the *Chaebols* are not exactly equivalent to the M-form corporations. In particular, the head offices in most *Chaebols* are deeply involved in the operating decisions of their affiliates, while a typical M-form corporate structure is characterized by the separation of strategic and operating functions (i.e. operating decentralization). Since the head office centralizes operating decisions as well as strategic and financial decisions, the *Chaebols* should be classified as having a CM-form structure rather than an M-form.

CM-form corporations have been regarded as sub-optimal in most cases because they lack some internal capital market characteristics of the M-form corporation. For example, by centralizing the operating decision, they cannot foster divisional accountability. Moreover, the boundary of accountability becomes ambiguous between divisions (affiliates) and the head office. For this reason, the CM-form has often been referred to as a corrupted M-form. Hill (1988) asserts that, "in the case of related firms, the CM-form control type is optimal, centralization being consistent with the exploitation of interrelationship" (p.73). If we follow this argument, then the *Chaebols* may have an inappropriate control system to fully realize benefits from an internal capital market because they pursue a strategy of unrelated diversification.

As market competition intensified, the mismatch between the control systems and strategy in *Chaebols* started to cause management inefficiency. After the onset of the financial crisis, some *Chaebols*, facing the government's reform policy and the emerging shareholder activism, have sought to change their organizational structure. For example, Hyosung, the 19th largest group in terms of asset size, consolidated its four major affiliates into one firm in an attempt to transform itself into an M-form corporation. Doosan, the 13th large group, merged its nine affiliates into Doosan Corp and reduced the number of affiliates from 27 in 1995 to 14 in 1999. Recently, the Hyundai group, whose diversification level is among the highest, spanning from the manufacture of computer chips to ships, separated Hyundai Motors and other automobile-related affiliates from the group.[4] Also LG, the 3rd largest group, has announced plans to transform itself into a holding-firm structure by 2003. We expect that in the coming decade the Korean conglomerates will put more effort into restructuring business portfolios as well as into organizational restructuring.

4. Pyramid Ownership Structure

Fourth, some interesting questions may arise as to the sustainability of the controlling family-centric governance structure in Korea. Table 1 shows that shareholding of the controlling family has decreased persistently from 15.8% in 1987 to 8.5% in 1997 and 5.4% in 1999. Despite this fact, the controlling family remained as the sole power in managing and controlling *Chaebol*s at least up till the recent financial crisis. How was this possible? Hwang and Seo (2000) explain this by the pyramid ownership structure, the lack of internal and market disciplining mechanisms, and the path-dependent remnants of the founding culture reflecting the short history of entrepreneurship in Korea, all of which have contributed to the managerial entrenchment in favor of the controlling shareholder. For example, the pyramid ownership structure facilitated entrepreneurs with the ability to control assets worth vastly more than their own wealth by holding

---

[4] After this separation in August 31, 2000, the number of affiliates that belong to the Hyundai group decreased from 35 to 25. Subsequently, Hyundai Motors became an independent group that ranked as the 5th largest.

controlling interests in companies, which in turn hold controlling interests in still more companies [Mork, et. al. (1998)]. In particular, the cross-shareholdings between affiliates and the lack of an adequate governance structure further reduced the minimum holdings necessary to control assets of affiliates, and thus reinforced the controlling shareholder-centric governance structure.

5. Controlling Shareholder Managerialism

Finally, the governance structure of the *Chaebols* can be characterized as "controlling shareholder managerialism," whereby the controlling shareholder participates in the management of all affiliates, and there is no effective independent mechanism to monitor and discipline the management [Hwang (2000 b)]. In a sense, the controlling shareholder and his family are part of the management in all the affiliates and, at the same time, act as the only agent that actively monitors and evaluates management performance. The controlling shareholder, often referred to as the chairman, does this through the Secretarial Office (the head office) which is at the apex of the authoritative and hierarchical structure of *Chaebols*.

While the head office has played a critical role as the control tower of internal capital markets to realize the benefits of the interrelationship among affiliates, it also has functioned as a conduit to serve the interest of the controlling family, sometimes at the sacrifice of the outside investors. As such, the *Chaebols* tend to maximize the value of the controlling family rather than the general shareholder value. In this sense, the controlling shareholder managerialism should be distinguished from the shareholder capitalism prevalent in the Anglo-Saxon economies because shareholderism emphasizes the fair treatment of all shareholders with the maximization of shareholder values as the utmost objective of management. It is also different from the stakeholderism that characterizes the European and Japanese corporate governance that attempts to harmonize the interests of employees and creditors with those of shareholders.

In the Korean conglomerates, the controlling families use the pyramid leverage to control assets worth much more than their own equity investment, and outside investors do not have any effective means to monitor and discipline the management as well as the controlling families. As such, they are allowed to have a large degree of freedom in managing the business groups for their own benefits such as family value maximization. From the theoretical perspective, this *Chaebol* governance supported by the pyramid control structure may magnify the agency problems and sometimes reduce the value of public shareholders. Recognizing the governance problems inherent in the *Chaebol* structure, it is easy to understand why people started to demand governance reform around the time of the economic crisis. However, the question remains as to why investors and scholars did not address these problems at an earlier time when the potential problems of governance failure were always present. Regarding this question, one may suppose that at the earlier period when the founding entrepreneurs managed their business group, potential problems were not reflected in the real world to the extent that the agency's theory may predict because the founders had the propensity to devote themselves almost entirely to the growth of their firms.[5]

III. Diversification Strategy: Extensive or Excessive ?

Although large corporations in almost every country tend to engage in multiple lines of business, it is true that the *Chaebol*s have pursued a relatively extensive diversification strategy. But the mere fact that the

---

[5] Using the data of the top 30 Chaebols, Hwang (2000 b) also explains that until the early 1990s the pyramid multipliers and the scopes of pyramid control were quite low as compared with those in later periods.

Chaebols are *extensively* diversified does not necessarily mean that they are *excessively* diversified beyond the point of profit maximization. The optimal level of diversification, if at all it exists, differs from one firm to another, depending on the characteristics of resources and the organizational capability that each firm has accumulated. It also differs in each country depending on the historical and institutional contexts that affect diversification behavior. But in Korea, it is generally admitted that the *Chaebols* have pursued excessive diversification with the term 'excessive' having two meanings: it refers to aggregate concentration or, on the other hand, refers to management performance. Here we briefly summarize previous literature dealing with the linkage between diversification and economic concentration, and the linkage between diversification and management performance.

1. The Perspective of Economic Concentration

Up to the crisis, the main reason for criticizing diversification behavior was that it tended to enable *Chaebols* to build a corporate empire and to increase economic concentration to their advantage. Many people feel that economic concentration remains at an abnormally high level in Korea and that is mainly due to the *Chaebols*' excessive diversification. Economists often share this belief and consider economic concentration as a Korea-specific phenomena, as if *Chaebols* are a Korea-specific business organization. Furthermore, the government has developed a wide range of regulatory policies aimed at prohibiting the concentration of economic power. In particular, the government has been concerned more about conglomeration and aggregate concentration than market concentration and has put the top 30 *Chaebols* under special monitoring and restrictive measures.

But Hwang (1997) asserts that the public perception and government policy about economic concentration are not usually supported by appropriate studies, and there exists considerable discrepancy between the generally held perception and reality. When the top 30 *Chaebols* are compared with other countries' 30 largest corporations, the employment-based aggregate concentration ratio in the manufacturing sector is found not to be relatively high; as of 1993, for example, the ratio for Korea is 18.5%, the U.S. 22.9%, Germany 31.7%, and the U.K. 32.6%.[6] Despite this fact, there remain some reasons to worry about the possibility for the *Chaebols* to abuse their economic power or exercise corporate hegemony, for example, through political-business connections. But it should be noted that the corporate hegemony in Korea has been problematic not just because of the amount of economic resources a certain group controls, but rather because of the lack of transparency in both political procedure and business management. From the economic efficiency point of view, public policy should have paid more attention to market concentration and the resulting inefficiency in resource allocation. The increase in aggregate concentration does not necessarily lead to increase in market concentration, and theoretical and empirical findings are somewhat mixed about the relationship between diversification of large firms, market concentration, and aggregate concentration [References, Bernheim and Whinston (1990), Berry (1974), Clarke and Davies (1983), Montgomery (1985), Mueller (1985)]. Hwang (2000a) using a panel data of 72 *Chaebols* from 1985 to 1997 examines this issue in Korea and finds that government policies to restrict *Chaebols*' diversification might have produced an undesirable outcome in that they tend to protect the market power of the incumbent firms thereby increasing market concentration.[7]

---

[6] Hwang (1997) also shows, however, that when different variables like sales and total assets are included, the aggregate concentration ratios in Korea are relatively high.

[7] Using a model that decomposes changes in aggregate concentration into changes in diversification and market concentration [as in Clarke and Davies (1983)], Hwang (2000a) shows that changes in the weighted sum of concentration in individual markets has strong tendency to move in the opposite direction with changes in the aggregate index of diversification, such as during the period of 1985-1997.

2. The Perspective of Management Performance

Following the onset of the financial crisis, the direction of discussions about diversification moved to the implications it has had on the business performance of *Chaebol*s and their long-term competitive advantage. Beginning with Hanbo in January 1997, six of the top 30 *Chaebol*s went bankrupt before the IMF bailout (see Table 2), and scholars suspected the leveraged diversification strategy as the primary cause. In this context, Lee and Eur (2000) analyze the cause of *Chaebol* bankruptcy, using the data of 35 *Chaebol*s during 1993-1997, and find that diversification is not the cause for bankruptcy but rather suggest that the aggressive investment financed by debt may be responsible. On the other hand, Lee and Han (1998) show that diversification, especially unrelated diversification had adverse effects on profitability, but their findings have limited implications on the recent series of *Chaebol* failure because they are based on cross-sectional data of 1992, which is long before the occurrence of the crisis.

Palich, et. al. (2000) report that "perhaps the most researched linkage in management literature is that involving diversification and performance, and yet this area of inquiry falls far short of the consensus" (p.155). This evaluation may be plausibly valid in the Korean case as well since previous literature reveals inconsistencies in their findings. The mixed results in empirical studies have been accompanied by various theories that attempt to explain the motivation for business diversification. The monopoly power

Table 2. Bankrupt *Chaebol*s Among Top 30 in 1997

	Hanbo	Sammi	Jinro	KIA	Haitai	New-Core	Halla
Default Date	Jan 23	Mar 19	Apr 21	July 15	Nov 1	Nov 4	Dec 5
Asset Size (Rank)	14th	25th	9th	8th	24th	28th	12th
Ownership							
-Controllers	80.6	12.7	15.1	21.0	9.9	35.6	22.4
-In-Group	85.4	28.4	45.6	25.6	28.4	99.4	55.6

* Note: Ownership statistics come from data published by the KFTC in April 1996.

hypothesis, for example, predicts the positive linkage of diversification and performance because the firm is depicted to diversify in order to increase its monopoly power in an anti-competitive way such as through cross-subsidization, mutual forbearance, and reciprocal buying. The transaction cost hypothesis, on the other hand, argues that the firm diversifies to internalize the high costs involved with market transaction that resulted from market imperfection, and thus predict a positive linkage as well. Another view, the agency theory, proposes a negative link between diversification and performance because firm managers, it is argued, tend to pursue goals other than corporate value maximization.

Beside these theories, the common resource hypothesis and the risk diffusion hypothesis make things more complicated. The resource view, argues that a firm's profitability and level of diversification are affected by its resource stocks, suggesting that it is difficult to find a systemic relationship between diversification and performance because firms will have varying optimal levels of diversification reflecting differences in the specificity of their resource stocks. For example, Montgomery and Wernerfelt (1988) argue that firms with more specific assets may have lower levels of diversification but earn higher profits (due to their specificity), while firms with less specific assets may pursue a diversification strategy, but will yield lower rent. The risk-dispersion view tends to deny any systematic linkage by arguing that the main reason for a firm to diversify may be to stabilize the profit stream rather than to increase the level of profitability [Cable and Yasuki (1985), Choi and Cowing (1999)].

Among the various theories, the transaction cost and the resource view deserve special attention when explaining why Korean conglomerates are so extensively diversified. Due to the relatively short history of capitalism and the discretionary policy of the government in Korea, market institutions for economic activity has been distorted and is far from perfect. And so far, most firms have not as yet accumulated productive factors that have high specificity sufficient enough to yield high rates of return. Along with these factors, the way in which Korean conglomerates diversify through the pyramid control structure further contributes to widen the breadth of diversification because it makes it possible for the controlling shareholder to launch a new investment project with little capital of his own while at the same time reducing the threat of take-overs.

As we have mentioned, an criticism about *Chaebols* is not just that they pursue extensive diversification but that they pursue reckless or excessive diversification. If this is true, then why do they intend to diversify beyond their optimal level? The agency theory might be one plausible explanation to this question because it has proposed that with the absence of significant ownership stakes, managers will tend to over-invest in diversification to maximize their utility rather than maximize shareholder-value. Managers will prefer higher levels of diversification compared to shareholders because shareholder utility is derived from firm value while management utility is derived not only from firm value but other factors such as firm size and employment risk as well. The agency theory, as such, predicts that the more diffusive the ownership structure, the higher the level of diversification, and thus more concentrated ownership leads to higher levels of firm monitoring which then would reduce agency costs paid through diversification [Hoskisson and Turk (1990)].

But it should be noted that the shareholdings in *Chaebols* have been rather concentrated while in the hands of the controlling family, which may contradict the agency theory based on ownership diffusion. The theory has further difficulty in explaining the successive bankruptcy of *Chaebols* in 1997 because their ownership concentration was higher than the average of the top 30 *Chaebols*. From Table 1 and Table 2, we see that as of April 1996, the average holdings of the controlling family in the top 30 are 10.3%, whereas most of the bankrupt *Chaebols* (except Haitai) exceeded this level and reached a maximum of 80.6% in the Hanbo group. Nevertheless, we may still suspect that there exist considerable conflict of interests between the controlling shareholder and general investors. In the case of the *Chaebols*, the agency problem does not come simply from the ownership diffusion because no matter what portion of equity capital it owns, the controlling family usually has complete control over the assets of all affiliates supported through pyramid ownership and cross-shareholding.

With the absence of internal and external governance monitoring systems, the controlling shareholder enjoyed almost full discretion without any challenge from outside shareholders and creditors.[8] Due to 'governance failure', the controlling shareholder tended to overvalue the expected benefits of diversification. On the other hand, the expected risks would be underestimated under the pyramid ownership structure and cross equity investment as these magnify the divergence of interests between the controlling family and the public shareholders of pyramid firms. With this distorted incentive structure, the controlling shareholder has motivation to expand the business scope and build a corporate empire, sometimes by investing in high-risk and high-return projects, which then lead to over-diversification.

But whether *Chaebol*s actually pursued an excessive diversification strategy is a question to be resolved by empirical evidence. As mentioned before, the founding entrepreneur did not pursue a diversification strategy in order to reduce the firm value, although this choice was always open to him. It should be noted that the existence of the pyramid control structure *per se* does not imply the inappropriateness of the *Chaebol* structure. At the early stages of economic development in which entrepreneurship, capital, and the institutional infrastructure for market transactions are rather limited, the controlling shareholder managerialism can not only contribute to the successful growth of a corporation but also the diffusion of entrepreneurship over all sectors in the economy. For example, in an empirical study on the top 30 *Chaebol*s during 1989-1996, Hwang and Seo (2000) show that there exists a reverse U-shaped relationship between the pyramid multiplier and *Chaebol* performance, with the pyramid control structure starting to reveal

---

[8] It was not until 1995 that investors questioned the problems inherent in the Chaebol governance structure and consequently, the government made the first attempt to improve management transparency and governance related institutions.

its limitation in the early 1990s. That is, the pyramid control variable was found to have a positive effect on performance in the sample period of 1989-1992, and a negative effect in the later period of 1993-1996.

In sum, the effects of the *Chaebol* structure on performance depend on the stage of economic development as well as the institutional environments and entrepreneurial capability. The various difficulties that the *Chaebol*s faced dating from the time of the economic crisis may have been caused by their maladaptation to the rapidly changing economic environment in Korea. Therefore, when one evaluates the linkage between diversification and performance, the agency problems inherent in the *Chaebol* structure as well as environmental changes that affect the marginal benefits and costs of diversification must be considered.

IV. An Empirical Analysis of Diversification and Performance

1. Some Stylized Facts

In this section we look into some of the stylized facts of the diversification strategy of Korean conglomerates, using an extensive panel data of 72 *Chaebol*s for the period of 1985-1997.[9] We do not include the state-owned enterprises such as POSCO, of Korea Telecommunication in the sample since they have different ownership and governance structures and besides this, the government directly protects their monopoly positions. But the sample in this study still represents a large share in the domestic economy and as of 1997, account for 51.8% in terms of total corporate assets and operate in 46 non-financial sectors among a total of 60 industries at the two-digit industry classification. The sample includes the 14 *Chaebol*s that are now bankrupt and the 9 *Chaebol*s that are involved in the current work-

---

[9] The database of Korea Investors Service, Inc. is used to construct the panel data in this paper.

out program, as well as the top 30.[10] We thus divide the sample into several subgroups to find some clues as to what may have happened to the *Chaebols'* business portfolio before the financial crisis that overwhelmed the economy at the end of 1997.[11]

Table 3 summarizes the diversification levels by *Chaebol* characteristics in selected years, and Figure 1 shows the trend of changes during the period of 1985-1997. In order to denote the level of diversification of each *Chaebol*, we use the Berry-Herfindahl index, which ranges from 0 (specialization) to 1 (maximum level of diversification) as this is easy to interpret. As can be seen, the diversification level of the Korean conglomerates in general increased from 0.694 in 1985 and reached the highest level of 0.765 in 1995, and then later declined. The first notable thing concerns the top 5, whose diversification level remained stable in the 1990s after reaching a peak of 0.80 in 1990. This suggests that the top 5 had already completed the expansion of their highly diversified business structures by the end of the 1980s. On the other hand, the failing *Chaebols* that became bankrupt and was placed under the workout program have been characterized by lower levels of diversification. In particular, the 14 bankrupt *Chaebols* show lower diversification than any other group, despite the fact that they pursued an aggressive diversification strategy after 1993. Thus interestingly, those *Chaebols* which adopted an extensive diversification strategy earlier on in the 1980s became less vulnerable to difficulties at the time of the financial crisis. Conversely, those that adopted a low diversification strategy and changed later in the 1990s to an aggressive expansion strategy ran into problems.

We observe another interesting fact by looking into the degree business relatedness and the different characteristics of *Chaebols*. The business relat-

---

[10] The workout program, as an alternative to the formal procedures of the insolvency law regime, is an informal procedure through which creditors and debtors can directly negotiate their debt-restructuring plan.

[11] Here the failing Chaebols are those that went bankrupt or were placed under the workout program as of April 1999. Since the Daewoo Group was included in the workout programs after this period, this paper does not consider Daewoo as a failing firm.

Table 3. Berry-Herfindahl Diversification Index by Group Characteristics

	1985	1988	1991	1994	1997	Avg Level (85~97)	Change Rate (85~96)	Change Rate (85~97)
By Chaebol Size								
Top 5	0.7427	0.7660	0.8027	0.8102	0.7968	0.7879	7.9%	7.3%
Top 30	0.7357	0.7481	0.7805	0.7899	0.7790	0.7705	7.3%	5.9%
Total 72	0.6944	0.7138	0.7444	0.7567	0.7542	0.7366	9.9%	8.6%
By Fate								
Surviving(49)	0.7074	0.7261	0.7574	0.7709	0.7658	0.7496	9.4%	8.2%
Failing(23)	0.6230	0.6463	0.6758	0.6863	0.6762	0.6658	13.8%	8.5%
-Bankrupt(14)	0.5739	0.6079	0.6195	0.6458	0.6149	0.6218	18.8%	7.1%
-Work-out(9)	0.6591	0.6835	0.7311	0.7266	0.7116	0.7062	11.2%	8.0%

Figure 1. Trend of Changes in Diversification Level: 1985-1997.

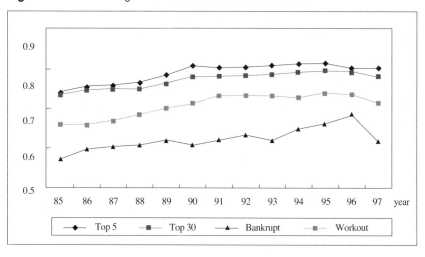

edness summarized in Table 4 is defined by the percentage ratio of related diversification over the total level of diversification and thus denotes the extent of relatedness or similarities among the multiple lines of businesses a *Chaebol* operates in. The business related ratio is based on the Entropy index of related and unrelated diversification. One notable point from Table 4 is that the 14 bankrupt *Chaebol*s have a feature of relatively higher

Table 4. The Business Related Ratios by Group Characteristics: 1985-1997

	1985	1988	1991	1994	1997	Avg Level (85~97)	Change Rate (85~96)	Change Rate (85~97)
By *Chaebol* Size								
Top 5	16.74	17.66	18.81	20.48	19.36	18.87	16.8%	15.7%
Top 30	18.62	19.27	20.96	22.31	20.97	20.56	11.4%	12.6%
Total 72	18.67	20.47	22.04	23.54	21.30	21.51	18.0%	14.1%
By Fate								
Surviving(49)	18.34	19.94	21.27	22.53	19.89	20.73	14.9%	8.5%
Failing (23)	20.48	23.39	26.06	28.53	30.33	25.75	30.9%	48.1%
-Bankrupt(14)	21.83	29.67	33.36	37.96	44.88	33.22	65.4%	105.6%
-Work-out(9)	19.49	17.29	18.90	19.17	21.95	18.92	-4.6%	12.6%

levels of business relatedness. Their average level of business relatedness during the period is 33.2%, which is much higher than that of the top 30 (21.5%) and, in fact, increased from 21.8% in 1985 to 44.9% in 1997. Caution, however, should be observed so as not to interpret this finding as implying that a high level of related diversification was a cause of the *Chaebol* failure. But the fact that the relatedness of the failing *Chaebol*s is higher than that of the surviving *Chaebol* is surprising when we consider that strategic management science emphasize that related diversification is preferable for sustained firm growth and that unrelated diversification may be bad for corporate performance.

What does it imply when on average, the failing *Chaebol*s had lower levels of total diversification and higher degree of related diversification as compared to the survivors? And what implications do the findings here have on government policy that strongly urges the *Chaebol*s to de-diversify and focus on core businesses?[12] As Khanna and Palepu (1999) emphasize, some preconditions should be met for the business focusing strategy to lead to improved performance. Among them, one important thing is the

---

[12] 'Focusing on core businesses' is one of the five principles for the Chaebol reform that the president-elect Kim Dae-Jung announced on January 13, 1998. See footnote 3 for further details.

institutional infrastructure supporting the economic activity, which involves government behavior to stabilize the economic environment as well as the legal and regulatory framework that serves the workings of the capital, labor and product markets, and the judiciary system for effectively enforcing impersonal contracts. If institutional mechanisms are not well developed, thereby resulting in high transaction costs, then highly diversified groups may outperform less diversified groups. Another important thing affecting the optimal choice of the business portfolio is the characteristic of the resource stocks that firms have accumulated so far. If firms have excess resources of multiple use and do not have a competitive advantage in their markets, then the business portfolio strategy focusing the source of cash flow on a few industries may endanger the long-run sustainability of the firm. Taking these arguments into account, we may say that at least until the mid-1990s, in Korea, the institutional infrastructures and the firms' capability were not sufficient enough to support the focusing strategy as being always desirable.

2. Regression Analysis of Failing Chaebols

Using the pooled data of failing *Chaebol*s in the manufacturing sector, we conduct a multivariate test to learn how their strategy of diversification affected their profitability. We take this sample because these *Chaebol*s have been criticized as having become vulnerable due to over-diversification. As of April 1999, we find that the data consists of nine bankrupt *Chaebol*s [13] and eight workout groups [14] that are subject to empirical tests. Whether they were bankrupt or put into the program, it is common that these *Chaebol*s underwent a very difficult period during the economy-wide financial

---

[13] The nine groups include Kia, Halla, Hanil, Jinro, Sammi, Tongil, Geo-pyung, Dae-nong, and Hanbo.

[14] The groups here include Ssangyong, Gohap, Anam, Sinho, Gangwon-sanup, Shinwon, Dongguk-muyuk, and Byuksan.

distress that started in early 1997.

In general, the linkage between diversification and performance is tested by regressing the diversification level on the profit rate with some control variables such as market share, debt ratio, firm size, and so on. The model here has the following specification:

$$ROA = b_0 + b_1 MSR + b_2 WAD + b_3 LTA + b_4 DEBT + b_5 DT + b_6 DRDT + b_7 WROR + \varepsilon$$

where
  ROA: returns on asset
  MSR: weighted market share
  WAD: advertising intensity
  LTA: log value of total assets
  DEBT: debt-asset ratio
  DT: Entropy diversification index in the manufacturing sector
  DRDT: business relatedness defined as the % ratio of related diversification to total diversification
  WROR: weighted industry return on asset

From the Hausman test, we find that the fixed effect model turns out to be more suitable to our panel data than the random effect model. At first, we estimate the above model [15] with the combined data of bankrupt and workout *Chaebols*. Table 5 summarizes the regression results and shows that the diversification level in these *Chaebols* had a negative effect on performance during the period of 1985-1996,[16] and the business relatedness or related diversification works in the direction of improving performance.

---

[15] The regression results based on the random effect model are not different from the findings here in terms of the sign and statistical significance of the variables of interest.

[16] We exclude the 1997 data from the analysis because this period was already affected by the financial crisis.

Table 5. Regression Results of the Panel Data of 17 Failing *Chaebols*: Fixed Effect Model (1985-1996)

Explanatory Variables	Dependent Variable: ROA					
	Model 1	Model 2	Model 3	Model 4	Model 5	Model 6
Intercept	-41.9217	-57.1083**	-62.7639**	-33.9936	-34.6743	-54.5393**
	(-1.5260)	(-2.1008)	(-2.2852)	(-1.2246)	(-1.2192)	(-2.0026)
MSR	-0.1496*	-0.2062**	-0.1912**	-0.1561*	-0.1555*	-0.1952**
	(-1.7325)	(-2.3983)	(-2.2526)	(-1.8144)	(-1.7991)	(-2.3068)
WAD			-0.2959		-0.0899	
			(-0.3971)		(-0.1169)	
LTA	2.5140*	2.7619**	2.9952**	2.4069*	2.4418*	2.7948**
	(1.9405)	(2.1841)	(2.3393)	(1.8647)	(1.8381)	(2.2456)
DEBT	-0.1117***	-0.1177***	-0.1188***	-0.1247***	-0.1244***	-0.1277***
	(-3.2084)	(-3.4650)	(-3.5451)	(-3.5096)	(-3.4843)	(-3.7394)
DT	-4.5207*	-6.0548***	-6.0829***	-14.0573**	-14.0337**	-12.2590**
	(-1.9639)	(-2.6401)	(-2.6930)	(-2.2551)	(-2.2436)	(-2.0352)
DT²				4.4013	4.3946	2.8710
				(1.6449)	(1.6373)	(1.1039)
DRDT		0.1529***	0.1610***			0.1534***
		(3.1956)	(3.3920)			(3.2455)
WROR			0.4233***			0.4067**
			(2.6506)			(2.5414)
Adjusted R²	38.1%	41.6%	44.0%	39.1%	39.1%	44.4%
F-value	1.878	2.138	1.916	1.981	1.839	2.062
N	204	204	204	204	204	204

Note 1) The figures in parenthesis denote t-statistics.
2) F-value to test for no fixed effect
3) Significant at 1% level (***), 5% level (**), and 10% level (*)

The results are also invariant even when the dependent variable (ROA) is replaced by returns on sale (ROS), as can be seen in the Appendix. Therefore from this, one may conclude that the failing *Chaebols* were excessively diversified and over-diversification was a cause of management failure. But caution should be taken in interpreting the empirical results because the study is based on the combined data of two rather different characteristics of *Chaebols*.

What is the difference between the bankrupt *Chaebols* and those that are placed in the workout program? One might say that the difference is just a matter of whether they have already exited the market or they are about to exit the market. But there are two reasons to indicate that they may differ in the extent and cause of managerial distress. Basically the workout program is designed to rehabilitate the ailing firms that have liquidity problems through the negotiation of debt restructuring between creditors and debtors. The creditors will agree to initiate the program only when the value of the firm as a going-concern is higher than its liquidation value.[17] Thus we may infer that for the bankrupt *Chaebol*s the liquidation value is higher than the value of the going-concern, while the opposite case is true for the workout *Chaebol*s. In addition, four of the bankrupt *Chaebol*s in the sample went into bankruptcy even before the IMF bailout, while all workout *Chaebol*s began to show signs of trouble after the start of the IMF bailout program, which called for destructive interest rates of up to 30%. Considering these facts, there might exist some qualitative differences between the bankrupt *Chaebol*s and the workout *Chaebol*s, and the regression results in Table 5 may then be misleading regarding the effect of diversification strategies in performance.

For the above reason, we examine the effects of the business portfolio structure on performance again by treating the bankrupt *Chaebol*s and the workout *Chaebol*s separately. Table 6 summarizes the regression results with the dependent variable as ROA. The first three columns represent the regression models on the bankrupt *Chaebol*s, whereas the last three columns represent the regression models on the workout *Chaebol*s. As can be seen here, the explanatory power improves conspicuously as compared with that of the combined model in Table 5.[18] We note that in the models

---

[17] After due diligence, the main bank usually proposes a restructuring plan. If this is agreed upon by the creditors that it represents more than 75% of the firm's debt, then the contract becomes binding to all the institutions. If the creditors cannot reach an agreement after two attempts, the case is referred to the Corporate Restructuring Coordination Committee (CRCC) whose decision then becomes effective.

[18] See Appendix 2 and 3 for detailed analysis on the bankrupt Chaebols and the workout Chaebols, respectively.

Table 6. Regression Results When Bankrupt and Workout Chaebols Are Separated: Fixed Effect Model (1985-1996)

Explanatory Variables	9 Chaebols in Bankrupt			8 Chaebols in Workout		
	Model 1	Model 2	Model 3	Model 4	Model 5	Model 6
Intercept	-79.6227*	-75.1518*	-74.9570*	11.5770***	10.2229***	36.4441
	(-1.9112)	(-1.9276)	(-1.9346)	(3.4717)	(3.1982)	(1.2322)
MSR	-0.1954	-0.2739	-0.2502*	-0.0371	-0.0152	-0.0157
	(-1.3183)	(-1.9813)	(-1.8079)	(-0.6245)	(-0.3358)	(-0.2444)
WAD		0.0382	0.3065	0.1838		0.5580
		(0.0343)	(0.2729)	(0.2991)		(0.8254)
LTA	4.8032**	4.8156**	4.8121**			-1.0722
	(2.4250)	(2.5773)	(2.5916)			(-0.7458)
DEBT	-0.1007**	-0.1435***	-0.1448***	-0.1692***	-0.1573***	-0.1698***
	(-2.0910)	(-3.2371)	(-3.2871)	(-4.4573)	(-4.3753)	(-3.8968)
DT	-15.1243***	-21.0861***	-20.9775***	3.0074**	3.0364***	3.3467***
	(-3.3408)	(-4.9153)	(-4.9198)	(2.5454)	(2.7467)	(2.7669)
DRDT		0.4308***	0.4195***			-0.0350
		(4.6598)	(4.5489)			(-1.2908)
WROR			0.3665		0.2669***	
			(1.4245)		(2.8714)	
Adjusted R^2	40.5%	53.0%	54.1%	70.3%	73.3%	71.1%
F-value	1.926	2.767	2.681	3.088	2.797	2.274
N	108	108	108	96	96	96

Note 1) The figures in parenthesis denote t-statistics.
2) F-value to test for no fixed effect
3) Significant at 1% level (***), 5% level (**), and 10% level (*)

that include the bankrupt *Chaebols* only, the regression results strongly support the hypothesis that they pursued excessive diversification, which led to lower profitability.

The most interesting point here is that the coefficients of the diversification variables have a positive sign in the models of the workout *Chaebols* and are statistically significant. This finding suggests that contrary to the widespread criticism about the failing *Chaebols* in general, the diversification strategy in the workout *Chaebols* may not have been a cause that led them to difficulty. Rather, the diversification strategy in these *Chaebols* turns out to be a factor that contributes to the improvement of conglomerate performance in terms of ROA. As hence, this study shows that even among the failing *Chaebol*s, the diversification-performance relationship is different depending on the *Chaebol* characteristics. While it is true that some *Chaebol*s, here bankrupt *Chaebol*s, have pursued the value destroying diversification, we also find the statistical evidence against the over-diversification hypothesis from the samples of surviving and workout *Chaebol*s. In addition, considering the fact that the diversification level in the bankrupt *Chaebol*s is not lower than those in two different samples of *Chaebol*s, the findings here confirm that the optimal level of diversification varies across *Chaebol*s, and that the extensive diversification *per se* does not necessarily mean it is suboptimal.

V. Summary and Discussions

The main purpose of this paper is to explore the relationship between diversification and economic performance, and thus derive some implications for direction of the business restructuring ahead. Because the *Chaebol*s have a feature of extensive breadth of unrelated diversification, they have been criticized as pursuing an excessive diversification strategy in order to build a corporate empire' at the expense of the public shareholder value. Recently, after the onset of the financial crisis, that strategy was believed to have caused subsequent management failures in many *Chaebol*s including Hanbo, Kia, Jinro, Sammi, and so on. As such, the government, under the rubric of 'Chaebol reform' strongly urges the *Chaebol*s to restructure their business portfolios and focus on core businesses. By examining the panel data of 72 *Chaebol*s during 1985-1997, we find however that in general the failing *Chaebol*s have lower levels of total diversification and higher levels of related diversification as compared with the surviving *Chaebol*s. This finding may suggest that at least until 1997, the institutional infrastructure and individual firm's competence were not sufficient enough to support a concentrated business structure as a winning strategy.

This finding itself does not exclude the possibility that some *Chaebols* actually pursued an over-diversification strategy. The *ex ante* motivation for over-diversification exists under the *Chaebol* governance structure of controlling shareholder managerialism, although whether this was exploted still remains an empirical question. We find the negative linkage between diversification and performance in the example of the bankrupt *Chaebols*. But we have completely different results from the regression models of the workout *Chaebols*, which reject the over-diversification hypothesis. In general the findings in this paper do not contradict the fact that the level of diversification is determined by the specificity and competitiveness of a firm's resource stocks. In this sense, the government policy strongly urging every *Chaebol* to de-diversify and focus on a small number of business lines may not be appropriate.

Especially in the rapidly changing environment, empirical results may yield somewhat misleading suggestions about what need to be done now and in the future because they are based on the past. As is well known, the Korean economy has drastically changed since the recent financial crisis of 1997. Outside shareholders and creditors started to challenge the controlling shareholder's monopoly position in governing and managing business groups. In addition, the government has taken various measures to improve management transparency, to vitalize the proper role of the boards at the firm level, and to enhance shareholder activism and the accountability of controlling shareholders. The government also put strict restrictions on intra-group trading and allowed large *Chaebols* to be liquidated, thereby ending the too-big-to-fail' legacy. We expect that together with the recent changes in the institutional environment, the intensified competition will increase the marginal cost of diversification and/or decrease its marginal benefit, thereby lowering the optimal level of diversification in the Korean conglomerates. But we believe that the most important task for restructuring the *Chaebols* will be that of adjusting the mismatch between the internal control system and the diversification strategy, rather than that of simply remanaging their business portfolios.

Appendix 1. Regression Results on the Panel Data of 17 Failing *Chaebols*: Fixed Effect Model, (1985-1996)

Explanatory Variables	Dependent Variable: ROS (Returns on Sales)					
	Model 1	Model 2	Model 3	Model 4	Model 5	Model 6
Intercept	-79.0848**	-98.9662***	-102.6058***	-73.1383**	-71.1150*	-99.7607***
	(-2.1978)	(-2.7795)	(-2.8341)	(-2.0010)	(-1.8993)	(-2.7717)
MSR	-0.1608	-0.2349**	-0.2194*	-0.1657	-0.1674	-0.2208**
	(-1.4219)	(-2.0859)	(-1.9608)	(-1.4627)	(-1.4718)	(-1.9745)
WAD			-0.0007		0.2674	
			(-0.0007)		(0.2640)	
LTA	4.6596***	4.9841***	5.1140***	4.5793***	4.4757**	5.0730***
	(2.7460)	(3.0091)	(3.0301)	(2.6943)	(2.5591)	(3.0842)
DEBT	-0.2162***	-0.2240***	-0.2261***	-0.2259***	-0.2267***	-0.2301***
	(-4.7425)	(-5.0370)	(-5.1202)	(-4.8304)	(-4.8242)	(-5.0968)
DT	-5.7929*	-7.8013**	-7.8423***	-12.9458	-13.0159	-10.8431
	(-1.9214)	(-2.5970)	(-2.6339)	(-1.5772)	(-1.5806)	(-1.3621)
DT^2				3.3012	3.3210	1.3969
				(0.9370)	(0.9399)	(0.4064)
DR/DT		0.2001***	0.2068***			0.2042***
		(3.1939)	(3.3062)			(3.2676)
WROR			0.4743**			0.4647**
			(2.2530)			(2.1972)
Adjusted R^2	44.7%	47.8%	49.3%	45.0%	45.0%	49.4%
F-value	2.972	3.128	2.949	3.002	2.876	3.028
N	204	204	204	204	204	204

Note 1) The figures in parenthesis denote t-statistics.
2) F-value to test for no fixed effect
3) Significant at 1% level (***), 5% level (**), and 10% level (*)

Appendix 2. Regression Results on the Panel Data of 9 Bankrupt *Chaebols*: Fixed Effect Model, (1985-1996)

Explanatory Variables	Dependent Variable: ROA					
	Model 1	Model 2	Model 3	Model 4	Model 5	Model 6
Intercept	-79.6227*	-75.1518*	-74.9570*	33.3203	25.7312	23.2750
	(-1.9112)	(-1.9276)	(-1.9346)	(0.8563)	(0.7402)	(0.6616)
MSR	-0.1954	-0.2739	-0.2502*	-0.1509	-0.2221**	-0.2177*
	(-1.3183)	(-1.9813)	(-1.8079)	(-1.2272)	(-2.0044)	(-1.9521)
WAD		0.0382	0.3065			
		(0.0343)	(0.2729)			
LTA	4.8032**	4.8156**	4.8121**	2.4933	2.7454*	2.8233*
	(2.4250)	(2.5773)	(2.5916)	(1.4830)	(1.8285)	(1.8647)
DEBT	-0.1007**	-0.1435***	-0.1448***	-0.2583***	-0.2787***	-0.2768***
	(-2.0910)	(-3.2371)	(-3.2871)	(-5.4815)	(-6.5934)	(-6.4977)
DT	-15.1243***	-21.0861***	-20.9775***	-112.8829***	-108.3222***	-106.8097***
	(-3.3408)	(-4.9153)	(-4.9198)	(-7.0502)	(-7.5633)	(-7.3002)
DT2				46.1996***	41.6873***	40.9981***
				(6.2803)	(6.2833)	(6.0523)
DR/DT		0.4308***	0.4195***		0.3611***	0.3581***
		(4.6598)	(4.5489)		(4.7125)	(4.6429)
WROR			0.3665			0.1205
			(1.4245)			(0.5629)
Adjusted R^2	40.5%	53.0%	54.1%	59.7%	68.3%	68.4%
F-value	1.926	2.767	2.681	4.880	6.129	5.794
N	108	108	108	108	108	108

Note 1) The figures in parenthesis denote t-statistics.
2) F-value to test for no fixed effect
3) Significant at 1% level (***), 5% level (**), and 10% level (*)

Appendix 3. Regression Results on the Panel Data of 8 Workout Chaebols: Fixed Effect Model, (1985-1996)

Explanatory Variables	Dependent Variable: ROA					
	Model 1	Model 2	Model 3	Model 4	Model 5	Model 6
Intercept	11.5770***	10.2229***	36.4441	14.0955	5.7056	23.5217
	(3.4717)	(3.1982)	(1.2322)	(0.5405)	(1.4074)	(0.8322)
MSR	-0.0371	-0.0152	-0.0157	0.0079	0.0153	0.0148
	(-0.6245)	(-0.3358)	(-0.2444)	(0.1308)	(0.3476)	(0.2405)
WAD	0.1838		0.5580	0.0207		0.2413
	(0.2991)		(0.8254)	(0.0348)		(0.3730)
LTA			-1.0722	-0.3072		-0.6568
			(-0.7458)	(-0.2357)		(-0.4810)
DEBT	-0.1692***	-0.1573***	-0.1698***	-0.1677***	-0.1589***	-0.1730***
	(-4.4573)	(-4.3753)	(-3.8968)	(-4.1232)	(-4.5768)	(-4.2003)
DT	3.0074**	3.0364***	3.3467***	10.5010***	11.0869***	10.3940***
	(2.5454)	(2.7467)	(2.7669)	(4.1188)	(4.7450)	(4.0653)
DT2				-3.3101***	-3.6148***	-3.1713***
				(-3.2609)	(-3.8266)	(-3.0815)
DR/DT			-0.0350		0.0047	-0.0227
			(-1.2908)		(0.2061)	(-0.8737)
WROR		0.2669***			0.2998***	
		(2.8714)			(3.3365)	
Adjusted R^2	70.3%	73.3%	71.1%	74.3%	77.9%	74.5%
F-value	3.088	2.797	2.274	2.276	3.191	2.304
N	96	96	96	96	96	96

Note 1) The figures in parenthesis denote t-statistics.
2) F-value to test for no fixed effect
3) Significant at 1% level (***), 5% level (**), and 10% level (*)

References

Bernheim, B Douglas and Michael D Whinston. (1990). Multimarket contact and collusive Behavior. *Rand Journal of Economics*, 21, pp. 1-26.

Berry, Charles H. (1974). Corporate diversification and market structure. *Bell Journal of Economics and Management Science*, 5, pp. 196-204.

Cable, John and Hirohiko Yasuki. (1985). Internal organization, business groups and corporate performance: An empirical test of the multidivisional hypothesis in Japan. *International Journal of Industrial Organization*, 3, pp. 401-420.

Chang, S. and Unghwan Choi. (1988). Strategy, structure and performance of Korean business groups: A transaction cost approach. *Journal of Industrial Economics*, 37, pp. 141-158.

Choi, Jeong-Pyo, and Thomas Cowing. (1999). Firm behavior and group affiliation: The strategic role of corporate grouping for Korean firms. *Journal of Asian Economics*, 10, pp. 195-209.

Clarke R. and Davies, S. W. (1983). Aggregate concentration, market concentration and diversification. *The Economic Journal*, 93, pp. 182-192.

Fershtman, Chaim and Ehud Kalai. (1993). Complexity considerations and market behavior. *Rand Journal of Economics*, 24, pp. 224-235.

Garvey, Gerald. (1994). Should corporate managers maximize firm size or shareholder wealth? *Journal of the Japanese and International Economies*, 8, pp. 343-352.

Ghemawat, Pankaj and Tarun Khanna. (1998). The nature of diversified groups: A research design and two case studies. *Journal of Industrial Economics*, pp. 35-61.

Granovetter, Mark. (1994). Business groups. Neil J. Smelser and Richard Swedberg. (eds.) *The Handbook of Economic Sociology*. Princeton University Press.

Hill, Charles W. L.(1988). Internal capital market controls and financial performance in multidivisional firms. *Journal of Industrial Economics*, 37, pp. 68-83.

Hoskisson, Robert E. and Thomas A. Turk. (1994). Corporate restructuring: Governance and control limits of the internal capital market. *Academy of Management Review*, 15, pp. 459-477.

Hwang, Inhak. (1997). *The Comparative Analysis of Korean Economic Concentration*, Seoul: Korea Economic Research Institute.

Hwang, Inhak. (1999). Diversification strategy of the Korean business group: Evidence and implications. *Journal of Korean Economic Studies*, 3, pp. 87-112.

Hwang, Inhak. (2000 a). Aggregate concentration, market concentration and diversification: The Korean case. *Korean Journal of Industrial Organization*, 8, pp. 49-74.

Hwang, Inhak. (2000 b). Limitations and reform of corporate governance structure in Korea. paper presented at the symposium of Case Studies of Economic Institution Reform in Korea, Yonsei University.

Hwang, Inhak, and Jung-Hwan Seo. (2000). Corporate governance and *Chaebol* reform. a paper for the 8th SJE symposium on Corporate Governance and Restructuring in East Asia, Seoul National University.

Lee, Jae-Min and Un-Sun Eur. (2000). Economic crisis and *Chaebol* bankruptcy. *Korean Journal of Economic Development*, 6, pp. 33-62.

Lee, Soo-Bock, and Sung-Duk Han. (1998). Diversification and profitability of Korean business group. *Korean Journal of Industrial Organization*, 6, pp. 55-69.

Lee, S., Jwa, Jung, and Kim. (eds.). *Corporate Governance Structure in Korea*. Korean Institute for Management Development.

Jensen, Michael.C. (1986). Agency costs of free cash flow, corporate finance, and takeovers. *AEA Papers and Proceedings*, 76, pp. 323-329.

Khanna, Tarun and Krishna Palepu. (1997). Why focused strategies may be wrong for emerging markets. *Harvard Business Review*, pp. 41-51.

La Porta, Rafael, Florencio Lopez-De-Silanes, Andrei Shleifer and Robert Vishny. (1997). Legal determinants of external finance. *Journal of Finance*, 52, pp. 1131-1150.

Markides, Constaninos C. (1995). *Diversification, Refocusing, and Economic Performance*. MIT.

Milgroms, Paul and John Roberts. (1992). *Economics, Organization and Management*. Prentice Hall.

Montgomery, Cynthia A. (1985). Product-market diversification and market power. *Academy of Management Journal*, 28. pp. 789-798.

Montgomery, Cynthia A.(1994). Corporate diversification. *Journal of Economic Perspectives*, 8, pp. 163-178.

Montgomery, Cynthia A. and Birger Wernerfelt. (1988). Diversification, Ricardian rents, and Tobin's q. *RAND Journal of Economics*, 19, pp. 623-632.

Mork, Randall. K. David Strangeland and Bernard Yeung. (1998). Inherited wealth, corporate control and economic growth: The Canadian disease? *NBER Working Paper*, 6814.

Mueller, D. C. (1985). Mergers and market share. *Review of Economic Statistics*, 67, pp. 259-267.

Palich, Leslie E., Laura B. Cardinal, and C. Chet Miller. (2000). Curvelinearity in the diversification-performance linkage: An examination of over the three decades of research. *Strategic Management Journal*, 21, pp. 155-174.

Seo, Jung-Hwan. (2000). Corporate bankruptcy system in Korea. Seoul: Korea Economic Research Institute.

Williamson, Oliver. (1975). *Markets and Hierarchies*. New York: Macmillan.

MANAGEMENT PHILOSOPHY & STRATEGIC CHOICES

1. The Impact of Confucianism on East Asian Business Enterprises
by Tai K. Oh and Eonsoo Kim

2. Asian Management Styles? The Evidence from Korea
by Dennis P. Patterson

3. Determinants of Competitive Advantage in the Network Organization Form: A Pilot Study
by Eonsoo Kim, Irene M. Duhaime, John C. Mc Intosh, and Sun-ah Yang

4. An Empirical Study on the Change of Organizational Culture and Performance in Korean Firms
by Young-Joe Kim

The Impact of Confucianism on East Asian Business Enterprises

Tai K. Oh[1] and Eonsoo Kim[2]

I. Introduction

The nations of East Asia constitute the fastest-growing part of the world economy and surpass the NAFTA sector at the turn of the century. In spite of the recent financial crisis and the economic slowdown in Japan and other East Asian countries in the past decade, their recovery has been noteworthy.

Over the past 30 years, four small nations in East Asia—South Korea, Taiwan, Hong Kong and Singapore—have been exhibiting an impressive rate of economic growth that rivals that of Japan, and today they rank among the world's most successful economies. This group of nations, sometimes referred to as "NIEs" (newly industrialized economies) exports three times more than the entire subcontinent of Latin America. The smallest of the four, Singapore, exports more with its population of 3 million than does the entire subcontinent of India with its population of 1 billion. In 1997, the per capita GNP for Singapore was $27,000, while for India it

---

[1] Professor, California State University, Fullerton, USA.

[2] Associate Professor, Korea University, Seoul, Korea.

was only $340. In 1989, *Fortune* predicted that during the 1990s, the four NIEs and Japan together would compose a market as big as North America or Europe, and this prediction appears to have come true (*Fortune*, 1989).

Many explanations for East Asia's phenomenal growth have been offered. Since every international executive knows that local social values have much to do with the way business is conducted throughout the world, much attention has been focused on finding a cultural explanation. Hicks and Redding (1984) and Redding (1984) attribute the East Asian economic miracle to favorable combinations of several factors: economic policies, political and legal factors, and cultural factors deriving from the country's history, carried partly by its religions, and evident in social values and ideals. In the area of cultural explanation, much attention has been focused on the possibility that Confucian values — the common ethical thread among East Asian nations — have had a positive influence on East Asia's economic development. This notion is supported by McFarquhar (1980), who identifies Confucian ideology as a main reason for East Asian economic success. Hofstede (1988) further supports the role of culture, specifically Confucianism, in East Asia's prosperity. Likewise, Jones and Sakong (1980) support the notion that Korea's Confucian heritage is a major factor in Korea's rapid economic development. Others, however, have argued that Confucianism is as much a liability as an asset. The purpose of this paper is to identify, explore, and evaluate Confucianism's real effect on East Asia's economy.

II. Foundations of East Asian Values

Just as Western values have derived from the Graeco-Roman heritage, the basic social values of East Asia originated with Chinese civilization. While a number of religions, particularly Taoism and Buddhism, have influenced the basic values of Chinese civilization, none have had a deeper or more practical influence on daily life than the religious/philosophical system known as Confucianism. Over the centuries, Confucianism has become more than just a creed which Asians can consciously accept or reject. It has become an inseparable part of East Asian cultural identity. So deeply is it ingrained that most Asians are only dimly aware, at best, that their values represent anything more than just a part of their ethnic identity. As Deverge has said, "Confucianism is not a creed to be adopted or rejected, but an inseparable part of what it means to be Chinese." (Deverge, n.d.: p. 4) It is not surprising, then, to find that East Asian business practices and customs are just as deeply influenced by what Confucius taught as any other area of East Asian life.

Defining Confucianism is not a simple task. In spite of its pervasiveness, Confucianism is not a monolithic repository of unchanging truth, but is as highly complex and varied as the social fabric of the nations of Eastern Asia. The influence of Confucianism in Japan has been largely limited to the warrior ethic, differing significantly from the situation in the four NIEs, where Confucianism permeates the entire moral value system and lifestyle (Morishima, 1982; Pye, 1985; Reischauer and Fairbank, 1958). Thus, Confucianism is deeply rooted in Taiwan and Hong Kong, which are ethnically Chinese to the core, as well as in Singapore, where the Chinese are the ethnic majority. In Korea, Confucianism began as a borrowed ideology without ethnic roots, but it eventually became even more dogmatic and rigidly confined to a narrow orthodoxy than in China (Reischauer and Fairbank, 1958).

The depth of Confucianism's influence on most of East Asia is mind-boggling. It forms the foundation of all ethics and morality in business as well as social and personal life, detailing the attitudes and behavior appropriate to every type of human relationship, from the top to the bottom of the social order, from the most intimate family relationships to the most distant associations, and in every area of daily life. In the NIEs of East Asia, it can be said that one's character is evaluated solely on the basis of how closely one adheres to the social forms and attitudes Confucius prescribed. This kind of propriety is the sole measure of one's virtue.

III. The Nature of Confucianism

1. A Formula for Relationships

According to Oh, "Confucianism is concerned with the correct observance of human relationships within a hierarchically oriented society" (1991: p. 46-56). The teachings of Confucius revolve around what are known as the "Five Cardinal Relationships" : father/son, monarch/subject, husband/wife, elder brother/younger brother, and friend/friend. Four of these relationships are hierarchically structured, and in each, the proper attitude of the subordinate party is prescribed. The proper attitude of the son towards the father is one of "filial piety" (a kind of self-sacrificing devotion and respect), the proper attitude of a subject is loyalty; of a wife, obedience to the husband; and of a younger brother, respect for his elder. Only within a friendship relationship can two people appropriately relate on an equal footing. Between friends, an attitude of mutual sincerity is considered appropriate.

2. Family First

The importance of the family in the Confucian value system is immediately apparent: of the five basic relationships, three involve the relationship of family members. To carry the emphasis even further, Confucianism teaches the "Model of Two," comparing and pairing the monarch/subject relationship to the father/son relationship, and the friend/friend relationship to that of brothers. From a very early age, people growing up in East Asia's NIEs are taught these values, which are characterized by exclusiveness in dealing with others (Hsu, 1984). While Confucian concepts of self-discipline and of the government of families and the nation form the basic principles of political philosophy in the NIEs of East Asia, the main emphasis in those societies is still on family relationships. Some of the more elaborate family customs and traditions have been modified by necessity in industrialized urban areas, but for the most part, they still observe the great family rites of Confucius much as they always have.

3. About Hierarchy and Harmony

The goal and purpose of establishing a rigid hierarchy of relationships has been to create and maintain a harmonious collective social order. Maintaining absolute loyalty and obedience to authority and fulfilling the obligations within relationships is supposed to guarantee an ordered collectivity in which overt conflict is absent. The emphasis on harmonious group life so widespread in East Asia today is a direct result of the value and importance Confucius placed on rigid hierarchical order.

In East Asia's NIEs, the Confucian principle of hierarchical order is the underlying cause for the predominantly vertical nature of the relationships in business organizations. The emphasis on obedience to authority certainly can be expected to affect the way individuals react to orders from their superiors in business organizations.

4. About Obligations

China and Korea emphasize the obligations of subordinates to superiors and say little or nothing about obligations of superiors towards subordinates. Japan differs by emphasizing the reciprocal nature of responsibilities in hierarchical relationships. This probably explains why Japanese companies tend to exhibit more employee solidarity and loyalty than Korean and Chinese companies do. In NIEs, the responsibilities of superiors are not usually stipulated in a clear-cut manner. Traditional morals were molded by a feudal society in which the rights of the ruled were ignored. Superior positions were for taking, not for giving. Consequently, being in a position of power is a very important goal in business, government, and other areas of life (Liebenberg, 1982).

5. About Formalities

One of the most striking characteristics of Confucian society is its formalism. Socialization in Confucian societies consists largely of teaching the stylized responses appropriate to every situation. Individuals are judged entirely by the way they fit into the prescribed patterns for interpersonal relations. Being polite means adhering to the prescribed formal model, and is the sole measure of one's virtue.

The well-known concept of face is directly related to formalism. When the group has confidence that individuals can be depended on to fit into the prescribed patterns at all times and on all occasions, they are said to have "face." If they should ever fail to meet these expectations, they have lost "face,"– which means they have lost the cooperation of their group, and have, in effect, lost everything worth having. Losing face is the ultimate social disaster in East Asian society.

The effect of loss of face is the feeling of shame. Shame, a direct result of violating Confucianism's formal requirements, is a major tool in the training and discipline of children in East Asia's NIEs. As adults, the feeling of shame continues to result from violations of the formal code (Bond, 1991).

Formalism sometimes leads to difficulties in organizational life. Because communication patterns outside one's own clan are highly ritualistic, it is difficult to communicate honestly in those areas. Impressive job titles are an important motivational tool, and employees often bear different job titles for external and in-house use in order to satisfy the demands of formalism. The emphasis on external appearances oftentimes presents a false face to outsiders while the true face is revealed only within the clan. Western society deplores this double standard and calls it deception and hypocrisy, but in Confucian society it is perfectly acceptable behavior, often implicitly encouraged for the clan's advantage.

6. The Value of Education

Education has long played a highly important role in Confucian tradition. Within Confucian societies of the past, the main qualification for leadership was "virtue," a quality that could only be acquired through intense, long-term study of the teachings of Confucius. Academic achievement was measured by a series of landmark examinations that determined young people's educational and personal futures within their society. The educational method involved much rote learning and copying of examples, with the development of theoretical and logical reasoning playing a minor role.

Education is still the pathway to power in East Asia today. Young people are highly motivated to obtain it, and diplomas and degrees are deeply respected achievements, still representing an important component of virtue. The method of education still places the major emphasis on accumulating a vast store of knowledge through rote memorization, producing a work force better suited to the regimentation of the manufacturing and service industries than to more innovative and creative fields like software development and biotechnology. The field of study chosen is of secondary importance: education in "virtue" as represented by a prestigious education is still considered a more important quality for a leader than technical competence or professional expertise. At times, the type of educational preparation some Asian businessmen have for their jobs may seem inappropriate to Westerners.

7. Family First in the Business Setting

The heavy emphasis on family so characteristic of Confucian tradition has made its impress on business life in East Asia in different ways. In Japan, the biological family plays a relatively minor role in national life, compared to other areas of East Asia. Instead, the *concept* of family has been transferred to the work environment, so that the work organization functions very much like a family in many ways, with corporate leaders playing the role of father and subordinates expressing attitudes of filial devotion.

Since the biological family in East Asia's NIEs is the single most important institution in the society, corporations are usually owned and operated by biological families as well (Business Groups in Taiwan, 1984; Chang, 1988).

IV. Negative Effects of Confucianism on East Asian Business

1. The Downside of "Family First"

While intense devotion to the family contributes a certain warmth to everyday social relations, it does have its disadvantages. Chang (1988) has observed a number of problem areas in Korean organizational behavior which tend to derive from the Confucian emphasis on family and personal friendships in Korean society.

When dealing with people outside their own personal family-type reference groups, Koreans tend to be highly individualistic. While most Korean corporations are family-owned, the corporations do not operate socially as families like they do in Japan. Motivation in Korean firms revolves around money, status and personal power, and personal advancement is highly competitive. Interpersonal trust and company loyalty are noticeably lacking, and personality-based factionalism is rampant. Good connections—with relatives or old school friends—are considered important stepping stones to personal achievement. The constant jockeying for position and power gives rise to a great deal of instability, and Korean executives tend to shoot for short-term goals rather than long-term planning.

As Liebenberg (1982) has pointed out, since the Confucian clan system dictated a narrow range of loyalty, Koreans have developed no sense of obligation to outsiders. As a result, they are good at competition, ruthless in opposition, and very poor at compromise and cooperation. The Korean mass media reports that some of Korea's most urgently needed organizational improvements are the separation of ownership and management, the development of professional management and managers, the elimination of familistic, paternalistic, and authoritarian personnel management practices, and the promotion of labor-management cooperation.

The situation with regard to family is much the same in the ethnically Chinese NIEs as in Korea. Teamwork is the relational style within the family, but in non-family business relationships, the Chinese tend to behave individualistically. The cooperative aspects of the family concept are not transferred to the society as a whole, with a resulting lack of social consciousness. Because of the dichotomy between family and non-family interests, Confucian society is in reality ruled by two sets of standards: family standards and public standards. Adherence to family standards, which takes precedence, often requires hypocrisy in the public domain, with lying an accepted means of protecting the family and maintaining the family reputation. No value is attached to the relational transparency which is so highly desirable in the West, so it is nearly impossible for someone brought up in the Confucian value system to conceive of being "transparent" in relationship with Westerners.

The family tradition has a strong negative effect on the longevity of business firms in East Asia's NIEs. There is a proverb that says "No family can stay rich for more than three generations," and much evidence supports it. In Hsu's (1986) study of 25 indigenous firms in Singapore, only one has been run by a single family for three generations. One reason that has been suggested is that the norms and traditions developed by family firms are in direct conflict with individual merit and rational organizational development. Objective impersonality is suppressed by family emotion and custom, inhibiting the rational growth of the organization (Parsons, 1949; Weber, 1951).

Unproductive inheritance of power and fortune

Another reason for the short life of family-owned business firms in East Asia's NIEs is the practice of inheritance among male heirs. In the Chinese family, the inheritance is equally divided among all sons while in Korea it more often goes to the eldest son than to the younger sons, but in both cases, business firms' ownership is inherited regardless of qualifications. In the extended family system practiced in family firms, father-son and brother-brother relationships play a critical role in management and decision-making, regardless of the age or competence of the decision-maker. The inner family circle tightly maintains its exclusive control of the firm.

As firms are passed from one generation to the next, a typical pattern can be observed. As the second generation matures and succeeds to the family fortune, a cycle of fragmentation begins. Multiple siblings attempt to share ownership in a going business and find themselves unable to break up the enterprise due to loss of economies of scale. Conflict erupts over shares of inheritance and power struggles develop into cliques battling for spheres of influence. A third generation matures and further fragmentation occurs. Under these circumstances it is very rare in East Asia's NIEs for a firm to survive for 200 or even 100 years, as is common in Japan (Wong, 1985; "South Korean Conglomerates," 1987).

Lack of trust between family members and non-family employees

Non-family employees of family-owned firms in East Asia's NIEs are in an unfortunate position. Permanently excluded from the inner circle, whose authority is unchallenged, they are seldom trusted, and feel alienated. What loyalty they do develop is directed towards their individual superiors rather than towards the organization. If the boss goes, the organization experiences the loss of all personnel who were loyal to him. When this happens, the organization suffers the loss of much accumulated experience. This kind of disenchantment and alienation is widespread in East Asia's NIEs. In Korea, the annual voluntary separation rate is 20%.

The lack of trust implicit in this system of doing business can have profoundly negative effects on economic welfare. Fukuyama (1995) makes a strong argument that economic success is determined by the moral bonds of social trust within a culture. Social trust facilitates transactions, empowers individual creativity, and justifies collective action. Trust, as social capital, is as important as physical capital, and cultural differences in social trust will be the ultimate determinants of economic success in global competition. Fukuyama sees Confucian society as characterized by a low level of trust, which impedes economic and social growth, but makes exception for Japan, which he classifies as a high trust nation.

The alienation between the family and its hired employees is reflected in, and enhanced by, gross salary differentials. In Korea, heads of family-owned enterprises earn more than 200 times as much as newly-hired college graduates, while in Japan, heads of firms make only about 10 times more than most junior members of their staff and just 4 times more than the salary of middle-aged workers (Fingleton, 1995).

2. The Downside of Harmony

According to Confucius, the highest achievement is harmony among individuals and between humans and the universe. The problem is that the harmony prescribed by Confucius is a harmony that is confined to unity and stability, within the context of a rigorous social hierarchy. It says very little about how to tackle disagreement, controversy or conflict, for they are rarely permitted to be acknowledged or expressed. Higher authority simply prevails, but it can never prevail fully over the inner emotional dissatisfaction of those whose interests have been denied and whose opinions have been discounted. The result is a hypocritical organization, that looks harmonious on the outside, but is seething with dissatisfaction on the inside.

This kind of harmony leads to a conformity that leaves no room for autonomy and creativity. Enforced harmony, masquerading as discipline, was a strength when manufacturing production was the most important area of the economy, but in today's world, where breakthrough ideas for products and services are critical components of productivity, conformity in an organization leads to deadly stagnation. Forced consensus and harmony produces workers who follow the same rationale, use the same language, accept the same assumptions, and are unwilling to take the risk of producing an original idea (Zhu, 1998).

3. The Downside of Obligations without Mutuality

Almost every society has some degree of hierarchy in at least some of its social relationship. One characteristic that distinguishes the Confucian hierarchy from other social hierarchies is the lack of superior-to-subordinate obligations required by the system.

Carried over into family relationships, the lack of superior-to-subordinate obligations has led to parental behavior patterns that sometimes border on the sadistic. Parents often feel free to demand what they will of their children, without considering the effects of their demands on their offspring, and children are expected to fulfill all demands cheerfully and without complaint as an expression of filial piety. The superior status of the father is well defined and unassailable, ranking him together with Heaven, Earth, the Emperor, and teachers. One Korean psychiatrist has termed filial devotion "moral masochism" in which filial piety functions as a defense mechanism to counteract the sadistic demands of totalitarian parenting (Cho, 1983).

In the society as a whole, the lack of superior-to-subordinate obligations has led to dysfunction in several respects. As children in East Asian NIEs grow up, they are severely restrained in their communication with their parents, leading at a later time to difficulty in communicating with all persons in authority. And just as Confucian children must repress hostility towards parents, so must subordinates repress hostility towards their superiors. The result, at home and away, is the displacement of hostility downward to the lower ranks in the hierarchy.

Mistrust and lack of delegation

This system, applied to business organizations, promotes a pervasive distrust from top to bottom. Managers hesitate to delegate authority to subordinates, limiting their opportunities to develop as managers. The higher the authority, the more absolute it becomes, and the greater the responsibility, the less willingness there is to delegate. As a result, decision-making is highly centralized. As Pye has observed, the "...ideal of omnipotent authority still persists, making divisions of responsibility awkward and the delegation of duties ambiguous" (Pye, 1985).

Co-dependency

The experience of playing a consistently subordinate role within this system gives rise to many powerful negative emotions and to maladaptive coping behaviors which exact a high psychological toll from the individual as well as the society as a whole. The maladaptive coping behaviors this system encourages look very much like the behaviors that have come to be called "co-dependency" in Western psychological literature. Around 1979, the concept of co-dependency began to appear with growing frequency in American psychological literature. Early definitions of the maladaptive behaviors the concept describes were developed within the context of alcoholism, but the concept gradually enlarged to encompass many other types of dysfunctional behavior as well. Eventually co-dependency came to be broadly defined as "a set of maladaptive, compulsive behaviors learned by family members to survive in a family experiencing great emotional pain and stress... Behaviors... passed on from generation to generation." A co-dependent is said to be "a person who has let someone else's behavior affect him or her, and is obsessed with controlling other people's behavior" (Beattie, 1989). Wegscheider-Cruse has (1985) characterized co-dependence as "a specific preoccupation and extreme dependence (emotionally, socially and sometimes physically) on a person or object. Eventually this dependence on another person becomes a pathological condition that affects the co-dependent in all other relationships." Behavior traits developed as a result of co-dependency in a family setting can be carried over into the workplace and affect the co-dependent's relationships with the people he or she supervises (Goff & Goff, 1988).

Beattie (1989) lists a number of traits she has observed to be common among co-dependents. One is the tendency to focus on others while ignoring self. Another is an inability to communicate reality to oneself or others. Characteristic emotional traits are worry and anxiety, and feeling angry and victimized. Other traits describe attempts to escape the pain of their condition such as looking for happiness outside of oneself, staying busy, becoming a workaholic, or becoming addicted to alcohol, drugs, achievement, gambling, religion, etc.

In the West, family systems that produce co-dependents are characterized by extreme imbalances of power, usually in the hands of an addict, which leaves the rest of the family to cope with the extreme frustration of powerlessness. In rigid Confucian societies, the total imbalance of power in the system appears to generate types of maladaptive and potentially self-destructive behaviors within the family as well as other groups in the society that look very much like the traits Beattie described. Filial piety encourages putting the focus on the father or superior and ignoring self. Absolute authoritarianism totally represses honest communication. Emotional needs of subordinate individuals are not met, and the result is anger that is either repressed or displaced. Dependency on alcohol, drugs, gambling or other escapes from pain and despair such as overwork and obsession with achievement are widespread. And when these remedies fail, death from stress-related illness is often the final outcome. Oh (1990) has analyzed and examined the relationship between the Western concept of co-dependency and the social ills prevalent in Confucian societies in detail.

4. The Downside of Formalities

While formalism is a very useful trait in establishing and maintaining harmony, predictability and stability in an organization, business people with very formal traditions tend to display a lack of adaptability when faced with unexpected and unprecedented events and situations, and they tend to find new faces—particularly Western faces from alien cultures—unsettling. The social distance inherent in formalism impedes honest and straightforward communication and delays the speedy development of new relationships that can be so important in the fast-paced business life of the West.

5. The Disadvantages of the Educational System

East Asia's highly demanding educational system develops in its young people a kind of discipline which prepares them well for future learning. They are well equipped for the demands of the heavy on-the-job training that goes with enterprise life, at least in the manufacturing sector. Having submitted themselves to school standards all their lives, they readily submit themselves to company standards as adults. However, in order to sustain an upward economic course within Confucian countries, the Confucian educational system, and the management systems it supports, will need to adapt to the demands of the contemporary world economy. In the past, the production of "hardware"—quantifiable, measurable, tangible production—has been the basis of the world economy, and this kind of production has flourished under the kind of educational and management system Confucianism has produced. But in today's world, the production of "software"—ideas, concepts, inventions and services that sell—is of increasing importance in determining the economic health and growth of a society. Unfortunately, Confucian educational systems do not promote the kind of positive, analytical, creative and original thinking that produces such "software" and Confucian management systems do not encourage it.

V. Summary and Conclusions

This paper has described a number of ways in which Confucian tradition has hindered effective economic activity. Redding has long argued that Confucianism has played a positive role in East Asia's economic miracle. Citing Kahn (1979), he has named several East Asian traits which derive from Confucian tradition as contributors to organizational success: intense family socialization promoting sobriety, a high level of education, the acquisition of skills, and seriousness about one's tasks, jobs, family and other obligations. He argues that the tendency to be cooperative within one's group has made East Asians good at teamwork in many instances. He sees respect for hierarchy and a sense of its naturalness as supporting the smooth exercise of authority.

This article reveals, however, that Confucianism has its dark side as well. Depending on circumstances, it can easily become more of a liability than an asset. The preeminence of family ties tends to lead to dishonesty and neglect of the public good. The emphasis on hierarchy and harmony can squelch creativity and leave conflict unresolved. The lack of superior-to-subordinate obligations creates an imbalance of power that is a threat to emotional health and well-being of individuals and to the collective welfare. The reliance on formality to guide human behavior creates a lack of adaptability to the unexpected and unprecedented encountered in the outside world. The emphasis on rote learning in the educational system fails to develop the critical thinking skills and creative capacity necessary for success in the contemporary global economy.

Pye (1998) has argued that what were once seen as Confucian virtues can just as easily lead to vice: "...the world has now found that the virtues of frugality, hard work, family values, respect for authority and close business-government cooperatives can become the vices of compulsive greed, single-minded inflexibility, nepotism, and outright corruption." The recent Asian economic crisis has pulled back the curtain of apparent prosperity just far enough for the Western world to get a glimpse of some of these dirty little behind-the-scenes secrets. The same cultural patterns that once appeared to promote economic prosperity now seem to have been responsible for its disasters as well. The liabilities of Confucianism described in this paper may provide some explanation for this paradox.

References

Beattie, M. (1989). *Beyond Codependency and Getting Better All the Time*. San Francisco: Harper & Row.

Bond, Michael H. (1991). *Beyond the Chinese Face: Insights From Psychology*. Hong Kong: Oxford University Press.

Business Groups in Taiwan, 1983-84. Compiled by China Credit Information Service Ltd.

Chang, Chan S. (1988). *Chaebol*, the South Korean conglomerates. *Business Horizons*, Mar-April.

Cho, D. A. (1983). Psychoanalytic study on *hyo* (filial piety) in oriental legends of filial children. *Korean Journal*, Vol. 23, No. 7.

Deverge, M. Confucianism: a guide for yesterday and tomorrow. Unpublished ms., n. d.

Fingleton, E. (1995). *Blindside*. New York: Houghton Mifflin.

Fortune. (1989). Fall, p. 11.

Fukuyama, F. (1995). *Trust: the Social Virtues and the Creation of Prosperity*. New York: Free Press.

Goff, J. Larry, and Patricia J. Goff. (1988). Trapped in co-dependency. *Personnel Journal*, December.

Hicks, G. and Redding, S. G. (1984). The story of the east Asian Economic Miracle', Parts I & II. *Euro-Asian Business Review*, Vol. 2, nos. 3 and 4.

Hofstede, Geert, and Michael Harris Bond. (1988). The Confucius connection: From cultural roots to economic growth. *Organizational Dynamics*, Vol. 16, No. 4, pp. 4-22.

Hsu, Paul S. (1984). The influence of family structure and values on business organizations in oriental cultures: A comparison of China and Japan. *Mimeo*.

Hsu, Paul S. (1986). Interpersonal relationships among family members in the Chinese firm as a function of generation. *Proceedings*, the Academy of International Business, Southeast Asia Regional Conference.

Jones, L. P. And Sakong, I. (1980). *Government, Business and Entrepreneurship in Economic Development: The Korean Case*. Cambridge, MA: Harvard University Press.

Kahn, H. (1979). *World Economic Development: 1979 and Beyond*. London: Croom Helm.

Liebenberg, Rualeyn Dereck. (1982). Japan incorporated' and the Korean troops: A comparative analysis of Korean business organization. Master's thesis, University of Hawaii.

Lim, UngKi. (1985). Ownership and control structure of Korean firms, with application of agency cost theory. *Mimeo*, April.

MacFarquhar, R. (1980). The post-Confucian challenge. *The Economist*, Vol. 9, pp. 67-72.

Morishima, Michio.(1982). *Why Has Japan Succeeded?* Cambridge: Cambridge U\niversity Press.

Oh, Tai K. (1990). Post-Confucian values in Korea and their psychological toll on Korean workers An exploratory study. *Proceedings*, Academy of International Business, Southeast Asia Regional Conference, Hong Kong, June.

Oh, Tai K. (1991). Understanding managerial values and behavior among the gang of four: South Korea, Taiwan, Singapore and Hong Kong. *Journal of Management Development*, Vol. 10, No. 2, pp. 46-56.

Parsons, Talcott. (1949). *The Social Structure of the Family in The Family: Its Function and Destiny*. R. N. Anshen. (eds.). New York: Harper.

Pye, L. W. (1985). *Asian Power and Politics*. Cambridge, MA: Harvard University Press.

Redding, S. G. (1984). Operationalizing the post-Confucian hypothesis: the overseas Chinese case. *Mimeo*.

Reed, J. D. (1989). Melody Beattie helps anguished readers kick the codependency habit. *People Weekly*, Vol. 32, p. 89.

Reischauer, Edwin O. and John K. Fairbank. (1958). *East Asia, the Great Tradition*. Boston: Houghton Mifflin.

South Korean Conglomerates. (1997). *The Economist*, Dec. 13.

Weber, Max. (1951). *The Theory of Social and Economic Organization*, translated by A. Henderson and T. Parsons. New York: Oxford University Press.

Wegscheider-Cruse, S. (1985). *Choice-Making for Do-Dependents, Adult Children and Spirituality Seekers*. Pompano Beach, FL: Health Communications.

Wong, S. L. (1985). The Chinese family firm: A model. *British Journal of Sociology*, Vol. 36, Mar.

Zhu, Zhichang. (1998). Confucianism in action: Recent development in oriental systems methodology. *Systems Research and Behavioral Science*, Mar-April. Vol. 15, No. 2, p. 16.

Asian Management Styles?
The Evidence from Korea[1]

Dennis P. Patterson[2]

I. Introduction

Why the nations of East Asia had grew so rapidly in the postwar period is a question that has attracted the attention of numerous scholars and journalists, and, over the last three decades, attempts to answer this question became a virtual growth industry. Many explanations have been offered for what has come to be known as the Asian miracle, and, as a result, it is difficult to categorize this writing in a way that accurately captures the various ideas that have been propounded. In spite of this, we can say that explanations for the rapid industrialization of East Asia in the postwar period have emphasized how the East Asian experience has been distinctive much more than how the nations of the region modeled themselves after the developed nations of the West.[3]

---

[1] I am thankful to Nic vande Walle and numerous conference participants for helpful comments.

[2] Assistant Professor, Michigan State University, USA.

[3] On these labels, see in particular Johnson (1982), Deyo (1987), Prestowitz (1988), and Fallows (1994).

Consequently, what has emerged is a view of economic development in Asia that is not simply different from the process elsewhere in the world but more importantly one that challenges our standard understanding of why it occurs in the first place.[4]

This ostensibly unique Asian approach to economic development has been given many names and, among the most prevalent, are neomercantilism, developmental statism, and Confucian capitalism.[5] Many factors are said to figure into this unique Asian approach to economic development, and perhaps the most important is strong state involvement in the industrialization and economic development processes that is driven by a nationalistic desire to catch up with, and even surpass, the world's other developed nations. State involvement is defined by an interrelated set of policies that attempts to, among other things, nurture the development of leading-edge, internationally competitive firms in high "value added" sectors by ensuring them a beneficially asymmetric access to corporate finance and trade protection and promotion.

Many specific policy tools have been employed by the states of Asia to advance this economic development agenda, and because the nations of the region experienced rapid rates of economic growth for a large portion of the postwar period, evaluations of this Asian approach have been universally positive.[6] The positive evaluations that exist have emphasized various aspects of the way that these nations have managed their economic development, and one notable focus concerned the idea that the Asian

---

[4] The reference here is to what is known as revisionism. For an introductory look at the revisionist view in the Japanese context, see Johnson (1995) and for Asia more generally see Deyo (1987) and Fallows (1994).

[5] For an overview of different models and theories of Asian economic development, see Calder (1993).

[6] There have certainly been criticisms of Asia's rapid economic developers, but these have focused mostly on their social and political practices and not their economic performances per se.

approach encouraged the development of a uniquely Asian style of management. Indeed, if one were to read the popular and scholarly business press in the 1970s and 1980s, one would readily notice an increasing amount of attention devoted to what was understood as a distinct school of Asian management.[7]

Asian-style management involves a number of features that vary from country to country as well as over time, and these different features have received different levels of emphasis from the scholars and journalists who have become its promoters. Despite this, certain features appear to be common to all discussions because of how they are touted as having generally positive impacts on economic development. Among the most of important of these features are those involving labor-management relations, especially lifetime employment and high levels of employee involvement in firm decision making, as well as other features that relate more directly to firm production processes such as quality control circles and just-in-time inventory management. While these are the most notable features of the model, there are certainly other features of Asian-style management that are difficult to ignore, including the idea that managers of Asian firms tend to be more representative of individuals trained in science and engineering than is typically found in Western firms, especially those of the United States.

Differences of emphasis exist to be sure, but what can be said is that, taken together, the features that define Asian-style management converge around a different model of firm behavior than is found in the neoclassical framework and that this different model of firm behavior has been at the heart of the Asian economic miracle. There are many characteristics that

---

[7] Writers have emphasized different aspects of this Asian style of management and, as a result, have given it different names. For example, writing about the manner in which management-labor relations are organized in large companies, William Ouchi (1981) referred to it as Theory Z while Peter Drucker, (1987) concerned about the way that Asian nations were engaging in international trade, coined the term, adversarial versus competitive trade.

describe this supposedly unique behavior of Asian firms but perhaps none more notable than those associated with firm profits and management time horizons. It is argued in many treatises that Asian-style management allows individuals in management positions to focus on long-term goals like market share maximization and value added maximization while managers in U.S.-style firms focus on short-term goals such as profit maximization. The reason for this differential in time horizons and corporate goals is said to derive from the contrasting ways that Asian and Western firms are structured and treat their respective work forces. Through such above-mentioned policies as lifetime employment and quality control circles as well as other methods of involving labor in firm decisions, Asian-style management builds employee loyalty because members of their respective work forces find their individual livelihoods tied to that of the firm, allowing if not encouraging management to take the longer term view. U.S. firms, on the other hand, treat employees much more as disposable resources which works to discourage their long-term loyalty to the firm and, thus, forces managers to behave in accordance with a short-term time horizon.

These features were long accepted not only as accurately describing management behavior in Asian firms but also as playing a positive role in the postwar economic rebirth of the nations of Asia. The Asian economic crisis of the 1990s, however, has forced proponents of Asian-style management to reexamine whether or not they oversold the effectiveness of the model if not the manner in which it was said to capture Asian corporate behavior as well. It is unfortunate that it took a severe economic crisis to force such a reexamination because there have been good reasons all along to suspect that the essential features of Asian-style management have been artifacts of the economic and other conditions that Asian firms have faced throughout the postwar period.

It is not coincidental that, in the 1990s, firms across Korea, Japan, and other parts of the region have been struggling to lower their break even points, like their U.S. counterparts did in the late 1970s and 1980s, and that such efforts has forced them to confront the issue of reducing the size of their workforces, something they reputedly would never do. The point is that the Asian economic crisis has raised a rather troubling question about Asian-style management. Specifically, if Asian firms are governed by different principles of management than their Western counterparts and this in turn has led them to follow a long-term trajectory whereby market share and value added are maximized rather than firm profits, then how is it that firms across the region now find themselves in the financial morass in which they are currently embroiled. The answer to this question is troubling in that it suggests that perhaps we never really understood Asian-style management in the first place, both how it came about and how it has actually been practiced.

This essay is dedicated to showing that this is exactly the problem with the concept of Asian-style management, and it will accomplish this task by showing how the concept itself has masked what are notably different management practices across the countries of Asia. This is particularly true for the case of Korea which not only deviated from many of the so-called features of Asian-style management but also for reasons that can be understood as a reaction by Korean firms to the economic incentives they faced over the last four decades. This effort begins with a more broadly-gauged discussion of Asian-style management itself, particularly its origins and applications as a concept and how its treatment in writing on Asian-style management corresponds to the actual developments that have defined the Asian economic development experience. Accomplishing this, however, temporarily takes us out of the Korean context to Japan where the concept was born, and, as will be demonstrated below, misunderstood and misapplied.

II. Asian Style Management: Japan's Misunderstood Corporate Governance System

Since Japan was the first Asian nation to achieve an economic miracle, it comes as no surprise that such things as lifetime employment, quality control circles, just-in-time inventory management, and close employee-management relations came to define Asian-style management through its own experience. Nonetheless, as the discussion provided above suggests, the argument promoting Japan as the nation responsible for developing Asian-style management is fraught with problems. First, while some features of Asian-style management are certainly visible in Japan, they do not describe the manner in which Japanese corporations are organized and behave nearly to the extent that the model suggests. For example, writing which has advanced the Japanese version of Asian-style management has not demonstrated clearly that such behavior as long-term market share maximization accurately described Japanese corporate (firm) behavior and that such behavior, to the extent that it has even occurred, was attendant to universally positive economic development results.

One aspect of the problem is that it is far from clear why the maximization of market share or value added should be preferable to profits or, in more accurate language, net present value maximization, which is hardly a short-term maximand and a more accurate way to understand firm behavior in the United States. In the neoclassical analysis of the firm, managers must put aside their own aversion to risk and maximize the net present value of the firm in a fashion that is risk neutral. This is because maximizing the net present value of the firm maximizes the value of claims on the firm (i.e. the firm's shares). Risk neutral management of a firm, while riskier than a strategy that manifestly avoids risk, will yield an overall greater net present value of the firm. Share holders needn't worry about this risk, since it can be diversified away through their portfolios. Managers, on the other hand, would prefer a risk averse strategy so as to maximize their tenure, but typically they will be unable to act on these preferences if an active takeover mechanism is present.

In spite of this intuitive economics-based understanding, proponents of Asian-style management nonetheless argue that market share and value added maximization constitute a kind of "strategic conquest," to use the words of Lester Thurow (1992), and, thus, are superior to the maximands of U.S. firms. Even if this were true, which the events of the 1990s say is not the case, there is a serious problem with the manner in which these ideas square with the economic realities Japanese companies have faced throughout the postwar period. Taking value added maximization for the moment, it must be remembered that a firm can maximize value added simply by buying raw materials and doing most of the processing in house, rather than buying processed materials on the market. In this sense, highly vertically integrated firms can be said to behave more like value added maximizers. In spite of this problem, Lester Thurow (1992), as a proponent of this view, asserts that Japanese firms are value added maximizers while recognizing that they tend to use networks of suppliers rather than vertical integration as U.S. firms have done.

What Thurow and others advocating his point of view have missed is that US firms are generally closer to value added maximization model than their Japanese counterparts since they tend to be more highly vertically integrated. The problem here is really one of simply failing to understand the definitions one is using. Thurow and many other proponents of Asian-style management became fixated on value added concepts without managing to understand them. Paul Krugman in his 1996 collection of essays, *Pop Internationalism*, carefully attacks this value added fixation and correctly notes that much of what proponents of this view assert to be high value added industries are not necessarily so. By showing that, in the United States, the highest value added firms are cigarette manufacturers, Krugman poignantly illustrates that value added in a firm is really a measure of the relative value of raw materials versus outputs and not firm strength and success.

Similar conceptual problems can be found in other aspects of the writing on Asian-style management, particularly those features that combine to give Japanese (Asian) management its ostensibly unique qualities. As was stated briefly above, when one subjects the operation of the Japanese economy to strict empirical scrutiny, one readily sees that the specific features that are said to define Japanese-style management are not nearly as prevalent as proponents have suggested. For example, lifetime employment which has been taken as synonymous with Japanese management applies only to large firms in Japan and, as a result, 30% of the labor force at most. Moreover, even in firms where lifetime employment is practiced and where the takeover mechanism is weak, managers still tend to perform in a risk averse fashion so as to maximize their own tenure with the firm. The problem here is that it is far from clear as to why risk averse behavior motivated in such a fashion promotes a well functioning organization. Also, the assumption that Japanese firms, and all Asian firms for that matter, are organized and function in the way that the Asian-style management model suggests carries with it the assertion that Western firms represent something quite different. Unfortunately, the Western, neoclassical model of the firm does not emphasize short-term profit maximization but, as was stated above, the maximization of net present value which is by no means a short-term concept.

For the professional observer of Japan, the treatises on Japanese, and thus Asian, management are something of a mystery for the additional reason that they eschew addressing a vitally important question. With no formal business education to speak of, with home grown executives, and with no proper business literature dedicated to the concept of management techniques, how could it be that Japan became the hotbed of management science and organizational theory? The simple answer to this question is that such assertions about Japan are untenable. Most of the techniques described by proponents of Asian-style management actually had no particular names associated with them until they were given names by the foreign analysts. Moreover, where such techniques accurately describe

Japanese firms, they did not simply emerge spontaneously in Japan but rather were put into practice by managers there because there were clear economic benefits from doing so. This is extremely important because it implies that, the economic incentives that have existed in postwar Japan and which made a particular management technique viable, may not exist in other Asian countries. As a result of this, the application of many techniques is not a matter of management prerogative but rather a response to incentives, and this in turn implies that the wholesale transplantation of such techniques to other countries, as has been advocated by proponents of Asian-style management, can be wholly inappropriate and even counterproductive unless the economic incentives faced by firms in importing countries are the same.

Because the essential features of Asian-style management emerged originally in Japan as a result of the economic incentives that firms there faced, it is necessary that more attention be devoted to explaining how and why such management techniques emerged in Japan. As stated briefly above, despite the theoretical and empirical problems that exist in the literature on Asian-style management, there are at least some management practices that appear to be somewhat unique in an international context and which appear to be applied in a fairly widespread fashion across firms in Japan as well as other Asian nations. The key question, however, is how such practices emerged and developed in Japan when there was no widespread system of management training in place and when Japanese managers, at least in the early part of the postwar period, emulated their American counterparts. Addressing this question must begin with the notion that what emerged in Japan was not the result of management prerogatives as has been suggested in the literature on American-style management. This conclusion stems in part from the fact that formal management training is all but absent in Japan and in part from the fact that, until foreign management scholars made note of them, there was generally no specialized terminology to describe many of the techniques that combine to form Asian-style management. The fact is that the bulk of what has come to be described as Japanese, and thus Asian, management resulted from the economic incentives which were present during much of the postwar period and from the corporate governance structure which has characterized Japan over the same time period. To explore this more fully, a brief examination of the Japanese corporate governance structure is necessary.

A complete examination of corporate governance in Japan is beyond the scope of this essay,[8] but a directed examination of certain features of the Japanese system, on the other hand, will help make the point that it is the economic incentives faced by Japan's business leaders in the postwar period that are at the base of the country's corporate governance system rather than management prerogatives expressive of some unique system of Asian-style management. The first feature to be examined concerns what has come to be known as just-in-time inventory management within Japan's extensive system of subcontractor relations. The issue to be examined here is not that Japan is rather distinct in the extent of its subcontractor system but rather how such a distinctive system emerged and developed over time.

During the first five decades of this century, American firms generally became more vertically integrated, acquiring their suppliers in an attempt to end supply disruption and ensure quality control. For Japanese firms, where large scale can represent a cost disadvantage due especially to the high price of the country's short supply of land, incentives existed for companies to rely more intensively upon outside suppliers for their inputs. This was no doubt a rational solution to the cost problems associated with large scale production in Japan, but it is necessary to note that, at the same time, this solution carried with it the possibility of increased costs associated with the quality control of the inputs provided by subcontractors. This is a potentially serious problem, but if the parent firm has some degree of control or leverage over the supplier, then these quality related costs could be minimized. In Japan, this was accomplished

---

[8] For an excellent discussion of this topic, see Sheard (1996) and Aoki (1988 and 1989).

in a number of ways. In addition to the fact that subcontractors are dependent on the large firms for technology and sales, large firms also exerted control with the assistance of a main bank in a *keiretsu* grouping and through the fact that this kind of group affiliation could effectively serve to blacklist the sub-contractor in the event of failure to deliver quality inputs on time.

In the case of just-in-time inventory management then, what we have is a predictable response to the economic incentives that firms faced in the postwar period and not a unique technique that evolved through management prerogative. This is important to understand because it also captures the manner in which the other management techniques emerged in Japan as well. The failure of the management prerogative view and the evidence supporting the response to economic incentives idea is perhaps best illustrated with respect to employment practices in Japan and their two most prevalent features, lifetime employment and the close relationship between labor and management. However, if one is to understand how the specific patterns of labor relations in postwar Japan emerged, one must look to the system under which and the processes by which workers in Japanese firms, especially large Japanese firms, are trained.

The higher education system in Japan acts primarily as a screen. What this means is that the best students test into the best universities but then generally learn little beyond what they have already acquired by the end of their secondary education. This includes a relatively high level of math and language ability albeit what is learned is very general. As a result, the major course of study is typically of little interest to the ultimate employer at least in the case where that employer is a large firm. This means that the firm typically assumes that the student has acquired little beyond general education and the quality of the university serves only as a screen so that the firm can judge the basic intelligence and trainability of the candidate.

III. Asian-Style Management: The Case of Korea

As was shown above, because actual management practices in postwar Japan diverged from those techniques that allegedly constitute the model of Asian-style management, it would be expected that management practices in post-1953 Korea would also diverge from the model. Just how and to what extent management practices in Korea actually diverged from the ideal types indicative of the model will depend on the economic conditions that defined the period of its initially rapid industrialization and the incentives and constraints such conditions thrust upon corporate Korea at the time. Identifying such conditions and the influences they carried requires not only a specification of Korea's economic circumstances in the post-Korean War period but also a brief explanation of how corporate Korea was put together at the time with attention to the structure of its system of corporate governance.

In the wake of the Korean War armistice in 1953, the principal task facing all Koreans, citizen and leader alike, was that of not simply rebuilding the war-shattered economy but more importantly of putting into place a set of institutions that would encourage the development of strong, self-sustaining, internationally competitive economy. The principal reason for this was that, while the armistice ended the actual fighting between the North and South, it did not end the war, and Korea has remained in a virtual state of war ever since. While North-South tensions have been significantly reduced in the last couple of years, being in a virtual state of was since 1953 forced upon Korean leaders the need to develop the capacity to provide for its own security as rapidly as possible. As has been well documented in the literature on economic growth in Korea, this was accomplished through the development of an economic structure where the state strictly controlled access to finance that was asymmetrically funneled to the country huge industrial conglomerates or *Chaebol*.

The standard interpretation of the Korean *Chaebol* is that the military regime of Park Chung-Hee turned to a small number of individual entrepreneurs to realize the industrialization plans that his administration had formulated. While this is a generally accurate description of the Korean government's behavior, it does not explain why the government chose the path of large industrial conglomerates (*Chaebol*) as opposed to something else. How such an interpretation begs this important question becomes clearer when one considers the case of Taiwan during the same period of time. In the wake of the communist revolution in China, the new Nationalist government on Taiwan faced a similar set of security imperatives as Korea, but its approach led to a very different solution, something that is manifested in the structure of the Taiwanese economy even today. What evolved in Taiwan was an economic structure based on a large number of small and medium sized enterprises rather than the *Chaebol* pattern that defines the Korean economic structure. Among other things, this was because Taiwan's relatively larger entrepreneurial class and more extensively skilled population made the development of a small and medium sized enterprise economy the prudent and, thus, expected response to the conditions Taiwan faced at the time. On the other hand, the rather small entrepreneurial class in Korea, encouraged by several decades of Japanese occupation, coupled with the presence of a large peasant, and thus industrially unskilled, population rendered the *Chaebol* approach the most appropriate there.

Despite the fact that the *Chaebol* structure of the Korean economy evolved in accordance with the economic incentives that confronted public and private actors at the time, it is important to note that the Korean economy at the time looked quite similar to the structure of the Japanese economy in the late prewar period. At that time, the Japanese economy was dominated by large industrial combines known as *zaibatsu* which many have argued are the precursors to Japan's well-known postwar business groupings known as *keiretsu*. What is noteworthy here, however, is that the late prewar period in Japan also looks like Korea from the 1960s through the late 1908s because of the fact that both nations were governed by military regimes. This is interesting because it tells us that we should expect a strong and active government presence in the Korean economy that is similar to the strong, active, and increasingly militaristic governments that steered economic decisions in late prewar Japan. More than this, however, this Japanese-Korean similarity is striking because it tells us that, since the features of Japanese management practices that combined to form Asian-style management were essentially postwar phenomena, Korea should diverge from the patterns of Asian-style management in the two to three decades prior to democratization.

The system of labor relations in Japan where full-time employees are guaranteed a job for life in exchange for company loyalty and where workers enjoy a high level of participation in the decision making processes of the firm because of their being organized at the firm and not the trade or cross-firm skill level emerged in the postwar period. As mentioned above, this was undoubtedly due to the conditions that corporate Japan faced at the time, particularly those relating to the supply of labor and the kinds of skills its respective members brought to the respective jobs, but it was also due to one other factor that was not mentioned above. Specifically, Japan's particular pattern of labor relations evolved in a period of political democracy which means that its firms had to evolve workable arrangements with laborers since the Japanese government was much less able to quell labor disturbances with an iron fist in the postwar period than in its militarist days. Korea under Park Chung-Hee and subsequent authoritarian administrations was able to use its monopoly of force to subdue Korean labor, and, as a result, there is little expectation that Korea would have evolved a similar system of labor relations as that which evolved in Japan.

Concerning the other features of Asian-style management that were ostensibly developed in Japan, like just-in-time inventory management and quality control circles, expectations are not quite as clear. First, while such techniques have been attributed to corporate managers in Japan, they are in fact American techniques that were imported by Japanese corporations in the early postwar period. The point here is that economic actors in Korea were also highly influenced by the United States presence in the country a fact suggesting that the situation might be the same as in Japan. On the other hand, this might not quite be the case if economic conditions were different and because the Korean regime was quite authoritarian while postwar Japan was quite democratic. In light of these expectations and the questions they leave unanswered, it is necessary to examine such features of the Asian model of management and determine of they correspond to actual corporate practices in Korea.

Taking labor relations in Korea first, our expectation is that they should contrast sharply with what we witness in Japan. Political differences between the two countries constitute one reason but another concerns the fact that Korean *Chaebol* are structured quite differently from their counterparts in postwar Japanese *keiretsu* groupings. The principal distinction relates to differences in the concentration of management in the two nations' corporations. Because Korean *Chaebol* tend to be dominated by the families of their respective founders, owners and managers are less distinct and, thus, run their corporations in a way that favors the interests of owners.[9] This is quite different from Japanese corporations where management is not only quite dispersed but also in many ways insulated from the influence of shareholders.

There is another factor that points to the differences that exist between Japanese firms and Korean *Chaebol* and suggests strongly that management practices relative to labor relations in the two countries would be different. The factor referred to here concerns the supply of labor and the fact that it was, at least temporarily, much more abundant in Korea than in Japan, especially when one examines the supply of labor at the time of each's economic development take-off.[10] As Keun Lee (1993) explains, when modernization in Korea began, the supply of available labor was much more exten-

---

[9] For a discussion of these Korean and Japanese management differences, see Lee (1999), especially Chapter 3.

[10] For a discussion of Japan's labor supply and its impact on Japan's system of lifetime employment, see Reed (1995), especially Chapter 4.

sive than it was in Japan. This fact, combined with the other factors mentioned above, led to labor-management relations in Korea having been much less cooperative than they were in Japan. Consequently, labor-management in Korea have never been characterized by Japanese-style lifetime employment. The evidence for this is witnessed in the higher rates of turnover in Korean corporations and the generally higher levels of dissatisfaction expressed by Korean workers in surveys of worker attitudes.[11]

In spite of this, conditions in Korea that encouraged the type of labor relations that were initially practiced there have not been immutable, and, as a result, patterns of labor relations in Korea have been changing. Perhaps the most notable and important changes have come with the decision by the Roh regime to permit democratic elections to take place, putting the Korean regime on the path to democratization. It is no coincidence that labor has been much more active in its efforts to organize and press for better wages and working conditions since democracy became consolidated in Korea. Such changes have been dramatic to be sure, but Korean labor had experienced at least some improvement in its ability to achieve stability in its employment conditions before the country democratized. While Korean labor was plentiful when industrialization began, the supply tightened up as Korean economic growth took off and the economy expanded. As a result of this, Korean *Chaebols* have been forced to devote more resources to human capital development. As would be expected, since labor has become less abundant and *Chaebols* have invested more in their respective work forces, the long-term employment rate in Korea has continually risen.[12]

The other features of Asian-style management, quality control circles and just-in-time inventory management, can both be found in Korea. The latter has a much longer history of use in Korea than the former because it

---

[11] For example, see the data presented by Lee (1993) in Table 4.3 on page 46.

[12] See e.g., Steers, Shin, and Ungson (1989).

evolved out of the Korean subcontracting system in much the same way that it evolved in Japan. The former management technique, however, was introduced later in the postwar period, specifically, after industrialization had already begun. By the late 1970s, Korean firms were attempting to stave off the upward pressure on wages that had been building for some time. While government repression was certainly employed to help keep labor's demands in check, Korean firms also needed to increase the productivity of their respective workers if they were to remain internationally competitive. Among other things, Korean firms began employing quality control circles to accomplish this, and, interestingly enough, it was through Japanese consultants that quality control circles were introduced to firms in Korea.[13]

IV. Asian-Style Management: Prerogatives Versus Incentives

The essence of the Asian-style management view as outlined above is that Asian managers employed rather different techniques than is witnessed in other parts of the world and, as a result, outperformed their Western counterparts in a conspicuous fashion. Attendant to this view is the assumption that Asian management is more capable of responding successfully to a changing economic environment than is its Western counterpart. Indeed, authors like Thurow (1992) cite what would normally be characterized as negative shocks, such things as oil embargoes and the rapid realignment of currencies, as providing impetus for Asian managers to succeed. Unfortunately for this view, large numbers of firms throughout Asia have not fared well in the 1990s for exactly the same reasons that were previously cited as sources of their managerial strength.

As the nations of Asia, one by one, achieved remarkable rates of

---

[13] On QQC's, see e.g., Amsden (1989) passim.

economic growth and became economic powers in their own right, the rest of the world took notice. Neoclassical economists viewed this Asian phenomenon as an example of how growth in inputs, combined with growth in the productivity in those same inputs, could yield phenomenal results. Others, however, viewed the nations of Asia as anomalies that neoclassical economists could not explain. Part of this criticism of neoclassical economics, particularly as it is practiced in the United States, involved management specialists asserting that special factors that were unique to Asian managers were also responsible for the Asian economic miracle. As a result of this, management specialists flocked to Japan, Korea, and the other nations of Asia and studied what those managers were doing.

Much was learned to be sure, but it is unfortunate that the result of this research effort was also the very biased view that, if the Asians were doing something different than managers in the rest of the world, it must be "right." This bias was supported by the fact that the United States was undergoing its major postwar restructuring at the same time, something that supported the conclusion that whatever American managers were doing was "wrong." Consequently, the management literature became packed with concepts like quality circles, just-in-time inventory techniques, and techniques that involved more active development of human capital with the implication being that, if American mangers would simply adopt the same techniques, they too would become successful. The problem here, as explained above, is that this view ignored the role played by economic incentives and the impact they had on the development of the management techniques that came to be known as Asian-style management.

What must be kept in mind is that American firms had realized tremendous gains over the first 50 years of the 20th century from the vertical integration of production. Input producers were purchased and brought under the roofs of the parent firms. These mega firms made sense in that era and did not fall prey to significant diseconomies, at least not initially. The firms of Japan and Korea, on the other hand, had realized their economies of scale differently. Rather than integrate vertically, Japanese firms relied upon a vast network of small sub-contractors while Korean firms utilized what is perhaps best referred to as a combination of both approaches. In both cases, the different approaches used were designed to avoid many overhead labor costs and maintain production that was internationally competitive. Given the economic incentives they faced, the choices made by managers of Japanese and Korean firms made sense.

Unfortunately, the economic incentives faced by Korean and Japanese managers are now quite different from those that they faced in the past. The presence of too many producers in specific markets, growing labor costs, and the inability of firms to respond to a rapidly changing global economic environment because of organizational inertia, have left and will continued to leave many managers in Asian firms high and dry. This will mean dismantling such institutions in Japan as seniority and lifetime employment where they exist, and in Korea it will mean continuing to invest more in human resource development and perhaps providing more stability to employees as well as *Chaebol* divesting out of certain production processes. In other words, what Korean and Japanese firms are facing now is a structural adjustment that the United States faced over two decades ago. Based on the experience of the United States and other developed nations, it is well known that the transition will be painful, challenging the institutions and practices that ostensibly led to success in the past. Institutions and practices deemed outdated by the adjustment will undoubtedly have their defenders, and, to the extent that defenders are successful in protecting past structures and practices from the changes they will inevitably experience, the transition will be longer and more painful.

In spite of this, it is hoped that the foregoing discussion provides a way for policymakers to understand that the best approach to the current economic problems is a set of policies that promotes the restructuring process while, at the same time, ameliorating its social consequences. This is because, as was shown above, that many of the management techniques that ostensibly led to the rapid economic development of Korea and other Asian countries did not in fact operate in the way that the model suggests and actually evolved out of the economic incentives faced by corporations throughout the postwar period.

References

Amsden Alice. (1989). *Asia's Next Giant: South Korea and Late Industrialization.* New York: Oxford University Press.

Aoki Masahiko. (1988). *Incentives, Information, and Managing in the Japanese Economy.* New York: Cambridge University Press.

_____(1989). The nature of the Japanese firm as a nexus of employment and financial contracts: An overview. *Journal of the Japanese and International Economies.* 3. 4. pp. 323-350.

Calder Kent. (1993). *Strategic Capitalism.* Princeton: Princeton University Press.

Deyo Frederick. (ed.) (1987). *The Political Economy of the New Asian Industrialism.* Ithaca, NY: Cornell University Press.

Drucker, Peter. (1986). *Wall Street Journal.* April 1.

Fallows James. (1994). *Looking at the Sun.* New York: Pantheon Books.

Johnson, Chalmers. (1982). *MITI and the Japanese Miracle.* Stanford, CA: Stanford University Press.

_____(1995). *Japan Who Governs? The Rise of the Developmental State.* New York: W.W, Norton.

Lee Keun. (1993). *New East Asian Economic Development.* New York: M.E. Sharpe.

Ouchi William. (1981). *Theory Z: How American Business Can Meet the Japanese Challenge.* New York: Avon Books.

Prestowitz Clyde. (1988). *Changing Places.* New York: Basic Books.

Sheard Paul. (ed.) (1996). *Japanese Firms, Finance, and Markets.* Melbourne: Addison Wesley.

Steers Richard, Yoo Keun Shin, and Gerardo Ungson. (1989). *The Chaebol: Korea's New Industrial Might.* New York: Harper and Row.

Thurow Lester. (1992). *Head To Head: The Coming Battle Among Japan, Europe, and America.* New York: Morrow.

Determinants of Competitive Advantage in the Network Organization Form: A Pilot Study

Eonsoo Kim[1], Irene M. Duhaime[2], John C. Mc Intosh[3], and Sun-ah Yang[1]

I. Introduction

Different environmental conditions require different organizational forms to conduct the value creating activities necessary to generate competitive products and services. As we move deeper into the information age, globalization, hypercompetition, and falling costs of computing and telecommunications are eroding the effectiveness of organizational forms based on hierarchy and bureaucracy (Lipnack & Stamps, 1994). Some organizations respond to this fundamental shift by using their knowledge of resource utilization to experiment with new forms (Miles et al, 1997). In particular, many organizations are either creating or joining networks to cope with ever intensifying competition.

Although they differ significantly from traditional organizational forms, networks, like hierarchy and bureaucracy, are considered a form of

---

[1] Associate Professors, Korea University, Seoul, Korea.

[2] Professor, Georgia State University, USA.

[3] Assistant Professor, Bentley College, USA.

organization (Dow, 1988). In today's highly uncertain business environment, pressures for greater speed, scope, and flexibility outstrip the resources and capabilities of many firms. Consequently, some firms choose to participate in networks to access critical resources that are either too risky to acquire or are beyond their control (Hamel & Prahalad, 1996).

This exploratory study examines the determinants of performance among the three networks that comprise the Korean furniture industry. Prior to 1997, that industry was dominated by large firms, some of which were part of highly integrated conglomerates. However, cataclysmic environmental change precipitated by a region-wide economic downturn in 1997 and the stiff requirements of the subsequent IMF bailout package forced many of those firms into bankruptcy. Among the surviving firms, many of which possessed narrow competencies appropriate to a limited range of value chain activities, were those that had adopted a hub and spoke network form to create a virtual vertically integrated organizations.

Previous studies of the determinants and outcomes of network formation have examined themes such as the reasons for network formation and the possible outcomes that might arise from a network relationship. However, few studies have focused on the connection between the way networks are managed and overall network performance. The purpose of this study is to address this gap in the literature. Our unit of analysis is the network formed by firms rather than individual firms participating in the networks. This study extends corporate strategy research by utilizing a resources and competencies lens to study the determinants of performance differences among competing networks in the same industry. It explores the question: "Do performance differences among networks within the same industry arise from differences in the way networks are managed?"

This study is interesting in three ways. First, the industry presents a rare opportunity and natural laboratory to study how small firms, in an industry formerly dominated by large ones, respond to a cataclysmic environmental shift. In Korea, full-fledged networks of firms with competencies in different value chain activities are rare. This is because the Korean government has historically crafted economic and public policies that favor the large, vertically integrated *Chaebols*. Nevertheless, the economic downturn, stipulations in the International Monetary Fund's bailout package, and chronic overcapacity of the furniture industry triggered widespread bankruptcies. Some small firms survived perhaps in part because they had adopted a hub and spoke network form.

Second, the industry's reorganization into networks composed of firms with particular value chain competencies offers an opportunity to test contemporary thought advanced by the resource-based view of the firm and competence-based competition. Our study shows that networks were organized by a focal firm which controlled critical resources such as a brand or company name. These firms also used critical competencies, such as activity coordination, to attract and exploit the capabilities of smaller specialist firms which could not survive independently.

Third, this study is notable because it surveyed the firms that comprise all three of the industry's networks. This was possible because the industry is very small, it is localized in the Seoul metropolitan area, and participation by the executive director of each network encouraged member firms to complete the study's survey.

II. Prior Research

Research on networks can be traced back to the 1970s when authors such as Aldrich (1979) and Williamson (1975) considered them a form of inter-organizational relationships. It was not until a decade later that Thorelli (1986) made the connection between competitive advantage and cooperation among networked organizations. Early research considered networks a structural form that leveraged the strengths of both markets and hierarchies (Jarillo, 1988; Powell, 1990; Thorelli, 1986). Since then, most network research has focused on the dyadic relationship between organizations, and later on cooperation among multiple organizations.

Osborn & Hagedoorn (1997) identified three distinct perspectives on networks. The first, and oldest, primarily focuses on why firms form networks. This research stream employs an economic lens to explain how transaction costs, R&D expenditures, and the costs of overcoming geographic limitations create incentives for network formation (Hagedoorn, 1993; Parkhe, 1993; Sakakibara, 1997; Thorelli, 1986). The second perspective, known as the interorganizational field perspective, focuses on organizational learning through networks (Lei et al, 1997), the influence of factors such as characteristics of member organizations on network features (Dickson & Weaver, 1997; Gulati, 1995), and the network as institutional pressure (Human & Provan, 1997). The third and most recent perspective employs a corporate strategy lens to study the phenomenon. This research stream, which casts the network as a tool for implementing corporate strategy, focuses principally on the problems associated with managing networks (Hamel et al, 1989; Osborn & Hagedoorn, 1997).

1. Economics-based Perspective

One of the first streams of network research studied the economic causes and consequences of network formation. This stream, advanced by research in transaction costs, R&D alliances, and international business, is discussed below.

Transaction costs and networks

Transaction cost economics argues that one can understand the power and limitations of markets and hierarchies only by examining each in relation to the other. Rather than studying the costs of producing a particular technology, attention is focused on reducing transaction cost (Williamson, 1975). Networks, from this perspective, can be considered a structural form that resembles a market yet also offers the lower transaction costs associated with internal hierarchies.

Networks in R&D collaboration

In their study of R&D collaboration, Osborn & Hagedoorn (1997) used game theory to analyze the role of cooperation in interfirm competition. They noted that incentives for participating in cooperative R&D arose from two distinct motives: cost-sharing and skill-sharing. Sakakibara (1997) analyzed the circumstances under which either cost sharing or skill sharing became the dominant motive in R&D consortia. She demonstrated that the relative importance of the cost-sharing motive increased either when participants' capabilities were homogeneous or when projects were large. In contrast, skill sharing increased in relative importance when participants had heterogeneous capabilities.

International business perspective and networks

This research stream views a network as a temporary mechanism for expanding multinational enterprises. Mowery (1988), for example, discovered that cooperative networks helped cope with national political restrictions. Much of the work in international business has incorporated arguments from transaction cost economics, which focuses on the individual firm and its use of alliances and networks to reduce the net costs of conducting business. This research stream has been extended by Park and Ungson's (1997) study of longevity and performance in international alliances.

Interorganizational field perspective

Osborn and Hagedoorn (1997) claim that the interorganizational field perspective, the second dominant perspective on networks, is rooted in sociology and organizations research. Sociological studies such as Warren (1967) examined how government agencies and nonprofit organizations created alliances and networks. The organizational literature, in contrast, examined the interaction between an organization and its environment (Emery & Trist, 1965; Hannan & Freeman, 1989; Pfeffer & Salancik, 1978). Early research on organizations offered a foundation for subsequent studies on technology, organizational learning, social and individual dynamics, and institutionalization.

The interorganizational field perspective views alliances and networks as mechanisms that facilitate organizational learning to keep abreast of technological change. Unlike the other perspectives, this research stream acknowledges the importance of individuals in the functioning of networks. This research addresses the critical questions: "How and why common alliance practices emerge, are copied over time, and eventually become generally accepted practice" (Osborn & Hagedoorn, 1997: p. 272).

Corporate strategy perspective
In contrast to the relatively long history of economics-based study of alliances, corporate strategy-based studies are more recent. Although a cohesive theoretical perspective has yet to be developed, "most share the presumption that senior managers rationally select an alliance option and craft each alliance to further the immediate interests of their firms" (Osborn & Hagedoorn, 1997: p. 266).

From a strategic perspective, the evidence of alliance success is mixed. Managing networks without control is reported to be difficult (Ohmae, 1989). The competencies and experiences of senior managers are important in successfully running networks (Hamel et al., 1989). In spite of the recognized benefits of the network form, in practice they are frequently viewed as temporary inter-organizational arrangements that are very difficult to manage.

III. Networks from a Competitive Strategy Perspective

The main question behind network studies from the economic, corporate strategy, and interorganizational field perspectives is "Why do firms create networks?" Indeed, the underlying assumptions are that networks can be used as a competitive weapon, they reduce transaction costs, and they build participants' skills for cooperation and learning. While previous research has well explored the origin of networks, this study addresses the important and unanswered question: what is the connection between the way networks are managed and overall network performance?

Today's firms often face a fast-changing, unpredictable, and highly competitive business environment. One way of coping with this uncertainty is to create competitive options that address the most likely environmental outcomes. However, very few firms possess the resources to create a sufficiently wide range of strategic options. As a result, firms form and manage networks that enable them to draw on each other's strengths and competencies. Long term membership in these networks often leads to closer and closer integration among participants and mutually dependent outcomes. The study reported in this paper is based on the belief that a network's performance depends on how it is managed (Madhok & Tallman, 1998; Ring & Van de Ven, 1994). In particular, it asks the question: "Do performance differences among networks within the same industry relate to differences in the way networks are managed?"

Corporate strategy is concerned with determining and managing the set of product/market domains in which a firm wants to compete. Business strategy, more narrowly focused, addresses how the firm might build and leverage competitive advantage in each of the product/market domains approved by its corporate strategy. Strategy scholars who study networks have focused on aspects of corporate strategy, such as organization construction or the CEO's intention. However, it is implausible that mere formation of a network will automatically result in superior performance. In much the same way that differences in resource and capability endowments across firms lead to performance differentials, it is logical to conclude that differences in resource and capability endowments across networks, including the capability for and nature of network management, will lead to differences in performance. This may occur because the aggregate resources and capabilities of member firms will differ from network to network. The foregoing suggests that a study of networks from a business or competitive strategy perspective can be informative.

There are very few network studies from the competitive strategy perspective. Human & Provan's (1997) exploratory study of networks of small and medium-sized enterprises addressed performance enhancement of individual firms arising from network participation. Provan & Milward's (1995) study of effectiveness of four mental health delivery systems dealt with dyadic links rather than multifirm networks. The present study's comparison of the determinants of performance differences across networks represents a new approach.

IV. Research Arena

The network form investigated by this study is an alliance of small and medium-size firms performing related value chain activities in the same manufacturing industry Figure 1. The resulting network forms a virtually vertically integrated organization. Each of this study's three networks was formed by a coalition of furniture manufacturing firms which survived an industry shakeout precipitated by the Korean economic crisis. By forming a network around a central or hub firm (hereafter referred to as a central office), participating firms sought to compensate for their respective lack of resources and competencies in procurement, marketing, manufacturing skill enhancement, activity coordination, and information dissemination. The primary purpose of each network was to exploit advantages from activities such as joint marketing, joint purchasing, and joint production—a range of activities typically beyond the reach of individual firms.

This type of network, typically called a hub and spoke form because of the centrality of the central office firm and the specialized roles played by peripheral member firms, is also found around the world in industries such as footwear, women's bags, leather goods, textiles, wood products, and clothing. These industries tend to be populated by small firms that perform specific value chain activities. Inzerilli's (1990) study of networks in Northern Italy showed that the successful growth of the networks in footwear, leather, and fashion was fueled by small-size enterprises.

Figure 1. Network Type under Study

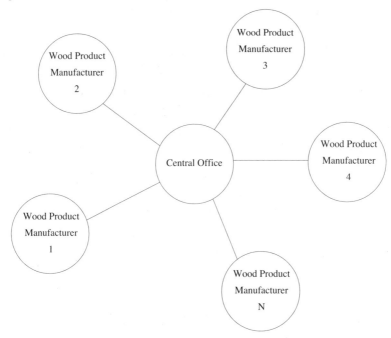

V. Research Hypotheses

This paper employs the definition of a network forwarded by Human & Provan (1997): "…intentionally formed groups of small- and medium-sized profit-oriented companies in which the firms (1) are geographically proximate, (2) operate within the same industry, potentially sharing inputs and outputs, and (3) undertake direct interactions with each other for specific business outcomes" (1997: p. 372). Although their study focused on individual firm performance, this paper assumes that Human & Provan's rationale for firm success can be applied at the network level. Comparing network firms with non-network firms, they found that network participants exhibited increased interactions, resulting in greater social capital, better information flows, greater access to business opportunities, and an increase in individual firms' competencies. Their study demonstrated that favorable outcomes for member firms were related to administrative aspects of network management that led to greater member involvement in the network.

Provan & Milward's (1995) comparative study of interorganizational networks of mental health service in four U.S. cities led to a preliminary theory of network effectiveness. Their study of four mental health delivery systems indicated that aspects of network structure and context, namely centralized integration, external control, stability, and resource munificence, explained differences in network effectiveness. In other words, network structure and dynamics, which govern the interaction among the focal firm and member firms, are success factors.

In this paper, structural factors of networks − coordination capabilities, resource sharing, and level of intranetwork competition--are considered independent variables. They are all expected to have a positive relationship with competitive advantage.

1. Network Member Coordination and Interaction

Results from initial interviews with network managers suggest that the existence of an administrative organization or central office and its quality of leadership are critical for effective network operation. In the Korean furniture industry, all networks are configured around a central office, or "node" in Thorelli's (1986) terminology. Interview results also indicated that the degree and frequency of interactions among member peripheral firms differed substantially across the three industry networks while all firms interacted with the central office.

Networks with a strong central office, one that actively coordinates and spreads information among member firms, are thought to achieve superior cross-learning, and pooling and transfer of information and resources. Because central offices tend not to possess significant amounts of information and resources, network effectiveness depend on extensive interaction among member firms. These observations suggest that the central office's principal function is that of a conduit for information and resources. Therefore, network effectiveness requires highly interactive peripheral members as well as a central office with strong coordinative capabilities. The preceding observation and conjecture are consistent with Provan & Milward's (1995) study, which demonstrated in a service industry context that centrally integrated networks achieved higher effectiveness than did decentralized networks. Their study showed that successful networks possessed both strong administrative links between the central office and peripheral members and a strong, largely centralized interactive structure.

Based on the preceding arguments, we offer the following two hypotheses:

H1-a. Competitive advantage of a network is greater when it has a strong administrative coordination arrangement.
H1-b. Competitive advantage of a network is greater when its structure facilitates strong interactions among peripheral member firms.

2. Network Resource Sharing

The central value of the network form derives from the fact that a network enables individual firms to tap resources that they could never obtain individually. Such resources can range from physical resources (such as equipment, manufacturing processes, and greater market access) to intangible resources (such as information). This paper examines separately two major categories of resources. In one category we group resources related to primary value chain activities such as purchasing, manufacturing, logistics, marketing, and service. In the other category we examine the intangible resource of information that supports value chain activities.

Human & Provan (1997) assert that network participation offers firms two fundamental opportunities. The first, potential opportunities, relates to the acquisition of information regarding new markets, new products, new designs, or new technologies arising from interaction with member firms. A network that encourages and facilitates cross-learning among member firms will increase the network's overall competitive advantage. The second, more tangible opportunities, includes shared benefits arising from joint production, new product development, collective marketing, employee training, joint purchasing of raw materials, joint branding, and joint distribution. By pooling and sharing resources among multiple members, a network can enjoy the economies of scale, scope, and speed.

The preceding arguments lead to the following hypotheses:

H2-a. Competitive advantage of a network is greater when the network facilitates active sharing of information among member firms.
H2-b. Competitive advantage of a network is greater when the network facilitates active sharing of resources other than information among member firms.

3. Competition among Network Participants

Whether a network relationship is truly synergistic or not depends on the level of competition and cooperation among member firms because network effectiveness depends on how competent the member firms are. Cooperation within a network will produce benefits when constructive, healthy competition among members improves the capabilities of individual firms.

A network may be viewed as a collection of 'nodes' or 'positions'(occupied by firms, households, strategic business units inside a diversified concern, trade associations and other types of organizations) and 'links' manifested by interaction between nodes (Thorelli, 1986). The positioning of a firm within a network may be of equal strategic significance to positioning its product in the marketplace. Thorelli indicated that cooperation is indispensable, and both intra- and inter-network competition is unavoidable. Potential competition from alternate members or alternate network configurations is also a highly relevant phenomenon in the network context. For example, if a member does not meet average performance expectations, that situation must be remedied among members. While this intranetwork competition raises the overall quality of the network, it produces continuing tension among members. In order to promote competence-enhancing competitive tension among members, every member must be considered replaceable. Inzerilli (1990) found that successful networks were characterized by easy change in member firms' functions or the possession of alternate technologies and production capacity.

This leads to the following hypothesis:

H3. Competitive advantage of a network is greater when competition among members exists.

VI. Methods

1. Industry Setting

The Korean furniture industry was chosen for the following reasons: This $3 billion industry steadily declined after two decades of explosive growth in the 1970s and 1980s. The economic decline also led to smaller firm size. By 1998, of the industry's 3,314 participants, only one half of one percent of these firms had more than 300 employees. These large firms, however, captured 23.3% of total industry sales. Approximately 60% of the remaining firms had fewer than 9 employees and together generated only 30% of total industry sales. Because of a downturn in home construction along with a poor economic climate, negative industry growth is expected to continue. With the exception of a few large mechanized firms, this industry is highly labor intensive. The 1997 economic crisis eliminated many large firms with well-known brand names, leaving only a few survivors. Some small and medium-sized firms, facing intensified competition in a rapidly shrinking market, used the network form to survive and to compete against the remaining large firms. These smaller firms were members of three networks in the Seoul metropolitan area; we surveyed all three for this study. To preserve the confidentiality of these networks, we refer to them as "A-net," "B-net" and "C-net ."

2. Data Collection

Participants were identified from each network's membership directory. A-net was composed of 44 member firms, B-net 39, and C-net 34 member firms. These numbers indicate that in terms of number of participating firms, the three networks are comparable. Table 1 presents descriptive

Table 1. Description of the Networks under Study

	A-net	B-net	C-net
Year formed	1996	1996	1997
Central office	non-profit organization with 11-member board of directors	non-profit organization with a full-time executive director and 8-member board of directors	profit organization with a full-time executive director and 10 full-time staff
Members	44	39	34
Focus	- stable distribution - healthy competition - enhancing credibility	- products at competitive prices	- building high-quality image - nationwide dealership network
Service provided	- joint purchasing of raw material - showroom - centralized contract - training workshop - trade shows/catalogs	- showroom - joint marketing - information sharing	- showroom - joint marketing - joint product development - joint service system - joint distribution and logistics
Member selection criteria	- excellence in quality and design - competitive price criteria - maintain at least one month's inventory for selected items - more than 20 full-time employees	- more than 10 full-time employees	- no systematic selection criteria - interview and reference
Total sales('98)	approximately $ 6 million	N/A	approximately $ 2 million

statistics for each network. The executive director of each network's administrative organization (central office) was selected as a key informant for developing our understanding of the characteristics of the networks. Each executive director played an active role in forming his respective network and was currently involved in maintaining his network. From interviews with the directors, we obtained information about industry dynamics, network structure, network governance, information flows, interaction patterns among members, and used our resulting understanding to develop a questionnaire which would be completed by the network member firms. With the aid of each director, the final instrument was administered to a pre-qualified sample of 73 firms across the three networks. Forty-seven usable questionnaires were collected for a response rate of 64%.

3. Measures of Competitive Advantage

Quantitative measurement of network performance (as distinguished from individual firm performance) is problematic. The particular difficulty of measuring network performance lies in the inherent objective of network participation, pursuit of non-quantifiable benefits such as rapid market entry, knowledge acquisition, or improved competitive status rather than the more readily quantifiable pursuit of efficiency (Sydow & Windeler, 1998).

In this industry, a comparison of the aggregated financial performance of network member firms was not viable because not all member firms were publicly traded. In addition, because a special consumption tax is levied on hand-made products, most firms underreport their actual sales and income. Consequently, even if sales data became available, it would be unreliable.

This study measured competitive advantage with two variables. These were tapped with questionnaire items based on a 5-point Likert scale. The first, enhanced firm reputation or credibility arising from network participation was based on Johanson & Mattsson (1987) and Larson (1992). Three questionnaire items were constructed to measure the network's perceived credibility in relation to the government, banks, and customers. That construct was measured by the average score across all three items. A reliability test (Cronbach's alpha: .7965) indicated that it was reliable. The second variable we developed was perception of a network's brand recognition, stability, and growth potential relative to the other two networks. Survey participants were asked to rank all three networks along these criteria.

Network structure

Administrative coordination (variable used in test of H1-a) was defined as the role played by the central office in providing a network environment that promotes active, frequent interaction among member firms. Administrative coordination was measured by a mixture of dichotomous questions regarding the existence of indicators such as regular meetings; regular newsletter, booklets, or other information sources; network-level exhibition projects; learning and training opportunities; jointly owned showrooms; and technology transfer programs. Respondents were also asked to state the number of events or items. The variable *interaction* (used in test of H1-b) was defined as the perceived value of and actual interaction of a member firm with other network members. Member-to-member interaction was measured by a Likert scale question, questions regarding the frequency of interaction, and questions concerning the nature of interactions.

Network resource sharing

Information-sharing (used in test of H2-a) was measured by four Likert scale questions regarding the value of network participation in terms of access to information about the market, product ideas, product and process technologies, and common issues facing member firms. This construct was measured by the average score across all four items. A reliability test (Cronbach's alpha: .9270) indicated that it was reliable. *Resource sharing* (used in test of H2-b) was measured by five questions that determined if participation in the network conferred benefits such as the joint purchase of raw material, joint branding, joint use of showrooms, joint marketing, and cooperation with outside entities specializing in design, training, and technology development. This construct was measured by the average score across all five items. A reliability test (Cronbach's alpha: .7961) indicated that it was reliable.

Competition among network participants
Competition (used in test of H3) was measured by three questions regarding a member firm's monitoring and benchmarking activities, and its sense of competition toward other network members. The Cronbach's alpha score of .9521 for the average score across these three items indicates that it is reliable.

VII. Results and Discussion

Analysis of differences in competitive advantage among the three networks showed consistently high rankings from all respondents for A-net on brand recognition, stability, growth potential, and credibility of the network. Results for differences between B-net and C-net were mixed. Assessments of each network's reputation and credibility relative to the others showed a statistically significant difference (p < .01) between A-net and B-net and between A-net and C-net. There were no statistically significant differences between B-net and C-net on the reputation/credibility dimension. Although A-net was the undisputed reputation/credibility leader, the ambiguous difference between B-net and C-net necessitated a one-way ANOVA test of the three networks' scores on all independent variables. ANOVA results indicated a statistically significant difference between A-net and B-net and between A-net and C-net. There was no statistically significant difference between B-net and C-net. Table 2 shows the result of one-way ANOVA of three networks.

The lack of a measurable performance difference between networks B and C provided an opportunity to level the respondent group size differences between A-net (24) and the other two networks (11 and 12 respectively). B-net and C-net were combined and renamed "group 2" while A-net was renamed "group 1." The remaining analyses examine whether and how differences in the independent variables relate to differences in competitive advantage of the two groups.

Hypothesis Testing: Results presented in Table 3 partially support H1-a: "Competitive advantage of a network is greater when it has a strong administrative coordination arrangement." Although a quantitatively rigorous analysis was not performed, Table 3 reports a clear difference between the two groups. Group 1 showed a higher level of administrative coordination activity in five of seven items: Monthly membership and board meetings; monthly newsletter; international trade show and demonstration projects; catalog and pamphlet; and training workshops.

Most notably, Group 1's central office created a communication channel to and among network members by providing monthly meetings and newsletters. Respondents from Group 2 reported no such activity. One hundred percent of responding Group 1 firms were aware of and partic-

Table 2. Results of One-way ANOVA of Three Networks

Variable	Mean	Network	Network A	B	C
Interaction	3.8750	A			
	2.7273	B	***		
	2.9167	C	***		
Information sharing	3.7396	A			
	2.3636	B	***		
	2.5833	C	***		
Resource-sharing	3.4666	A			
	2.9545	B	***		
	2.7083	C	***		
Competition	2.9375	A			
	2.6363	B	***		
	2.7222	C	***		

***: significantly different at p < .01

ipated in national and international exhibition fairs, whereas only 27.3% of Group 2 firms were either aware of or participated in such activity. Group 1 developed promotional catalogs but Group 2 did not. Most responding Group 1 members (91.6%) were aware of and participated in training and education workshops offered by the central office, but Group 2 offered no such activities. Both Group 1 and Group 2 did, however, invest in jointly shared showrooms. (Group 1 had four (A-net=4) and Group 2 had six (B-net=5 and C-net=1).) Neither of the two groups offered any technology transfer-related projects. This may be attributable to the industry's high labor intensity, low levels of technological sophistication among small furniture firms, and a lack of funds for capital investments.

The preceding results show that network effectiveness is associated with a strong central administration that actively coordinates network members. Results also suggest that merely offering a shared physical resource, i.e., jointly used showrooms, without active management does not necessarily improve network effectiveness.

Hypothesis 1-b: "Competitive advantage of a network is greater when its structure facilitates strong interactions among peripheral member firms" was supported. Table 4 reports that Group 1 firms (mean=3.8750) believed

Table 3. Comparison of the Central Offices' Administration Activities

Item	Group 1	Group 2
1. Monthly membership and board meetings	100%	0
2. Monthly newsletter	83.3%	0
3. International trade show, demonstration projects	100% (three times/year)	27.3% (one-two times/year)
4. Catalog, pamphlet	100%	0
5. Training workshops	91.6% (one to three times/year)	0
6. Showroom	100% (4)	100% (B-net: 5, C-net: 1)
7. Technology transfer project	0	0

Group 1 = 24 firms
Group 2 = 23 firms

that the network provided significantly more opportunities to interact with member firms than did Group 2 firms (mean=2.7727). This finding is supported by comparing responses to questionnaire items concerning frequency of contact between network members. Group 1 firms averaged 28 contacts per year with member firms while firms in Group 2 averaged 7.16 contacts per year. Analysis of motives for contact among Group 1 firms showed the following: discussing market issues and other business information (100%), building group cohesiveness (83.3%), purchasing raw material (50%), discussing products (41.6%), and discussing manufacturing skills (33.3%). These results suggest that network effectiveness relies not only on a central office with strong coordinative capabilities but also on frequent member-to-member interaction. Members of Group 1 regarded network participation as an opportunity to build social capital and to renew friendships. Group 1 members were also more likely to view each other as equals and they hoped to gain strategic advantage through cooperation.

Hypotheses 2-a and 2-b: Results presented in Table 5 support both Hypotheses 2a and 2b. For H2-a: "Competitive advantage of a network is greater when the network facilitates active sharing of information among member firms," Group 1 firms (mean=3.7396) reported a greater possibility

Table 4. T-test for Difference in Interactions among Member Firms

	N	Mean	S.D.	T - value	Degree of freedom	Significance level
Group 1	24	3.8750	0.741	4.79	42	0.004
Group 2	23	2.7727	0.813			

Table 5. T-tests for Differences in Sharing and Competition among Member Firms

Item	Group	Mean	S.D.	t-value	Degree of freedom	Significance level
Information-sharing	1	3.7396	0.544	7.55	44	0.000
	2	2.4783	0.598			
Resource-sharing	1	3.4666	0.516	7.76	44	0.000
	2	2.2608	0.547			
Competition	1	2.9375	0.676	9.01	45	0.000
	2	2.6811	0.631			

Group 1 = 24 firms, Group 2 = 23 firms

of gaining market information, product information, operations procedures, and technology reports through the network than did Group 2 firms (mean=2.4783). The network was also perceived to provide opportunities for members to discuss common interests. For H2-b: "Competitive advantage of a network is greater when the network facilitates active sharing of resources other than information among member firms," Group 1 firms (mean=3.4666) made more use of the network's resources such as material purchases, common brand names, jointly owned showrooms, and joint promotion and marketing than did Group 2 firms (mean=2.2608). These findings suggest that network effectiveness is related to pooling and sharing of information and other resources.

Hypothesis 3: Results presented in Table 5 also support H3: "Competitive advantage of a network is greater when competition among members exists." Group 1 firms (mean=2.9375) considered member firms as competitors more than did Group 2 firms (mean=2.6811). Group 1 firms showed a higher level of curiosity about member firms, monitored them more closely, benchmarked members when considering future product lines, and felt more strongly about member firms producing the same line of products than did Group 2 firms. These results support the assertion that competition is an important element in network effectiveness.

VIII. Conclusion

The objective of our study was to ascertain the determinants of competitive advantage among networks in the same industry. The major conclusions of this study are as follows. First, creation of a network is a necessary but not sufficient condition for performance of the focal firm and its affiliates. Because the networks under study were collections of small firms performing similar value chain activities (manufacturing), member firms needed an entity to coordinate other value chain activities. Therefore, the role of the central office was particularly important to the success of the network.

Second, network effectiveness in regard to coordination and innovation was related to the level of information sharing and interaction between affiliates. Third, healthy competition among member firms was important to the effectiveness of the entire network. We believe that this preliminary study offers research implications for understanding effectiveness at the network level as opposed to the individual firm level.

Because the ability to create and participate in networks is becoming almost a competitive necessity in today's business arena, this study has implications for practitioners. This is particularly applicable to the multitude of Korean industries that have been traditionally dominated by a small number of large corporations. Retailing provides a compelling example. The traditional street retail shop town (localized clusters of small retailers) has experienced a resurgence because they are more competitive than clusters of large-scale department stores owned by giant retailers. Although individual small retailers cannot compete with industry giants, by mimicking the resource sharing and coordination of furniture manufacturers, these clusters have become competitive. Furthermore, legislative and economic pressures are forcing traditional, vertically integrated large-scale corporations to either spin-off unprofitable units or outsource some activities. Lacking experience in managing collaboration beyond the corporate boundaries, these firms may uncover valuable lessons from the furniture industry.

This study also carries an important implication for public policy. The Korean government plays a vital role in the development of domestic industries through funding, infrastructure projects, and leadership. Because networks are an important mechanism for leveraging resources and dealing with great environmental uncertainty, government-sponsored initiatives to promote and facilitate network arrangements become important for national competitiveness.

We recognize that this study has certain limitations. First, the application of its findings may be most appropriate to labor intensive, highly fragmented industries. Additional studies of networks in a variety of industry settings are required to extend this study's applicability. Second, in the absence of a critical mass of relevant theory, this study developed an industry-specific questionnaire. Consequently these results should be considered exploratory rather than rigorous theory testing. Third, performance metrics and the research instrument need to be refined. The use of perceptual data as opposed to objective, quantitative data is a noticeable weakness.

Future research should investigate how to successfully utilize network management capabilities (Gulati, 1998; Khanna, 1998). This may help identify generally applicable network management capabilities as well as capabilities specific to different types of networks in different industries. For example, collective learning is an important factor for network success. It is argued that relative power, opportunism, suspicion, prior relationships among members, trust, and long-term prospect either positively or negatively influence the learning process (Larsson, et al, 1998). This may be augmented by study of additional factors such as the capability to spot collaboration opportunities and candidates, the capability to exploit a governance mechanism, the capability to lead necessary changes, and the capability to manage counterparts' expectations (Gulati, 1998).

Obviously, networks are not a panacea, as many have failed to achieve their intended benefits. The network form is one of a variety of organization forms a firm may adopt. Firms need to assess the advantages and disadvantages of networks, and how those advantages can be achieved, before deciding to form or join a network. However, with adequate understanding, networks may prove to be a valuable competitive weapon in an ever-changing competitive landscape.

References

Aldrich, H. E. (1979). *Organizations and Environments*. Prentice-Hall.

Dickson, P.H. & Weaver, K.M. (1997). Environmental determinants and individual-level moderators of alliance use. *Academy of Management Journal*, 40(2), pp. 404-425.

Dow, G. K. (1988). Configurational and coactionvational views of organizational structure. *Academy of Management Review*, 13, pp. 53-64.

Emery, R. & Trist, E. L. (1965). The causal context of organizational environments. *Human Relations*, 18, pp. 21-32.

Gulati, R. (1995). Does familiarity breed trust? The implications of repeated ties for contractual choices in alliances. *Academy of Management Journal*, 38(1), pp. 85-112.

Gulati, R. (1998). Alliances and networks. *Strategic Management Journal*, 19, pp. 293-317.

Hagedoorn, J. (1993). Understanding the rationale of strategic technology partnering: Interorganizational modes of cooperation and sectoral differences. *Strategic Management Journal*, 14(5), pp. 371-385.

Hamel, G., Doz, Y. & Prahalad, C. (1989). Collaborate with your competitors and win. *Harvard Business Review*, 67, pp. 137-139.

Hamel, G. & Prahalad, C.K. (1996). Competing in the new economy: Managing out of bounds. *Strategic Management Journal*, 17, pp. 237-242.

Hannan, M. & Freeman, J. (1989). Setting the record straight on organizational ecology. *American Journal of Sociology*, 95, pp. 425-435.

Human, S. & Provan, K. (1997). An emergent theory of structure and outcomes in small-firm strategic manufacturing networks. *Academy of Management Journal*, 40(2), pp. 368-403.

Inzerilli, G. (1990). The Italian alternative: Flexible organization and social management. *International Studies of Management and Organization*, 20(4), pp. 6-21.

Jarillo, C. (1998). On strategic networks. *Strategic Management Journal*, 9, pp. 31-41.

Johanson, J. & Mattsson, L. (1987). Interorganizational relations in industrial system: A network approach compared with the transaction-cost approach. *International Studies of Management and Organization*, 17, pp. 34-48.

Khanna, T. (1998). The scope of alliances. *Organization Science*, 9, pp. 340-355.

Larson, A. (1992). Network dyads in entrepreneurial settings: A study of the governance of exchange relationships. *Administrative Science Quarterly*, 37, pp. 76-104.

Larsson, R., Bengtsson, L., Henriksson, K. & Sparks, J. (1998). The interorganizational learning dilemma: Collective knowledge development in strategic alliances. *Organization Science*, 9, pp. 285-305.

Lei, D., Slocum, J. & Pitts, R. (1997). Building cooperative advantage: Managing strategic alliance to promote organizational learning. *Journal of World Business*, 32(3), pp. 203-223.

Lipnack, J. & Stamps, J. (1994). *The Age of the Network*, Essex Junction: Oliver Wight.

Madhok, A. & Tallman, S. B. (1998). Resources, transactions and rents: Managing value through interfirm collaborative relationships. *Organization Science*, 9, pp.326-339.

Miles, R., Snow, C., Matthews, J., Miles, G. & Coleman, Jr., H. (1997). Organizing in the knowledge age: Anticipating the cellular form. *Academy of Management Executive*, 11(4), pp. 7-24.

Mowery, D. C. (1988). Collaborative ventures between U.S. and foreign manufacturing firms: An overview. In D. C. Mowery (Ed.), *International Collaborative Ventures in U.S. Manufacturing*, Cambridge, MA: Ballinger, pp. 37-70.

Ohmae, K. (1989). The global logic of strategic alliances. *Harvard Business Review*, 67(2), pp. 143-154.

Osborn, R. & Hagedoorn, J. (1997). The institutionalization and evolutionary dynamics of interorganizational alliances and networks. *Academy of Management Journal*, 40(2), pp. 261-278.

Park, S.H. & Ungson, G. (1997). The effects of national culture, organizational complementarity, and economic motivation on joint venture dissolution. *Academy of Management Journal*, 40(2), pp. 279-307.

Parkhe, A. (1993). Strategic alliances structuring: A game theoretic and transaction cost examination of interfirm cooperation. *Academy of Management Journal*, 36(4), pp. 794-829.

Pfeffer, J. & Salancik, G. R. (1978). *The External Control of Organization*, New York: Harper & Row.

Powell, W. W. (1990). Neither market nor hierarchy: Network forms of organization. In L. L. Cummings & B. M. Staw (Eds.), *Research in Organizational Behavior*, Greenwich, CT: JAI Press, 12, pp. 295-336.

Provan, K. & Milward, H.B. (1995). A preliminary theory of interorganizational network effectiveness: A comparative study of four community metal health systems. *Administrative Science Quarterly*, 40, pp. 1-33.

Ring, P. S. & Van de Ven, A. H. (1992). Structuring cooperative relationships between organizations. *Strategic Management Journal*, 13, pp. 483-498.

Sakakibara, M. (1997). Heterogeneity of firm capabilities and cooperative research and development: An empirical examination of motives. *Strategic Management Journal*, 18, pp. 143-164.

Sydow, J. & Windeler, A. (1998). Organizing and evaluating interfirm networks: A structurationist perspective on network processes and effectiveness. *Organization Science*, 9, pp. 265-284.

Thorelli, H. (1986). Networks: Between markets and hierarchies. *Strategic Management Journal*, 7, pp. 37-51.

Warren, R. L. (1967). The interorganizational field as a focus for investigation. *Administrative Science Quarterly*, 12, pp. 396-419.

Williamson, O. E. (1975). *Markets and Hierarchies: Analysis and Antitrust Implications*, New York: The Free Press.

An Empirical Study on the Change of Organizational Culture and Performance in Korean Firms

Young-Joe Kim[1]

I. Introduction

The rapid constant change of a business environment requires the change of organization. The environmental changes are characterized as: increasing globalization, technological revolution, and variability of customer needs resulting in a new competitive landscape, which in turn requires new types of organization and management. Recently, to respond to environmental change and to build and maintain a competitive advantage, many new management techniques, such as business process reengineering, customer satisfaction management, self-directed work teams, learning organization and knowledge management have been introduced, and many Korean firms have actively adopted them. However, there has been little research investigating whether the changes in organization and management have actually occurred after the adoption and implementation of new management tools, and if so, the direction and extent of the change. Under such circumstances, this study aims to examine empirically whether the cultural traits of Korean firms have changed

---

[1] Assistant Professor, Pukyong National University, Pusan, Korea.

recently using a longitudinal study method.

Organizational culture (or corporate culture) was a hot topic of management in the 1980s and early 1990s for the practitioners as well as scholars. The tremendous popularity of an organizational culture started with the basic understanding that it is a source of sustainable competitive advantage and an important determinant of organizational performance. Even though interest in culture has decreased recently compared to a decade ago as various new management techniques were introduced, the importance of organizational culture is still emphasized in that the success of new management systems may depend on the creation and management of relevant organizational culture. In other words, without transformation of prevailing organizational values and mind-sets, the efforts to change the organization and management end in failure or only temporary success. Thus, as Morgan (1997, p.143) maintains, the challenge of creating new forms of organization and management is very much a challenge of cultural change.

Cho and Kim (1995), Choe (1994a,b), Hahn, Hwang, and Park (1997), Jeon and Kim (1997), Jun and Shin (1995), Jung, Park, and Kim (1996), Kang (1997), Kim and Lee (1997), Kim and Park (1998), Park (1997), and Park and Kim (1995) can be given as examples of the recent research on the organizational culture of Korean firms. These studies can be summarized into four strands. The first branch of research focuses on the relationship between corporate culture and other organizational variables such as organizational structure, business strategy, leadership, and the like. The second is a trait approach that addresses the relationship between cultural attributes and organizational performance. The third investigates whether strength of culture (consistency or homogeneity) leads to excellent performance. Finally, the fourth one is a contingency approach asserting that the success and performance of an organization relies upon the meshing of the organizational culture and other variables, including business environment, corporate strategy, leadership, and so on.

In spite of much interest and research on the organizational culture, there has been scant research that investigates empirically whether the organizational culture of Korean firms has actually changed, and if so, the nature and extent of the change. In order to evaluate the efforts of change, and to plan a future strategy, research on the change of the organizational culture is definitely required. Thus, this research basically aims to investigate change of the organizational culture in Korean firms over a period of five years (1994-1999) using the longitudinal study method.

II. Theoretical Background

1. Organizational Culture and Corporate Performance

The study of organizational culture has proposed numerous definitions of 'culture' including shared meaning (Louis, 1985), shared values (Barney, 1986), beliefs (Lorsch, 1985), and basic assumptions (Schein, 1985). Among these definitions, the view that culture is "shared values" is widely held. Thus, in this paper, organizational culture is defined as shared values that are developed within an organization over time.

The study on the relationship between organizational culture and corporate performance might be classified as three strands. First, most research that tries to relate culture to an organizational outcome has pursued the trait approach. The trait approach to culture suggests that a specified type of value or belief, i.e., specific cultural characteristics, has particular effects such as involvement and commitment of organizational members, corporate competitiveness and performance. Based on this assumption, many studies have focused on the search for distinctive cultural traits that could lead to high corporate performance. Probably the most widely known study is Peters' and Watermans' (1982), outlining eight characteristics of excellent companies. Similarly, Kilmann (1985) maintained that well-performing companies should have adaptive cultures that involve a risk-taking, trusting and proactive approach. Some scholars have also done empirical research on the impact of corporate culture on performance, and proposed their own cultural traits (Calori & Sarnin, 1991; Denison, 1984, 1990; Gordon & DiTomaso, 1992; Hansen & Wernerfelt, 1989).

Second, many authors have emphasized the fact that organizations with strong culture have been related to high employee involvement and corporate performance. This perspective could be called 'strong culture hypothesis,' which proposes that a strong culture leads to an extraordinary corporate performance. Cultural strength has been also defined in various ways which include coherence (Deal & Kennedy, 1982), homogeneity (Ouch & Price, 1978), stability and intensity (Schein, 1985). Some empirical research based on this perspective, such as Denison (1990), Calori & Sarnin (1991), Gordon & DiTomaso (1992), and Kotter & Heskett (1992), supported the hypothesis.

The third strand is the contingency approach to culture, which claims that the organizational performance depends on the fit between corporate culture and situational factors. According to the contingency approach prevalent in organizational studies, the culture trait of an organization should match such factors as organizational structure, corporate strategy, industrial and environmental characteristics in order to contribute to superior performance (Gordon, 1985, 1991; Saffold, 1988; Schwartz & Davis, 1981; Wilkins & Ouchi, 1983). Based on this perspective, Gordon (1985) investigated the relationship between corporate culture and industry characteristics, and its impact on corporate performance. He found that organizations in highly dynamic industries were characterized by cultural values that emphasized adaptability, whereas those in the more static industries were characterized by cultural values that enhanced stability. Furthermore, he found that corporate growth and profitability depended on a match between cultural values and industrial characteristics.

2. Competing Values Model (CVM)

This study focuses on the four culture types classified and assessed by the competing values model. The competing values framework was originally developed to explain differences in the values underlying various organizational effectiveness (Quinn & Rohrbaugh, 1981). Since its introduction, the competing values framework has extended to study organizational forms (Quinn & Hall, 1983), organizational life cycles (Quinn & Cammeron, 1983), and leadership styles (Quinn, 1988). Furthermore, many studies have applied the framework to investigate organizational culture, and have demonstrated its utility and validity (Cameron & Freeman, 1991; Denison & Spreitzer, 1991; Park & Kim, 1995; Quinn & Kimberly, 1984; Quinn & McGrath, 1985; Quinn & Spreitzer, 1991; Yeung et al, 1991). The framework seems to be useful, as Quinn & Kimberly (1984, p.298) suggest, in that the value orientations inherent in the framework can be used to explore the deep structures of organizational culture, the basic assumptions that are made about such things as the means to compliance, motives, leadership, decision-making, effectiveness, values, and organizational forms. In addition, the culture types classified by this framework have a common denominator with previous classifications of organizational culture such as Handy (1978), Harrison (1972), Ouchi (1981), and Wallach (1983).

This framework focuses on the competing demands and conflicts inherent in every organization. It is based on two main dimensions. The first axis reflects the competing demands of change (i.e., flexibility and spontaneity) and stability (i.e., control and order). The second axis reflects the conflicting demands created by the internal organization (focusing on integration and buffering to sustain the existing organization) and the external environment (focusing on competition, adaptation, and interaction with the environment). From the juxtaposition of these two dimensions, four types of cultural orientations emerge: group culture, developmental culture, rational culture, and hierarchical culture.

According to the descriptions provided by Cameron & Freeman (1991), Denison & Spreitzer (1991), and Quinn (1988), each cultural orientation can be summarized as follows. The *group culture*, which emphasizes flexibility and maintains a major focus on the internal organization, has a primary concern with human relations. The development of human resources, trust, teamwork, participative decision-making, attachment and commitment are emphasized in the organizations that have a strong group culture. The *developmental culture*, which emphasizes flexibility and change, but maintains a major focus on the external environment, has a primary concern with adaptation to the external environment. This cultural orientation gives emphasis to growth, resource acquisition, creativity, innovation, entrepreneurship and risk-taking. The *hierarchical culture*, which focuses on the logic of the internal organization and stability, has an orientation reflecting values associated with bureaucracy. This orientation sets high value on internal efficiency, uniformity, centralization, coordination and evaluation. Thus, chain of command, rules, procedures and policies are emphasized. Finally, the *rational culture*, which emphasizes stability, but maintains a major focus on the external environment, has a primary concern with goal achievement, productivity and performance. The organizations with high rational culture tend to focus on the attainment of well-defined objectives, goal clarity, efficiency, and competitiveness.

Figure 1. The Competing Values Model

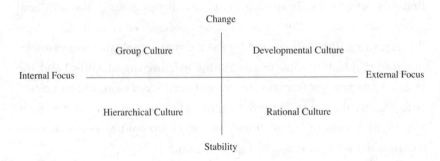

3. Change of Organizational Culture

Starting from the standpoint that corporate culture is a major determinant of the organizational performance, many scholars and practitioners have been interested in the issue of changing and managing the organizational culture. There have been two conflicting views about the possibility of cultural change (Gagliardi, 1986; Kilmann et al., 1985, 1986). On the one hand, some scholars maintain that it is very difficult to change the culture, since the organizational culture defined as a coherent system of basic assumptions and values shared throughout the organization is, of its nature, a tenacious and unalterable phenomenon. That is, the more deeply-seated and widely-diffused these values are, the more tenacious and unalterable the culture is. On the other hand, some suggest that it is possible to change and manage the organizational culture deliberately, since one can see that the organizations have evolved and cultural traits have changed, especially by the influence of charismatic leadership.

The literature on cultural change has focused on describing the process by which organizational cultures form and evolve. The antecedents, processes and consequences of cultural change have been investigated relying on the case analysis method, and then the model for explaining the stages of culture change and specific methods for this have been proposed. For example, Dyer (1985) proposed a six-stage model to represent the complex processes of cultural change derived from the histories of five organizations. Porter and Parker (1992) investigated two companies' cases for the conditions and processes of cultural change, and then discussed the lessons and implications. In addition to these, Allen (1985) proposed a four-phase systematic program for changing cultures, and Kilmann (1989) also suggested a five-step participative process to assess and change the corporate culture: (1) examining existing norms, (2) articulating new directions, (3) establishing new norms, (4) identifying culture-gaps (the difference between actual and desired norms), and (5) closing culture-gaps.

In addition, many scholars have tried to find out specific methods for changing and managing an organizational culture. Among them, the role of leader (Dyer, 1985; Sathe, 1985; Schein, 1983, 1985), organizational reward system (Sethia & Von Glinow, 1985), human resource management practices such as recruitment and selection, training and education, career management, reward system (Porter & Parker, 1992), and using symbols, including rites and rituals (Deal & Kennedy, 1982; Trice & Beyer, 1985) have been widely emphasized.

Whereas most of this work has relied on the normative argument or case analysis of specific companies, there has been little empirical research using quantitative methodology. Under such circumstances, this research basically aims to investigate empirically the change of organizational culture in Korean firms during the recent five years (1994-1999) using longitudinal study method.

III. Research Method

1. Research Framework

In the 1990s, many Korean firms tried to change their management styles and organizational culture in order to enhance corporate competitiveness and improve organizational performance. But, there has been scant empirical research investigating and evaluating whether their efforts to change have produced the intended outcome. Accordingly, in this research I investigated the change of organizational culture and effectiveness in Korean firms between 1994 and 1999 using a panel survey design (Bryman, 1989; Green, 1975). The data was collected at two points in time using the same survey questionnaire. The first survey was conducted in 1994, and the second wave of data collection took place five years after.

Specifically, as can be seen from Figure 2, this study aims to investigate (1) the change of organizational culture in Korean firms between 1994 and 1999, (2) the change of organizational members' attitudes, including job

Figure 2. Research Framework. Panel Survey Research Design

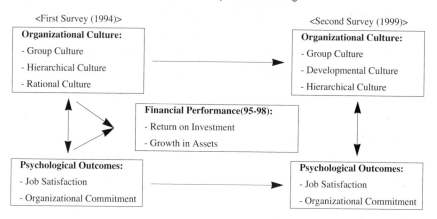

satisfaction and organizational commitment, (3) the relationship between organizational culture and psychological outcomes longitudinally as well as cross-sectionally, (4) the impact of organizational culture and psychological outcomes on corporate financial performance, and finally (5) the influence of cultural change on attitudinal change.

2. Sample

The survey was administrated to multiple respondents of the same sample companies in 1994 and 1999 using the same survey questionnaire. The first survey was administered from January to April in 1994. The data was obtained from 1,571 employees of 82 Korean listed companies. As for the second survey, it was administrated from August to September in 1999. The second survey was administered to the same companies which participated in the first survey. The data was obtained from 1,051 employees in 47 out of 82 companies. The reason for a loss of samples between the first and second survey is because (1) bankruptcy or M&A took place in some companies during this period, (2) several firms didn't agree to administrate the survey, and (3) 8 firms didn't return the survey questionnaires. Therefore, in this study, only the 47 companies completing the first and second survey were analyzed. In the end, only 835 respondents of the 47 companies were used in the analysis.

This study adopted the 'organization' as the level of analysis in that this study investigates organizational culture and corporate performance. Thus, the data collected from the individuals of each company were aggregated across the organization: that is, the collective scores for each organization were created by averaging individual members' scores, and then used in the subsequent analysis.

As for the size of the sample firms, 2 firms (4.3%) out of 47 firms have less than 300 employees, 14 firms (29.8%) have 300-999 employees, 18 firms (38.3%) have 1,000-4,999 employees, and 13 firms (27.7%) have more than 5,000 employees. In terms of industry, 27 firms (57.4%) belonged to manufacturing industries, 3 firms (6.4%) to construction industries, 6 firms (12.8%) to wholesale and retail industries, 3 firms (6.4%) to transportation and communication industries, and 8 firms (17.0%) to financial service industries.

Of the individuals who responded to the survey, 89.1 percent in 1994 and 86.0 percent in 1999 were male employees. The respondents' average age was 30.8 and 32.4 years old respectively, and average tenure was 5.3 and 7.1 years.

3. Measurement

Organizational Culture

In this study, organizational culture was classified into four types based on the competing values model. These four types of organizational culture were measured using 6 items respectively. The instrument developed by Quinn (1988) was used, but modified a little by the researcher to make it relevant to the contingencies of Korean companies. The responses were assessed using five-point Likert-type scales ranging from (1) strongly disagree to (5) strongly agree.

To confirm the existence of four cultural types, the iterative exploratory factor analyses were used for the first and second survey data. Principal component factor analyses with varimax rotation were performed on the 24 items, and four common factors between the two data sets were extracted. The results show four interpretable factors defined by 19 of the 24 items. Table 1 shows the results of the factor analysis.

As can be seen from Table 1, the patterns of factor loading for the data of two different time points are very similar and support the conceptual classification. The first factor, clearly defined by six items, can be labeled *developmental culture*. Five items loading on the second factor reflect *group culture*. The third and fourth factors containing four items respectively reflects *rational culture* and *hierarchical culture*.

Internal consistency reliability estimates (Cronbach's alpha) were calculated for the four factors. Reliability coefficients for the developmental culture (Factor 1) were .7575 for the first survey data and .7574 for the second survey data. Reliability coefficients for the group culture (Factor 2) were .8010 and .7932, respectively. Reliability coefficients were .6424 and .6487 for the rational culture (Factor 3), .6064 and .6279 for the hierarchical culture (Factor 4), respectively. As such, the internal consistency reliability estimates were quite acceptable.

Organizational Performance

Psychological Outcomes

Job satisfaction was measured using seven items taken from the Job Descriptive Index (JDI; Smith et al, 1969) and developed by the author. The items ask about the respondents' specific satisfaction with compensation, promotion, the job itself, career development, managerial philosophy, corporate social responsibility, and general satisfaction. Respondents were asked to indicate on a five-point scale their level of agreement (1=strongly disagree, 5=strongly agree). The reliability coefficients were .8394 for the first survey data and .8436 for the second one.

Organizational commitment was assessed using eight items taken from the Organizational Commitment Questionnaire (Mowday and Steers, 1979) that measures employee's identification with and involvement in the organization, and desire to maintain membership in the organization. In order to avoid potential wording confounds, only eight items were used from the original fifteen. The reliability coefficients were .8693 and .8702, respectively.

Corporate Financial Performance

To analyze corporate financial performance, return on investment (ROI) and growth in assets were used. These indicators including profitability and growth reflect on the company's overall performance. The data for each company was obtained from Korean Investors Service's *Annual Reports of Korean Companies (1996-1998)* and *Annual Business Reports* that the listed company submitted to the Financial Supervisory Service. The four years' financial performance data (from 1995 to 1998) was used.

IV. Results

1. Descriptive Statistics

Table 2 shows means, standard deviations, and correlations of all variables for the first (1994) and second (1999) survey data. First, overall cultural profiles of sample companies in 1999 were not so different from those in 1994. The results showed that whereas the hierarchical culture was quite strong in 1999 as well as in 1994, developmental culture was relatively weak. Second, according to the inter-correlation between cultural types analyzed by cross-sectional data, developmental culture was significantly related to group culture and rational culture. The correlation between developmental culture and rational culture was especially very high. Third, concerning corporate financial performance, the ROI of sample companies was low, but growth in assets was considerably high. The results support the fact that Korean firms have preferred growth to profitability.

Table 1. Factor Analyses for 4 Types of Organizational Culture (N=47)*

	Factor 1 (DC)	Factor 2 (GC)	Factor 3 (RC)	Factor 4 (HC)
Encourage innovative thinking and creative ideas	.85147	.05376	.32593	.12473
	.80754	.18022	.35019	-.03133
Work in one's own way	.79585	.15601	.03326	-.18259
	.66458	.08646	-.09518	-.48167
Try new things; trial-and-error learning	.73269	.04334	.45412	-.08445
	.87948	.09951	.01793	.15061
Emphasize creative and risk-taking propensities	.71023	.19134	.39987	.09501
	.80063	.19998	.29353	-.16015
Emphasize organizational change and managerial reform	.70911	.04582	.14018	.43468
	.62849	.12316	.39327	.13442
Adopt new insights aggressively in management	.67186	.34787	.40276	.04202
	.73980	.34042	.40484	.05307
Family-like organizational climate	-.04649	.90519	-.18969	-.06847
	.02165	.80891	-.36924	-.07256
Good human relations among employees	.11381	.89722	-.05335	.04867
	-.06227	.92236	.13582	.03940
Encourage cooperation and teamwork	.24028	.84401	.20146	.15923
	.37356	.77933	.11721	.31400
Emphasize cohesion and identification	.17338	.84073	.32766	.19437
	.45966	.68604	.04721	.35332
Try to build consensus and commitment	.42848	.61310	.40412	.25208
	.62633	.55774	.05168	.36143
Respect the expertise and capability needed to perform tasks successfully	.27133	.26438	.80048	-.12324
	.21883	-.05355	.80064	-.11783
Emphasize competitive atmosphere and task accomplishments	.30980	-.37411	.76159	.24074
	.51673	-.17892	.71698	-.04261
Prefer rational goal achievement to rules and procedures	.43006	.09579	.72005	-.14001
	.75427	.14281	.44881	-.21471
Appraise employees based on ability and performance	.38420	.10401	.50975	.47613
	.36167	.02989	.82375	.07972
Emphasize the hierarchy	-.15354	.18332	.03622	.87452
	.04805	.05191	-.36731	.86895
Follow the formal rules, procedures, and policies	.05660	.00264	-.25499	.86617
	-.10277	.14632	.15090	.86201
Strict chain of command, and communications through it	.28471	.20632	.30922	.70405
	.29814	.33498	.27489	.71238
Coordinate and control the work process strictly	-.39876	-.37787	-.45620	.52665
	-.48292	.02729	-.02450	.70915
EigenValue	7.7667	3.2141	2.8079	1.0493
	7.9291	4.0074	2.1028	1.0356
Percentage of Variance(%)	40.9	16.9	14.8	5.5
	41.7	21.1	11.1	5.5
Cummulative Percentage(%)	40.9	57.8	72.6	78.1
	41.7	62.8	73.9	79.3

* upper numbers. analysis based on the first survey data (1994)
  lower numbers . analysis based on the second survey data (1999)

Table 2. Descriptive Statistics of Variables and Inter-correlations Among Variables (N=47)

Variables **		Mean	StdDev	First Survey (1994)						Second Survey (1999)						ROA
				GC	DC	HC	RC	JS	OC	GC	DC	HC	RC	JS	OC	
First Survey (1994)	GC	3.2192	.3549													
	DC	2.9042	.3377	.42*												
	HC	3.4674	.2626	.19	.00											
	RC	3.1349	.2999	.26*	.71*	-.04										
	JS	3.0966	.3213	.75*	.57*	.21	.43*									
	OC	3.2750	.3448	.77*	.37*	.25	.23	.88*								
Second Survey (1999)	GC	3.3603	.2633	.33*	.16	.17	.09	.20	.18							
	DC	2.9695	.2953	.11	.47*	.21	.26*	.32*	.12	.48*						
	HC	3.4953	.2582	.06	-.10	.43*	-.13	-.04	.12	.40*	-.00					
	RC	3.2666	.2778	.01	.32*	.22	.39*	.29*	.11	.26*	.75*	-.07				
	JS	3.1234	.2851	.16	.13	.16	.19	.32*	.21	.64*	.63*	.22	.61*			
	OC	3.2539	.2783	.30*	.11	.03	.21	.33*	.26*	.66*	.43*	.18	.35*	.84*		
ROA ***		.7690	3.3439	.00	-0.9	.17	.03	.16	.29*	.05	-.28*	.25	-.07	.09	-.00	
GA ***		20.4562	15.8478	.13	.41*	.19	.14	.09	.04	-.18	.24	-.14	.19	-.12	-.22	-.14

* $p<.05$ ($r>.26$, $p<.05$; $r>.35$, $p<.01$; $r>.42$, $p<.001$)
** GC. group culture, DC. developmental culture, HC. hierarchical culture, RC. rational culture, JS. job satisfaction, OC. organizational commitment, ROA. return on investment, GA. growth in assets
*** ROA & GA. 4 years' average (1995-1998).

2. The Change of Organizational Culture

In this study, the change of organizational culture between 1994 and 1999 was investigated across four cultural type classifications based on the competing values model. In the 1990s, many Korean companies tried to change their organizational culture in order to heighten competitiveness in the face of the rapidly changing environment and global competition. Their cultural change efforts over this period of time could be described as an attempt to move from hierarchical culture to the direction of group, developmental, and rational culture. Therefore, it may be expected that the hierarchical culture became weaker during the recent five year period, whereas the three other cultural traits became stronger.

T-tests for the first and second survey data were also conducted. As Table 3. shows, it is found that group and rational culture showed a significant difference between 1994 and 1999, but developmental and hierarchical culture showed no significant difference at all. According to the gap in the average score, group culture of the sample companies was strengthened by .1411 and rational culture by .1317. In this regard, it may be reasonable to say that even in the case of group and rational culture there was a statistically significant, but not substantially outstanding, difference Figure 3. Thus, contrary to the expectation, such results don't suggest that sample companies gave rise to dramatic cultural change during the recent five years.

Table 3. Change of Organizational Culture. t-test (N=47)

Organizational Culture	1994	1999	Difference (1999-1994)	t-test
Group Culture	3.2192	3.3603	.1411	t=2.65 p=.011
	(.3549)	(.2633)		
Developmental Culture	2.9042	2.9695	.0652	t=1.37 p=.176
	(.3377)	(.2953)		
Hierarchical Culture	3.4674	3.4953	.0279	t=0.69 p=.494
	(.2626)	(.2582)		
Rational Culture	3.1349	3.2666	.1317	t=2.84 p=.007
	(.2999)	(.2778)		

Figure 3. Cultural Profiles of 1994 and 1999

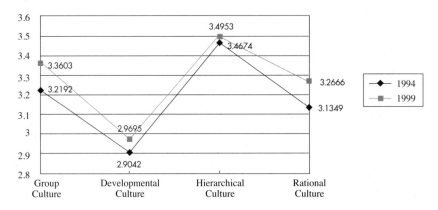

3. The Change of Psychological Outcomes

Next, the change of psychological outcomes such as job satisfaction and organizational commitment between 1994 and 1999 was examined. During the recent five years, an economic crisis took place in 1997, and in response to this crisis there has been drastic restructuring, downsizing and wage cuts in order to reduce cost in many Korean firms. It seems reasonable to anticipate that job satisfaction and organizational commitment of organizational members have decreased accordingly.

As can be seen from Table 4, contrary to the expectations, the results show nonsignificant t-values for job satisfaction and organizational commitment. It is not easy to explain the reasons why there is no significant difference in the organizational members' attitudes. It seems possible to interpret that since the respondents to the survey were survivors of the severe layoffs and still had jobs even under the gloomy economic conditions, they might not show any negative attitudes towards their job and organization.

Table 4. The Change of Psychological Outcomes. t-test (N=47)

	1994	1999	Difference (1999-1994)	t, p
Job Satisfaction	3.0966 (.321)	3.1234 (.285)	.0268	t=.52 p=.605
Organizational Commitment	3.2750 (.345)	3.2539 (.278)	-.0211	t=-.38 p=.706

4. The Relationship between Organizational Culture and Psychological Outcomes

The relationship between organizational culture and psychological outcomes was investigated in various ways. First, the correlation between culture and outcomes was analyzed in each point of time with the cross-sectional data. As can be seen from Table 2, the results for the first and second survey showed a very similar pattern. Hierarchical culture was not significantly related to job satisfaction and organizational commitment, while group, developmental, and rational culture were positively related to the psychological outcome. Specifically, group culture showed the strongest relationship with the psychological outcome. These results imply that group, developmental, and rational culture has a positive influence on employee attitudes.

Second, using the longitudinal data, the causal relationship between culture and outcome was examined. The impact of organizational culture at the time of the first survey (1994) on psychological outcome at the time of second survey (1999) was analyzed. The results showed that only a relationship between group culture and organizational commitment was significant ($r=.3039$, $p<.05$). This implies that group culture may influence the organizational commitment of employees for quite a long time. However, since other correlations were not significant at all, in general the results do not support the causal impact of organizational culture on the psychological outcome.

The reverse causal relationship between the psychological outcome at the time of the first survey and organizational culture at the time of the second survey was examined as well. As Table 2 shows, job satisfaction was positively related to developmental and rational culture. This result implies that previous job satisfaction of organizational members could be helpful for a company to shape and maintain developmental and rational culture over time. However, most, if not all, causal relationships between the psychological outcome and organizational culture were not supported.

5. Organizational Culture, Psychological Outcomes, and Corporate Financial Performance

Multiple regression analyses were performed to address whether four types of organizational culture and two psychological outcomes influence the corporate financial performance, including profitability and growth. As can be seen from Table 5, neither organizational culture nor psychological

Table 5. Multiple Regression Analyses on Effects of Culture and Results on Financial Performance

Dependent Variable	Independent Variables*	B	SE B	Beta	t	p	statistics
Return on Investment (95-98)	GC	-3.2111	2.3552	-.3530	-1.363	.1823	R2=.2297
	DC	-1.4604	2.3728	-.1496	-.615	.5426	R2(adj.)=.0853
	HC	2.2262	2.3134	.1696	.962	.3431	F=1.5908
	RC	2.2463	2.5831	.1920	.870	.3910	p=.1820
	JS	-2.1602	4.0263	-.2098	-.537	.5953	
	OC	6.9896	3.6232	.7334	1.929	.0626	
	(Constant)	-15.9073	11.6499		-1.365	.1816	
Growth in Assets (95-98)	GC	4.8952	10.2318	.1089	.478	.6351	R2=.2852
	DC	35.8861	10.0382	.8565	3.574	.0010	R2(adj.)=.1724
	HC	10.1586	9.6757	.1574	1.050	.3005	F=2.5272
	RC	-15.9417	11.0897	.3085	-1.438	.1586	p=.0371
	JS	-18.5688	17.8031	.3830	-1.043	.3035	
	OC	.4997	15.4232	.0110	.032	.9743	
	(Constant)	-32.2751	48.7068		-.663	.5116	

* GC. group culture, DC. developmental culture, HC. hierarchical culture, RC. rational culture, JS. job satisfaction, OC. organizational commitment

outcomes were significant in explaining the return on investment (ROI). Unlike the significant influence of organizational culture on psychological outcomes, organizational culture was not a significant predictor of corporate profitability. Moreover, contrary to general predictions, job satisfaction and organizational commitment of employees were not related to corporate profitability either.

As for growth in assets, the result indicates that the model was significant (F=2.5272, p=.0371, R2=17.24). However, only developmental culture had a positive significant effect on corporate growth. Since organizations high in the developmental culture are characterized by an emphasis on innovation and risk-taking, and an aggressive pursuit of new opportunities, such cultural traits seem to have influenced corporate growth strategy and subsequent performance.

6. Relationship between Change of Organizational Culture and Psychological Outcome

The psychological outcome may be influenced not only by the past or present cultural traits but also by the change of cultural traits within a certain period of time. For example, if organizational culture changes in the direction that organizational members think is desirable, then their job satisfaction and organizational commitment may be enhanced accordingly. First, this study investigated whether the cultural change in specific companies during the recent five years had influenced the level of psychological outcomes at the time of the second survey. In this analysis, the change of organizational culture was measured by the gap in average scores between two points of time; that is, the average score at the time of first survey (1994) was subtracted from the average at the time of second survey (1999). As Table 6 shows, while the change of group, developmental, and rational culture was positively related to job satisfaction, the change of hierarchical culture was not significantly related. This implies that strengthening the group, developmental, and rational culture leads to a high level of job satisfaction. As for organizational commitment, the only outstanding effect in achieving

Table 6. Relationship between Change of Organizational Culture and Psychological Outcomes

Variables[1]	The Change of			
	GC[2]	DC[2]	HC[2]	RC[2]
Change of Job Satisfaction	.7729***	.6229***	.2676*	.4297***
Change of Organizational Commitment	.6949***	.4550***	.2082	.1866
Job Satisfaction (1999)	.3033*	.4317**	.0550	.3583**
Organizational Commitment (1999)	.1828	.2764*	.1335	.1068

* $p<.05$, ** $p<.01$, *** $p<.001$
1) Changes of organizational culture and psychological outcomes are measured by the gap in average scores between 1994 and 1999. that is, the subtraction of 1994's average score (the first survey data) from 1999's average score (the second survey data).
2) GC. group culture, DC. developmental culture, HC. hierarchical culture, RC. rational culture

significance was developmental culture, but its correlation coefficient was relatively low.

The second analysis focused on whether the change of organizational culture between the two time frames caused the psychological outcome to change within a given period of time. The results show that the change of four culture types is all related to the change of job satisfaction. Notedly, the change of group and developmental culture was closely related to the change of satisfaction, while the change of hierarchical culture showed a relatively low correlation. In addition, the change of group and developmental culture had a significant relation to organizational commitment as well. In summary, the change of group and developmental culture within a certain period of time is a good indicator in explaining the change of employees' psychological outcomes.

V. Discussion

1. Implications for Organizational Culture and Performance

In order to investigate the change of organizational culture and performance in Korean firms during the recent five years, two waves of survey were administered using a panel survey design in 1994 and 1999. First, with regard to the overall cultural traits of sample companies, the results showed that the cultural profiles of 1994 and 1999 were very similar. Simply put, while hierarchical culture was quite strong, developmental culture was relatively weak. The results of the t-test present that group and rational culture showed a significant difference between 1994 and 1999, but developmental and hierarchical culture showed no significant change. In addition, it is hard to evaluate that even group and rational culture had a substantially outstanding difference. Therefore, it seems reasonable to appraise that Korean firms did not succeed in changing their organizational culture greatly in spite of their continuous efforts to change.

In the 1990s, through the Corporate Culture Movement, many Korean firms tried to overcome the bureaucratic and hierarchical control systems and to move toward 'harmony among employees, trust and teamwork,' 'innovation, creativity, and adaptation to the changing environment,' and 'efficiency, expertise, and rational goal achievement' (The Federation of Korean Industries, 1993). Thus, their change efforts can be summarized as an attempt to escape from hierarchical culture and move directly towards group, developmental, and rational culture Figure 4. In this respect, the results of this study imply that the sample companies were not so successful in reinplementing the cultural traits in that way. In other words, although Korean firms had emphasized on organizational change and managerial reform, new values did not have roots planted deeply in the organizations yet, while managerial practices emphasizing hierarchy, order, and rules still remain predominant.

Such phenomena may be attributed to two reasons. The one reason is that most, if not all, change efforts of Korean firms have been inclined to formalism. When pursuing the Corporate Culture Movement, many firms have focused on crafting a plausible corporate mission and behavioral credos, and then initiating the campaign with a sloganery. Or, they have

Figure 4. The Direction of Organizational Culture Change (Denison & Spreitzer, 1991)

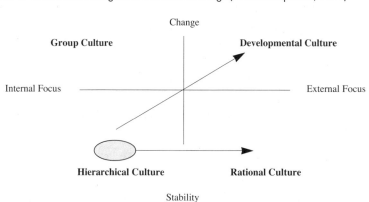

placed stress on changing overt features such as company symbols and logos as a part of the corporate identity program (CIP). On the contrary, within the corporate power structure, including the corporate governance structure and control system, the basic assumption and philosophy of CEOs and their leadership have almost remained unchanged. As such, giving priority to change the visible artifacts and creations rather than to transform the base structure of corporate culture, may bring to the fore formalism, which in turn leads to distrust and cynicism. Evidence to support this explanation is that more than half the respondents (55.5%) agreed to the questionnaire item that, "Even though top management emphasize and advocate a transition in the way of thinking and behavior in words, in fact they want employees to be obedient to them," while only 15.3% of respondents disagreed and 29.2% of respondents took a neutral attitude.

The other reason is that it is not easy to immediately change the organizational culture since it is characterized as deep-seated values, norms, and practices shared throughout the organization over a long period of time. Wilkins and Patterson (1985) suggested in the same manner that cultures cannot be changed by using methods that focus on rational planning, nor by imposing the values of a few upon the many, nor by eliminating the muddling and growing time required to change human institutions. The results of this study also support the persistence of organizational culture. As can be seen from Table 7, the correlations of

Table 7. Correlations of Culture Types between the First and Second Survey (N=47)

Variables		Second Survey (1999)			
		Group	Developmental	Hierarchical	Rational
First Survey (1994)	Group	.3304*	.1187	.0628	.0175
	Developmental	.1605	.4769***	-.1065	.3203*
	Hierarchical	.1775	.2105	.4316***	.2237
	Rational	.0996	.2677*	-.1395	.3957**

* p<.05, ** p<.01, *** p<.001

culture types between 1994 and 1999 were analyzed using longitudinal data. The results show that while most correlations among different culture types exhibited no significance, all auto-correlations between same culture types exhibited a significant relationship (correlation coefficients on the diagonal). This result implies the persistence or historical property of each organizational culture.

Second, the results show that psychological results such as job satisfaction and organizational commitment, had no significant difference between 1994 and 1999. During that time, it was expected that employees' quality of working life and level of involvement and loyalty to their organizations decreased, since there had been drastic restructuring, downsizing and wage cuts in many Korean firms in response to the 1997 economic crisis. Contrary to that expectation, however, the results present no significant difference in job satisfaction and organizational commitment between 1994 and 1999. Since the respondents to the survey were survivors of the severe layoffs and still had jobs under the very gloomy economic conditions, they might not show negative attitudes to their job and organization directly. But, to explain this result more systematically, further research, including extensive interviews are required.

Third, this study investigated the relationship between the organizational culture and psychological outcome from various angles. According to the cross-sectional analysis, the group, developmental, and rational culture were positively and significantly related to the psychological outcome, whereas hierarchical culture was not significantly related. Next, this study examined the impact of culture change on the change of psychological outcomes using longitudinal data. Consistent with the cross-sectional study, the finding was that the strengthening of group and developmental culture led to the increase of job satisfaction and organizational commitment. In addition, the influence of the culture change on the psychological outcome at the time of the second survey was analyzed. It is found that the group, developmental, and rational culture had a significant and positive relationship with job satisfaction. In short, these results support the significant relationship between the organizational culture and psychological outcome. In conclusion, in order to heighten the level of employees' job satisfaction, involvement and loyalty to the organization, any efforts to strengthen the group, developmental, and rational culture should be implemented.

Fourth, most causal relationships between the organizational culture and psychological outcome was not supported. This study aimed to investigate the causal relationship between culture and effectiveness through longitudinal study, but the results did not exhibit a significant causal relationship.

Finally, unlike the studies of Denison (1990), Hansen and Wernerfelt (1989), and Gordon and DiTomaso (1992) that reported a significant impact of organizational culture on corporate financial performance, in this study the predictive power of organizational culture on financial performance, including return on investment (ROI) and growth in assets, was quite low. The results show that only developmental culture was a significant predictor of growth in assets. Consistent with the expectations, organizations with high developmental culture emphasizing innovation and risk-taking are likely to grow faster.

2. Advantages and Disadvantages of This Study

This research has several implications for theory and management. First, this research has strength in that it utilized the longitudinal study method. Even though the importance of longitudinal study has been emphasized, most previous research has focused on cross-sectional study. Especially in Korea, there has been scant research that either analyzes the organizational change or addresses the relationship among the organizational variables using longitudinal data. Therefore, this research has an advantage in filling a gap and helping one understand organizational properties more systematically through the longitudinal study method.

Second, this study administered two surveys and analyzed the data statistically, whereas most, if not all, previous research on the change of organizational culture has relied on qualitative methodology, such as case study. The quantitative research has an advantage in that it enables one to compare the organizational traits among the organizations, examine the change of organizational culture across different points of time, and analyze the relationship among organizational variables objectively using a statistical method.

Third, this study dealt with not only psychological outcomes, such as job satisfaction and organizational commitment, but also corporate financial performance, including profitability and growth. In other words, this study examined the organizational performance comprehensively in that both perceptual response of organizational members and corporate financial data were included in the analysis.

Fourth, this study may be helpful in evaluating the outcome of prior change efforts and plan the future direction of culture change. In particular, this study suggests that in order to build up positive attitudes to job and organization, the organization should focus on strengthening the group, developmental, and rational culture.

However, several limitations of this study should be acknowledged when interpreting the findings. First, this study retains the inherent shortcomings from which quantitative study on culture can usually suffer. On the one hand, the quantitative research enables a statistical analysis using objective data: that is, it enables one to compare the organizational traits among companies, examine the change of culture and its direction and extent, and analyze the relationships among the organizational variables statistically. On the other hand, it suffers from the deficiency that it cannot afford the "thick description" on the cultural phenomena. Especially, when relying on quantitative research exclusively, it is difficult to capture the idiosyncratic and dynamic process of culture change properly.

Second, this study does not address the important contexts that would be considered to understand the change of organizational culture and performance. For example, this study does not deal with the subculture issues, the factors that influence the change of organizational culture, and the specific circumstances of each individual firm such as its environment, corporate strategy, leadership, and the like. Thus, in order to comprehend the cultural phenomena, any future research should address the antecedents, contexts, processes, and consequences of culture change.

Third, the concern of representativeness can be raised. Reliance on the convenient sampling and the small sample size might raise questions about the representativeness, which in turn make it difficult to generalize the findings.

Finally, the two surveys were administered to the same sample companies, but not to the same respondents. Due to the lengthy interval and guarantee of anonymity, it was not feasible to administrate the repeat survey to the identical respondents in the same company. However, the lack of correspondence from the respondents might suffer from the perceptual variability of individual respondents, and therefore, it might provide a bias in the direct comparison of the first and second survey data.

VI. Conclusion

This study investigated the change of organizational culture and effectiveness in Korean firms between 1994 and 1999. Based on a panel survey design, the data was collected from 47 Korean listed companies at two points in time, 1994 and 1999. The results were as follows: First, while the change of group and rational culture between 1994 and 1999 was significant, the change of developmental and hierarchical culture was not significant. Second, the change of job satisfaction and organizational commitment was not significant. Third, satisfaction and commitment were positively associated with group, developmental, and rational culture, but not significantly associated with hierarchical culture. Fourth, the change of organizational culture was positively related to the change of satisfaction and commitment. Fifth, the effects of organizational cultures and psychological outcome on corporate financial performances were not significant, except for the effect of developmental culture on asset growth. The implications of these findings for theory and practice were then discussed.

References

Allen, R. F. (1985). Four phases for bringing about cultural change. In R. H. Kilmann et al. (Eds.). *Gaining Control of the Corporate Culture,* San Francisco: Jossey-Bass, pp. 332-350.

Barney, J. B. (1986). Organizational culture: Can it be a source of sustained competitive advantage? *Academy of Management Review,* 11, pp. 656-665.

Bryman, A. (1989). *Research Method and Organization Studies.* London: Unwin Hyman.

Calori, R., & Sarnin, P. (1991). Corporate culture & economic performance: A French study. *Organizational Studies,* 12, pp. 49-74.

Cameron, K. S., & Freeman, S. J. (1991). Cultural congruence, strength, and type: Relationships to effectiveness. In R. W. Woodman & W. A. Pasmore (Eds.). *Research in Organizational Change and Development, vol.5,* Greenwich, CT: JAI Press, pp. 23-58.

Cho, Y. H. & Kim, I. S. (1995). Corporate culture and organizational performance. *The Korean Personnel Administration Journal,* 19, pp. 119-145.

Choe, M. K. (1994a). An empirical study of corporate strategy types, culture types, and financial performance, *Korean Management Review,* 24, pp. 1-39.

Choe, M. K. (1994b). Cultural types, strategic types, and behavioral performance in organizations. *The Korean Personnel Administration Journal,* 18, pp. 283-328.

Deal, T. E., & Kennedy, A. A. (1982). *Corporate Cultures,* Reading, Mass.: Addison-Wesley.

Denison, D. R. (1984). Bringing corporate culture to the bottom line. *Organizational Dynamics,* 13(2), pp. 5-22.

Denison, D. R. (1990). *Corporate Culture and Organizational Effectiveness.* New York: John Wiley & Sons.

Denison, D. R., & Spreitzer, G. M. (1991). Organizational culture and organizational development: A competing values approach. In R. W. Woodman & W. A. Pasmore (Eds.). *Research in Organizational Change and Development, vol.5,* Greenwich,CT: JAI Press, pp. 1-21.

Dyer, W. G. (1985), The Cycle of Cultural Evolution in Organizations, In R. H. Kilmann et al. (Eds.), *Gaining Control of the Corporate Culture,* San Francisco: Jossey-Bass, pp. 200-229.

Federation of Korean Industries. (1993). *Corporate Culture of Korean Big Companies*, Seoul: Federation of Korean Industries.

Gagliardi, P. (1986) The creation and change of organizational culture: A conceptual framework. *Organization Studies*, 7(2), pp. 117-134.

Gordon, G. G. (1985). The relationship of corporate culture to industry sector and corporate performance. In R. H. Kilmann et al. (Eds.). *Gaining Control of the Corporate Culture*. San Francisco: Jossey-Bass, pp. 103-125.

Gordon, G. G. (1991). Industry determinants of organizational culture. *Academy of Management Review*, 16, pp. 396-415.

Gordon, G. G., & DiTomaso, N. (1992). Predicting Corporate Performance from Organizational Culture. *Journal of Management Studies*, 29, pp. 783-798.

Green, C. N. (1975). The reciprocal nature of influence between leader and subordinate. *Journal of Applied Psychology*, 60(2), pp. 187-193.

Hahn, J. H., Hwang, W. I. & Park, S. K. (1997). The impact of the characteristics of organizational culture on the bases for organizational commitment. *Korean Journal of Management*, 5(2), pp. 95-134.

Handy, C. (1978). *Gods of Management*. London: Souvenir.

Hansen, G. S., & Wernerfelt, B. (1989). Determinants of firm performance: The relative importance of economic and organizational factors. *Strategic Management Journal*, 10, pp. 399-411.

Harrison, R. (1972). Understanding your organization's character. *Harvard Business Review*, May-June, pp. 119-128.

Jeon, S. G. & Kim, L. S. (1997). A study on the relationship between leadership and organizational culture : Focusing on the moderating effects of technology. *Korean Journal of Management*, 5(1), pp. 1-49.

Jun, S. H. & Shin, Y. J. (1995). An empirical study on the behavior effectiveness by fitness of organizational culture and leadership. *Korean Management Review*, 24(4), pp. 153-186.

Jung, J. G., Park, S. E. & Kim, Y. J. (1996). An empirical study on the relationship between organizational culture and organizational performance. *Journal of Industrial Relations*, 6, pp. 295-327.

Kang, J.A. (1997). A study on the organizational effectiveness based on the organizational culture categories. *Korean Management Review*, 26(3), pp. 513-530.

Kilmann, R. H. (1985). Five steps for closing culture-gaps. In R. H. Kilmann et al.

(Eds.). *Gaining Control of the Corporate Culture*. San Francisco: Jossey-Bass, pp. 351-369.

Kilmann, R. H. (1989). *Managing Beyond the Quick Fix*. San Francisco: Jossey-Bass.

Kilmann, R. H., Saxton, M. J., & Serpa, R. (1985). Introduction: Five key issues in understanding and changing culture. In R. H. Kilmann et al. (Eds.). *Gaining Control of the Corporate Culture*. San Francisco: Jossey-Bass, pp. 1-16.

Kilmann, R. H., Saxton, M. J., & Serpa, R. (1986). Issues in understanding and changing culture. *California Management Review*, 28(2), pp. 87-94.

Kim, N. H. & Lee, J. H. (1997). Empirical study on organizational culture types, CEO leadership styles, and behavioral performance. *Korean Journal of Management*, 5(1), pp. 193-238.

Kim, Y. J. & Park, S. E. (1998). An empirical study on the relationships between cultural type, strength and organizational performance in Korean firms. *Korean Journal of Management*, 6(2), pp. 195-238.

Korean Investors Service. *Annual Reports of Korean Companies (1996-1998)*. Seoul: Korean Investors Service.

Kotter, J. P., & Heskett, J. L. (1992). *Corporate Culture and Performance*. N.Y.: The Free Press.

Lorsch, J. W. (1985). Strategic myopia: Culture as an invisible barrier to change. In R. H. Kilmann et al. (Eds.). *Gaining Control of the Corporate Culture*. San Francisco: Jossey-Bass, pp. 84-102.

Louis, M. R. (1985). An investigator's guide to workplace culture. In P. J. Frost et al. (Eds.). *Organizational Culture*. Beverly Hills: Sage, pp. 73-93.

Morgan, G. (1997). *Images of Organization*. 2nd edition. Thousand Oaks, CA: Sage.

Mowday, R., & Steers, R. M. (1979). The measurement of organizational commitment. *The Journal of Vocational Behavior*, 14, pp. 224-247.

Ouch, W. & Price, R. (1978). Hierarchies, clans, and theory Z: A new perspective on organizational development. *Organizational Dynamics*, 7(2), pp. 25-44.

Ouchi, W. (1981). *Theory Z*, Reading, Mass.: Addison-Wesley Publishing.

Park, R. Y. (1997). The exploratory study on the relationship between organizational culture and strategy. *Korean Management Review*, 26(2), pp. 303-329.

Park, S. E. & Kim, Y. J. (1995). A study on the relationships between cultural profiles and organizational effectiveness: An empirical test of competing values model on the Korean firms. *Korean Management Review*, 24(3), pp. 213-237.

Peters, T. J., & Waterman, R. H. (1982). *In Search of Excellence : Lessons from America's*

Best Run Companies. N.Y.: Harper & Row.

Porter, B. L., & Parker, W. S. (1992). Culture change. *Human Resource Management*, 31, pp. 45-67.

Quinn, R. E. (1988). *Beyond Rational Management: Mastering the Paradoxes and Competing Demands of High Performance*. San Francisco: Jossey-Bass.

Quinn, R. E., & Cameron, K. S. (1983). Organizational life cycles and shifting criteria of effectiveness. *Management Science*, 29, pp. 33-51.

Quinn, R. E., & Hall, R. H. (1983). Environments, organizations, and policymakers: Toward an integrative framework. In R. H. Hall & R. E. Quinn (Eds.). *Organizational Theory and Public Policy*. Beverly Hills: Sage, pp. 181-298.

Quinn, R. E., & Kimberly, J. R. (1984), Paradox, Planning, and Perseverance: Guidelines for managerial practice. In J. R. Kimberly & R. E. Quinn (Eds.). *Managing Organizational Transitions*. Homewood,Ill.: Richard D. Irwin, pp. 295-313.

Quinn, R. E., & McGrath, M. R. (1985). The transformation of organizational cultures: A competing values perspective. In P. J. Frost et al. (Eds.). *Organizational Culture*. Beverly Hills: Sage, pp. 315-334.

Quinn, R. E., & Rohrbaugh, J. (1983). A spatial model of effectiveness criteria: Toward a competing values approach to organizational analysis. *Management Science*, 29(3), pp. 363-377.

Quinn, R. E., & Spreitzer, G. M. (1991). The psychometrics of the competing values culture instrument and an analysis of the impact of organizational culture on quality of life. In R. W. Woodman & W. A. Pasmore (Eds.). *Research in Organizational Change and Development*, vol.5. Greenwich, CT: JAI Press, pp. 115-142.

Saffold, G. S. (1988). Culture traits, strength and organizational performance: Moving beyond 'strong' culture. *Academy of Management Review*, 13, pp. 546-558.

Sathe, V. (1985). How to decipher and change corporate culture. In R. H. Kilmann et al. (Eds.). *Gaining Control of the Corporate Culture*. San Francisco: Jossey-Bass, pp. 230-261.

Schein, E. H. (1983). The role of the founder in creating organizational culture. *Organizational Dynamics*, 12(1), pp. 13-28.

Schein, E. H. (1985). *Organizational Culture and Leadership*. San Francisco: Jossey-Bass.

Schwartz, H., & Davis, S. M. (1981). Matching corporate culture and business strategy. *Organizational Dynamics*, 10(1), pp. 30-48.

Sethia, N. K., & Von Glinow, M. A. (1985). Arriving at four cultures by managing the reward system. In R. H. Kilmann et al. (Eds.). *Gaining Control of the Corporate Culture*. San Francisco: Jossey-Bass, pp. 400-420.

Smith, P. C., Kendall, L. M., & Hulin, C. L. (1969). *The Measurement of Satisfaction in Work and Retirement*. Chicago: Rand McNally.

Trice, H. M., & Beyer, J. M. (1985). Using six organizational rites to change culture. In R. H. Kilmann et al. (Eds.) *Gaining Control of the Corporate Culture*. San Francisco: Jossey-Bass, pp. 370-399.

Wallach, E. J. (1983). Individuals and organization: The cultural match. *Training and Development Journal*, 37, pp. 29-36.

Wilkins, A. L., & Ouchi, W. G. (1983). Efficient cultures: Exploring the relationship between culture and organizational performance. *Administrative Science Quarterly*, 28, pp. 468-481.

Wilkins, A. L., & Patterson, K. J. (1985). You can't get there from here: What will make culture-change projects fail. In R. H. Kilmann et al. (Eds.). *Gaining Control of the Corporate Culture*. San Francisco: Jossey-Bass, pp. 262-291.

Yeung, A. K. O., Brockbank, J. W., & Ulrich, D. O. (1991). Organizational culture and human resource practices: An empirical assessment. In R. W. Woodman & W. A. Pasmore (Eds.). *Research in Organizational Change and Development*, vol.5, Greenwich, CT: JAI Press, pp. 59-81.

INDUSTRIAL RELATIONS & HUMAN RESOURCE MANAGEMENT

1. **The Korean Industrial Relations System: from Post-Independence to Post-IMF**
   by Richard N. Block, Jeonghyun Lee, and Eunjong Shin

2. **Rapid Changes in Earning Inequality in Korea after the Financial Crisis**
   by Sung-Joon Park

3. **HRM in Korea: Transformation and New Patterns**
   by Woo-Sung Park and Gyu-Chang Yu

4. **Changes in Gender Differences in the Employment Structure**
   by Hae Un Rii

The Korean Industrial Relations System: from Post-Independence to Post-IMF [1]

Richard N. Block[2], Jeonghyun Lee[3], and Eunjong Shin[3]

I. Introduction

What is an industrial relations system? It may be defined as all aspects of industrial society that are linked to the employment relationship. An industrial relations system may be "viewed as analytical subsystem of an industrial society on the same logical plane as an economic system" (Dunlop, 1958, 1993, p. 45). An industrial relations system consists of the actors in the industrial relations system and the constraints of the system. The major actors in the system are (1) employers and their representatives, usually managers; (2) workers and their representatives, if any; and (3) government agencies concerned with work and the employment relationship. The constraints are primarily technological, market/budgetary, and the distribution of power in the larger society.

---

[1] The authors thank Peter Berg and Duck Jay Park for helpful comments on an earlier draft of this paper.

[2] Professor, School of Labor and Industrial Relations, Michigan State University, USA.

[3] Ph.D. Candidate, School of Labor and Industrial Relations, Michigan State University, USA.

The observed outcomes of the system are procedural rules, which determine how decisions will be made, and substantive rules, which determine the terms and conditions of employment.

Technological constraints determine how work is organized and carried out. For example, the technology of transportation creates a set of employment issues that are different from the technology of a manufacturing plant. Market/budgetary constraints determine the scope of competition for the enterprise, and, generally, the resources any enterprise can allocate to employment. In general, firms that operate in concentrated markets or in markets that are sheltered from competition have more resources to allocate to employment than firms in more competitive markets. The distribution of power in society determines the relative status of the actors in the system.

At some points, such as with the establishment of compensation, the industrial relations system intersects with the economic system. At other points, such as establishing procedures for union recognition, it may be separate from the economic system. The industrial relations system may also touch other subsystems, such as the political system and the legal one. This is especially true when one focuses on the distribution of power in a society.

Once an economy develops from an agrarian economy based on self-sufficiency to an industrial economy with paid wage labor, or if a portion of the economy becomes industrialized, an industrial relations system is created. This is because an industrial economy is based on paid employment, and paid employment creates the two essential actors in the system, employers and workers. Moreover, paid employment, by its very nature, creates substantive and procedural outcomes, or rules. Such rules can be as minimal as how much employees will be paid and how employment is obtained and lost. Even in a situation in which there is no formal government involvement in this decision or in any employment-related decision, the government has acted even by inaction.

Because an industrial society with wage employment creates an industrial relations system, a fundamental question for any government is the nature of the industrial relations system in the country. All countries have enacted laws to regulate the employment relationship in some way. Some countries have decided that it is in the country's best interest to heavily regulate the employment relationship. Other countries have chosen less regulation. Some countries have chosen a system in which the government is deeply involved with employers and/or employees. Other countries have opted for less involvement.

The result is a range of industrial relations systems. For example, for most of the twentieth century, Great Britain has opted for relatively little regulation of industrial relations (Hyman, 1995). Governments in the United States and Canada are more heavily involved in industrial relations than the government in Britain (Block, 1996; Adams, 1997; Block, 1997). On the other hand, governments in Europe and Australia tend to be involved to a greater extent than the United States (see, for example, Davis and Lansbury, 1998; Furstenberg, 1998; Pelligrino, 1998; Hammerstrom and Nilsson, 1998). In Japan, the government has been indirectly involved through support of the large corporations (Fajnzylber, 1990; Kuwahara, 1998).

The purpose of this paper is to explore how the industrial relations system in Korea has evolved over the last three decades, with special attention to the 1997 intervention of the International Monetary Fund (IMF) in Korea. External shocks to an economic system can affect the industrial relations system because of the links between the two, and the IMF intervention in the Korean economy was a momentous shock. As the Korean economy adjusts and changes in the post-IMF era, the industrial relations system will also change. The key question that must be asked is whether it is in the interest of the Korean government to influence this change, and, if so, how? Put differently, what should be the characteristics of the Korean industrial relations system? Part II of the paper will briefly examine the pre-IMF industrial relations system in Korea and its relationship to economic development. Part III will examine the relationship between the IMF intervention and the Korean industrial relations system. Part IV will propose an option for organizing the Korean industrial relations system in the post-IMF era. Part V will provide a summary and conclusions.

II. The Pre-IMF Industrial Relations System in Korea

1. Characteristics of the Korean Economy

Korea is an emerging country in Asia characterized by rapid economic growth over the last three decades (Amsden, 1989; Deyo, 1989). Its population is 45 million and almost 80 per cent of the population was urban by the late 1990s (Park and Leggett, 1998). Rapid industrialization since the mid 1960's through export-oriented manufacturing has resulted in an increase in per capita GNP of Korea from US$87 in 1962 to more than US$10,000 in 1997 (The Bank of Korea, 2000). Korea showed an annual average growth rate of 8 per cent during 1980s and 1990s (Park and Leggett, 1998). Korea is now the world's twelfth largest economy, and it became a member of the Organization for Economic Cooperation and Development (OECD) in 1996 (Park and Leggett, 1998).

Table 1.1 Recent Major Economic Index of Korea

	'87	'89	'91	'93	'95	'97	'98	'99
GPD Growth (Percent change from previous year)	11.5	6.4	9.1	5.8	8.9	5.5	-5.5	9.9
Workforce (1,000's)	14,979	15,644	16,306	16,830	17,384	17,955	18,212	18,462
Unemployment Rate (annual)	3.1	2.6	2.3	2.8	2.0	2.6	6.8	6.3
Union Density (annual percentage)	13.8	18.6	15.9	14.2	12.7	11.2	11.5	
Export Increase (percent change from previous year)	36.2	2.8	10.5	7.3	30.3	5.0	-2.8	8.6
CPI (annual percent increase)	3.1	5.7	9.3	4.8	4.5	4.5	7.5	0.8

(Source: Yearbook of Labor Statistics, Ministry of Labor; The Bank of Korea; KLI, each year)

As will be discussed below, however, this remarkable record of economic development was associated with structural characteristics of the Korean economy that developed during the process of concentrated growth during 1970s and 1980s. These underlying fractures were abruptly revealed toward the end of 1997. Consequently the Korean economy experienced a currency crisis, which was ignited by the East Asian currency crisis in mid-1997. At present, Korea is pressing ahead with thoroughgoing structural reform through which the Korean economy may escape the influence of the IMF bail-out program (The Bank of Korea, 2000).

2. The Importance of the Chaebols

The *Chaebols* and the Government

A key feature of the Korean economy in the post-Korean War era has been the importance of the *Chaebols* in combination with succesive government policies of import substitution and export-oriented industrialization (EOI) (Bamber and Leggett, 1996). Not unlike the Japanese economy, with the zaibatsu in the pre-war era and the keiretsu in the post-war era, the *Chaebols* were the engine of Korean economic policy, and the government, the fuel. The engine was the productive capacity of the *Chaebols*, and the fuel was the favorable financial arrangements created by government policy. The fuel took multiple forms: (1) government subsidies to the *Chaebols* to permit the *Chaebols* to implement the EOI; (2) favorable financial conditions from banks, with the government encouraging banks to make loans to *Chaebols* on the basis of EOI rather than on a business rationale; (3) limitations on imports; and (4) high tariff rates (Woo, 1996).

During the period 1948-79, the *Chaebols* had three main sources of capital accumulation: repatriated property after Japanese colonization ended in 1945, selective allocation of aid funds, materials, and related support by government. This latter source included support for investment, maintenance of an undervalued currency (thereby reducing the costs of Korean exports), restrictions on imports of foreign merchandise, and privileged access to financing at low interest rates in a time of high inflation, resulting in a negative real interest rate. These latter loans were really policy loans so that *Chaebols* could purchase government properties and foreign aid goods and services, and expand business operations. The dominant source of cheap credit was bank loans and international borrowing, access to which was controlled by government. The *Chaebols* received long-term loans and a grace period for repayment. Then, as the *Chaebols* grew, the ease with which they could obtain loans increased. (Woo, 1991; Lee, 1996)

From the point of view of this paper, the key period is the Park Chung-hee regime, from 1961-79. During this period, following the regime of Rhee Syngman, the economic development policy of the state changed from an import substitution policy to an EOI policy (Woo, 1991; Lee, 1996). The state played the role of entrepreneur in economic development. It planned development, invested in the public sector, and provided the private sector with massive financial support (Lee, 1997). Specific industries were targeted for support, as exemplified by the Heavy and Chemical Industry program, instituted from 1973-79 (Stern, Kim, Perkins, and Yoo, 1995; Kim, 1997). Under this program, large government investments were made in *Chaebols* in such heavy industries as steel, autos, shipbuilding, petrochemicals, and machinery. These investments were for the export market, as the domestic market could not possibly absorb this level of production (Stern, Kim, Perkins, and Yoo, 1995).

Lee (1997) points out, however, that despite the close relationship between the *Chaebols* and the government during the Park Chung-hee regime, the government was always the patron of the *Chaebols*, rather than the reverse. As a result, the government retained its autonomy and authority. Thus, in the early 1980's, when the regime of Chun Doo-hwan succeeded the Park Chung-hee regime, the government responded to public criticism of the wealth and power of the *Chaebols* by adopting regulations designed primarily to restrict the market power of the *Chaebols* (Lee, 1997). Government support for the *Chaebols* did not end. Rather, support was tempered by recognition of the need for balance in the economic system (Lee, 1997). The policy of regulation of the *Chaebols* was continued under the regime of Roh Tae-woo, from 1988-93 (Lee, 1997).

In 1993, the Kim Young-sam government, the first civil government since 1960, began to promote a policy of economic liberalization. This included reduced intervention in the private sector, relaxation of administrative regulations, reduction of the size of government, and reduced intervention in the financial system (Lee, 1997). As will be seen, this deregulation and reduced intervention in the financial system was to be a key factor in the financial developments that led to IMF intervention in 1997.

The Growth of the *Chaebols*

As mentioned, the rapid economic development in Korea during past four decades depended on the *Chaebols*; thus the process of economic growth meant the growth of *Chaebols* in the Korean economy. In April 1998, the top 30 *Chaebols* totaled 804 affiliated companies (Choi, 1998). On average, each *Chaebol* consisted of 26.8 affiliated companies. For the five largest *Chaebols*, moreover, the average number of affiliated companies for each *Chaebol* was over 50. For example, the largest and the second largest *Chaebol*, Hyundai and Samsung, had 62 and 61 affiliated companies, respectively (Choi, 1998).

Some indicators reveal the huge influence of *Chaebols* over Korean economy. The share of permanent employees in the entire economy hired in the top 30 *Chaebols* increased from 7.94% in 1994 to 8.44% in 1996. As the crisis occurred in 1997, however, the share of the top 30 *Chaebols* decreased to 7.70% in 1997 and to 7.48% in 1998 due to a rise in bankruptcies, massive layoffs in many industries, and organizational restructuring in firms (Choi, 1998).

The importance of the *Chaebols* is demonstrated by examining the concentration of assets in the top 30 *Chaebols*. The share of the total assets of the Korean economy held by the top 30 *Chaebols* increased continuously from

41.56% in 1994 to 46.61% in 1996 to 47.79% in 1998 (Choi, 1998). Focusing on the top five *Chaebols*, the trends of asset concentration become still more stark. While the share of the top five *Chaebols* in terms of the number of permanent employees in the economy increased marginally from 4.49% in 1994 to 5.02% in 1997 and 1998, the share of the 5 *Chaebols* in terms of total assets increased considerably, from 23.39% in 1994 to 31.61% in 1998 (Choi, 1999). Thus, in 1998, a mere five *Chaebol* owners control about one third of the total assets in the economy. In sum, the degree of concentration of economic power into the top 5 or top 30 *Chaebols* in Korea is enormous and exceeds the degree by Zaibatsu in Japan during the pre-war period or other business groups in other countries (Kang et al., 1991).

3. Historical Overview of the Industrial Relations System in Korea

Unions and Government Policy

The history of industrial relations in Korea may be traced to the Japanese occupation (1905-1945), during which Korean unions were restrained by the Japanese imperial authorities (Park and Leggett, 1998; Song, 1999). At the same time, the labor movement drew support from nationalist and socialist leaders (Park and Leggett, 1998). During this time, the union movement was more of a political movement addressing national issues — i.e. national independence — than a trade union movement representing the economic interests of workers (Vogel and Lindauer, 1989).

After World War II, with Korea divided by the occupation forces of the Soviet Union and the United States, the labor movement in South Korea was split into *Jeonpyeong* (General Council of Korean Trade Unions), the pro-communists, and *Daehan Nochong* (Federation of Korean Trade Unions), the anti-Communists (Vogel and Lindauer, 1989). In 1947, the leftist *Jeonpyeong* was banned by the American military government and soon replaced by the *Daehan Nochong* (Vogel and Lindauer, 1989).

Economic development depended on an ample supply of low paid, cooperative workers. Government labor policy assured this by repressing labor rights and controlling trade unions (Kim, 1994; Woo, 1996). When the Park government took power through a military coup in 1961, a policy of modern industrialization was initiated. Korean industrial relations continued to be controlled by the government. Park's government put the first priority on economic growth by means of the "market-clearing wage" which was sufficiently low for Korean products to be price-competitive in international markets and to provide positive patronage for *Chaebols* (Song, 1991; Jang, 2000). In order to discipline the working class, the government relied on authoritarian control policies (Choi, 1992; Deyo, 1987; Song, 1999). In 1961, unions were obliged to affiliate with industry federations under a government-sponsored national center, the Federation of Korean Trade Unions (FKTU); rival organizations were outlawed and oppressed (Park and Leggett, 1998). Through the 1970s, unions were usually officially sponsored organizations controlled by management and backed by the government (Vogel and Lindauer, 1989).

In 1980, although the political liberalization, so-called "Seoul Spring," followed Park's assassination in 1979, Chun Doo-hwan repressed the political protest led by students and union leaders in 1981. Chun's government established a system of enterprise unionism through the Trade Union Act, which prohibited political activity by unions, and locked out 'third parties' who were not employed by the enterprises concerned (Choi, 1992). Moreover, labor disputes were not permitted in the public and defense sectors (Lee, 1992).

In spite of the repressive control, unions protested for the right to organization. Protests in the 1980's led by students and union activists against Chun's government came to a head in June 1987 when the presidential candidate Rho Tae-woo promised political liberalization, including direct elections (Park and Leggett, 1998).

This political democratization provided the momentum for modern Korean unionism. Independent unions began to organize and labor disputes dramatically increased. By the mid-1980 the same political pressures that caused the Chun regime to replace the Park regime and to change government policy toward the *Chaebol*s also began to cause unrest among workers. In 1986, the government acquiesced to continuing pressure from the FKTU, then the only officially recognized federation of unions, to revise or repeal the Labor Union Law of 1980 which prohibited higher-level labor organizations from bargaining with business firms, and limited bargaining to workers and employers so that wage increases would comply with the guideline of the government and the Korean Employers Association (KEA) (Rhee, 1994). In 1986, the labor law was revised, permitting the FKTU to bargain with employers (Rhee, 1994).

Finally, in 1987, following student and union demonstrations against the government in June 1987, which resulted in the death of two students, presidential candidate Roh Tae-woo (the successor to Chun in the Democratic Justice party) and the government revised labor policy to emphasize equity rather than efficiency in their campaign. They promised the realization of distributive justice and the promotion of workers' welfare through a democratic relationship between labor and management, a guarantee of proper wage levels, and improvement of working conditions (Lee, 1997). Such laws were enacted in 1987 during the transition from the Chun regime to the Roh regime, which started in February 1988 (Lee, 1992; Lee, 1996; Woo, 1996).

While a full review of the industrial relations laws is beyond the scope of this paper, it should be pointed out the laws gave unions that are voluntarily established the right to represent employees, required that employers bargain in good faith, and prohibited certain employer unfair labor practices, mainly interfering with employees' union activities (Lee, 1992).[4] The laws also established dispute resolution mechanisms (Lee, 1992). The basic principle was a government withdrawal from its authoritarian approach as an ally of employers and a repressor of labor to become a neutral coordinator within its legal framework, while still

---

[4] For a more detailed discussion of the post-1987 labor laws in Korea, see Lee, 1992.

committed to the maintenance of economic growth (Park and Lee, 1994; Woo, 1996; Park & Leggett, 1998).

In 1995, the Korean Confederation of Trade Unions (KCTU), which consisted of unions from both manufacturing and service industries, and from public and private sectors, was formed. Although its leaders were immediately jailed and it was officially outlawed until 1999, the KCTU expanded its number of affiliates and its membership to 500,000 by 1997 and managed to gain de facto legality and recognition competing with the conservative FKTU (Kwon & O'Donnell, 1999).

In April 1996, the government announced new directions for industrial relations reform, for which the Industrial Relations Reform Commission (IRRC) was established to discuss labor law reform. This was an important step toward the institutionalization and recognition of the trade union movement, because representatives of labor, including the KCTU, were formally involved in the discussion of national policy toward labor. In particular, it is very meaningful that the government, management and the unions reached a compromise on labor relations reform through the tripartite IRRC (Choi, Y. K., 1999).

But the conservative ruling party—the New Korea Party—did not commit to the compromised bill and passed its unilateral bill through the National Assembly at 2 a.m. on 26 December 1996, in the absence of the opposition and without debate or public scrutiny (Ranald, 1999). This bill contained restrictions on the recognition of multi-unionism, the continued restriction of legal recognition at the national federation level to only the FKTU, continued restrictions on the right of public sector workers and teachers to organize, and the continuation of limits on the union political activities, while easing employer constraints on dismissing employees. The KCTU initiated a national campaign of action, while easing the FKTU supported. The campaign included the largest national strike since *Jeonpyeong*'s general strike in 1946. Eventually, the government was forced to withdraw the bill. (Kim, 1998)

Employment Security

Despite the variability of government policy toward labor since the Rhee Syng-man regime, a constant theme in Korea has been employment security. Macroeconomic growth has been a key factor underlying employment security in Korea. At the same time, laws have encouraged employment security at the firm (micro) level. At the macro level, Woo (1996) points out that unemployment in Korea dropped from 16.4% in 1963 to 3.0% in 1988 and remained below 5% through the mid 1990's. Park and Lee (1995) note that the unemployment rate continued to drop after 1988, down to only 2.3% in 1991. Moreover, it continued to be low through 1995 (Woo, 1996).

Other economic indicators tell a similar story. Employment more than doubled from 1965 to 1991, increasing from 8.1 million to 18.6 million (Park and Lee, 1995). The percentage of employed persons who were employees (the rest being self-employed, often at a subsistence level) increased from only 32.2% in 1965 to 60.9% in 1991 (Park and Lee, 1995). The percentage employed in agriculture declined from 58.5% in 1965 to only 16.7% in 1991, while, during that same time period, the percentage employed in manufacturing rose from 9.4% to 26.3% (Park and Lee, 1995). To a large extent, this employment was driven by exports. Exports increased, from US$32 million in 1967 to US$62 billion in 1991. It was also, however, driven by cheap labor, relative to productivity gains (Woo, 1996).

At the micro level, employees in firms of five or more are covered by the Labor Standards Act (LSA) and are protected from dismissal (Park and Lee, 1995).[5] Under the vast majority of collective agreements, unless a worker is unable to work for mental or physical reasons, or commits a criminal offense, or is given a penalty according to the company's regulations, the worker may not be temporarily laid off. Courts also limit

---

[5] Because coverage was limited to firms of five or more, 6 million employees were not covered by LSA in the mid 1990's (Park and Lee, 1995).

layoffs for business restructuring unless there is no other way of solving business problems. Ministry of Labor guidelines say layoffs for business restructuring are only recognized if the company would go bankrupt, business operations have stopped, or workers can't be transferred. (Park and Lee, 1995)

This inflexibility, in turn, has led to firm employment reduction strategies that are focused away from incumbents. These strategies include not replacing workers who leave jobs (attrition), reducing new openings, contracting out work (through "small president" and job agencies), and laying off daily workers not covered by LSA.

It is clear that the economic success of Korea from the 1960' s through the mid-1990's in combination with laws severely restricting employers options for employment reductions through layoffs led to an expectation of long-term or even lifetime job security among Korean workers. While wage rates and compensation remained relatively low to permit Korean firms compete in the international market, as in Japan, lifetime employment became the expectation in Korea. In essence, an implied agreement evolved among Korean employers, Korean workers, and the government, at least since the early 1980's. Korean employers would have available relatively low cost, high-skilled labor as well as government subsidies. Korean workers would trade high wage rates for lifetime employment (e.g., continuous job security). Despite the occasional strike and demonstration of unions, the government obtained some semblance of Confucian social harmony (Lee, 1997) through lifetime job security. The government used employers, primarily *Chaebol*s, as the vehicle for providing lifetime job security for employees. The actors in the industrial relations system, government, employers, workers, and to some extent, unions, had established a set of rules that incorporated job security and income security.

III. The Korean Financial Crisis, The IMF, and Industrial Relations

The Asian financial crisis, which began in Thailand on July 2, 1997, and spread to Indonesia, Malaysia, and Korea, has been called a global economic crisis because it spread beyond Asia to Russia and Latin America (World Bank, 1999). Among these four Asian countries, only Malaysia did not seek emergency IMF financial assistance. This economic crisis in Southeast Asia caused an unfavorable economic environment in Korea by making foreign investors and creditors more sensitive to financial problems in Korea that prior to the crisis.

1. Financial Problems in Some Sectors of the Korean Economy

The IMF point of view (Sugisaki, 1997) was that the crisis in Korea (and Hong Kong, Indonesia, Malaysia, and the Philippines) was caused by contagion effects from the crisis in Thailand, with the observation that many of the factors that were present in Thailand were present in Korea. These included concerns about the health of the financial sector, overvalued property, floating exchange rates combined with an unwillingness to raise interest rates to market levels, and providing some firms with favorable treatment through development-related government intervention in financial markets and investment decisions.

In the corporate sector, the *Chaebol*s accumulated very high levels of debt (OECD, 1998). Because the government allocated low interest loans to firms according to level of exports and policy considerations rather than financial considerations, larger firms had an advantage in securing the loans. As a consequence, the top 30 *Chaebol*s recorded a debt-to-equity ratios double the average ratios of the 448 firms that are listed on the Korea Stock Exchange in 1997 (UN, 1999). The average debt-to-equity ratio for top 30 *Chaebol*s was 519% in 1997 and would be increased to 603.6% in 1998 if financial companies are included (OECD, 1999a). The high levels of debt incurred by the *Chaebols* required them to bear enormous financial costs. For example, the financial costs of debt service accounted for nearly 17% of total Korean business costs in 1997; comparable costs were below 6% in the U.S. and Japan (OECD, 1998).

In the financial sector, banks lacked objective assessment measures for determining the risks associated with loans. Rather, loans were made to firms through the influence of government policies; it is not surprising then, that some loans made more political sense than economic sense. As a result, the financial institutions in Korea have been exposed to huge non-performing loans (OECD, 1998 and 1999a; UN, 1999).

The economic crisis in 1997 triggered a series of bankruptcies among the *Chaebols*, such as Hanbo, Jinro, Daenong, New Core, and Kia. Among them, Hanbo was the fourteenth and Kia was the eighth largest *Chaebol* (OECD, 1999a). The bankruptcies of Hanbo Steel and finally the Hanbo business group in early 1997 were associated with a debt-to-equity ratio of 674.9% in 1995. Kia had a debt-to-equity ratio of 516.9% in 1996 (OECD, 1999a). A few weeks after the crisis in Thailand in mid-1997, Kia Motors requested a "debt work-out" of program with its major creditors of involving about $8 billion. The incident sparked market volatility. In addition, the bankruptcies of Kia and Hanbo, the eighth and the fourteenth largest *Chaebol* respectively, were followed by a series of bankruptcies of small and medium-size firms due to credit crunch and rapidly increased interest rates.

2. The IMF Intervention

The IMF intervention was broad, falling into three main areas, macroeconomic policies, financial sector restructuring, and "other structural measures." The macroeconomic policy requirements called for a tight monetary policy to minimize the impact on inflation of the won depreciation and a tight fiscal policy to provide for the possible costs of financial sector restructuring. The restructuring of the financial sector included the closing or restructuring of troubled financial institutions, a changing of accounting principles to international standards, the disposal of nonperforming loans, and the acceleration of foreign entry into the domestic sector. The "other structural measures" included trade liberalization, capital liberalization (increasing foreign involvement in the Korean equity market), changes in corporate governance, including the elimination of government involvement in bank lending decisions, greater provision of financial data, and most important from the point of view of this paper, strengthening "the capacity of the new Employment Insurance system . . . to facilitate the redeployment of labor, in parallel with further steps to improve labor market flexibility." (International Monetary Fund, 1997)

3. The IMF Intervention and the Industrial Relations System

Academic and other non-IMF observers have also added various perspectives on the IMF intervention in Korea, and these are relevant to understanding the impact of the IMF intervention on industrial relations in Korea. Chang, Park, and Yoo (1998) argue that the crisis has its roots in the decision of the Korean government to liberalize financial regulations in the early 1990's as a response to the success of the *Chaebols* in the 1980's, pressure from the United States to open the Korean financial market to foreign firms, and Korea's interest in membership in the OECD, which required financial market liberalization.[6] But because the regulations were much more liberal for short term than for long term debt, Korean corporations accumulated the former relative to the latter. Chang, Park, and Yoo (1998) also argue that the abandonment by the Kim Young-sam regime in the mid-1990's of generalistic industrial policies in favor of particularistic policies, showing preference for particular *Chaebols* caused industrial policy decisions to be made on political, rather than economic,

---

[6] See also Wade, 1998.

terms.

Finally, Chang, Park, and Yoo (1998) contend that the financial problems were not due to the means by which Korean firms were financed themselves. Although Korean firms had a very high debt-to-equity ratio of over 300%, during the period 1973-96, it was no higher than those of Japanese firms. They attribute the IMF intervention not to any fundamental deficiencies in the Korean economic system, but rather to a general financial panic associated with Asia.

Wade (1998) and Wade and Veneroso (1998) argue that the intervention was not due to fundamental problems in the Korean economic system nor to a generalized financial panic, but rather to an attempt by the United States to "open the Korean markets" for the benefit of Wall Street and to "Americanize" the Korean economy. To Wade (1998) and Wade and Veneroso (1998), what appeared to the IMF and the United States to be a problem, the high debt-to-equity ratio of corporations, was simply a manifestation of the Asian economic system with its high savings rates and low equity ownership. In such a system, debt is likely to be high because of the supply of liquidity in bank savings and because of the paucity of funds to purchase equity.

Krugman (1998) attributed the crisis to overlending by Korean financial institutions. He argued that the institutions obtained funds at low interest rates and lent it at high rates for speculative investments, believing that they had government guarantees in the event of losses.

Stiglitz (1998) argues that, although the macroeconomic fundamentals in Korea were strong (Korea, like other east Asian countries "had high saving rates, government surpluses or small deficits, low inflation, and low levels of external debt relative to other developing regions."), the crisis was caused by an aggregation of firm decisions that resulted in overinvestment in relatively risky instruments, such as speculative real estate, an overemphasis on short-term debt in international markets and very high levels of corporate debt relative to equity. Stiglitz argued that much of this was caused by financial liberalization in the 1990's that was unaccompanied by appropriate and adequate government controls, such as reserve requirements and deposit insurance with the requisite monitoring of loans. Thus, in Stiglitz' view, the absence of regulations and restrictions on banks permitted them to make loans that might not be considered prudent. In addition, financial liberalization and opening of capital markets increased the supply of credit to the corporate sector, with the result being risky loans to Korean firms in the international market.

Common to all these views is the central thesis that the Korean crisis was primarily a financial crisis triggered by problems in the financial sector. Although it has been argued that low productivity and low profit, caused at least in part by labor market inflexibility, contributed to the crisis (Park, 1999), there is no reason to believe that these factors would cause a financial crisis if financial markets were efficient. In the presence of efficient financial markets, low firm productivity and profit would be capitalized into the interest rate charged or would result in a loan denial. Thus, for the purposes of this paper, we argue that neither the official IMF view nor the views of commentators would support the position that the industrial relations system in Korea contributed to the crisis.

Yet, the IMF, in its agreement with the Korean government, incorporated a condition that would prove to be most disruptive to the Korean economy and to the Korean industrial relations system, a requirement for increasing labor market flexibility. Issues of "labor market flexibility," are said to arise when the attachments between employers and their employees are so strong as to prevent the movement of labor from less productive to more productive uses (Clarke, 1992). Labor market inflexibility generally arises in labor markets that are characterized by employee job security and limitations, either legal or cultural, on the layoff of redundant employees. These are precisely the conditions that existed in Korea in late 1997.

Labor market inflexibility can generate inefficiencies in an economy experiencing large-scale structural change, as when an economy experiences a rapid decline in one sector (for example, software manufacture). Labor markets in such a situation are viewed as being inflexible in the short run. In the long run, employment in the declining sector shrinks through attrition as retirees and quitters are not replaced with new hires/labor force entrants. Rather, demand pressures force new labor force entrants into the expanding sectors. There was no consideration in the IMF intervention regarding the extent to which any adjustments could be accommodated through the attrition model, consistent with the existing "rules" created through the Korean industrial relations system. In addition, there was no encouragement either through the IMF, through the government, or through the *Chaebol*s of exploring Japanese-style money compensation reductions and worker reallocations to healthier sister *Chaebol* companies (Koshiro, 1992; Mizuno, 1992; Seike, 1992) and reductions in working time (Clarke, 1992) as alternatives to large scale layoffs.[7]

Fundamentally, the IMF requirement of labor market reform in Korea went far beyond the problems in the financial sector that the IMF intervention was designed to solve. Indeed, Wade (1998) and Wade and Veneroso (1998) argue that the entire IMF intervention went well beyond the particular problems in Korea and attempted to establish a Western financial system in Korea. One need not go as far as Wade and Wade and Veneroso to point out that the requirements for labor market restructuring went far beyond the contribution of the labor market to the problem that necessitated IMF intervention. The rationale for the labor market flexibility provision was simply to facilitate corporate restructuring. It would not, in and of itself, solve any of the financial problems that caused the crisis. Rather, the IMF intervention created an external influence that was inconsistent with the industrial relations system that had evolved in Korea. Thus, it is not surprising that the result was disruptions in the industrial

---

[7] While employment security arrangements can result in short-term labor market inflexibility, evidence indicates that, over the long run, firms adjust to such arrangements by reducing hiring during economic upswings so that it is unnecessary to reduce employment during downturns. Hiring, then, shows less cyclical variation than is found in the absence of employment security provisions. Adjustments in hours worked are also used to address fluctuations in labor demand. (Cazes, Boeri,Bertola, 1999)

relations system that would hamper Korea's attempts to comply with the IMF agreement.

While a detailed discussion of the all the industrial relations matters that arose following the IMF intervention in Korea is beyond the scope of this paper, some examples will suffice to provide a sense of the industrial relations situation in 1998 and early 1999. In February 1998, the South Korean National Assembly accepted a key condition from the IMF that would increase the flexibility of labor markets by reducing restrictions on the right of firms to lay off workers. Unions, as expected, resisted the bill. (South Korean Parliament · · ·, 1998).

The *Chaebol*s then began to announce restructurings, which involved layoffs, and labor conflict began. Unions at Kia Motors called an indefinite strike on April 16, 1998 to protest possible sale of the company to a third party ("Shares Sink· · · 1998). The strike ended on April 23 as government announced it had no immediate plans to sell Kia. President Kim Dae Jung became involved, stating at a meeting with unions and management that Kia issues should be addressed transparently and openly for all to understand. The Korea Development Bank, Kia's, main creditor, said the creditors would support Kia if labor and management reconcile differences. ("Kia Motors will end· · ·, 1998).

Meanwhile, continuing layoffs by *Chaebol*s sparked street protests in May, 1998 ("South Korean Stocks · · ·, 1998). In response, President Kim Dae Jung promised to take strong action when unions interfered with management and violated the law, stating that it was important that the labor market be more flexible (House and Schuman, 1998; "South Korea's Kim · · · 1998). At the same time, however, he said unemployment, which reached 6.5% in March 1998 (1.38 million unemployed), double the March 1997 rate, posed the greatest threat to Korea's economic recovery, and that he would propose government support for unemployed workers ("South Korea's Kim · · · 1998). Moreover, Kim's finance minister, Lee Kyu Sung, was quoted as saying that "without social stability, we couldn't accomplish our reform program," but that without strong reform efforts, "the economy will drop into longtime sluggishness" ("South Korea's Kim ··· 1998).

Meanwhile the KCTU, with a large membership in automobile manufacturing and shipbuilding, announced on May 20 that it would call a strike on May 27 to protest layoffs (Schuman, 1998). Kim Dae Jung was reported as saying that labor unrest was the biggest obstacle to economic reform and promising strong action against unions (Schuman, 1998a).

In June, workers called a two-week strike at Kia to protest unpaid wages. Prior to that workers had been receiving half pay. When management said it would close plants for 10 days, about 30 union members entered management office with pipes, injuring fifteen people (Schuman, 1998b). In September, 1998, following the merger of five small banks with larger banks, banking industry executives retreated from their claimed need to reduce jobs by 50% after the union representing financial services workers threatened a strike ("South Korean Financial Watchdogs · ·· 1998). Eventually, the banks agreed to limit the job reductions to 32% (Burton, 1998a).

News analyses reported that labor problems could reduce confidence on the part of investors and the business community in the ability of Korea to implement the IMF reforms (Burton, 1998b; Mufson, 1998). These incidents demonstrate the costs associated with the absence of labor-management-government structures to deal with economy-wide issues such as the IMF agreement.

Workers and the labor market were being asked to bear a substantial portion of the burden of restructuring. This perceived inequity was aggravated by the fact that the KCTU, at least, perceived that it had little voice in the actual restructuring decision that was made at the national level. As a result, the KCTU took direct action at the firm level, disrupting the restructuring process with the resulting loss of confidence in Korean business.

The foregoing discussion suggests a need for a structure of industrial relations at the national level. The next section of the paper will discuss such potential system.

IV. The Korean Industrial Relations System in the Post-IMF Era: Does Tripartitism Make Sense?

The increased democratization of the Korean political system and the importance of unions in the Korean industrial relations system suggest that a vehicle must be created to accommodate and listen to the views of labor in order to redomesticize the industrial relations system in Korea. The IMF has brought to the Korean economy a western (European/American/Canadian) influence that is likely to persist for a long period of time. Thus, it is important for the Korean industrial relations system to establish structures that can accommodate to this western influence. While a U.S. and Canadian-style model of decentralized unionism is compatible with a western economy, we believe that it is incompatible with a small country like Korea, with a dynamic export-driven economy and where the Confucian principle of harmony is highly valued (Lee, 1997). Therefore, we believe that Korea should continue to experiment with the tripartite structures it created in the 1990's.

1. Previous Experiences with Tripartite Structures

In light of the tradition of Korean industrial relations driven by authoritarian government from 1960s to the early 1990s, it is easily understood that there had been no distinct predecessor of the 1998 tripartite committee. Only a few attempts to establish such corporatist[8] institutions are found from the late 1980s and early 1990s (You, 1998).

The first attempt to create a tripartite, corporatist structure was the Central Labor-Management Council. Created by Labor-Management Council Act in 1980, the Council included a corporatist structure, which consisted of labor, management, and public representatives. It was considered a failure, however, because its agreements were not binding and it did not cover labor in practice (Choi, Y. K., 1999). The Minimum Wage Committee from 1987 had a structure similar to the Central

Labor-Management Council in that labor, management, and public representatives participated together. Despite this corporatist structure, however, the Committee was viewed as too limited to be effective because government did not join and the scope of issues that the Committee handled was narrow, being limited to the annual renewal of the minimum wage (Choi, Y. K., 1999).

The National Council for Economy and Society (NCES) was created by a proposal of the FKTU in 1990. It was comprised of representatives of management and the FKTU. The purpose of the NCES was to make recommendations on national economic issues. Like the Central Labor-Management Council and Minimum Wage Committee, the NCES did not include the non-authorized union labor federation, the Korean Trade Unions Congress (KTUC), the predecessor of the KCTU. Although, through the NCES, the representatives of management and the FKTU in 1993 and 1994 reached agreement on a national wage increase scheme that ranged from 4% to 8%, the agreement faced severe resistance from the KTUC and even from some of the affiliated enterprise union leaders within the FKTU (Choi, Y. K., 1999). Eventually, the NCES dissolved.

Excluding the economic emergency caused by the Korean currency crisis in 1997 and emergence of a new president as a result of the victory of the opposition party, two incidents that are regarded as pre-history of the tripartite committee from 1998 should be mentioned. One is the experience of the tripartite IRRC of 1996-1997. The other is the general strike by KCTU in the early 1997. The purpose of the IRRC was the revision of labor laws covering representatives of labor, management, and government. The IRRC is also important because the representatives of the KCTU, the officially unrecognized federation, participated. The experiences from the IRRC allowed all three actors in the industrial relations to system work together, an essential aspect of the creation of Tripartite Commission (TC) in 1998 (Choi, Y. K., 1999).

Through the efforts of TCIS, an agreement on labor law reform was reached between the labor and public members. The ruling party, however, passed a revised bill that was viewed by the KCTU as unfair. This unexpected incident provoked the first general strike in history by the KCTU and at last government had to retreat and promise to revise the labor laws again after two-months general strike. These incidents, including the general strike, reminded all three actors in industrial relations that the exclusion of either union federation from tripartite structure must be ineffective (Kim, 1998).

2. A Proposal for a New Tripartite Structure

The experiences of tripartite institutions in Korea indicate an absence of success in the sense that most of the institutions were not viable and no longer exist. These entities generally failed to produce agreements of any duration or lasting impact on Korean industrial relations. In spite of the creation of social pact in February 1998, the TC in 1998 also suffered from the retreat of labor representatives (Yoon, 1999), such as the first retreat of the KCTU in March 1998, its return in June, another retreat of both FKTU and KCTU in February and April 1999, respectively, FKTU's return in August 1999 and non-participation by KCTU since February, 1999.

On the other hand, these multiple attempts to develop a tripartite structure demonstrate that tripartitism and corporatism are generally compatible with Korean culture. Korea appears to be searching for a system that encourages the parties of the Korean industrial relations system to work together to address industrial relations issues.

A tripartite industrial relations structure is compatible with a small, open, and vulnerable economy of, such as that of Korea, which relies heavily relying on export and multi-national capital. As Katzenstein (1987) argues, the vulnerable economic structure of small open economies in

---

[8] A corporatist structure, or corporatism: is defined as a model of governance in which predefined interest groups are given exclusive representational status through a recognized entity in return for some constraints on selection of leadership and articulation of demands (Schmitter, 1979; Lee, 1997).

Europe such as Sweden, Austria, and the Netherlands was a driving force for those countries to adopt and develop a corporatist industrial relations system. These countries must maintain their international competitiveness, and stable industrial relations is an indispensable precondition for maintaining competitiveness. As a result of continuous market liberalization in Korea since the late 1980s, the Korean economy has become more open dependent on exports. At the same time, it is still dependent on exports. In that situation, Korea would be well-served by a system that facilitates stable domestic industrial relations in order not only to continue to be attractive to multi-national capital but also to achieve steady economic growth on the basis of stable politics.

In this sense, a European corporatist model may be more consistent with Korean situation than the decentralized industrial relations model of the U.S and Canada. Although previous attempts at tripartitism in Korea have been unsuccessful, they may have been overly ambitious in theirs goals. It is difficult for the parties in a tripartite system to work together if they have minimal experience in such structures and those structures must make fundamental decisions regarding the Korean economy and the Korean industrial relations systems. The parties' stakes in the decisions are simply too great to permit new structures to work at solving them.

Accordingly, we believe that a more modest form of tripartitism than has previously been attempted is appropriate for the Korean industrial relations system at this time. Thus, we recommend the creation of a national, tripartite entity that issues nonbinding recommendations on matters within its area of interest. Such an entity will permit tripartitism in Korea to evolve and grow slowly. It will permit union representatives, employer representatives, and government/public representatives to interact and become acquainted with one another in the post-IMF era. At the same the system will minimize the actual political effect of what is done, thereby, at this initial stage, reducing the probability of disagreement, as the cost of any decision to any of the three parties will be low.

We recommend an entity with 15 members, divided equally among employer representatives, union representatives, and public representatives. Given the large number of employers, we make no recommendations on how the five employer representatives could be constituted. The five union representatives could consist of three representatives from the FKTU and two representatives from the KCTU, as the FKTU is the larger of the two federations. The five public representatives should consist of three from the government and two from the public, perhaps academics in industrial relations with credentials for neutrality between labor and management.

A recommendation or decision could require the support of 9 of the 15 members of the entity. At any point in time, either management or labor will have greater influence with the government than the other. The public and the aggrieved party would lose confidence in the decisions of the body if it were perceived that an alliance between one of the two parties and the government representatives was sufficient to generate a recommendation. By requiring a recommendation to have the support of at least nine members, it would mean that the government and the more influential party would need the support of at least one of the nongovernmental public members in order to generate a recommendation from the body. This would create a system where negotiations could take place among the members to assure that no recommendation is strongly offensive to the other party, as that party would be able to inform the nongovernment public members about its concerns and have those concerns addressed. If, despite such concerns, decisions and recommendations were made that did not address the concerns of the party, that party could in theory withdraw, compromising the entire system. Such withdrawal is less likely than otherwise in this system, however, where only recommendations would be forthcoming. Even if withdrawal did occur, the costs to the country would not be great.

It is hoped that such a system could evolve into an entity that has some formal authority to make policy. This is more likely to occur, however, if the parties have worked together on nonfundamental issues before addressing the fundamental one.

V. Summary and Conclusions

The 1997 Korean financial crisis has highlighted the importance of developing a consensus on industrial relations in a small, but dynamic economy like Korea. Through the early 1980's, there was acceptance of the importance of economic development and the role of the industrial relations system, given the priority of growth. From the late 1980's through the late 1990's, a consensus developed on industrial relations, with the development of enterprise unions. The 1997 IMF intervention will bring a strong western influence into the Korean economy (Wade, 1998; Wade and Veneroso, 1998). Thus, it is important for the country to develop an industrial relations system that is compatible with this influence in the Korean economy in order to avoid disruptions such as occurred in 1998 and 1999.

The nature of the industrial relations system in a country has always been determined by domestic political, economic, and cultural factors (Dunlop, 1958; Sisson, 1987). Focusing on systems in developed countries, those that are most similar economically to Korea, although all recognize the right of free association and collective bargaining, all have important structures and features that have their roots in the culture of the country. Thus, for example, the United States, with a strong tradition of individualism, decentralization, and minimal government involvement in the market, emphasizes the importance of decentralized collective bargaining, governmental noninvolvement in the outcomes of collective bargaining, and not imposing unionism and collective bargaining on unwilling bargaining units (Block, Beck, and Kruger, 1996). The highly decentralized, largely unregulated system in Great Britain is a function of the strong laissez faire tradition in that country (Hyman, 1995). The Canadian system has broad structures that are much like that of the United States, its large neighbor to the south, although, compared to the United States, its more collectivist tendencies have resulted in less emphasis on elections and greater government involvement to protect collective bargaining (Lipset, 1989; Adams, 1997; Block, 1997). Centralized, multi-employer bargaining systems emerged in the European countries on the continent in the late nineteenth and early twentieth century as a vehicle for mainly small and medium-sized employers to minimize the influence of trade unionism at the workplace (Sisson, 1987). Enterprise bargaining in Japan can be traced to the creation of the Zaibatsu by the state in the late nineteenth century (Kuwahara, 1998).

The IMF intervention in Korea was an exogeneous shock to the industrial relations system in Korea that was evolving in a manner consistent with Korean needs, traditions, and culture. That system, forged to a great extent through direct action, was a combination of enterprise bargaining, formal rules and informal understandings regarding employee job security, and occasional attempts at tripartitism. This system, still in its formative stages, could not accommodate the shock to the system imposed by the IMF, a non-Korean actor. As a result, when the IMF required that one of the pillars of the system, job security, be ended, the unions reverted to direct action. They had no other choice.

Korea, in the aftermath of the IMF intervention, must begin to reestablish the industrial relations system that existed prior to the IMF intervention. The multiple attempts to establish tripartite structures in the 1990's suggest that there is compatibility between tripartitism and Korean industrial relations. Since the great protests of June 1987, increased democracy has facilitated a dialogue among employers, labor, and government. Government no longer represses or ignores the voice of labor in the national level. The extremely decentralized collective bargaining structure owing to enterprise union system would benefit from national level coordination by the actors. The Korean industrial relations system, which had been characterized by political exclusion of labor by authoritarian government and bureaucratic order and coercion, would be strengthened by a tripartite system based on political inclusion, participation, open persuasion, and compromise between actors at the national level.

When a system is created that recognizes the legitimate interests of employers, unions, and government, legitimate conflicts between labor and management can be resolved. For example, in November, 2000, financially troubled Daewoo and the union representing its employees agreed on a restructuring plan that included layoffs ("Daewoo Motor, Union...," 2000). At the same time, the ad hoc unstructured nature of the industrial relation system in Korea does not provide for consistency. Thus, Daewoo unions have protested the possible sale of Daewoo to General Motors ("Daewoo Motor Workers...," 2001).

The minimalist tripartite system proposed here, with high level participants but nonbonding recommendations is a first step in the road to a Korean corporatist and tripartite industrial relations system that may lead to a "social pact" (Song, 1999) that would make Korean trade unions a full partner in the continuing economic and political development of Korea. By establishing a system with modest aims that will permit the parties to come together and get to know one another, the prospects for long-term success are enhanced.

References

Adams, George W. (1997). *Canadian Labour Law*, 2nd Ed. Aurora, Ont.: Canada Law Book (May).

Amsdsen, Alice H. (1989). *Asia's Next Giant: Economic Backwardness in Contemporary Perspective: South Korea's Industrialization Through Learning*. London: Oxford University Press.

Bamber, Greg J. and Chris Leggett. (1996). Tiers of change in the Asia-Pacific region: Reflections on democratization, industrial relations, and human resources. *The Transformation of Industrial Relations Under Democratization: Democratization, Globalization, and the Transformation of Industrial Relations in Asian Countries*. Proceedings of the International Industrial Relations Association 3rd Asian Regional Congress, Taipei, Taiwan, R.O.C., Vol. 1, September 30 - October 4, pp. 21-46.

Block, Richard N., John Beck and Daniel H. Kruger. (1996). *Labor Law, Industrial Relations and Employee Choice: The State of the Workplace in the 1990's*. K Kalamazoo, Mich.: W.E. Upjohn Institute for Employment Research.

Block, Richard N. (1997). Rethinking the national labor relations act and zero-sum labor law; An industrial relations view. *Berkeley Journal of Employment and Labor Law*, Vol. 18, No. 1, pp. 30-55.

Burton, John. (1998a). Bank protest strike cancelled. *Financial Times*, September 30.

Burton, John. (1998b). Radical measures are needed. *Financial Times*, October 2.

Cazes, Sandrine, Tito Giuseppe Bertola (1999), *Employment Protection and Labour Market Adjustment in OECD Countries: Evolving Institutions and Variable Enforcement*, Employment and Training Papers 48, Geneva: International Labour Office.

Chang, Ha Joon, Hong-Jae Park, and Chul Gyue Yoo. (1998). Interpreting the Korean crisis: Financial liberalization, industrial policy, and corporate governance. *Cambridge Journal of Economics*, Vol. 22, pp. 735-746.

Choi, Jang-jip. (1992). *Labor Movement and the State in Korea*. Seoul: Nanam (in Korean).

Choi, Sung-No. (1998). *The Korea Big Business Groups*. Seoul: Centre of Free Enterprise (in Korean).

Choi, Young-Ki. (1999). The tradition of social pact and the tripartite committee in

Korea. paperpresented at the Joint Conference of the Korean Academy Association of Industrial Relations, Korean Academy Association of Labor Economics, and Korean Academy Association of Labor Law, January, Seoul (In Korean).

Clarke, Oliver. Employment adjustment: An international perspective. *Employment Security and Labor Market Flexibility.* In Kazutoshi Koshiro. (ed.). Detroit, Michigan: Wayne State University Press, pp. 218-244.

Daewoo Motor, Labor Union Agree on Restructuring, Including Layoffs. (2000). *Wall Street Journal Interactive Edition,* November 27.

Daewoo Motor Workers Hurl Eggs to Protest GM's Takeover Offer. (2001). *Wall Street Journal Interactive Edition-Associated Press,* June 4.

Davis, Edward M. and Russell D. Lansbury. (1999). Employment relations in Australia. *International and Comparative Employment Relations.* In Greg J. Bamber and R. Lansbury. (eds.). London, Thousand Oaks, and New Delhi: Sage Publications, pp. 110-143.

Deyo, Frederic C. (1989). *Beneath the Miracle: Labor Subordination in the New Asian Industrialism.* Berkeley: University of California Press.

Dunlop, John. (1958, 1993). *Industrial Relations Systems.* Boston, Massachusetts: Harvard Business School Press.

Fajnzylber, Fernando. The United States and Japan as models of industrialization. *Manufacturing Miracles: Paths of Industrialization in Latin America and East Asia.* In Gary Gereffi and Donald L. Wyman. (eds.). Princeton, N.J.: Princeton University Press, pp. 323-352.

Fursternberg, Friedrich. (1998). Employment relations in Germany. *International and Comparative Employment Relations.* In Greg J. Bamber and R. Lansbury. (eds.). London, Thousand Oaks, and New Delhi: Sage Publications, pp.201-223.

Hammerstrom, Olle and Tommy Nilsson. (1998). Employment relations in Sweden. *International and Comparative Employment Relations.* In Greg J. Bamber and R. Lansbury. (eds.) London, Thousand Oaks, and New Delhi: Sage Publications, pp. 224-248.

House, Karen Elliott and Michael Schuman. (1998). Kim says unemployment poses biggest threat to Korea's reform. *Wall Street Journal Interactive Edition,* May 5.

Hyman, Richard. (1995). The historical evolution of British industrial relations. *Industrial Relations: Theory and Practice in Britain.* Oxford, United Kingdom: Blackwell Publishers, pp. 27-49.

International Monetary Fund. (1997). Republic of Korea - IMF stand-by arrangement: Summary of economic program. December 5 at http://www.imf.org/external/np/oth/ KOREA.HTM.
International Monetary Fund. (1999). *World Economic Outlook*. Washington, DC.
Jang, S. C. (2000). *Driving Engine or Rent-seeking Super-Cartel?: the Business-State Nexus and Economic Transformation in South Korea: 1960-1999*. unpublished Ph.D Dissertation, Department of Political Science, Michigan State University.
Kang, Chulkyu, Jeongpyo Choi, and Jisang Jang. (1991). *Chaebol: Seongjang juyeok-inga Tamyokye Hwasin-inga (Hero of Development or a Perfect Picture of Avarice*, Seoul: Beebong Publishers (in Korean).
Katzenstein, P. J. (1987). *Small States in World Markets: Industrial Policy in Europe*. Ithaca and London: Cornell University Press.
Kia Motors union will end 9Day strike. (1998). *Wall Street Journal Interactive Edition*, April 23.
Kim, Eun Mee. (1997). *Big Business, Strong State: Collusion and Conflict in South Korean Development*. Albany, New York: State University of New York Press.
Kim, Yong-Cheol. (1998). Industrial reform and labor backlash in South Korea: Genesis, escalation, and termination of the 1997 general strike. *Asian Survey*, Vol. 38, No. 12, December, pp. 1142-1160.
Koshiro, Kazutoshi. (1992). Bonus Payments and Wage Flexibility in Japan. *Employment Security and Labor Market Flexibility*. Detroit, MI: Wayne State University Press, pp. 102-126.
Krugman, Paul. (1998). What happened to Asia? unpublished paper. Department of Economics, Massachusetts Institute of Technology, January, at www/DISINTER.html.
Kuwahara, Yasuo. (1998). Employment relations in Japan. *International and Comparative Employment Relations*. In Greg J. Bamber and R. Lansbury. (eds.). London, Thousand Oaks, and New Delhi: Sage Publications, pp. 249-274.
Kwon, S. and O'Donnell M. (1999). The state, the *Chaebol* and trade unions in South Korea: an historical analysis. *Journal of Industrial Relations*, Vol. 41, No. 2, pp. 272-293.
Lee, Michael Byungnam. (1992). Korea. *Industrial Relations Around the World*. Miriam Rothman.
Lee, Yeon-ho. (1997). *The State, Society, and Big Business in South Korea*. London and

New York: Routledge.

Lipset, Seymour Martin. (1989). *Continental Divide: The Values and Institutions of the United States and Canada*. Toronto and Washington, D.C.: D.C. Howe Institute and National Planning Association.

Mizuno, Asao. (1992). Japanese Wage Flexibility: An International Perspective. *Employment Security and Labor Market Flexibility*. Detroit, MI: Wayne State University Press, pp. 102-126.

Mufson, Steven. (1998). Experts divided on region's fate. *Washington Post*, November 13, p. F1.

Organization for Economic Co-operation and Development. (1999a). *OECD Economic Surveys Korea (Special Features: Financial Sector Reform Corporate Restructuring The Labour Market)*, No. 1, August, Paris.

Organization for Economic Co-operation and Development. (1999b). *OECD Economic Outlook*, No. 66, December, Paris, pp. 95-97.

Park Young-bum and Chris Leggett. (1998). Employment relations in Korea. *International and Comparative Employment Relations*. In Greg J. Bamber and R. Lansbury. (eds.). London, Thousand Oaks, and New Delhi: Sage Publications, pp. 275-293.

Pellegrini, Claudio. (1998). Employment relations in Italy. *International and Comparative Employment Relations*. In Greg J. Bamber and R. Lansbury. (eds.) London, Thousand Oaks, and New Delhi: Sage Publications.

Ranald, P. (1999). Analysing, organizing, resisting: Union responses to the Asian economic crisis in east asia, South Korea and the Philippines. *The Journal of Industrial Relations*, Vol. 41, No. 2, pp. 295-325.

Rhee, Jong-Chan. (1994). *The State and Industry in South Korea*. London and New York: Routledge.

Schuman, Michael. (1998a). Seoul increases funds to buoy banks, but $35 billion may not be enough. *Wall Street Journal Interactive Edition*, May 21.

Schuman, Michael. (1998b). Unpaid wages are on the rise for workers in South Korea. *Wall Street Journal Interactive Edition*, July 6.

Schmitter, Phillipe C. (1979). Still the century of corporatism. *Trends Toward Corporate Intermediation*. In Philippe C. Schmitter and and Gerhard Lehmbruch. (eds.). Beverly Hills, Ca,: Sage Publications.

Seike, Atsushi. (1992). The Employment Adjustment Patterns of Japan and the United Stated. *Employment Security and Labor Market Flexibility*. Detroit, MI:

Wayne State University Press, pp. 245-263.
Shares sink on labor unrest. (1998). *Wall Street Journal Interactive Edition*, April 16.
Sisson, Keith. (1987). *The Management of Collective Bargaining: An International Comparison.* Oxford, U.K. and New York: Basil Blackwell.
Song, Ho Keun. (1991). Authoritarian state and wage policy in Korea, 1970 1987. *Labor Politics and Market in Korea.* Seoul: Nanam.
Song, Ho Keun. (1999). *Labour Unions in the Republic of Korea: Challenge and Choice.* Labour and Society Programme, International Institute for Labour Studies, International Labour Organization, at http://www.ilo.org/public/english/bureau/inst/papers/1999/dp107/index.htm.
South Korean financial watchdogs waver on tough bank reforms. (1998). *Agence France Presse,* September 20.
South Korean parliament adopts economic reforms in IMF pact. (1998). *Wall Street Journal Interactive Edition,* February 14.
South Korean stocks falter as labor unrest worsens. (1998). *Wall Street Journal Interactive Edition,* May 4.
South Korea's Kim asks nation to endure a 'Very Difficult' year. (1998). *Wall Street Journal Interactive Edition,* May 11.
Stern, Joseph J., Ji-hong Kim, Dwight H. Perkins, Junh-ho Yoo. (1995). *Industrialization and the State: The Korean Heavy and Chemical Industry Drive.* Harvard Institute for International Development and Korea Development Institute, Distributed by Harvard University Press.
Stiglitz, Joseph. (1998). Sound finance and sustainable development in Asia. Keynote Address to the Asia Development Forum, Manila, The Philippines, March 12.
Sugisaki, Shigemitsu. (1997). Address to symposium on capital flows and financial system stability in Asia by the deputy managing director of the International Monetary Fund. Institute for International Monetary Affairs International Monetary Fund, Tokyo, Japan, December 8 at http://www.imf.org/external/np/speeches/1997/120897.htm.
Taylor, George W. (1947). Voluntarism, tripartitism, and wage stabilization. *The Termination Report of the National War Labor Board: Industrial Disputes and Wage Stabilization in Wartime,* January 12-1942 December 31, 1945, pp. xv-xxxi
The Bank of Korea. (2000). Introduction at

United Nations. (1999). *Economic and Social Survey of Asia and the Pacific (Asia and the Pacific into the Twenty-first Century: Information Technology, Globalization, Economic Security and Development)*, New York.

Vogel, E. F. and Lindauer, D. (1989). *Toward a Social Impact for South Korean Labour.* Cambridge: Harvard Institute for International Development.

Wade, Robert. (1998). The Asian debt-and-development crisis of 1997: Causes and consequences. *World Development*, Vol. 28, No. 8 , August, pp. 1535-1553.

Wade, Robert and Frank Veneroso. (1998). The Asian crisis: The high-debt model versus the Wall Street-Treasury-IMF complex. *New Left Review*, Vol. 28, March-April, pp. 3-23.

Woo, Jung-en. (1991). *Race to the Swift: State and Finance in Korean Industrialization.* New York: Columbia University Press.

Woo, Seoghun. (1996). Approaching the 21st century: Perspectives on Korean industrial relations. *The Transformation of Industrial Relations Under Democratization: Democratization, Globalization, and the Transformation of Industrial Relations in Asian Countries.* Proceedings of the International Industrial Relations Association 3rd Asian Regional Congress, Taipei, Taiwan, R.O.C., Vol. 4, September 30 - October 4, pp. 155-176.

World Bank. (1999). *Global Economic prospects and the Developing Countries: Beyond Financial Crisis*, 1998/1999. Washington, DC.

Yoon, Jinho. (1999). The tripartite committee, A new paradigm of industrial relations? Paper presented in the Conference, Political Economy of Structural Adjustment and Korean Economy in the 21st Century, by Korean Institute of Social Science and Korean Academy Association of Sociological Economics, December (in Korean).

You, Hyun-Seok. (1998). An experiment of corporatism in Korea: Viability and conditions for the tripartite committee, Paper presented in Korean Political Science Association (in Korean).

Rapid Changes in Earning Inequality in Korea after the Financial Crisis

Sung-Joon Park[1]

I. Introduction

We found out recently through the news and several research papers that since the financial crisis income distribution has become worse. The reason is that the top quintile benefited from the high interest rates while the lower quintiles suffered from declining wages and rising unemployment. However, this explanation is not sufficient in explaining worsening income inequality during and after the economic recovery. The purpose of this paper is to examine the source of change in income inequality after the financial crisis by using raw data from the 'Family Income and Expenditure Survey'published by the National Statistical Office of Korea. The focus of this paper is the earnings of household heads rather than family income, because information about the former is better and their earning averages 70 percent of their family's. Therefore, earning inequality among household heads is a good proxy of income inequality between families.

This paper is organized as follows. Section II explains the data. Section

---

[1] Senior Research Fellow, Korea Economic Research Institute, Seoul, Korea.

III describes the facts on earning inequality. Section IV decomposes inequality into components associated with observed differences (education and experience) and residual or unobserved components, while section V identifies the pattern of the returns to alternative measures of skill. Section VI attempts to explain the reasons for the overall rise in the returns to skill. Section VII is the conclusion.

II. Data

The data used in this paper is the raw data of the 'Family Income and Expenditure Survey' published annually by the National Statistics Office of Korea. The survey covers households with more than two people residing in seventy-two selected cities across Korea. The survey excludes households whose head is a farmer, a fisherman, or self-employed, single-person households, and jobless households. The purpose of the survey is to collect information on urban households' incomes and expenditures. The income information contained in the survey consists of earned and unearned income. Earned income consist of the earnings of the household head, and the spouse's and other members' earnings. Unearned income consists of interest, dividends, and so on. We use the earning of the household head in this paper because unearned income represents a very little portion of the household's income and the earnings of the household head represents about 70 percent of the total household income. In addition, personal information such as age, sex, schooling, industry and occupation are available only for the household head. So we assume that if we examine the inequality between earnings of household heads, we can find out income inequality.

III. Overall Earning Inequality

Figure 1 graphs the tenth, median and ninetieth percentiles of the real earning distribution of household heads[2] for 1991-1999. For ease of comparison, the earning for the three groups are indexed at 100 in 1991. The real earning of the three groups increases relatively steadily from 1990 through to 1997, before the financial crisis, declines sharply in 1998, and then recovers somewhat after 1999. As is clear from the figure, the story is significantly different for the tenth percentile compared to the other two samples used. For the tenth percentile, earning rose similar to the other percentiles before the crisis but declined much more sharply than the other groups during the crisis. Even during the economic recovery in 1999, real earning rose relatively less than the other groups.

Figure 2 displays the substantial widening of earning distribution by plotting the 90-10, 90-50 and 50-10 earning differentials from 1991 to 1999. There is little change in the 90-10 earning differential from 1991 until the

Figure 1. Indexed real earning by percentile

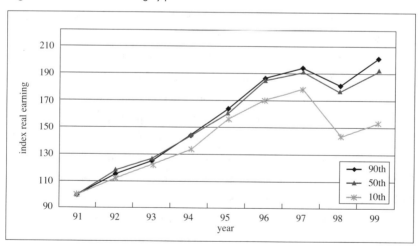

---

[2] From this, we use the earning instead of the earning of the head of the household.

Figure 2. Trend in the Change of Earning Distribution

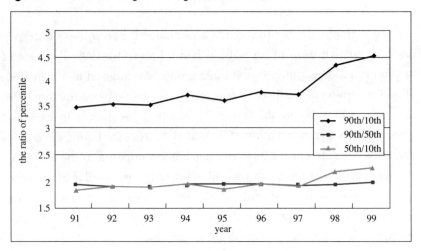

crisis. However, after the crisis the earning gap between these two groups widens very rapidly. The figure also displays the trends of the 90-50 and 50-10 earning differentials. It was found that the 90-50 earning differential did not change even after the crisis, but that the 50-10 earning differential widened after the crisis so that the increase in inequality has been larger than for the higher median.

Table 1 quantifies these changes by giving inequality measures for 1991 and 3 years average surrounding years from 1991 to 1999. The standard deviation for earning is about .53 before the crisis but increase to .66 after the crisis, an increase of about 13 percent. Similarly, the log earning differential between the ninetieth and tenth percentiles increase from 1.24 to 1.33, an increase of 9 percent before the crisis, but, after the crisis, from 1.33 to 1.52, an increase of 19 percent. The differential between the ninetieth and the fiftieth percentiles increases from .65 to .67, an increase of about 2 percent before the crisis, and, after the crisis, from .67 to .70, an increase of 3 percent. Therefore, we find there is no change in the differential between the ninetieth and the fiftieth percentiles before and after the crisis. However, The story for the fiftieth and tenth percentiles' differential is

Table 1. The Inequality Measure for Log Earning

	1991	1992	1993	1994	1995	1996	1997	1998	1999
s.d.	0.5310	0.5264	0.5320	0.5359	0.5324	0.5480	0.5369	0.6363	0.6635
Percentile differential									
p90-p10	1.2445	1.2680	1.2599	1.3193	1.2901	1.3370	1.3269	1.4736	1.5181
		(0.0120)	(0.0322)	(0.0297)	(0.0237)	(0.0247)	(0.0819)	(0.1000)	
p75-p25	0.6598	0.6488	0.6324	0.6891	0.6723	0.7134	0.7116	0.7249	0.7916
		(0.0138)	(0.0292)	(0.0291)	(0.0207)	(0.0232)	(0.0072)	(0.0429)	
p90-p50	0.6517	0.6248	0.6306	0.6506	0.6710	0.6571	0.6660	0.6707	0.6951
		(0.0142)	(0.0135)	(0.0202)	(0.0105)	(0.0070)	(0.0069)	(0.0156)	
p50-p10	0.5927	0.6432	0.6293	0.6688	0.6190	0.6799	0.6609	0.8029	0.8230
		(0.0261)	(0.0200)	(0.0263)	(0.0324)	(0.0311)	(0.0771)	(0.0884)	
p75-p50	0.3547	0.3303	0.3476	0.3568	0.3587	0.3567	0.3691	0.3635	0.4022
		(0.0125)	(0.0135)	(0.0059)	(0.0011)	(0.0067)	(0.0062)	(0.0209)	
p50-p25	0.3050	0.3185	0.2848	0.3323	0.3137	0.3567	0.3425	0.3614	0.3894
		(0.0170)	(0.0244)	(0.0239)	(0.0216)	(0.0219)	(0.0099)	(0.0236)	

( ) : Standard deviation.

different. The differential between these groups increases from .66 to .82, an increase of about 16 percent after the crisis while the differential increases from .64 to .66, an increase of only 2 percent before the crisis. Once again, Table 1 shows that the earnings distribution of the below the 50th percentile got much worse after the crisis than before the crisis.

IV. Inequality within and between Group

The results presented so far refer only to changes in the overall earning distribution and do not display how these changes break down in to changes within groups (defined by education and experience) and changes between groups. They do not illustrate whether the changes have been greater for some subgroups than the others. Figure 3-1 addresses both of these issues by looking at log earning changes by percentile separately for workers with 1-10 years of experience and workers with 21-30 years of experiences. The percentile numbers on the bottom refer to percentiles of the individual groups' earning distribution. As the figure shows, earning differentials across experience groups have increased at all percentiles. Overall, there exists the positive earning differential between those with 21-30 years of experience and those with 1-10years of experience. Now, looking at the within each groups, a very interesting pattern is found. For the more experienced group, the tenth percentile gain 10 percent and the gain steadily increases as we move up percentiles until it reached 45 percent gain for the sixtieth percentile and then gain steadily decreases to the ninetieth percentile 35 percent. This trend shows that middle percentile groups gain relative to the extreme lower and upper percentile. However, the story is different for young group. The gain differentials among them are very small; workers at tenth percentile gain 10 percent and workers at ninetieth percentile gain around 23 percent. However, when we look at before and after the crisis, The figure 3-2 shows the very striking facts. It is found that the earning differential is relatively stable at all percentiles between the old and young groups before the crisis. In contrast, even if workers in both groups and in all percentiles suffered from lower income after the crisis, the young group lose much more than the old group so that the earning differential between two group increased. When we look at

Figure 3-1. Estimated Change in Earning by Experience. 91-99

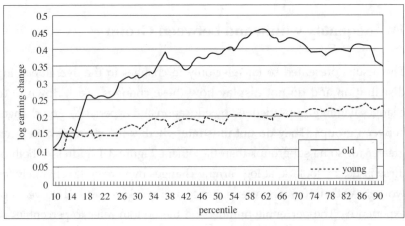

Figure 3-2. Estimated Change in Earning by Experience. 91-97 and 97-99

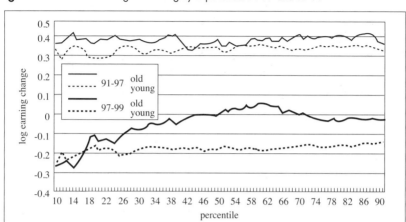

earning over time, we see no evidence of growing inequality within groups before the crisis, In contrast, after the crisis, while we cannot find any earning differential in the young group, we can see evidence of it the old group; the lower 25% of workers lost about 30 percent of their earning while the upper 25% lost almost nothing. In addition, the group between fiftieth and sixtieth percentile gains about 5 percent. The both figure show that the earning inequality increase both between groups and within groups after the crisis.

One of the most striking facts is found in Figure 4-1, which shows the real earning changes in earning for workers with 1-10 years of experience depending on whether they are high school or college graduates. The differential between groups changed at around the seventy-fourth percentile. That is, until that mark college graduates gain much more than the high school graduates, but the gain gaps become gradually smaller at all percentiles until roughly the seventy-fourth percentile and then the pattern is reverse. High school graduates gains more than the college graduates, even though the gain gaps are small, but it becomes gradually larger at all percentile above the seventy-fourth one.

However, when we look at before and after the crisis, we can see that

Figure 4-1. Estimated Earning Change by Education Level, 1991-99

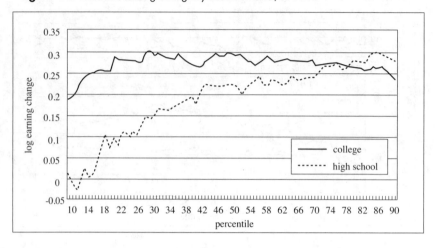

Figure 4-2. Estimated Change in Earning by Education Level, 91-97 and 97-99

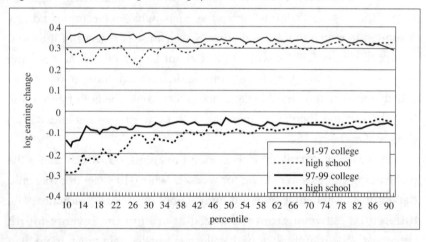

high school graduate lose much more than the college graduate group after the crisis. The inequality within a group is also striking. High school graduates in the upper earning strata gained about 30 percent, whereas the lower strata lost about 2-3 percent because the lost gap of the lower group is larger than the other group after the crisis. However, the pattern of the college graduates is different. While the tenth percentile and ninetieth percentile gain about 20 percent, the other percentiles also gain only 25 percent. This means that it is easy to find the increase of earning inequality among the high school graduate, whereas it is very difficult to find the same phenomenon among college graduates.

Table 2 takes the analysis one step further by looking at the distribution of regression residuals from a regression of log earning on a specification of education and experience effects. Looking at regression residuals allows us to look within very narrowly defined education and experience categories.

Apparently there was very little change in inequality within groups before the crisis. However, the period after the crisis is characterized by an increase in equality. Workers at the ninetieth percentile of the residual distribution gain about 15 percent relative to workers at the tenth percentile. It is also found that the inequality above and below the fiftieth are different; the inequality above the fiftieth percentile is 2 percent and the inequality below the fiftieth percentile is 13 percent. These facts mean that the large earning inequality occurred below the fiftieth percentile (median) after the crisis.

Table 2. Inequality Measure Based on Regression Residual

	1991	1992	1993	1994	1995	1996	1997	1998	1999.
s.d.	0.4885	0.4790	0.4912	0.4895	0.4859	0.4922	0.4840	0.5757	0.5918
Percentile differential									
p90-p10	1.1623	1.1227	1.1377	1.1466	1.1398	1.1727	1.1548	1.2570	1.3162
		(0.0200)	(0.0121)	(0.0123)	(0.0174)	(0.0165)	(0.0546)	(0.0816)	
p75-p25	0.5967	0.5821	0.5917	0.6102	0.6065	0.6167	0.6143	0.6101	0.6472
		(0.0074)	(0.0143)	(0.0153)	(0.0051)	(0.0053)	(0.0033)	(0.0203)	
p90-p50	0.5815	0.5564	0.5667	0.5777	0.5814	0.5834	0.5812	0.5998	0.6039
		(0.0126)	(0.0106)	(0.0135)	(0.0029)	(0.0012)	(0.0102)	(0.0121)	
p50-p10	0.5808	0.5663	0.5710	0.5689	0.5584	0.5894	0.5737	0.6572	0.7123
		(0.0074)	(0.0024)	(0.0054)	(0.0157)	(0.0155)	(0.0444)	(0.0698)	
p75-p50	0.3052	0.2969	0.3044	0.3092	0.3093	0.3016	0.3129	0.2992	0.3147
		(0.0046)	(0.0062)	(0.0071)	(0.0044)	(0.0058)	(0.0073)	(0.0084)	
p50-p25	0.2915	0.2851	0.2873	0.3010	0.2972	0.3151	0.3014	0.3109	0.3325
		(0.0033)	(0.0086)	(0.0083)	(0.0094)	(0.0094)	(0.0070)	(0.0160)	

( ) : Standard deviation.

V. Components of Change in Earning Inequality

So far, we saw in part III that the change in overall earning inequality is assessed by decomposing it into change in between group (observable component) and within group (unobservable component).

A further issue concerning this approach is the extent to which changes in between-group earning inequality reflects changes in the returns to observed skills as opposed to changes in the distribution of worker characteristics. The full-sample distribution accounting scheme developed by Juhn et al. (1993) is a useful approach that allows us to make such assessments for any measure of inequality. This approach begins with a simple earning equation such as

$$Y_{it} = X_{it}\beta_i + u_{it}$$

where Y_{it} is the log earning for individual i in year t, Y_{it} is a vector of individual characteristics(experience and education effects), and is the component of earning accounted for by the unobservable factors. For our purpose it will be useful to conceptualize this residual as two components: an individual's percentile in the residual distribution, θ_{it}, and the distribution function of the wage equation residuals, $F_t(\ )$. By definition of the cumulative distribution function, we have

$$u_{it} = F_t^{-1}(\theta_{it} \mid X_{it})$$

where $F_t^{-1}(\ \cdot\ \mid X_{it})$ is the inverse cumulative residual distribution for workers with characteristics X_{it} in year t.

In this framework changes in inequality come from three sources: (1) changes in the distribution of individual characteristics (i.e., changes in the distribution of the X's), (2) changes in the prices of observable skills (i.e., changes in the β's), and (3) changes in the distribution of the residuals. By defining $\bar{\beta}$ to be the average prices for observable factors over the whole period and $\bar{F}(\cdot \mid X_{it})$ to be the average cumulative distribution, the level of inequality is decomposed into corresponding components as following

$$Y_{it} = X_{it}\bar{\beta} + X_{it}(\beta_i - \bar{\beta}) + \bar{F}^{-1}(\theta_{it} \mid X_{it})$$
$$+ [F_t^{-1}(\theta_{it} \mid X_{it}) - F_t^{-1}(\theta_{it} \mid X_{it})].$$

The first term captures the effect of a changing education and experience distribution at fixed prices. The second term captures the effects of changing skill prices for observable factors at fixed X's, and the final term captures the effects of changes in the distribution of earning residuals. This framework allows us to reconstruct the (hypothetical) earning distribution that would be attained with any subset of components held fixed. For example, with fixed observable prices and a fixed residual distribution, earnings would be determined as

$$Y_{it}^1 = X_{it}\bar{\beta} + \bar{F}^{-1}(\theta_{it} \mid X_{it})$$

In practice, we can estimate how this distribution would have changed through time by predicting earnings for all workers in the sample in year t using the average coefficients, $\bar{\beta}$, and computing a residual for each worker based on his actual percentile in that year's residual distribution and the average cumulative distribution over the full sample[3]. We can determine how changes in the distribution of observable factors have affected other inequality measures such as the interquartile range or the ninetieth-tenth percentile differential or how the effects have been different for inequality above and below the mean.

If we want to allow both observable prices and observable quantities to vary through time, then we can generate earning as following

---

[3] The major advantage of this over the more standard variance accounting framework is that it allows us to look at how composition changes have affected the entire earning distribution and not just the variance.

$$Y_{it}^2 = X_{it}\beta + \bar{F}^{-1}(\theta_{it} \mid X_{it})$$

In this case we predict each worker's earning in year t given his observable characteristics and the earning equation estimated for year t and again assign him a residual based on the cumulative distribution for all years. Finally, if we allow observable prices and quantities and the distribution of residuals to change through time, we obtain

$$Y_{it}^3 = X_{it}\beta + \bar{F}^{-1}(\theta_{it} \mid X_{it}) = X_{it}\beta + u_{it} = Y_{it}$$

which replicates the actual earning distribution since $u_{it} = \bar{F}^{-1}(\theta_{it} \mid X_{it})$ by definition of the cumulative earning distribution.

Our basic technique will be to calculate the distribution of Y_{it}^1, Y_{it}^2, Y_{it}^3 and for each year and attribute the change through time in inequality in the Y_{it}^1 distribution to changes in observable quantities. We then attribute any additional change in inequality in Y_{it}^2 to changes in observable prices, and finally we attribute any additional changes in inequality for Y_{it}^3 beyond those found for Y_{it}^2 to changes in the distribution of unobservable factors (i.e., changes in unmeasured prices and quantities).

The A panel in figure 5 plots the time series of overall earning inequality as measured by log earning differential between the ninetieth and tenth percentiles of the earning distribution. As the figure shows, the overall inequality was stable until before the crisis. After crisis, however, the inequality rapidly increases. The remaining three panels in figure 5 give the part of the ninetieth-tenth percentile log earning differential accounted for by each of these three components. The B panel gives the effects of changes in the distribution of observable characteristics. The changes in observable characteristics have had less impact on the overall inequality after the crisis than before. This means that the change in the experience and education composition of the workforce have not had a direct effect on the level of inequality after the crisis. The C panel looks at the component of changes in inequality due to changes in observable prices(i.e.,

Figure 5. Ninetieth-tenth Percentile Log Earning Differential and Components, 1991-1999

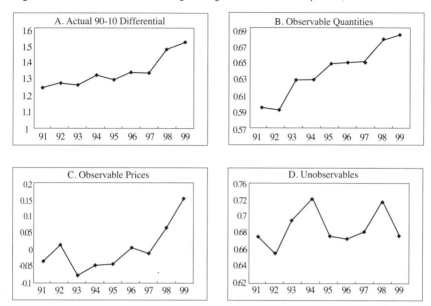

changes in the returns to education and experience). As the figure shows, this component has the most impact on the overall inequality after the crisis; the increases in the education differentials and returns to experience have almost no impact on the inequality until crisis. After crisis, however, the increase in observable prices very rapidly increases the ninetieth-tenth percentile log earning differential, about 15 percent. The D panel shows the component of change in inequality attributable to changes in unobservable prices and quantities (i.e., residuals). As the figure illustrates, even if we can not find any trend, this component has the least impact on the inequality.

Table 3 displays the contribution of observed quantities and prices and the unobservable factors to the increase in the ninetieth-tenth percentile differential over the period 1991 1999.

As the table shows, for the 1991-1999 period the observed prices account for the dominant portion of the increase in inequality of all

Table 3. The Observable and Unobservable Components of Change in Earning Inequality

	Total Change	Observed Quantities	Observed Price	Unobserved Pri. and Quan.
		1991-1999		
90th-10th	0.27362	0.08546	0.18704	0.00112
90th-10th	0.04331	0.04958	0.05903	-0.06530
50th-10th	0.23031	0.03588	0.12801	0.06642
		1991-1997		
90th-10th	0.08569	0.05319	0.02655	0.00595
90th-10th	0.01700	0.02292	0.00312	-0.00904
50th-10th	0.06869	0.03027	0.02343	0.01499
		1997-1999		
90th-10th	0.18793	0.03227	0.16049	-0.00483
90th-10th	0.02631	0.02666	0.05591	-0.05626
50th-10th	0.16162	0.00561	0.10458	0.05143

percentile differentials[4]. However, if we look at before and after the crisis, the table reveals very interesting facts. While the observed quantities are the major portion of the ninetieth- tenth percentile differential before the crisis, the observed prices are the major portion of the ninetieth -tenth percentile differential after the crisis. This table, however, does not show which prices in the observable prices (i.e., among the returns to education, to experience, and the within group) has more impact on the inequality.

The figure 6 plots three skill prices for education, experience, and within-group (unobservables) skills. The price series were derived from yearly regression of log earning on education and experience effects, as follows; Within-group skill price is the ninetieth-tenth percentile log earning differential from the regression residuals. The education skill price is an unweighted average of the college-high school log earning differential. Similarly, skill prices for experience are constructed from the average log earning differential between the 1-10 and the 21-30 experience

---

[4] For the ninetieth-fiftieth percentile differential, the major contributor of the total change in equality is the unobservables though the sign is negative.

Figure 6. The Trend of Skill Indexes

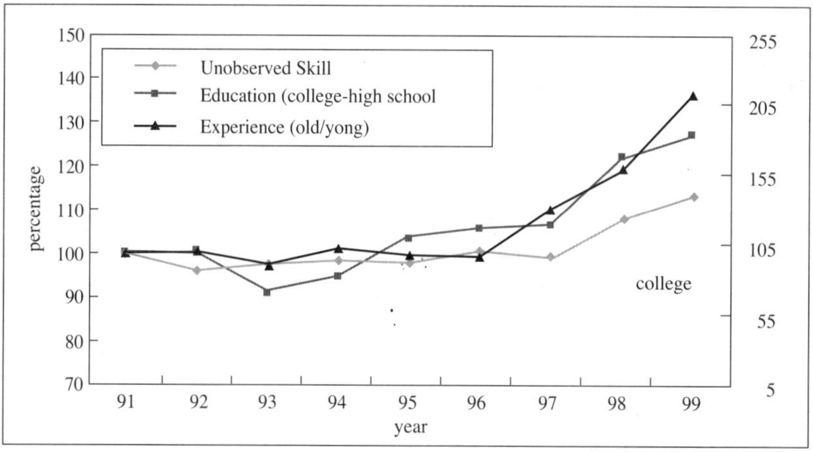

Legend:
- Unobserved Skill
- Education (college-high school)
- Experience (old/yong)

groups. Each of these differentials is indexed to 1991.

Skill differentials within-group were steady until the crisis occurred, but, increased greatly after the crisis so that within-group differential is about 13 percent larger in 1999 than in 1991. The price of education shows very different pattern. By 1993 the education premium had fallen more than 10 percent below its value in 1991. Since then the price of education steadily increase so that the price is the same as that of 1991 when the crisis occurred. However, after the crisis the price of education rapidly increases 27 percent above its value in 1991. The most striking fact is the experience price trend. The experience's price was very stable until 1997 and then sky-rocketed, so that by 1999 it stood about 113 percent above its value of 1991.

VI. The source of the rapidly rise in returns to skill after the crisis

The Figure 6 shows that the prices of a wide variety of skills have increased over the 1990's, especially, after the crisis. Given the rapid rise in the entrance rate to higher levels of education (entrance rate of college increases from 33.2 percent at 1990 to 64.1 percent at 1998), such a large increase in skill premiums must have results from a significant demand shift toward the most skilled. Such a shift in labor demand can be due to either a shift across industries toward industries that demand more skilled workers or a technological shift within industries toward production methods that favor the most skilled.

To find these shifts empirically, we divided the economy into 6 industries and 4 occupation categories. The columns of Table 4 are the fractions of workers in the bottom 10 percent, the middle 10 percent, and the top 10 percent of the earning distribution employed in each industry and occupation. As the table shows, the higher skilled workers were employed mostly in the public sectors industry and were manager / professionals by occupa-

Table 4. Industry and Occupation Distribution by Percentiles, 1994-1999

	Percentiles		
	0-10	45-55	90-100
Industry			
Agriculture / Mining / Fishery / Construction	35.13	18.43	6.99
Manufacturing / Transportation / Communication	18.27	34.51	20.73
Utilities	8.35	10.19	8.62
Retail / Wholesale / Repairing / Lodging / Restaurant / Others	17.23	16.71	8.41
Finance / Insurance / Real estate	15.46	8.56	14.06
Public administration / Education / Welfare	5.56	11.61	41.17
Occupation			
Laborer	37.56	6.80	0.84
Craft / Operator	45.19	49.69	17.31
Clerk / Sales	10.30	21.04	17.97
Manager / Professional	6.95	22.48	63.88

tion, while the least skilled are largely employed in the agriculture/mining/ construction industries and were laborer / operator by occupations. We can find that shifts in industry/ occupational composition generate changes in relative demand.

To measure the change in the labor demand associated with a given change in the industrial and occupational composition, we use the following equation [5];

$$dX_d = \sum_{i,j} \frac{dY_{ij}}{Y_{ij}} X_{ij}$$

where X_{ij} is the 100 x 1 vector of employment by percentile in industry/ occupation cell ij, Y_{ij} is the output produced by industry/ occupation cell ij, dY_{ij} is the change the output in industry/ occupation cell ij.

We measure the change in output of an industry/ occupation cell by the change in factor inputs at fixed reference prices [6](this means factor-neutral technological change within industry/ occupation) and measure X_{ij} employment distribution across industries and occupations by percentile in the 94 sample. Demand growth for any group of workers is measured as a weighted average of the growth in factor inputs in industry/ occupation cells. Therefore, groups employed largely in expanding sectors will experience rising demand, and groups employed largely in contracting sectors will experience decreasing demand.[7]

Figure 7 presents the percentage change in relative demand at each percentile of the overall earning distribution accounted for by shifts in employment across the industry and occupation categories for the whole period and two subperiods.[8] The figure shows that there is excess demand

---

[5] To derive this equation, we assume that the production function is the constant return to scale.

[6] This paper use the average earnings in the '94 sample as the fixed reference price.

[7] The weights are industry/occupation shares for that group.

[8] The industry and the occupation classification is changed at 1993. We examine the periods from 1994 to 1999.

Figure 7. The Changes in Labor Demand by Earning Percentile

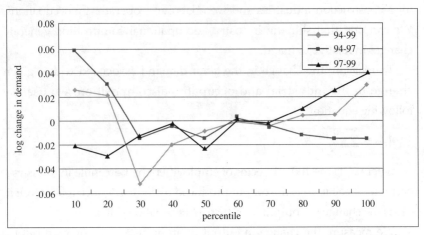

in both low quartile and in top quartile in the whole period from 1994 to 1999. However, when the whole periods is divided into two, before and after the crisis, we can find a very different pattern. Before the crisis, the demand rose by between 3 and 6 percent in the low quartile and fell(excess supply)by between roughly 1 and 2 percent in the remaining quartiles, especially in the high quartile. Therefor, as we found, the earning inequality is decreasing or remained stable in this period. In the contrast to the before the crisis, the demand fell (excess supply) by roughly 2 percent for workers below the 75 percentile and increases by between 1 and 4 percent for the top quartile after the crisis, a period during which earning inequality increased. From this figure, we can see that there is little change in demand between the low quartile and the middle quartile, while there is a large change in demand between the middle quartile and the top quartile. This leads to the little change in the earning inequality demand between the low quartile and the middle quartile, and leads to the large gap between the middle quartile and the top quartile. However, this pattern is contrast to the trend in the earning distribution at the Figure 2. We can interpret such a conflict as the followings: We have unions that consist of the manufacturing workers in the large firms, whose earning distribution is in the middle quartile. The large firm unions have the strong bargaining power which restrains the fall in the wage. Therefore, there is a little earning gap between the middle quartile and the top quartile after crisis when the demand for skill is increasing. However, the workers in the low quartile have no union or the weak unions so that they experienced the fall in the fall in the wages. This leads to the large gap between the low quartile and the middle quartile .

Anyway, the growing demand for skill is the main factor leading to an increase in the earning inequality after the crisis. However, we do not know why the demand for skill increases after the crisis. We can only guess that the growing demand for skill is related to changes in technology (Davis and Haltiwanger (1991), Bound and Johnson (1992), Krueger (1991), Mincer (1991)), organizational and personnel practices, globalization (Murph and Welch (1991)) and changes in unionization and other labor market institutions (Blackburn, Bloom, and Freeman (1990, 1991), Freeman (1991), and Mitchell (1989)). We think that these changes have happened after the crisis in Korea economy.

VII. Conclusion

Using raw data of the 'Family income and expenditure survey', we find that the earning distribution worsened in Korea after the financial crisis; the gap between ninetieth and tenth percentile grew larger after the crisis more than before. Such a phenomenon is apparent within narrowly defined education and labor market experience variables. We found that the increase in earning inequality came from the rapidly increasing return to the components of skill other than the schooling and experience, which is caused by the increasing demand of skill after the crisis. Therefore, we can interpret the growing demand for skill is an important factor leading the increase in the earning inequality after the crisis. And then, we think that the reason for the increasing demand for skill after the crisis can be found in the changes of the technology, the organizational and personnel practice, the globalization, and the labor market. We can derive policy implications from this: To narrow the inequality we must invest the industrial demand-oriented skill education/training.

References

Autor, David H and Katz, Lawrence F. (1999). Changes in the wage structure and earnings inequality. *Handbook of Labor Economics*, Vol. 3, pp. 1464-1555.

Blackburn, M., D. Bloom, and R. Freeman. (1990). The declining position of less skilled American males. *A Future of Lousy Jobs?* In G. Burtless. (ed.). Washington, D.C.: Brookings Institution, pp. 31-67.

_____. (1991). Changes in earning differentials in the 1980's: Concordance, convergence, causes, and consequences. Discussion Paper Series No. 554, Department of Economics, Columbia University.

Borjas, George J. and Valerie Ramsey. (1995). Foreign competition, market power and wage inequality. *Quarterly Journal of Economics*, 110, pp. 1075-1110.

Bound, John and George Johnson. (1992). Changes in the structure of wages in the 1980s: an evaluation of alternative explanations. *American Economic Review*, 82, pp.371-392.

Buchinsky, Moshe. (1994). Changes in the U.S. wage structure 1963-1987: an application of quantile regression. *Econometrica*, 62, pp. 405-458.

Davis, S., and J. Haltiwanger. (1991). Wage dispersion between and within U.S. manufacturing plants, 1962-1986. *Brookings Papers on Economic Activity: Microeconomics*, pp. 115-180.

DiNardo, John, Nicole Fortin and Thomas Lemieux. (1996). Labor market institutions and distribution of wages, 1973-1992: a semi-parametric approach. *Econometrica*, 64, pp. 1001-1044.

Freeman, R. (1991). How much has de-unionization contributed to the rise in male earnings inequality? NBER Working Paper, No. 3826.

Johnson, George. (1997). Changes in earning inequality: the role of demand shifts. *Journal of Economic Perspectives*, 11, pp. 41-54.

Juhn, Chinhui, Kevin M. Murphy and Brooks Pierce. (1993). Wage inequality and the rise in returns to skill. *Journal of political Economy*, 101, pp. 401-442.

Katz, Lawrence F. and Kevin M. Murphy. (1992). Changes in relative wages, 1963-87: supply and demand factors. *Quarterly Journal of Economics*, 017, pp. 35-78.

Kim, Dae-il and Robert Topel. (1995). Labor markets and economic growth: lessons from Korea's industrialization, 1970-1990. In Richard Freeman and Lawrence Katz (eds.). *Differences and Changes in Wage Structures*. University of Chicago Press.

Krueger, A. (1991). How computers have changed the wage structure: Evidence from micro-data, 1984-1989. Mimeo. Princeton University.

Levy, Frank and Richard J. Murnane. (1992). U.S. earnings levels and earnings inequality: a review of recent trends and proposed explanations. *Journal Economic Literature*, 30, pp. 1215-1244.

Mincer, J. (1991). Human capital, technology, and the wage structure: what do time series show? NBER Working Paper No. 3581.

Mitchell, D. (1989). Wage pressures and labor shortages: The 1960s and 1980s. *Brookings Papers on Economic Activity: Microeconomics*, 2, pp. 191-232.

Murphy, K., and F. Welch. (1991). The role of international trade in wage differentials. *Workers and Their Wages*. In M. Kosters. (ed.). Washington, D.C.: The AEI Press, pp. 39-69.

Topel, Robert H. (1993). Regional labor markets and the determinants of wage inequality. *American Economic Review*, 83(2), pp. 110-115.

Pyeong Tak Nahm. (1997). Changes in wage inequality and the effect of human capital in Korea: 1972-89. *Korea Journal of Labor Economics*, 23(2).

HRM in Korea: Transformation and New Patterns

Woo-Sung Park [1] and Gyu-Chang Yu [2]

I. Introduction

Recently, HRM practices in Korean firms have undergone an important transformation, under a rapidly changing environment. The first-order motive for transformation has come from the economic crisis which took place at the end of 1997. The shock emanated by the so-called "IMF crisis" was beyond imagination. The deep-rooted myth that banks and big conglomerates ("*Chaebol*"), the symbols of Korean economic success, would never go bankrupt has gone away, and financial difficulties made Korean firms doubt the traditional Korean management style and HRM model. They began to reexamine the growth-driven strategy and to adopt the profitability-driven strategy (Cho, 2000a). This reorientation in business strategy has made Korean firms be very cost-conscious, and to actively pursue innovative changes in HRM practices, such as a new compensation system based on performance.

---

[1] Assistant Professor, Kyung Hee University, Kyunggi-do, Korea.

[2] Assistant Professor, Sookmyung Women's University, Seoul, Korea.

The economic crisis and subsequent downsizing has had a profound impact on HRM in Korean firms. After the economic crisis, many Korean firms were forced to reduce their workforce: 66% of listed companies were reported to lay-off their workforce[3] (Korea Labor Institute, 2000). The companies learned an important lesson in regards to securing the flexibility in managing their workforce, which was not a consideration in the previous growth era. On the employees' side, this unemployment experience has changed their attitude vis-à-vis the company: the implicit tie between company and employees have loosened, and employees have begun to actively search out opportunities in the external labor market. These changes on both sides have rocked the foundation of a traditional HRM system, which is based on long-term employment and seniority-based compensation. At the same time Korean companies are forced to find a way to develop and motivate their core workforce under the increasingly severe global competition.

Another important factor of changing the HRM picture in Korean firms is the digital revolution and rapid growth of venture businesses. Venture firms based on information technology and the internet do not adhere to the traditional Korean HRM model: they don't guarantee job security and prefer recruiting their workforce from the external labor market by offering attractive compensations, including stock option. Many young employees with high potential quited the large companies to find a job in venture companies. High turnover in managerial and R&D employees is a serious problem in Korean traditional firms. This forces Korean firms to change their traditional HRM practices, and they are now trying to introduce various incentive systems and the autonomous and creative work environment

The rapid growth of foreign direct investment in Korea also plays an important role in reshaping the management style and HRM in Korean firms. Having remained at 1 billion dollars in yearly average till to the

---

[3] Includes early retirement and honorary retirement.

middle of 1990s, FDI soared up to 8.8 billion dollars in 1999. The sum of FDI in 1998 and 1999 was three and half times larger than the total amount of FDI from 1980 to 1996 (Korea Bank, 2000). HRM systems different from the Korean are introduced in wholly owned foreign subsidiaries, and, more importantly, their HRM systems are benchmarked by many Korean firms as global standard. The recent diffusion of job and performance-based HRM system can be partly explained by this growth of FDI in Korea.

As pointed out above, Korean firms are now facing an important environmental change at multiple levels. It would be interesting to examine the recent changes of HRM which the environmental pressure has produced on Korean firms. First, we will try to identify the important changes in HRM practices after the economic crisis. Second, we will discuss whether these changes in practices mean the transformation of the HRM paradigm in Korean firms. And we will describe the emerging new patterns of the HRM model. Finally, we will examine the changing role of HRM toward strategic human resource management.

For these purposes, we used the results of two surveys conducted in 1998 and in 2000 respectively by the Korea Labor Institute. It is not easy to identify the changes in HRM after the economic crisis, because reliable surveys are rare, and because they are focused only on particular areas of HRM, such as compensation, employee participation, etc. The two surveys are vitally important sources of information in that they cover almost every part of HRM, and were done twice, maintaining similar contents in each questionnaire, which allows us to examine and compare recent changes of HRM practices in Korean firms.

A sample of the two surveys consists of listed companies on the Korea stock market. At the time of the survey, the total number of listed companies was 744 in 1998 and 712 in 2000. The numbers were reduced over the two years as some companies were dropped out from the list, mainly due to M&A and bankruptcy. The numbers of responses from the surveys were 417 and 376, representing 56% and 53% of response rates respectively. The distribution of industry and employee size has shown very similar distribution. The sample is mainly composed of large firms: for example, the average number of employees in respondent firms came to 2,180 in 2000 and 76.5% of the respondents employed more than 300 persons.

II. Changes of HRM Practices

According to the KLI survey 2000, Korean firms have undergone important changes in their HRM practices. More than 80% of respondents reported to changes in almost every area of HRM practices after the economic crisis. This shows that the changes in HRM practices are very extensive and general in Korean firms. In particular, more than 50% of firms reported to have had important changes in their compensation and evaluation system, which could be explained by the rapid diffusion of merit pay ('*Yeonbongje*'), as we will show later.

1. Staffing

The survey results show no significant change in selection criteria but rather, important change in recruitment sources and use of contingent workers. Korean firms began to search workforce more actively from external resource pools, and to use more contingent workers. The principal motive for this change is flexibility in managing the workforce, mainly coping with a rapidly changing environment.

Changes in Recruitment

An important change of staffing in Korean firms is that they began to use the external labor market as a source of recruitment. The KLI survey 2000 shows that 25% of respondents have the policy of getting the necessary workforce by staffing it from the external labor market. It also indicates that 78.5% of respondents have experienced recruitment from outside the firm in the last two years; this percentage is particularly high in the distribution and finance industry. There is no previous survey data exactly matching this figure, but the promotion from within has long been taken for granted in Korean firms, with the exception of certain R&D jobs. A survey in 1997 gives some evidence to this general rule in demonstrating that less than 10% of managerial jobs were filled from outside the firm (Park and Ahn, 1998). Internal recruitment, often a synonym of promotion, is one of the cornerstones of the HRM system in large Korean firms, based on the internal labor market (Park, 1995).

Changes in Selection Criteria

In regards to the criteria for selection, it seems that there is no significant change in Korean firms. In a 1998 survey, some important criteria for selection were reported to be creativity, challenge, integrity, cooperation, and technical competence, in their order of importance. This criteria and the order of importance did not change in survey 2000. And another study done in 1994 reported similar results in selection criteria (Park, 1995). We can conclude that the selection criteria have stayed unchanged through the economic crisis.

More interesting to note is the relative importance between cooperation and technical competence. Cooperation represents a selection criterion based on long-term perspective, related to a long-term employment practice; while technical competence can be considered a short-term selection criterion, related to job-based management. Two surveys asked respondents to choose between two extreme choices: a candidate with good technical competence but un-cooperative, and a candidate with good cooperation but low technical competence. In the two surveys, more than 70% of respondents showed their intention to select the latter. This implies that Korean firms still maintain a long-term relationship with their employment policy, and that they consider technical competence being developed in the firm after selection.

Table 1. Increase of Contingent Workers

	Number of employees in average (person)	Portion of contingent workers (%)
1997	2,230	5.5
1998	1,940	7.0
1999	2,181	8.6

Source: KLI survey 2000 (KLI, 2000)

Utilization of Contingent Workers

Another important change staffing practice is active utilization of contingent workers. The economic crisis and changing environment force Korean firms to actively pursue flexibility in managing their workforce. On one hand, they downsized their workforce through lay-offs with two of three firms responding to the KLI survey of 2000 that they were required to lay-off their employees after the economic crisis. On the other hand, a new workforce, consisting of contingent workers is actively utilized. This resulted in a rapid increase of the contingent workforce in Korean firms. As the table below indicates, the average number of employees was reduced by 13% from 1997 to 1998, and increased by 12.4% due to the economic recovery. However, the portion of contingent workers among the total employees rapidly increased from 1997; 5.5% in 1997 but 8.6% in 1999. The number of contingent workers are increasing in almost every industry but the increase is particularly noticeable in the beverage and food, whole sale and retailing, transportation, and finance industry, with special significance to the portion of contingent workers in the finance industry more than doubling, from 8% in 1997 to 20% in 1999.

2. Employee Development

Career Development
Developing a career is an important element of employee development. Career development is not a one-shot training program. Rather, it is an ongoing organized and formalized effort that recognizes people as a vital organizational resource (Leibowitz, 1987). Recent surveys do not show any

significant change in career development in Korean firms. In 1995, career development was implemented in 23.4% of Korean firms employing more than 300 persons (Ahn, 1996). In the KLI survey of 1998, it is reported to be 23% and with no change in the survey of 2000. The limited use of career development seems to be related to the weakening long-term employment practice and internal labor market.

Evaluation and Employee Development

In contrast to organized career development, individual development based on performance evaluation is rapidly progressing in Korean firms. Traditionally, the evaluation is mainly used for promotion decisions. However, Korean firms begin to apply evaluation results to employee development. In the KLI survey of 2000, we can find that although the principal purpose of evaluations is still to use as the criteria for promotion, its application is widened to employee development. More than 50% of firms actually make use of the evaluation to develop employees and help their career development.

Management by Objective (MBO)

Management by objective (MBO) is used not only to evaluate individual performance but also to develop employees in Korean firms. In the KLI survey of 1998, 63% of firms are reported to have used MBO for the two purposes at the same time. In recent years, MBO has been introduced into many Korean firms. As table 2 shows, in 1995 MBO was implemented in 24.4% of large Korean firms, but the rate of implementation increased to 35% in 1998, and peaked at 49% in 2000.

Table 2. Implementation of MBO

	Percentage of firms implementing MBO
1995*	24.4%
1998**	35.0%
2000**	49.0%

Source: * Ahn (1996), ** Korea Labor Institute (1998; 2000)

3. Compensation

Employee compensation is the area in which the most important change has been taking place after the economic crisis. Traditionally, the Korean pay system is largely based on seniority. In Korean firms, seniority has been an important element in determining base salary. This system has long been the subject of critics in that it doesn't reflect the performance of employees. This system is now rapidly changing toward a performance based system: on one hand, Korean firms begin to introduce "merit pay" determining a pay increase according to personal performance, and on the other hand, they actively promote the group incentive systems.

Merit Pay

The table below summarizes a rapid diffusion of the merit pay system ("*Yeonbongje*") in Korean firms. The merit pay being introduced in only 3.6% of Korean firms employing more than 100 persons in 1997, more than tripled over the next two years, reaching 12.7% in 1999. In listed companies, it is now implemented in 45.2% of them, and 22.6% of them are planning to adopt it within one year. Therefore, we can consider merit pay as a dominant practice, at least among Korean listed companies. The economic crisis and environmental pressure seems to play an accelerating role in changing the pay system in Korean firms to merit pay. The majority of the firms having introduced merit pay did away with the seniority based increase in pay, while 35% of them still maintain it to avoid the abrupt change in their pay system.

Group Incentives

The change in pay, moving toward the performance-based system, can be verified in the diffusion of various group incentives in Korean firms. According to recent surveys of the Korea Labor Institute, group incentives, especially profit sharing and gain sharing, show a sharp increase from 1998 to 2000. Now, the profit sharing scheme is used in two out of five listed

Table 3. Diffusion of merit pay

	Percentage of firms having merit pay system
Ministry of Labor*	
1999	1.6%
1997	3.6%
1999	12.7%
Korea Labor Institute**	
1998	35.0%
2000	45.2%

Source: * Ministry of Labor (2000), ** Korea Labor Institute (1998; 2000)

Table 4. Adoption rate of group incentives

	Profit sharing	Gain sharing	Team incentive
Korea Labor Institute*			
1998	25.9%	17.7%	23.7%
2000	40.7%	23.9%	25.8%

Source: * Korea Labor Institute (1998; 2000)

firms.

The concept of group incentives has been actively adopted by Korean firms for the purpose of motivating employees, and complementing the side effect of merit pay, easing harsh individual competition between employees. In addition, Korean firms hope to make labor cost more flexible in tying it to overall performance (Park, 1999).

4. Employee Participation and Team-based Organization

Employee Participation

Employee participation practices were widespread before the economic crisis but many Korean firms abandoned them after the economic crisis. As the table below shows, the implementation rate of employee participation practices has dropped sharply from 1996 to 1998. We can infer that economic difficulties and downsizing undermined the base of participative management. On the other hand, it is possible that before the economic cri-

Table 5. Changes in Implementation Rate of Participative Practices (%)

	Year 1996*	Year 1998**	Year 2000**
Employee survey	78.4	26.1	32.2
Employee suggestion	97.1	74.8	77.7
Job enlargement	90.5	41.7	42.3
Job enrichment	83.3	38.1	43.9
Quality circle	91.8	58.3	58.8
Problem solving team	81.9	58.5	59.6
Work council	96.6	90.4	88.6
Joint committee	71.1	40.5	33.8
Self-directed work team	43.5	28.5	29.8

Source: * Lee and Yu (1997), ** Korea Labor Institute (1998; 2000)

sis, the participative practices were introduced in large part from imitative pressure or as a managerial fad, and was not strongly anchored in the management system and employee relations.

From 1998 to 2000, the implementation rate revealed no important changes. However, they are administered and utilized more actively and constructively than in 1998. When comparing results of the survey 2000 to 1998, the number of firms responding that the participative practices functions constructively has significantly increased in 2000. It seems to us that the economic crisis played a role of litmus testing the solid base of participative practices in Korean firms. Those who practiced them without clear policy and vision gave them up when faced with financial difficulties, while those who realized their benefits during the economic downturn now invest more actively in participative practices.

Team-based Organization
Another important change in Korean HRM practices is flattening structure. Traditionally, structure has been characterized by extended hierarchy and concentration of authority, and this often results in many negative effects, including conforming and bureaucratic attitudes (Cho, 2000). Recently, firms have been flattening their structure by reducing the grade system and decision making procedure.

Table 6. Implementation Rate of Team-based Organization

	Percentage of firms implementing team-based organization
1998*	54.2%
2000**	80.1%

Source: *Korea Labor Institute (1998), **Korea Labor Institute (2000)

Changes toward the team-based organization can be considered as a typical example of these recent trends happening in Koran firms. Under the team-based organization, the heavy burden of administrative work and inefficient decision-making procedures are eliminated, and a long grade system is reduced to team coordinators and team members. The team-based organization began to be actively implemented by Korean firms in 1995 and rapidly diffused to reach the 80.1% of implementation rate in 2000.

III. Transformation and New Patterns of HRM

Based upon two consecutive surveys of listed companies, we identified recent functional changes of each HRM practice in Korea. Because these surveys were drawn from large firms, it is difficult to generalize the results to the population of small and medium firms. However, we may conclude that the trend of changes in HRM practices of small and medium firms would not be that far from those of large firms. Generally large firms play the role of pattern setter in shaping new HRM practices. In particular, isomorphic institutional pressure is very strong in Korean society (Orru et al., 1991).

Then, the next question is, "Would functional changes of HRM practices in Korea be a paradigm shift of HRM from the traditional system to the new HRM system?"

1. New Paradigm in HRM

Recently we have observed the trend of transformation of HRM practices in several countries (Appelbaum & Batt, 1994; Bae et al., 1998; Nakamura & Nitta, 1995). Universal environmental pressure, especially globalization and borderless market competition, led firms in industrialized countries to change their HRM practices toward getting a more competitive advantage (Pfeffer, 1994). Under similar environmental pressure, it seems that HRM and industrial relations practices across countries tends to converge into a similar system which aims at more flexibility in the workplace (Kuruvilla and Erickson, 2000). On the other hand, some researchers argue that such changes are neither fundamental nor transformational, rather they are continuous adjustments to or extensions of the basic framework, embedded in national cultural settings (Nakamura & Nitta, 1995).[4]

We have seen many functional changes of HRM practices in large Korean firms. However, from these observations, it is not easy to answer the question of whether such changes are fundamental transformation toward a new paradigm of HRM or only functional adjustments to environmental pressures.

The traditional Korean HRM system has been defined as one that cultivates long-term loyalty and organizational attachment from employees by providing job security and various seniority-based HRM practices (Kim & Yu, 2000). We have seen some functional changes in the HRM which apparently depart from the traditional HRM system. However, we have also seen HRM practices which seem to still be related to the traditional HRM system.

In order to identify how extensively the transformation has already occurred (or will occur), we conducted another survey in 1999. There were

---

[4] One important issue for the 12th IIRA World Congress in Tokyo, Japan (May 29 June 2) was the impact on globalization and regional systems of industrial relations and employee relations: divergence and convergence.

107 HRM specialists that responded to the survey, including university professors (in human resource management and industrial relations field), consultants, researchers, and top HRM executives in large Korean firms (Yu & Park, 2000). In the survey we presented items related to contrasting HRM perspectives, traditional HRM perspectives and new HRM perspectives and asked respondents to choose the one representing the exact situations in Korean firms.

As can be seen in Table 7, the majority of respondents agreed that there are fundamental shifts of HRM perspectives in Korean firms. Table 7 shows that traditional seniority-based, paternalistic, autocratic and generalist HRM perspectives, based on the socio-cultural background of Korean society, are expected to be transformed to new performance and contract based, democratic and specialist HRM perspectives. Traditional HRM perspectives are based on the socio-cultural background of Korean society. Accordingly, the traditional Korean HRM system reflects the features of traditional Korean management styles, which are often summarized as family-oriented paternalistic leadership (Kim & Kim, 1989). The new HRM perspective reflects environmental pressures based on market and competition mechanism.

The various functional changes described earlier are closely related to

Table 7. HRM Specialists' Opinion Regarding Paradigm Shift of HRM Perspectives in Korean Firms

Present Paradigm	Future Paradigm
Seniority based HRM	Performance based HRM
(70%)	(96%)
Paternalistic HRM	Contract based HRM
(62%)	(91%)
Autocratic HRM	Democratic HRM
(70%)	(91%)
Generalist HRM	Specialist HRM
(62%)	(84%)
People based HRM	Job based HRM
(50%)	(47%)

such a paradigm change in HRM perspectives. For example, the shift from seniority-based HRM perspective to performance-based HRM perspective is closely related to the change in the pay system. The individual performance based pay system—merit pay (or "*Yeonbongje*")—has diffused rapidly, starting before and containing through the IMF crisis. It is based on the difference in individual performance, not in seniority. In the same token, it is not surprising that various group incentive pay schemes have also been diffused widely and rapidly.

Transformation from the paternalistic HRM to a contract based HRM is also an important feature of a new HRM paradigm. Traditionally Korean firms have maintained paternalistic family-oriented management styles (Kim & Kim, 1989; Shin, 1992). The family ideology has been widely used by Korean firms (in particular, *Chaebol*) to develop long-term psychological relationships between employees and management. Accordingly, massive layoff was rare for Korean firms before the IMF crisis. However, as we have seen, more than sixty percent of firms have adopted various sorts of lay-offs for structural adjustments, so long-term psychological relations based on family ideology can no longer be the norm.

The transformation from autocratic HRM to democratic HRM is also another feature of the new HRM paradigm. The other side of the coin of family-oriented management styles would be autocratic managerial leadership. Utilizing an autocratic leadership style could have been very effective for rapid economic development by providing concrete guidance for direction. However, recent environmental pressures forced Korean firms to change their leadership styles. Active utilization of human resources becomes one of the most critical success factors for Korean firms. Transformation into democratic HRM is closely related to diffusion of employee participation and a team-based organizational structure, as we have seen.

Emphasis on specialist HRM rather than generalist HRM is deeply related to the change of staffing practices. Traditional staffing practices in Korea were primarily based on the internal labor market, generally characterized by a job ladder with entry only at the bottom and then movement up (Althauser & Kalleberg, 1981). Unlike the internal labor markets in western firms, however, traditional Korean internal labor markets did not provide a career ladder for specialists. Even R&D specialists must transfer to managerial positions after a certain stint within the firm if they want to receive opportunities for more compensation and promotion. The reason for such staffing practices was because Korean firms prefer generalists who can play versatile roles in organization and thus provide internal flexibility during a rapid economic expansion period (Shin, 1992). However, now Korean firms have begun to realize the important roles of specialists to get a competitive advantage, in particular in the development of information and communication technology. As we have seen in functional HRM changes, a specialist HRM perspective is closely related to both externalization of staffing practices and provision of career ladders and incentive schemes for specialists, such as R&D engineers and marketing.

Although the majority of respondents agreed that Korean HRM has undergone an important paradigm shift from traditional HRM to new HRM perspectives, there was an important issue that remains to be controversial: people-based HRM vs. job-based HRM. The traditional HRM system in Korea is known to be based on people, which means that the most important basis for HRM decisions is on general characteristics of the employees. The seniority-based compensation and generalist staffing practices are closely related to the people-based HRM perspective. Korean firms generally did not have specific job descriptions or job classifications. Rather they had broadly-defined position grades ("*Jik-geup*") which is quite different from the job grade concept (Jeong, 2000). As we have discussed so far, there is an apparent consensus that such a people-based traditional HRM system would not be adequate for the current environment. Then would the new HRM perspective be the job-based HRM? Certainly there is some evidence that Korean HRM practices are somewhat moving toward a job-based HRM. However, as traditional job-based HRM practices in the U.S. has been widely criticized recently and many US firms are moving toward a competence-based HRM (Lawler, 1994; Dubois, 1998), HRM specialists in Korea hesitate to come to a conclusion about job-based HRM perspectives. No more than fifty percent of specialists agreed that Korean HRM is moving toward job-based HRM.

2. New Patterns of HRM

We examined earlier recent changes in HRM practices and the paradigm shift of HRM in Korean firms. This clearly shows that many important changes have occurred through, and after, the economic crisis, and that these can be explained by the paradigm shift of HRM in Korean firms. However, Korean firms are not homogeneous in their HRM systems. The HRM system of a specific firm is the product of many external factors, such as the industry where it belongs, the market environment, and internal factors such as the history, and the strategic choice it takes in managing its employees. Each firm has its specific HRM system but it can be grouped into certain dominant HRM systems. Two KLI surveys allow us to examine the changes in these HRM models and new emerging patterns strengthened after the economic crisis.

The HRM models of Korean firms can be classified and analyzed according to two dimensions: the relationship-transaction dimension and the utilization-control dimension (Kim and Yu, 2000). The relationship is related to the nature of the association between employer and employee. In the relationship-oriented HRM, a long-term relationship is sought, and firms cultivate the loyalty of employees for the firm, guaranteeing long-term employment and compensating seniority. In transaction-oriented HRM, the opposite side of the relationship, the nature of employer and employees relations is transactional, and the short-term contribution of employees is emphasized. Therefore, a firm would be positioned in the dimension according to the degree of whether its HRM is relationship or transaction.

The utilization-control dimension indicates the nature and degree in utilization of human resources. In the utilization approach, the firm tries to maximize the positive potential of its employees. In this approach, the firm makes an important investment in employee development and wants to reap high performances by fully utilizing its human resources. On the contrary, the control approach is focused on minimizing the negative aspects of labor force, for example minimizing the absence rate and discontent of employees. In other words, in the control approach, the firm' objective is principally to prevent labor unrest and to build up a disciplined work force.

Using this theoretical framework, we created the following typology of HRM models in Korean firms.

It is interesting to note that in the 1998 survey, Type I and Type IV models reach about 70% of the sample. Both Type I and Type IV represent HRM models emphasizing relationship rather than transaction. Previous authors (Kim, 1993; Kim and Park, 1997) insist that the important characteristics of HRM in Korean firms be long-term based relations. In fact, the results of the 1998 survey show that HRM systems based on relationship orientation take a predominant place in the total distribution.

However, the results of the cluster analysis using the 2000 KLI survey show that there have been some important changes in HRM systems of larger Korean firms. A remarkable change is the movement from the relationship dimension to the transaction dimension. The two HRM systems emphasizing the relationship orientation have decreased at the same time, while the transaction model based on short term performance and the external labor market have increased sharply. On the other hand, we have not seen much change between control orientation and utilization orientation. It seems that many Korean firms have adopted a more transactional approach in their HRM systems after the economic crisis.

The examination of Korean HRM systems from the two strategic dimensions seems to support the changes in HRM practices and paradigm we have described earlier in this paper. The results of various surveys

Figure 1. Typology of HRM and Recent Changes

	Relationship		
Control	Type I Relation-Control 1998: 96(35.6%) 2000: 88(32.7%)	Type IV Relation-Utilization 1998: 93(34.4%) 2000: 48(17.8%)	Utilization
	Type II Transaction-Control 1998: 52(19.3%) 2000: 64(23.8%)	Type III Transaction-Utilization 1998: 29(10.7%) 2000: 69(25.6%)	
	Transaction		

Source: Adapted from Kim and Yu (2000)

examined earlier show clearly the transition from the relationship dimension to the transaction dimension. On the other hand, while Korean firms have moved toward transactional orientation under short-term economic pressures, the number of the firms having strategic intention to invest their workforce and utilize their potential has not increased significantly yet.

IV. The Changing Role of HRM: How Strategic Is HRM in Korea?

Recently HRM literature has largely focused on the strategic role of HRM to get a competitive advantage of firms (Martell & Carroll, 1995; Wright & McMahan, 1992). Along with the changes in HRM practices, the strategic role of HRM within an organization in Korea has also been stressed (Yu, 2000). The question should then be: How much has HRM in Korean firms taken strategic roles?

On the 2000 KLI survey, we asked strategic planning executives to

Table 8. Changing Role of HR Department

	Yes	No
The role of HRM has significantly increased after IMF crisis	51.8%	9.5%
The role of HRM will significantly increase in the future	57.8%	8.8%
The HR executive participates in strategic planning process	53.5%	17.5%
The HR executive significantly influences the decision-making of CEOs	56.0%	10.5%
The HR department should play a significant role in implementing organizational strategy	53.5%	9.8%
The HRM department plays a significant role in implementing organizational strategy	30.8%	22.3%

evaluate the role of HRM departments within an organization.[5] Not surprisingly, as shown in Table 8, the survey results indicated that the majority of strategic planning executives think that the role of HRM within an organization has significantly increased after the IMF crisis, and that this trend will continue in the future. Also, HR executives in the majority of large Korean firms currently participate in the strategic planning processes of the organization and significantly influence the decision-making of CEOs. Similarly, the majority of respondents agreed that the HR department should play a significant role in implementing organizational strategy. However, in reality, the HR department in only thirty percent of responded firms actually plays a significant role in implementing organizational strategy. Based on the survey results we can tentatively conclude that Korean firms have begun to realize the strategic role of HRM within an organization, but only a few firms actually implement those roles.

Interestingly, the survey respondents identified that a lack of CEOs'

---

[5] We sent separate questionnaires to strategic planning managers (executives) to get reliable evaluations regarding the roles and effectiveness of the HR department.

understanding of the strategic role of the HRM department would be the most significant impediment to the changing role of HRM. The executives with whom the CEO's consult most frequently were first, marketing executives (49.8%) and second, finance executives (24.5%). Only seven percent of respondents were HR executives.

However, another important barrier to the changing role of HRM is the lack of competence of HR executives themselves. According to the survey on HR specialists, the most important skills that today's HR managers must possess is not only an extensive knowledge of various HRM issues and specific skills in the HRM field, but also extensive knowledge in management and business, leadership, vision and communication skills. The latter skills are relatively new to HR managers in Korea, but important ones for them to competently perform their strategic roles in the HRM field (Yu & Park, 2000).

V. Conclusion

We have discussed the recent changes of HRM practices and the paradigm shift of HRM in Korea. It is clear that, under the strong market pressure for performance and flexibility, extremely intensified through the economic crisis, the Korean traditional perspectives and practices of HRM has been found to be less effective to cope with the domestic and foreign competition. Many changes witness the important efforts of Korean firms to innovate their HRM system. The new direction of HRM practices and perspectives is the one that gives firms more flexibility in the workplace and the one that emphasizes better performance from employees. It resembles the one that we can find in recent literature of industrial relations and human resource management (Towers Perrin, 1992; Appelbaum and Batt, 1994;.Yu, 1998; Morishima, 2000; Voos and Kim, 2000).

And these changes have led to the important role-change of the HR department: its role has increased in a significant way during recent years, especially after the economic crisis, and more and more it is asked to play a strategic role to facilitate the rapid organizational change. There is, however, clear discrepancy between its new role and competency. The leadership, vision for future HRM and communication, ability to analyze the impact of the internal and external environment are, among others, essential factors newly required for HR specialists. It is therefore expedient that Korean firms develop these competencies in order to succeed in the transformation of their HRM.

It is worthy to note that HRM practices of Korean firms are not completely disconnected from the traditional pattern; certain original Korean HRM practices are still maintained. For example, in the promotion decision making, one's performance record is the highest criteria, but service years are still of important consideration. And the ability to cooperate with other employees or to work as a team is considered more important than job expertise or potential job performance. No small number of Korean firms having introduced the merit pay still keep seniority as the determinant of base pay. All this shows that there is also continuity in this change and transformation of the Korean HRM. The new trends are certainly moving toward flexibility and performance, but some practices based on the long-term relation perspective are staying unchanged. In short, Korean HRM passes a transitional period in which new innovative practices and traditional practices are present at the same time.

However, it needs to pay attention to the fact that the HRM systems in Korean firms are not homogeneous. The cluster analysis we conducted resulted in 4 different HRM systems, including the traditional model. The direction and intensity of changes in HRM would not be the same among the firms having a different HRM system. It will be important work to analyze them in coming years. Although we found some shifts in HRM models from a relation dimension toward a more transaction dimension, we failed to observe a significant change between the control dimension and the utilization dimension. This may result from the time necessary to change a specific HRM model into a different one, in particular into a HRM model fully utilizing the potential of the employees. More precise examination will be needed by future research.

An important issue we did not handle in this paper is the strategic choice an individual firm makes in managing its employees. Traditionally, large Korean firms have shown a high degree of isomorphism in their management and HRM (Orru et al, 1991), and have previously shown almost identical HRM practices. Recently, however, we have seen large difference of HRM practices between firms. For example, the compensation of executives in conglomerates has been determined by the common rule based on the internal consistency among the member firms of the conglomerate. Now, many conglomerates are changing it in consideration of the size and the performance of a specific firm. This change coincides with the strategic reorientation in management underlining the survival of each affiliated member firm and its performance, an important lesson of Korean conglomerates learned from the IMF bailout. It would increase hereafter the necessity for Korean firms to be more autonomous and strategic in their choice of HRM practices and models.

A different environmental context and firms' business strategy require different configurations of HRM practices in Korean firms (e.g., Kim & Yu, 2000). What type of HRM configurations can we find and how these configurations change over time should be included in the next research agenda of Korean HRM.

References

Althauser, R. P. & Kalleberg, A.L. (1981). Firms, occupations, and the structure of labor markets: A conceptual analysis. In Berg (ed.). *Sociological Perspectives on Labor Markets*, pp. 119-149. New York: Academic Press.

Appelbaum, E. & Batt, R. (1994). *The New American Workplace: Transforming Work Systems in the United States*. Ithaca and London: ILR.

Ahn, H. T. (1996). *New Human Resource Practices in Korean Firms*, Korea Employers Federation. (in Korean)

Bae, J., Chen, S., & Lawler, J.J. (1998). Variations in human resource management in Asian countries: MNC home-country and host-country effects. *The International Journal of Human Resource Management*, Vol. 9, No. 4, pp. 653-670.

Cho, Y. H. (2000a). Changes in environment and transformation in Korean management. *Human Resource Management in the 21st century*. Korea Labor Institute (Ed.). Seoul: Myeong-Gyeong Publishing Co. (in Korean)

Cho, Y. H. (2000b). Designing Flattening structure. *Human Resource Management in the 21st century*. In Korea Labor Institute (Ed.). Seoul: Myeong-Gyeong Publishing Co. (in Korean)

Dubois, D. D. (1996). *The Competency Casebook: Twelve Studies in Competency-based Performance Improvement*. Amherst: HRM Press.

Jeong, Y. A. (2000). A paradigm shift of Korean HRM. *Human Resource Management in the 21st century*. In Korea Labor Institute (Ed.). Seoul: Myeong-Gyeong Publishing Co. (in Korean)

Kim, D.K. & Kim, W.C. (1989). Korean value systems and managerial practices. *Korean Managerial Dynamics*. In Chung, K.H. & Lee, H.C. (Ed.). New York: Praeger.

Kim, D. O. (1993). Analysis of labour disputes in Korea and Japan: The search for an alternative model. *European Sociological Review*, Vol. 9, No. 2, pp. 139-154.

Kim, D. O. and Park, S. (1997). Changing patterns of pay systems in Japan and Korea: From seniority to performance. *International Journal of Employment Studies*, Vol. 5, No. 2, pp. 117-134.

Kim, D., & Yu, G.C. (2000). Emerging patterns of human resource management in Korea: evidence from large Korean firms. Presented at 12th IIRA World

Congress, Tokyo, Japan.

Korea Bank. (2000). *Monthly Statistics.* Seoul: Korea Bank.

Korea Labor Institute. (2000). *Survey On The Changes In Human Resource Management* (unpublished).

Korea Labor Institute. (1998). *Survey On The Human Resource Management In Korean Firms* (unpublished).

Kuruvilla, S. & Erickson, C. (2000). The impact of globalization on industrial relations in Asia: A comparative review and analysis. Presented at 12th IIRA World Congress, Tokyo, Japan.

Lawler III, E.E. (1994). From job-based to competency-based organizations. *Journal of Organizational Behavior,* Vol. 15, pp. 3-15.

Leibowitz, Z. B. (1987). Designing career development systems: Principles and practices. *Human Resource Planning,* Vol. 10, pp. 195-207.

Martell, K. & Carroll, S.J. (1995). How strategic is HRM? *Human Resource Management,* Vol. 34, No. 2, pp. 253-267.

Ministry of Labor. (2000). *Results Of Survey On Merit Pay And Group Incentives.* Seoul: Ministry of Labor. (in Korean).

Morishima, M. (2000). Pay innovations in Japan: Do they lead to high performance organizations? *Proceedings of Korean Industrial Relations Research Association Congress,* Seoul.

Nakamura, K. & Nitta, M. (1995). Development in Industrial Relations and Human Resource Practices in Japan, in Locke, R., Kochan, T., & Piore, M. (ed.) *Employment Relations in a Changing World Economy.* Cambridge: MIT Press.

Orru, M., Biggart, N.W., & Hamilton, G.G. (1991). Organizational isomorphism in East Asia. *The New Institutionalism in Organizational Fields.* In Powell, W.W., & DiMaggio, P.J. (ed.). Chicago: The University of Chicago Press.

Park, J. S. (1995). Characteristics of workforce management in Korean large firms. *Management Characteristics In Korean Large Firms,* Shin, Y. K. et al. (ed.). Seoul: Se-Kyung Publishing Co. (in Korean)

Park, K. K. and Ahn, H. T. (1998). *A Comparison Of Human Resource Management Between Korean And German Firms.* Korea Employers Federation. (in Korean)

Park, W. S. (1999). *Wage Flexibility: Model And Cases In Korean Firms.* Korea Labor Institute. (in Korean)

Pfeffer, J. (1994). *Competitive Advantage Through People.* Boston, MA: HBS Press.

Shin, Y. (1992). *Korean Management.* Seoul: Bakyeong-sa. (in Korean)

Towers Perrin. (1992). *Priorities for Competitive Advantage*.

Wright, P. & McMahan, G.C. (1992). Theoretical perspectives for strategic human resource management. *Journal of Management*, Vol. 18, pp. 295-320.

Yu, G.C. (1998). *New Trend of Human Resource Management in Korea*. Korea Labor Institute (in Korean).

Yu, G.C. (2000). The changing role of HR department and career development of HR managers. *Human Resource Management in the 21st century*. Korea Labor Institute (Ed.). Seoul: Myeong-Gyeong Publishing Co. (in Korean)

Yu, G.C. & Park, W.S. (2000). The survey of HR specialists. *Human Resource Management in the 21st century*. Korea Labor Institute (Ed.). Seoul: Myeong-Gyeong Publishing Co. (in Korean).

Voos, P. B. and Kim, H. (2000). High performance work systems: The U.S. industrial relations consensus and its critics. *Proceedings of Korean Industrial Relations Research Association Congress*. Seoul.

Changes in Gender Differences in the Employment Structure

Hae Un Rii[1]

I. INTRODUCTION

Korea earned its reputation as one of the "Asian Tigers" with a remarkable economic growth rate of up to 10 % annually through the mid-1990s. However, Korea's breathless economic development slowed dramatically and it has experienced an economic crisis since 1997. The nation's remarkable economic development and recent economic crisis have greatly influenced the changes in socio-economic structure as well as people's daily lifestyle.

Korea is a traditionally male dominant society and the concept that the householder should be a man (or husband) and has to support his family financially is widespread, even though young female family members are used to sacrificing for their male family members. The belief occurs under the pretext that "the son is a pillar of the household or of the family, so everyone should support him for his success." In other words, most female workers have the family-oriented ideology to sacrifice themselves for their family. Younger sisters quit school in order to make money which is sent to

---

[1] Professor, Dongguk University, Seoul, Korea

the family to be used for their brother's tuition and family expenses. This was common until the 1980s.

However, with the changes in the socio-economic structure, the school attendance rate and the number of females receiving a higher education are gradually increasing. More female workers are seeking a secure job rather than a temporary job before marriage. Such a tendency has made great changes not only in people's perception of female workers but also in their own attitude toward work. Many job opportunities are now open to female workers and they can hold higher position in the workplace and participate in professions, even though there encounter gender discrimination in certain positions. In fact, many more female workers got jobs in large enterprises within the last 10 years (DongA Daily Newspaper, Feb. 9, 2001). The number of females earning doctorates has increased over 30 times during the last 20 years. But, the number of female doctorates who found jobs is half that of their male counterparts (DongA Daily Newspaper, Feb. 12, 2001). The result from a recent survey on females' employment reports that 45.5% of male respondents and 25.9% of female respondents answered the category of "if I were a chairperson and 2 candidates had the same abilities, I would hire the male worker rather than the female worker" (http://www.donga.com/fbin/news? f=print&n=20010260076).

The issue of 'female employment' changed in quantity and quality with the socio-economic development in Korea. In other words, economic changes with rapid growth, crisis, recovery, etc. over the past 30 years, especially in the later 1990s, resulted in a great transformation of employment structure in both gender issues and people's perception of work. For this reason, it is necessary to review the changes in gender differences in the employment structure of Korea.

II. Economic Development and Economic Activities by Gender

1. Economic Development in Korea

The Korean economy has greatly developed due to the 'Five-Year Economic Development Plans,' which were launched in 1962. These plans were accomplished in six phases over 30 years. Each phase had a different purpose for the development of the Korean economy (Table 1). Each phase sought to establish a self-supporting economy in different fields. During the 5th Plan, the name, 'Five-year Economic Development Plan' was changed to 'Economic and Social Development Plan.' This implied that the Korean economy had become a self-supporting system and it was time to think about social welfare.

One result from the completion of these six phases was the change of the economic structure of the Korea from an agricultural society to an industrial society. In the early 1980s, the Korean economy reached a mass-production stage and people started to turn their eyes to social life. In fact, people's daily lifestyle changed from an economy-oriented lifestyle, with a focus on making money, to a socio-economy oriented lifestyle such as

Table 1. Five-Year Economic Development Plan

	Purpose
1st (1962-1966)	Establishment of infrastructure for achieving self-supporting economy
2nd (1967-1971)	Modernization of industrial structure and accelerating the establishment of self- supporting economy
3rd (1972-1976)	Establishment of self-supporting economy structure and balance of regional development
4th (1977-1981)	Establishment of self-supporting growth structure and improvement of technique and efficiency
5th (1982-1986)	The name was changed to "Economic and Social Development Plan." Improvement of social welfare through economic growth and social development
6th (1987-1991)	Achievement of advanced economic structure and promotion of social welfare

Source: Doosan Donga, 1996, Doosan World Great Encyclopedia.

working only during working hours, saving money, and enjoying life with diverse cultural activities.

In 1965 when the results from the first five-year economic development plan started to appear, the Korean economy was based on primary industries employing 58.5% of all employees rather than the secondary and tertiary industries (Figure 1). In fact, for centuries, Korea had been a traditional agriculture society and had just begun to place an emphasis on manufacturing at that time. Manufacturing centered on mainly light industries like textile and clothing industries. Korea, thus, was rated as one of the undeveloped countries indicating U$105 of GNP per capita (KNSO, 1995).

With the accomplishment of the five-year economic development plans, the economic structure started to be changed to emphasize the secondary industries, especially heavy industries and export-oriented industries. Korea experienced an oil shock in the 1970s, but economic development continued at a 10% growth rate. As a result, the employment rate working in secondary industries was recorded at 22.5% in 1980, while the percentage of employees in primary industries dropped to 34.0%. In the case of tertiary industries, the percentage also increased to 43.5% (Figure 1).

Such a trend continued until 1997 when the economic crisis hit Korea.

Figure 1. Employed Persons by Industry (1965-1998)

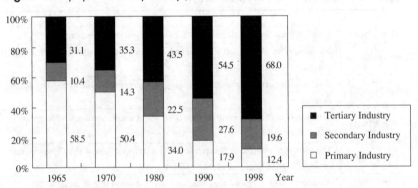

Source : Korea National Statistical Office, 1995, *Transformation of Korea Through Statistical Data*; Seoul Metropolitan Government, 1999, *Seoul Statistical Yearbook*.

From the 1970s, Korea stepped into an industrial society, and was termed one of the NICs, Tigers or Dragons along with other Asian countries having a similar experience in economic development. The proportion of production by secondary industries continuously increased, even though the economic growth rate decreased in the 1990s, as compared with rates in the 1970s and 1980s.

The employment rate in the primary industries continued to drop to 17.9% in 1990 and 12.4% in 1998, while that in the tertiary industries it increased to 54.5% in 1990 and 68.0% in 1998. The secondary industries traced a different course from other industries. The employment rate in the secondary industry reached 27.6% in 1990, but it dropped to 19.6% in 1998. These changes indicate that Korea has stepped to a post-industrial society in some sense. After the economic crisis in 1997 and the development of information technology in the late 1990s, the information industry became an important part of the Korean economy and emerged as a new type of industry.

As is the tendency worldwide, the tertiary industries could be divided into a more detailed classification such as tertiary, quaternary and quinary industries. The restructuring of the Korean economy after the economic crisis had an influence on the changes of socio-economic development and employment structure.

2. Changing Economic Activities by Gender

There is a great change in the participation rate of economic activities by gender within the last 30 years. The proportion of female workers involved in economic activities among the total number of women increased 10% from 37.0% in 1963 to 47.0% in 1998, while the economic activities participation rate by males slightly decreased by 3.2% from 78.4% in 1963 to 75.2% in 1998 (Figure 2). In other words, there has not been much change in the economic activities of men over the years, while many more women found jobs in the same time period. These trends might be proven with the

Figure 2. Economic Activities Participation Rate by Gender (1963-1998)

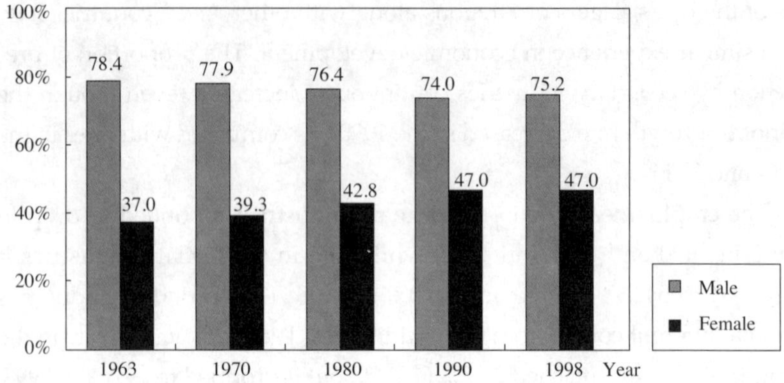

Year	Male	Female
1963	78.4	37.0
1970	77.9	39.3
1980	76.4	42.8
1990	74.0	47.0
1998	75.2	47.0

Source: Korea National Statistical Office, 1976 & 1999, *Korea Statistic Yearbook*.

comparison of the number of doctorates between males and females, and the increase of married women as workers. The increase rate of women in employment was much larger than the same rate of men in employment from 1970 to 1980. In particular there was an increased number of married women getting jobs in the same period (Ahn, 1988). Persons who obtained a doctoral degree, potential laborers for professional jobs, increased by a different rate according to gender from 1980 to 2000. The increase rates for male doctorates were recorded at 283.8% from 1980 to 1990 and 89.1% from 1990 to 2000, while the rates for female doctorates were at 822% from 1980 to 1990 and 226.0% from 1990 to 2000 (DongA Daily Newspaper, Feb.12, 2001). This indicates that a social trend of more women than men trying to receive a higher education in order to find a higher position in employment, is continuing over time. In fact, there has been a continued increase in the number of women graduating from colleges and universities, entering new employment of large enterprises, especially in the late 1990s (DongA Daily Newspaper, Feb. 9, 2001). These aspects explain the transformation of social perspectives on women's labor as well as women's attitudes on holding a job over the past 30 years.

Upon deeper examination, one can trace back the path of gender differences in the employment structure. Before rapid economic development, most young female workers used to work in private houses as a live-in maid (housekeeper) to support their brother's tuition and family expenses. Due to economic development and Korea's transformation into an industrial society, there were many job openings for both male and female workers. Especially after 1980, the economic activities participation rate by females increased greatly.

This finding might be explained by a partially hidden female labor force getting employment in factories and other service sectors. Most female workers were able to get blue-collar jobs in factories of light industries, while male workers got jobs in factories of both light and heavy industries as white or blue-collar workers. In terms of position in the factory, mostly male workers occupied higher positions over a certain level. In most cases, however, female workers were expected to resign the job in almost all workplaces after they got married. Since the 1980s, married female workers have been allowed to continue working. This tendency has resulted in a sharp increase in the economic activities participation rate by females.

Just before the economic crisis in 1997, the economic activities participation rate reached 50.0% for females and 75.8% for males in June, 1997 (Figure 3). But after the economic crisis, the rate declined continually for both genders. When the decreased participation rate of male and female workers

Figure 3. Economic Activities Participation Rate by Gender after Economic Crisis

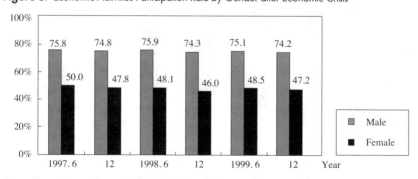

Source: Korea National Statistical Office, 1999, Annual Report on The Economically Active Population Survey.

is examined, there is a great gender gap. The rate of male workers was reduced by only 1.6% from June, 1997 to December, 1999, while at the same time a drop of 2.8% was recorded for the economic activities participation rate by female workers during the same period. This means that more female workers had to quit their job than male workers. For example, if a husband and wife worked together at the same company, the wife was forced to resign first. This, of course, was not the official course of action, but the moral, social and environmental one. Moreover, part-time female workers lost their jobs as a result of the increased employment of part-time or temporary male workers after the economic crisis in 1997 (200008070462). In recent years, a tendency has emerged for more female workers to get a part-time or low-level type of blue-collar or low income job (200008070462).

III. Transformation of Social Structure

Economic development has accelerated industrialization and urbanization in Korea. Since the 1960s, these trends have influenced the rapid increase of urban population, finally resulting in changes to the social structure. Figure 4 shows the changes of regional distribution of population by gender over

Figure 4. Distribution of Population by Gender

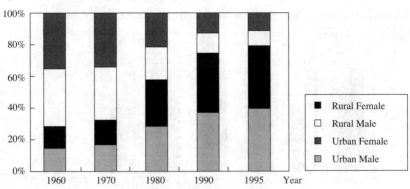

Source: Korea National Statistical Office, 1999, *Korea Statistic Yearbook*.

the designated time period. A transformation to an industrial society and the growth of urban areas created job opportunities in the city and led to a sharp increase of population in urban areas. In fact, the job opportunities in urban areas played an important role as a pull factor for the migration from the rural area to the urban area.

From 1970 to 1980, in particular, a great change took place in the gender percentages of population living in rural and urban areas. Between 1960-1980, young unmarried females came to the city to earn money to support family expenses and a brother's tuition as well as to prepare for their own wedding. In the 1960's, they came to the urban areas to find jobs mainly in the service sector, but, from the 1970s, people were able to find jobs in the secondary industries in general. Industrialization and urbanization continued to progress in Korea, and the urban population has grown continuously.

Economic development and changes in the socio-economic structure have led to a changed family structure as well. More job opportunities for women and the increased participation in economic activities by female laborers led naturally to a tendency of women seeking to reduce housework and increase activities outside of the home. As shown in Figure 5, the number of persons per household was reduced from 5.6 persons in

Figure 5. Persons per Household (1960-1995)

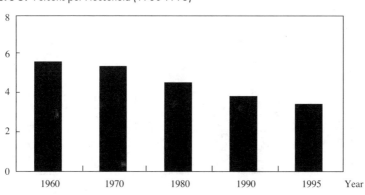

Source: Korea National Statistical Office, 1999, Korea Statistic Yearbook.

1960 to 3.4 persons in 1995. This dramatic drop was a result of family planning, extension of the nuclear family project, and an increase in the social participation of women.

Figure 6 and 7 present the employment rate of occupation by gender

Figure 6. Employment by Occupation of Male (1963-1998)

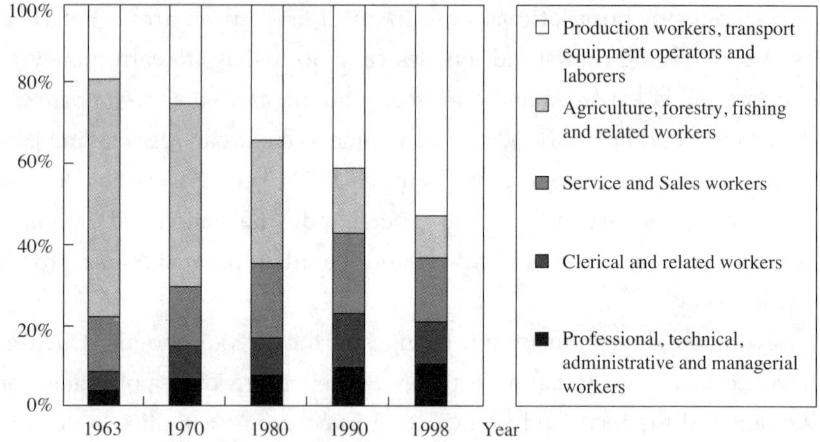

100%
80%
60%
40%
20%
0%
1963
1970
1980
1990
1998
Year
Production workers, transport equipment operators and laborers
Agriculture, forestry, fishing and related workers
Service and Sales workers
Clerical and related workers
Professional, technical, administrative and managerial workers

Source: Korea National Statistical Office, 1964, 1976 and 1999, *Korea Statistic Yearbook*.

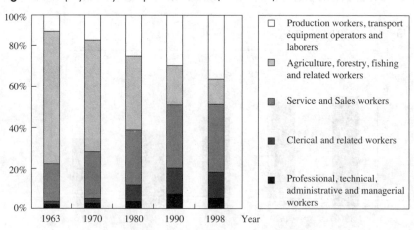

Figure 7. Employment by Occupation of Female (1963-1998)

100%
80%
60%
40%
20%
0%
1963
1970
1980
1990
1998
Year
Production workers, transport equipment operators and laborers
Agriculture, forestry, fishing and related workers
Service and Sales workers
Clerical and related workers
Professional, technical, administrative and managerial workers

Source: Korea National Statistical Office, 1964, 1976 & 1999, *Korea Statistic Yearbook*.

over the 30 year period. The number of male workers, production workers, transport equipment operators and laborers increased greatly from 1963 to 1998, while the numbers of agriculture, forestry, fishing and related workers fell sharply. Professional, technical administrative and managerial workers have continued to increase over time. However, service and sales workers as well as clerical and related workers saw a similar increase in employment rate until 1990, but then decreased in 1998.

A similar trend can be found for female workers. The percentage of agriculture, forestry, fishing and related workers fell sharply from 1963 to 1998, while the percentage of workers in other occupations gradually increased. Service and sales workers as well as clerical and related workers recorded almost the same level of employment in 1990 and 1998, while the percentage of professional, technical, administrative and managerial workers decreased from 1990 to 1998, in contrast to the case of male workers.

Even though there are similar tendencies of the employment structure by occupation for both genders, there is a gender difference between male and female workers in the employment structure in 1998. Male workers predominated in the category of production workers, transport equipment operators and laborers with almost half of the total employment rate. However, it is not possible to identify a single dominant job category for female workers. The categories of clerical and related workers and production workers, transport equipment operators and laborers are occupied by about two-thirds of the total employment percentage of female workers. In sum, male workers were mainly employed in the secondary industries, while most female workers were employed in both the tertiary and secondary industries. More male workers than female workers have jobs in the category of 'professional, technical, administrative and managerial workers.' In other words as a general rule, male workers have higher positions in the employment structure than female workers.

After the economic crisis, trends in employment patterns have changed. Enterprises which experienced economic stagnation have sought flexibility of labor and reduction of wage, prefer to hire irregular workers like temporary and daily-based workers instead of regular workers. Managers believe that discharging a male will put into effect a serious menace to his family and society. As an alternative, female workers were first dismissed from their jobs and employed for irregular work more frequently than men. As a result, the proportion of daily workers and temporary employees is increasing, while that of regular employees has decreased from June, 1997 to December, 1999 (Figure 8). These tendencies have resulted in an increase of part-time, temporary, low-income or day-labor workers among female workers in the recent periods, as mentioned above.

On the other hand, an increasing number of women with an education level higher than college, the changes of the occupational view by women themselves, and a changing view by society of women holding jobs resulted in an ongoing hiring of women by enterprises or/and searching jobs by high qualified, potential female workers. It is true that more female workers are involved in part-time, temporary, low income or low skill jobs, but it is also true that the number of female workers finding jobs in the professionals or/and higher managerial positions has increased.

The attitude towards women taking jobs has changed both for women themselves, and for men. Traditionally Koreans thought that working outside of the home was a man's role and that a woman should stay home

Figure 8. Employment Patterns of Female Workers

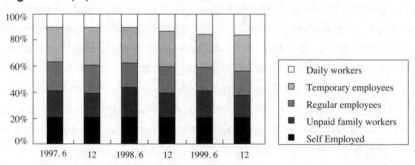

Source: Korea National Statistical Office, 1999, Annual Report on The Economically Active Population Survey.

and concentrate only on housework, raising the children and supporting the husband. However, traditional thoughts have shifted along with socio-economic development through time. Table 2 shows how attitudes towards working women have changed over a period of 10 years from 1988 to 1998. The percentage of those 'working without considering housework' has gradually increased. Also the percentage of other categories which have some constraints to work outside of the home for female workers has continuously decreased over time for both men and women. It seems that holding a job for women is becoming a normal and acceptable statement in Korean society. Comparing men and women, more women than men tend to hold aggressive attitudes about holding jobs without considering housework. Such a change of people's attitude towards female workers might have an influence on reducing job discrimination by gender. The number of women considering a future as a professional career woman and working in professional positions has increased. These aspects, therefore, explain that female workers having a higher education are able to find jobs in large enterprises in competition with male workers.

Table 2. Attitudes on Getting a Job by Female

(Unit : %)

		Stay home	Before marriage (A)	After kids are grown(B)	A & B	Working without considering housework	
Male	1988	25.4	28.7	19.3	18.2	8.4	
	1991	25.7	22.9	20.9	20.2	10.3	
	1995	19.6	15.1	16.1	32.3	16.8	
	1998	11.6	13.1	15.0	25.2	23.1	
Female	1988	17.5	17.8	23.9	24.6	16.7	
	1991	17.0	17.8	23.9	24.6	16.7	
	1995	12.1	11.3	16.1	35.8	24.7	
	1998	8.5	10.3	14.0	27.6	30.4	

Source: Korea National Statistical Office, 1999, Korea Society Indicator.

IV. Conclusion

Economic development over the past 30 years and the economic crisis after 1997 have greatly influenced the changes in socio-economic structure as well as our daily lifestyle in Korea. As a traditionally male dominant society, gender discrimination in the employment structure existed from a very early period. Young female workers used to sacrifice themselves for family and/or brothers. With Korea's economic development, however, they could gain a higher education than before and find jobs in factories and other sectors rather than housework. Married women are now aware that they can work after marriage as well. In fact, the number of married female workers has increased over time.

After the economic crisis in 1997, gender discrimination worsened in many cases. However, the sharp boundaries on working area and position by gender are not so clearly defined and people's perception of work by gender has also changed. The gap of gender differences in the employment structure has been reduced, even though Korea is still a male dominated society and preferences of men to women as working partners and/or their superiors remain widespread.

Things are changing. The society is slowly being transformed in many ways, often in contrast to the past. Female workers have gained highly qualified abilities on certain jobs and their perception of an occupation has also changed. It is also true that female workers have superior abilities than male workers in some areas. These trends will continue into the new century. Thus, in the future, business managers and enterprise owners will realize and accept such changes in the gender labor structure and be able to hire employees on the basis of their ability at work, without any gender discrimination.

References

Ahn, Mi-Kyung. (1988). Geographical research on economic activities population by female. Master's thesis, Graduate School of Education, Ewha Womans University.

Cho, Soon-Kyoung. (1998). Economic crisis, women's work and employment politics. *Han'Guk YeoseongHak (Journal of Korean Women's Studies)*, Vol. 14, No. 2, pp. 5-34.

Kim, Eun Hye. (2000). Status of female from the geographical perspectives: the case study of Seoul. Unpublished Master's thesis, Graduate School, Dongguk University. *Han'Guk YeoseongHak (Journal of Korean Women's Studies)*, Vol. 16, No. 1, pp. 37-64.

Kim, Hyun Mee. (2000). Modernity and women's labor rights in South Korea.

Lee, Sook-Jin. (1998). Economic recession and women's employment: Centering on working hours and opening hours in distribution industry. *Han'Guk YeoseongHak (Journal of Korean Women's Studies)*, Vol. 14, No. 1, pp. 111-143.

Rii, Hae Un, Eun Hye Kim and Na young Im. (1999). Changes of gender mobility with the socio-economic development in Korea. A paper presented at the conference of Gendered Mobilities in Asia conference, November 24-26, Hong Kong.

Slater, Christopher L., Joseph J. Hobbs, Jesse H. Wheeler, Jr. & J. Trenton Kostbade. (2000). *Essentials of World Regional Geography*, 3rd ed., Harcourt College Publishers.

Korea National Statistical Office. (1964). *Korea Statistic Yearbook.*

Korea National Statistical Office. (1976). *Korea Statistic Yearbook.*

Korea National Statistical Office. (1995). *Transformation of Korea Through Statistical Data.*

Korea National Statistical Office. (1999). *Annual Report on The Economically Active Population Survey.*

Korea National Statistical Office. (1999). *Korea Society Indicator.*

Korea National Statistical Office. (1999). *Korea Statistic Yearbook.*

Seoul Metropolitan Government. (1999). *Seoul Statistical Yearbook.*

'Female wind in new employment of large enterprises.' (2001) DongA Daily Newspaper, February 9.

Female doctorates. (2001) DongA Daily Newspaper, February 12.
<?=print&n=200008070462>
<?=print&n=200011010252>
<?=print&n=200101230076>
DongA Daily Newspaper, February, 9, 2001: "Female Wind in New Employment of Large Enterprises"
Dong A Daily Newspaper, February, 12, 2001: "Female Doctorates"
<http://www.donga.com/fbin/news?=print&n=200008070462>
<http://www.donga.com/fbin/news?=print&n=200011010252>
<http://www.donga.com/fbin/news?=print&n=200102130076>

Index

Administrative coordination 258, 264, 266
Advertising intensity 192
Affiliates 64, 84-87, 90-95, 97, 110-111, 114-115, 123-126, 128, 133, 172, 174-179, 186, 269-270, 319
Agency costs 149, 154, 158, 169, 185, 202
Agency problems 8, 49, 131, 151-157, 167-170, 180, 187
Agency theory 184-185
Antitrust policy 50
Asian approach (or Asian style management) 228-229, 232
Authoritarian administrations 240
Bank Supervisory Commission 33
Bankruptcy 32-33, 45, 54, 86-87, 124, 171, 182-183, 185, 194, 202-203, 250, 283, 369
Berry-Herfindahl Index (BHI) 72, 188
Blockholders 137, 142-143, 145
Book-to-market equity ratio 156, 159, 165-166
Bureaucracy 34, 249, 280
Business portfolio 129, 171, 173, 178, 188, 191, 194, 196-197

Capital liberalization 324
Capital structure 38, 170, 172, 174
Career development 372-373, 390-391
Central Labor-Management Council 330-331
Centralized multidivisional form (CM-form) 176-177
Chaebol 8, 16-18, 32-33, 41-42, 48, 52-55, 58, 64, 67, 72-79, 81-86, 88, 90-92, 94-100, 102, 104-105
Citizens Coalition for Economic Justice 35
Co-dependency 218-220, 224
Confucian capitalism 228
Confucianism 9, 14, 16, 205, 207-210, 212, 214, 221-222, 224-225
Compensation 285, 310, 321, 327, 367-370, 374, 381, 388
Competing Values Model (CVM) 278-280, 284, 288, 304
Competitive advantage 183, 191, 205, 249, 251, 255, 258-261, 263, 265-269, 275-276, 302, 378, 381, 384, 390-391
Competitive weapon 254, 271
Conglomerates 27, 32, 38, 132, 135-136,

140, 165, 172, 178, 180, 184, 187-188, 197, 216, 224-225, 238-239, 250, 367, 388
Contingent workers 370, 372
Core businesses 25, 82-83, 86, 126, 128, 172, 190, 196
Corporate culture 134, 276, 278, 281, 295-296, 302-306
Corporate governance 17-20, 32, 37, 49, 78, 82-84, 116-117, 128-129, 131, 133, 135, 138-139, 147, 149-152, 168, 170, 179, 202, 232, 236, 238, 296, 324, 338
Corporate identity program (CIP) 296
Corporate strategy 250, 252, 254-255, 276, 278, 300, 302
Corporatism 332, 341, 343
Cost-sharing 253
Cross-debt guarantees 38, 176
Cross-funding 132, 134-136, 138, 140
Cross-learning 258, 260
Cross-shareholding 165, 174, 179, 186
Cross-subsidization 184
Daenong 323
Debt consignment 135
Debt-equity ratio 38, 172, 174
Decentralized unionism 330
Deconcentration 56, 58, 62, 74-75, 77
Democratization 240, 242, 317, 330, 338, 342
Developmental statism 228
Distributive justice 318
Doosan 178, 394
Diversification 17, 49, 52, 56-58, 61, 70, 72-73, 76, 78, 136, 152, 155, 157, 161, 163, 167, 169, 170-174, 176, 178, 180-197, 200-202
Earning differential 347-348, 350, 356-358, 365
Earning distribution 347-349, 350, 355-356, 360-362
Economic and Social Development Plan 395
Economic concentration 49, 51-60, 62-63, 65-68, 70-78, 172-173, 180-181, 202
Economic miracle 208, 222, 224, 229, 232, 244
Economics-based perspective 252
Employee involvement 229, 278
Employee suggestion 376
Employee survey 376
Employment distribution 360
Employment security 320, 326-327, 339-340
Environmental uncertainty 270
Entropy Index (EI) 55, 72, 189
Ethical competence 27, 30-31, 33, 35, 46
Fair Trade Act 49, 51, 78, 172
Fair Trade White Book 52, 76, 78
Federation of Korean Trade Unions 316-317
Financial Supervisory Services (FSS) 36, 41, 46
Fiscal policy 323
Five Cardinal Relationships 210
Five-Year Economic Development Plans 24, 28, 395-396

Foreign Capital Inducement Act 60
Foreign Exchange Management Act 37
Formalism 212, 220-221, 294, 296
Free cash flow 152, 153, 155, 157-158, 160, 162-170, 202
General Council of Korean Trade Unions 316
Going-concern 194
Global Political-Economic System 21, 23-24, 26-27, 29, 39, 44, 46
Globalization 43, 47, 131, 249, 275, 338, 341, 343, 362-363, 378, 390
Group incentive system 374
Hanbo 32-33, 81, 182-183, 185, 190, 196, 322-323
Hayekian philosophy 14
Hierarchy 44, 211, 217-218, 222, 248, 273, 286, 295, 376
Human capital 242, 244, 266
Human resource development 245
Human resource management (HRM) 282, 305, 369, 377, 386, 389-391
Hyosung 176
Hypercompetition 249
Hyundai 84, 86-89, 93, 114, 125, 132, 134-138, 142-145, 148, 176, 178, 315
Industrial relations 6, 303, 307-312, 316-321, 324, 326-332
Industrial Relations Reform Commission 319
Information age 249
Insurance Supervisory Commission 33
Intangible resources 259
Interaction 25-26, 253, 257-260, 262, 264, 266-279
Internal labor market 371, 373, 379-380
International business 224-225, 252-253
International Monetary Fund (IMF) 22, 26, 47, 251, 311, 324, 338, 340, 342
Interfirm competition 253
Inter-subjective competence 26, 30, 45
Intra-group transaction 54, 56-59, 63-65, 76, 82-83
Intranetwork competition 258, 261
Jinro 32, 81, 115, 183, 191, 196, 323
Job Descriptive Index 285
Job enlargement 376
Job enrichment 376
Job satisfaction 282-284, 288, 290-294, 297-298, 300
Job security 320-321, 326, 336, 368, 378
Keiretsu 144, 237, 239, 313, 341
Kia 32, 80, 92, 138, 140, 183, 191, 196, 323, 328-340
Korea Development Bank 328
Korea Industrial Technology Association (KITA) 42
Korea Stock Price Index 39
Korean Fair Trade Commission (KFTC) 51, 165, 172
Korean Air 41
Korean Confederation of Trade Unions 319
Korea Listed Companies Association 155-156, 158
Korea Securities Research Institute 155-156, 158
Korean Stock Exchange 147, 152, 155-

156, 158, 160, 162, 166
Korean Trade Unions Congress 331
Labor-management relations 229, 242
Labor movement 316, 338
Labor Standards Act (LSA) 38, 320
Layoff 38, 130, 290, 296, 315, 321, 326-328, 337, 339, 380
Leadership 34, 130, 141, 213, 258, 270, 276, 279, 281, 298, 300, 303-305, 332, 379-380, 386-387
Lifetime employment 229-230, 232, 234, 237, 242, 245, 321
Liquidation value 194
Loans 24, 33, 36-37, 40, 80, 82, 94, 108, 110, 152, 168, 313-314, 322-324, 326
Lucky-Goldstar (LG) 89, 136, 138, 176, 178
M-form 176-178
Management by objectives (MBO) 373
Management prerogatives 235-236
Market-clearing wage 317
Market share 192, 203, 230-233
Mergers 60, 78, 131, 149, 169, 203
Merit pay 370, 374-375, 380, 387, 390
Minimum Wage Committee 330, 331
Modernization 241, 395
Monetary regulation 66-67
Monitoring 19, 46, 64-65, 114, 137-138, 142-144, 172, 181, 185-186, 265, 326
Monopoly market structure 58
Monopoly Regulation and Fair Trade Act (FTA) 51
Moral hazard 16, 36, 128, 135, 152, 319
Multi-unionism 319

Mutual forbearance 184
National Assembly 331
National Council for Economy and Society (NCES) 331
National Statistical Office of Korea 345
Neoclassical analysis 232
Neomercantilism 228
New Core 323
New Foreign Investment Promotion Act (FIPA) 37
Newly industrialized economies 207
Network effectiveness 258-260, 267, 269, 270, 274
Network organization 205, 249
Nonprofit organizations 253
OECD 19, 26, 312, 322-324, 338, 341
Oligopoly market structure 58
Organizational Commitment 283, 285, 288, 290-294, 296-297, 299-300, 303-304
Organization construction 255
Ownership deconcentration 56, 58, 62, 74-75, 77
Ownership concentration 52, 54-57, 75, 136, 144, 152, 154, 185
Ownership structure 73-74, 76, 84, 90, 92, 94, 110, 124, 126-127, 129, 134-135, 140, 143, 145, 147, 149, 152-155, 165, 167, 169-170, 175, 178, 185-186
Participative management 374
Physical resources 258
Planning and Coordination Office 19, 176

Politico-economic collusive structure 55
POSCO 187
Presidential Decree 61-63
Private Capital Inducement for Social Overhead Capital Act 62
Profit maximization 181, 230, 234
Quality circles (QC) 244
R&D alliances 252
R&D consortia 253
Reciprocal buying 184
Reorganization 251
Restructuring 17-18, 24, 36-38, 40-41, 45-46, 49, 79-80, 82, 84-86, 88, 90, 92, 94, 96-97, 99-100, 102, 105, 107-108, 110-112, 121-123, 125-130, 171-172, 178, 188, 194, 196, 201-202, 244-245, 290, 297, 315, 320, 322, 324, 327-329, 337
Returns on asset 192
Return on investment (ROI) 283, 286, 288, 292, 298
Sammi 32, 182, 190, 196
Samsung 88, 132, 136, 138, 176, 315
Seniority 245, 268, 274, 278, 378-380, 382, 387, 389
Security rights 60
Self-directed work team 275, 376
Shareholder capitalism 179
Shareholder managerialism 179, 186, 197
Shin-Dong-Ah 33
Short-term debt 39, 152-153, 157-158, 162, 164-168, 324
Skill-sharing 352

South Korean National Assembly 328
Strategic alliances 273
Strategic conquest 233
Takeovers 60, 168, 202
Taoism 14-15, 208
Technical competence 27, 30, 213, 371
Tobin's Q ratio 139, 145
Transaction costs 54-55, 191, 252, 254
Trade liberalization 324
Trade Union Act 317
Tripartite Commission 38, 40, 331
Tripartitism 330, 332-333, 336, 342
U-form 177
Unemployment rate 312, 320
United Nations 26, 48, 243
Value added fixation 233
Value added maximization 230, 233
Vertical integration 233, 244
Voting rights 59-61, 63-64, 66, 76, 141, 149
Wage rates 320-321
Work council 376
World Bank 36, 43, 45-46, 48, 131, 322, 342
Zaibatsu 239, 312, 316, 336

About the Contributors

Editors

Eunmi Chang, Ph.D.
Assistant Professor, Michigan State University

Zusun Rhee, Ph.D.
Research Fellow, Korea Economic Research Institute

Contributors

Sung Hee Jwa, Ph.D.
President, Korea Economic Research Institute

Gill-Chin Lim, Ph.D.
Distinguished Institute Professor, KDI School of International Policy and Management, Seoul, Korea.
MSU Endowed Professor of Asian Studies in a Global Context Michigan State University

Zusun Rhee, Ph.D.
Research Fellow, Korea Economic Research Institute

Hasung Jang, Ph.D.
Professor, Korea University

Y. Peter Chung
Associate Professor, University of California

Byung-Mo Kim
Korea Advanced Institute of Science and Technology

Inmoo Lee, Ph.D.
Assistant Professor, Korea University

Inhak Hwang, Ph.D.
Research Fellow, Korea Economic Research Institute

Tai K. Oh, Ph.D.
Professor, California State University

Eonsoo Kim, Ph.D.
Associate Professor, Korea University

Dennis P. Patterson, Ph.D.
Assistant Professor, Michigan State University

John C. McIntosh, Ph.D.
Assistant Professor, Bentley College

Irene M. Duhaime, Ph.D.
Professor, Georgia State University

Sun-ah Yang
Korea University.

Young-Joe Kim, Ph.D.
Assistant Professor, Pukyong National University

Richard N. Block
Professor, Michigan State University

Jeonghyun Lee
Michigan State University

Eunjong Shin, Ph.D.
Michigan State University

Sung-Joon Park, Ph.D.
Senior research fellow, Korea Economic Research Institute

Woo-Sung Park, Ph.D.
Assistant Professor, Kyung Hee University

Gyu-Chang Yu, Ph.D.
Assistant Professor, Sookmyung Women's University

Hae Un Rii, Ph.D.
Professor, Dongguk University